Democracy and War

Democracy and War

Institutions, Norms, and the Evolution of International Conflict

DAVID L. ROUSSEAU

Stanford University Press
Stanford, California
2005

Stanford University Press
Stanford, California

Printed in the United States of America on acid-free, archival-quality paper

Library of Congress Cataloging-in-Publication Data
Rousseau, David L.
    Democracy and war : institutions, norms, and the evolution of international
conflict / David L. Rousseau.
        p.   cm.
    Includes bibliographical references and index.
    ISBN 0-8047-5081-5 (cloth : alk. paper)
    1. War—Political aspects—Case studies.   2. Democracy.   I. Title.
JZ6385.R68 2005
327.1′17—dc22   2004018552
Original Printing 2005

Last figure below indicates year of this printing:
14   13   12   11   10   09   08   07   06   05

Typeset by G&S Book Services in 10.5/12.5 Bembo

For Ellie, Nate, and Lynn

Contents

Tables and Figures

FIGURES

Acknowledgments

THIS PROJECT COULD NOT have been completed without the support and assistance of a number of people. For comments and advice at various stages of the project, I would like to thank Chris Achen, Bear Braumoeller, Lars-Erik Cederman, Erich Duchesne, Avery Goldstein, Joanne Gowa, Hyung Min Kim, Pierre Landry, Ian Lustick, Ellen Lust-Okar, Ed Mansfield, Susan Martin, Pat McDonald, Sara McLaughlin Mitchell, Chuck Myers, Bruce Newsome, Dan Reiter, Anne Sartori, Maurits van der Veen, Claude Welch, Frank Zagare, and Frank Zinni. Special thanks go to my dissertation coadvisors, Paul Huth and Ted Hopf, for comments on early drafts of the project and for teaching me to be a social scientist.

The research foundations at the State University of New York at Buffalo and the University of Pennsylvania provided financial assistance for the project. The Christopher Browne Center at the University of Pennsylvania provided grant support for experiments and simulation development. For programming the agent-based computer simulation in Chapter 7, I would like to thank Maurits van der Veen. For advice during the production process, I would like to thank Amanda Moran of Stanford University Press.

For permission to publish a revised version of our coauthored paper in Chapter 2—David L. Rousseau, Christopher Gelpi, Dan Reiter, and Paul Huth, "Assessing the Dyadic Nature of the Democratic Peace, 1918–1988," *American Political Science Review* 90 (September 1996): 512–33—I thank Dan Reiter, Chris Gelpi, Paul Huth, and Cambridge University Press. I, of course, am responsible for all changes and additions.

Finally, I am grateful to my family. My wife, Lynn Warner, read and commented on every draft of the manuscript. Her conceptual critiques, editing skills, and indefatigable spirit greatly improved the final product. Our children, Nate and Ellie, who arrived during the long gestation of the project, patiently waited more often than anyone thought was fair for their father to finish his "big paper." For their sacrifices and support, I dedicate this book to my family.

Democracy and War

Introduction: Domestic Institutions, Political Norms, and the Evolution of International Conflict

DO DOMESTIC INSTITUTIONS and political norms influence foreign policy decisions? This book examines this question by focusing on one of the most important decisions a political leader will make: whether or not to use military force to resolve inter-state conflicts. When facing conflicts such as territorial disputes, treaty violations, or threats to nationals abroad, political leaders must determine if military force is an appropriate response to the external challenge. Leaders must carefully weigh the probability of success associated with a military solution with the potential domestic and international costs of the policy. Domestic political institutions and norms can influence this decision process in a number of ways. Over the long term, institutions socialize current and future political leaders regarding acceptable means for resolving political conflicts both at home and abroad. More immediately, political institutions determine which members of the political elite participate in the decision regarding the use of force. After a use of force, institutions can facilitate the punishment of leaders who choose to use force and fail to achieve foreign policy objectives, succeed but at a socially unacceptable cost, or violate social standards in pursuit of victory.

More broadly, one can ask whether political institutions influence public policy in general; the answer to this question seems to be an obvious yes. It is common knowledge that the choice of a voting rule for elections, such as proportional representation versus "first-past-the-post," can have a decisive influence on subsequent policy choices (Lijphart 1977). Similarly, institutional theorists have shown that the structure of the decision-making process in the legislature can induce equilibrium despite the potential for voting cycles (Shepsle and Weingast 1981). Research has also demonstrated that institutional structures can affect problem definition, agenda formation, information flows, participation, and policy implementation (Kingdon 1984; Krehbiel 1992). As far as domestic policy decisions are concerned, then, it seems obvious that institutions matter.

When discussion turns to the field of international affairs, however, the situation becomes more muddled. Traditionally, security issues have been viewed as categorically different from domestic policy issues. In part, this difference stems from the importance of the issue at hand; if the very existence of the state is at stake, domestic political conflicts must be suppressed in the interest of national security. The difference is also due to the dominance of the executive in foreign policy decision making. Typically, the complex nature of the costs and benefits to be evaluated coupled with the rapidly changing external environment leads to a centralization of decision-making power within the executive. Legislators and even cabinet members are often excluded from the decision-making process; case studies have demonstrated that during intense crises most key decisions are made by a handful of individuals regardless of the state's institutional structure (Elman 1997b; Mendelson 1993). Finally, most noncrisis security issues are typically seen as overly abstract and essentially irrelevant from the perspective of the average citizen. With the exception of international trade issues, only a narrow segment of the attentive public actively follows foreign policy debates. This indifference tends to leave foreign policy in the hands of the chief executive.

For these reasons, many theorists have argued that domestic politics and institutional structures are irrelevant to the foreign policy decision-making process (Gowa 1999).[1] Political realists have long argued that power politics drive inter-state relations; the balance of military and economic power between the two adversaries is believed to determine the dynamics of a conflict and its ultimate outcome (Mearsheimer 2001). For political realists, the internal structure of the state is largely *irrelevant* because when the security of a state is threatened, all decision makers will behave in a similar manner. Democrats, dictators, monarchs, and oligarchs will all seek to maximize a state's ability to meet the external threat. Failure to do so would result in their elimination from the system in the long run (Waltz 1979).

Criticism of the realist claim that institutions are irrelevant has come from both within and outside the realist camp.[2] One realist faction has argued that although internal factors should not influence foreign policy, domestic politics often do creep into the policy process with unfortunate, if not disastrous, consequences (Gulick 1955; Machiavelli 1950). For these individuals, realism is a normative theory rather than an accurate description of behavior in the modern world; the realist tenets are goals to be strived for rather than an inevitable result of systemic forces. Many individuals who adhere to this vein of criticism have argued that democratic institutions are a *hindrance* to the development and implementation of coherent foreign policies. Implicitly or explicitly, these observers contend that polities with centralized and unchallenged authority have greater capacity for making sound foreign policy decisions over the long term. Machiavelli (1950) argued that democratic regimes were inherently expansionary or imperialist. Hintze ([1906] 1975) concluded that democratic institutions clashed with military efficiency.[3] Lippmann (1922, 1925) believed that the volatility of domestic public opinion undermined the president's ability to design a coherent foreign policy.

From outside the realist camp, a school of thought has rejected both the irrelevance and the hindrance arguments. Idealists, at least since the days of Immanuel Kant, have argued that democratic institutions improve decision making within states and that democracies in general serve as a positive force for peace in the international arena. Rather than hindering foreign policy formation, the democratic process encourages broad participation in the setting of foreign policy goals, ensuring that state policy serves the interests of the entire state rather than those of an individual or interest group. Reiter and Stam (2002) argue that this broad support helps democracies fight harder on the battlefield, contributing to the outstanding win-lose record of democratic polities.[4]

Kant ([1795] 1971), writing in an era in which a single republic existed, argued that the spread of the republican form of government would lead to a decline in international violence.[5] Kant claimed that the autocratic monarchs of his day chose a policy of war because they reaped the benefits of war without having to pay any of its costs. Plunder, monopoly trade links, and new revenue-producing land increased the wealth, power, and prestige of monarchs; human and financial costs were borne by mercenaries, unfortunates, and the taxpaying public. Kant argued that expanding the accountability of monarchs to a legislature would decrease the incentive for war by reintegrating the cost variable into the decision-making process.

Early empirical research did not support the Kantian hypothesis (Wright [1942] 1965; Small and Singer 1976). However, subsequent research found that although democracies are not particularly pacific overall, they seem to avoid large-scale conflict with other democracies (Doyle 1983, 1986; Maoz and Abdolali 1989; Bueno de Mesquita and Lalman 1992; Bremer 1992, 1993; Maoz and Russett 1993; Russett 1993; Rousseau et al. 1996; Huth and

Allee 2002; Russett and Oneal 2001; Dixon and Senese 2002; Peceny et al. 2002; Rasler and Thompson 2001; Bennett and Stam 2004). This "joint democracy" or "dyadic" finding has become the cornerstone of the democratic peace literature.

Central Questions

This book refines and extends research on the relationship between domestic political institutions and foreign policy decisions by examining six specific questions, presented sequentially in chapters 2 through 7. *First, are more democratic states less likely to initiate violence regardless of the regime type of their opponent, or are democracies more pacific only when dealing with other democracies?* This monadic versus dyadic effect of democratic institutions has been the central question in the debate on the relationship between regime type and international conflict. Although the vast majority of studies have produced strong support for the dyadic argument, research with respect to the monadic argument has produced mixed results.[6] Whereas several studies have rejected the monadic argument (Wright [1942] 1965; Small and Singer 1976; Chan 1984; Weede 1984; Maoz and Abdolali 1989; Dassel and Reinhardt 1999), others have found support for the argument either directly or indirectly (Rummel 1983; Bremer 1992; Schweller 1992; Dixon 1993; Benoit 1996; Rioux 1998; Schultz 1999, 2001; Ireland and Gartner 2001; Russett and Oneal 2001; Huth and Allee 2002; Bennett and Stam 2000, 2004).

Supporters of the monadic argument propose that leaders of democratic states are less likely to resort to military force to resolve an international conflict due to political norms or institutional structures (or some combination of the two). The political norms variant argues that democratic leaders are less likely to initiate violence because they are socialized to accept compromise and to use nonviolent means of conflict resolution. The institutional structure variant contends that democratic leaders are reluctant to use force because opposition groups in society can punish leaders for failures or costly mistakes. According to either variant, democratic polities should be less likely to resort to military force *regardless of the regime type of the opposition.*

Proponents of the dyadic argument begin with similar building blocks: peaceful norms of conflict resolution and constraining institutional structures. However, the dyadic argument adds a critical assumption that makes the behavior of democracies conditional (or interactive). The dyadic model assumes that democratic leaders *expect* that their nondemocratic opponents will quickly resort to force and/or will refuse to negotiate in good faith. This expectation leads democratic decision makers to adopt more coercive for-

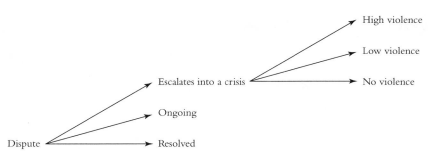

FIGURE I.I. Evolution of disputes into crises

eign policies when facing nondemocracies, including the willingness to use force first.

Although the "monadic" versus "dyadic" hypotheses have been tested in the literature, research design flaws ranging from theoretically inappropriate dependent variables to unsuitable units of observation render findings from previous research inconclusive. The empirical tests in Chapter 2 represent a unique contribution to the growing body of literature by employing the most recent version of the International Crisis Behavior data set (1918–2001), using dependent variables that measure the number of regular and irregular troops used in operations, focusing on conflict initiation rather than involvement, employing a directed dyad data structure, and testing competing explanations such as the selectorate model of Bueno de Mesquita and colleagues (2003).

Second, has the literature, which has focused almost exclusively on wars and militarized crises, underestimated the importance of institutions by neglecting the fact that democratic institutions may inhibit the escalation of a nonmilitarized dispute into a war or militarized crisis? Most of the democratic peace literature neglects the fact that political conflicts evolve over time.[7] Examining this evolutionary process is important because norms and structures could have different influences at different stages of the conflict. In this book, a *dispute* is defined as a political-security conflict between two independent states.[8] Disputes can be triggered by a variety of issues, ranging from disagreements over territorial boundaries to clashes over ideology. As Figure 1.1 depicts, disputes can evolve in a number of ways. A dispute can be permanently resolved through negotiation or third-party mediation. Alternatively, a dispute can be ongoing in the sense that the underlying conflict is never resolved to the liking of both parties, yet neither party chooses to escalate the dispute. Finally, a dispute can escalate into a *crisis*, defined as a confrontation in which at least one party actively contemplates using military force to resolve the dispute. Some crises are resolved without either party resorting to force; in others, one or both sides might use low or high levels of force with the aim of permanently and favorably resolving the dispute.

It is quite likely that selection effects have a powerful impact on the relationship between regime type and the use of external violence. Selection effects occur when individuals, such as foreign policy leaders, can choose whether or not to be in a sample. Whether or not to enter a dispute or escalate a dispute into a crisis is a choice. If democratic leaders systematically choose not to escalate disputes, then an analysis of a "crisis" data set that does not control for the self-selection process can lead to a misinterpretation of the relationship between regime type and the use of force. For example, we could conceivably discover a strong monadic effect at the dispute level but only a dyadic effect at the crisis level. An analysis of crises would incorrectly conclude there is no monadic effect of institutions. Conversely, we may find that norms and structures have powerful effects at the dispute level, but only structural concerns remain at the crisis level.

The empirical tests in Chapter 3 fill an important gap in the literature by employing a unique data set of international disputes. Unlike other research that has focused on a single-issue area (for example, the class of territorial disputes explored by Hensel [2001] or Huth and Allee [2002]), this data set contains disputes from a broad range of issue areas, including antiregime and ethnic conflict disputes. Moreover, broader data sets such as "all dyads" or "politically relevant dyads" (for example, Reed [2000]) cannot shed light on the central issue addressed in Chapter 3: why do some disputes escalate to military conflict whereas others do not?

Third, has the almost exclusive focus on regime type led to a neglect of how domestic institutions can either constrain or encourage armed conflict?[9] Critics of the democratic peace contend that regime type and institutional constraint are not perfectly correlated because the level of constraint can vary widely in both democracies and autocracies. Elman (2000) argues that prime ministers leading a coalition in a parliamentary democracy face greater *ex ante* and *ex post* constraints than either the leaders of presidential systems or a parliamentarian system dominated by a majority party. Prime ministers in coalition governments typically must obtain approval in the cabinet prior to commencing hostilities; in addition, after the commencement or conclusion of the operation, the government can be toppled in a vote of no confidence.[10] Similarly, Peterson (1996) argues that the distribution of decision-making power in the executive can constrain leaders. She contends that opposition within the Politburo in the post-Stalin years constrained leaders such as Nikita Khrushchev because the opposition could threaten to punish Khrushchev for failures or costly successes.[11]

In addition to neglecting variance within regime types, most studies of the democratic peace that have gone beyond the use of a dummy variable to measure regime type (that is, democracy or not) have relied on a single source of data on institutional constraint: the Polity data sets developed by Ted Robert Gurr and his colleagues. This dependency raises the issue of robustness with respect to the results. I address the institutional structure versus regime type debate in Chapter 4 by developing entirely new measures of institutional constraint. I examine how the existence of collective decision-making bodies in the executive, opposition parties in the legislature, and rival factions in the ruling party influence decisions to use military force to resolve international disputes.

The institutional constraint model developed and tested in Chapter 4 represents an important contribution to the literature because the analysis employs the new dispute data set, examines constraint in both democracies and autocracies, probes the impact of informal factions in both political parties and the executive branch, and measures political opposition in the legislature more precisely than have most previous studies.

Fourth, are institutional structures or political norms more important in constraining democracies from using force? The norms approach focuses on the socialization of leaders within the domestic sphere whereas the institutional approach emphasizes the domestic political costs of using force. In the political norms model, individual decision makers are constrained by their internal value systems; the decision maker believes that force is either a legitimate or illegitimate means for resolving political conflicts. In the structural model, political leaders are constrained by their domestic political environment. If opposition groups—regardless of their location in the political system—can punish decision makers for failures or costly successes, decision makers will be reluctant to use force.

Distinguishing the relative importance of structures and norms for foreign policy outcomes has been difficult for several reasons.[12] First, norms and structures are theoretically, at least to some degree, interactive. As leaders overseeing a transition to democracy would certainly attest, any attempt to develop stable democratic institutions requires at least some minimal acceptance of norms traditionally associated with democracy (for instance, resolving disputes within institutions and not resorting to physical force). The interactive relationship also results from the fact that the establishment and maintenance of democratic institutions in a society inevitably shape the socialization of future leaders. Second, developing measures of political norms independent of institutional structures is notoriously difficult. Some researchers have used institutional measures such as those found in the Polity data sets as a proxy for political norms.[13] Finally, most attempts to distinguish norms from structures have employed the problematic nondirected dyads as the unit of analysis (for example, did Ecuador and Peru go to war?) rather than the directed dyad (for example, did Ecuador initiate war? Did Peru initiate war?) used in this project.[14] For these three reasons, drawing any firm conclusions about the existing empirical literature on the norms–structure debate is difficult, if not impossible.

Distinguishing the relative importance of norms versus structures is more than a mere academic exercise; it has important implications for policy making and the democratic process. If domestic structures and the threat of punishment constrain leaders, we should see presidents and prime ministers attempt to use third parties and covert action in order to minimize domestic costs and circumvent legislative oversight. Conversely, if norms constrain presidents and prime ministers, citizens are relieved from having to worry about the diversion of force to less visible sources. The migration of covert operations from the Central Intelligence Agency (CIA) following the Church Committee's investigation of the CIA in the mid-1970s to the National Security Council (NSC) staff during the Reagan Administration provides at least anecdotal evidence in support of the structural explanation. The repercussions of the Iran-Contra scandal clearly indicate that the norms–structures debate has important policy implications and warrants further investigation.

Although interest in norms has increased over the last few years, no strong consensus has emerged in the literature. Whereas several studies have argued that norms constrain democratic behavior (Dixon and Senese 2002; Cederman 2001a; Cederman and Rao 2001; Kahl 1998/99), others reject the normative argument on logical grounds (Gowa 1999, 12; Bueno de Mesquita et al. 2003, 221) or empirical grounds (Huth and Allee 2002, 286; Reiter and Stam 2002, 163). This study contributes to this debate by employing new methods (for example, laboratory experiments and computer simulations), new data sets (the dispute data set), new independent variables (the means used to obtain office), and new causal arguments (institutional constraint is likely to apply only to large scale uses of force).[15]

Fifth, does regime transformation, which is the process of becoming more or less democratic, influence decisions to resolve an ongoing dispute with force? The monadic and dyadic democratic peace hypotheses have a very static flavor; country X is classified as regime type Y, and we investigate whether or not it used force to resolve a dispute. The theoretical framework neglects how

TABLE I.I
Regime type versus regime change

Year	Regime	Regime type	Regime change
1970	Autocratic	0	0
1971	Democratic	1	1
1972	Democratic	1	0
1973	Democratic	1	0
1974	Democratic	1	0

regime change may influence decisions to resort to violence. Moreover, Mansfield and Snyder (1995a, 1995b) have presented controversial evidence that democratization—the process of moving from some point along the autocracy-democracy continuum toward the democratic end of the continuum—*increases* the probability of conflict. This creates an interesting puzzle: how could the *process* of becoming more democratic increase the probability of conflict while simultaneously the *condition* of being more democratic decreases the probability of conflict?

The simplest way to conceptualize the distinction between process and condition is to image regime type as a dichotomous variable: a state is either democratic ($X_i = 1$) or autocratic ($X_i = 0$). Regime change involves a shift from one category to the other. Table 1.1 gives an example of a regime change from autocracy to democracy in 1971. The question is, Does the regime change variable provide information above and beyond the regime type variable? If the *process* of democratization were to increase the probability that a state uses force but the *condition* of being a democracy were to decrease the probability that a state uses force, we would expect a higher probability of force in 1970 (condition increases and process has no impact), a medium probability of force in 1971 (condition decreases but process increases), and a lower probability of using force in 1972 (condition decreases and process has no impact).[16]

Analyzing the impact of regime change will also shed light on the relative importance of norms versus structures. The structural argument leads one to expect that constraint emerges once democratic institutions are established. In contrast, the norms argument points to a much more gradual rise of constraint as norms of peaceful conflict resolution and compromise become entrenched in the population.

The quantitative analysis in Chapter 6 extends the democratization literature by employing a new data set of international disputes, testing Mansfield and Snyder's most recent operationalizations (2002a, 2002b), and controlling for competing explanations such as the selectorate model of Bueno de Mesquita and colleagues (2003). Although Mansfield and Snyder's work is some of the most cited in the literature, the statistical analysis provides no support for their dire predictions.

Sixth, how does the evolution of conflict, institutions, and norms influence deci-sions to use force and the amount of violence in the system overall? All too often, we examine conflicts as "snapshots" in time. Did El Salvador or Honduras fire the first shot in 1969? What was the size of the Honduran army relative to the Salvadoran army in that year? Were the states democratic or auto-cratic? Although these questions focus on the behavior and characteristics of the states in a particular year, they neglect the dynamic element of do-mestic politics and inter-state relations. For instance, the intensity of the ter-ritorial dispute between the countries rises and falls across time. Behavior by each party in the preceding years shapes perceptions and the nature of the conflict in the current year. Political leaders enter and leave office over the course of time. Overwhelming legislative majorities created in one election evaporate in the next. Dominant political parties in one period split into disputing factions in the next. Autocratic polities transition into democra-cies and either consolidate their new institutional framework or once again devolve into more autocratic structures. Relative military capacity, whether it is the number of soldiers or the quality of their arms, rises and falls across the life of an international dispute. In sum, many central dimensions in the study of regime type and violence vary across time, including the conflict (for example, peace, dispute, crisis, and war), institutions (democratization and autocratization), domestic political opposition (shifts in public opinion from strongly supportive to strongly opposed), and norms (the birth, life, and death of ideas).

The use of an evolutionary perspective to study the democratic peace has been extremely rare. Cederman and Rao (2001) employ a regression model with dynamic coefficients to study the strengthening of the dyadic demo-cratic peace across time. Cederman (2001b) employs an agent-based model to explore the implications of strategic tagging, regime-influenced alliance formation, and collective security for the emergence of a peaceful liberal world. I contribute to this emerging literature by creating a unique agent-based model that links institutional constraint and domestic political oppo-sition to the use of military force. For the first time, a computer simulation is used to explore the emergence of the democratic peace (rather than its consequences, as in Cederman [2001b]). The results indicate that a very simple model of domestic politics can produce both a monadic and dyadic peace over time.

Methodology

To address these six central questions, I draw on both qualitative and quantitative methodologies. Historically, there has been in important division in international relations research between those who focus on explaining unique events (such as why did the Spanish-American War occur) and those seeking to explain classes of events (such as why does war in general occur). Although some observers emphasize the importance of both approaches (Russett 1970), the "case study" approach is often pitted against the "large-N statistical" approach. In some cases, this competition occurs because different methods can lead to very different conclusions. For example, the quantitative study by Maoz and Russett (1993) finds that democracies are much less likely to use force against other democracies, but the qualitative analysis by Layne (1994) provides no evidence that knowledge of an opposing state's regime type plays a vital role in the suppression of conflict. In addition, the tension between methods derives from important differences in the training of scholars. Case study researchers develop the skills of a historian whereas large-N researchers are typically trained in econometrics.

Every method of inquiry has both strengths and weaknesses. Case studies are ideal for process tracing, but it is often difficult to generalize from them. Large-N statistical studies are useful for generalizing from the sample to the population and assessing the relative power of competing explanations, but they are rarely used for process tracing and tend to be vulnerable to spurious correlation. Formal models are ideally suited for ensuring logical consistency, but they cannot be used to test arguments. The strength of simulations lies in their ability to deal with complexity and emergent properties, but they are often dependent on critical assumptions and must be evaluated with real-world data. Finally, experiments are perfectly suited for controlling for competing explanations and establishing causality, but the external validity of the results is often open to question.

Kinder and Palfrey (1993, 3) argue that "triangulation" is the solution for dealing with the weaknesses associated with each approach: "Dependable knowledge has its base in no single method, but rather in triangulation across multiple methods." One of the unique contributions of this book is the use of several different methodologies to address the causes and consequences of the democratic peace (for example, large-N studies in chapters 2–6, case studies in chapters 2–6, experiments in Chapter 5, and a simulation in Chapter 7). Although the use of multiple methods is not a panacea, it expands our ability to test different aspects of the causal claims and ensure the robustness of our conclusions (Bueno de Mesquita 2002).

In terms of case studies, I do not randomly select cases in order to systematically test arguments. Rather, I use case studies for three specific purposes. First, the case studies are used to generate new hypotheses (Eckstein 1975). For example, the Suez Crisis case in Chapter 2 and the Greco-Turkish case in Chapter 3 are used to develop hypotheses about institutional constraint that are systematically tested with quantitative data in Chapter 4. Second, the case studies are used for process tracing (George and McKeown 1985). Whereas statistical analysis can produce a negative correlation between institutions and initiation, case studies can illuminate the process through which institutions constrain decision makers. For example, the process tracing in the Suez Crisis case contributes to the development of a domestic opposition model that is tested in a simulation in Chapter 7. Third, the case studies are used to examine outliers or deviant data points in the statistical analysis (King et al. 1994, 55; Van Evera 1997, 22). For example, the statistical results in Chapter 2 support the dyadic proposition that democracies are less likely to use force against fellow democracies. This raises an interesting question: why didn't the presence of joint democracy inhibit the escalation of conflict between Ecuador and Peru in the 1980s?

Each case study has been selected for two reasons: a *micro-objective* and a *macro-objective*. The micro-objective of each case study is to explore theoretical and empirical issues arising in each chapter (for example, constraint in autocracies in Chapter 4 and normative constraints in democracies in Chapter 5). These case studies complement the statistical analysis through hypothesis generation, process tracing, and an examination of outliers. The macro-objective of the case studies is to examine the universe of large-scale initiations of violence by democratic states. In each chapter the reader will be presented with several cases of democratic initiation so that by the final chapter we can examine the set of initiations as a whole. Although the macro-objective implies that the cases will have greater breadth than a purely micro-analysis would require, the alternative format of grouping all the cases in a single chapter after the statistical analysis would undermine the micro-objective of the cases. In the concluding chapter, I examine the collection of democratic initiations *as a group* in order to identify factors that contribute to the breakdown of normative and institutional constraints on the use of force. This cross-case examination highlights several factors that have been neglected in previous research on the relationship between political structure and military force. Therefore, the macro-objective of the cases is to promote hypothesis generation for future research.[17]

Overview of the Book

The book is divided into eight chapters. Each of the substantive chapters (chapters 2 through 7) focuses on one of the five central questions posed earlier. In Chapter 2, I examine the monadic and dyadic hypotheses within the context of international crises from 1918 to 2000. I find that within militarized crises, democracies are only less conflictual when dealing with other democracies. I conclude the chapter with an examination of two case studies: the Suez Crisis and the Ecuador-Peru territorial dispute. The Suez Crisis is used to probe the failure of the monadic hypothesis; the Ecuador-Peru case sheds light on the robustness of the dyadic findings.

In Chapter 3, I explore the selection bias question through the use of a new data set of international disputes. I find that democratic institutions inhibit the emergence of crises regardless of the regime type of the opponent. This chapter concludes with two case studies (Israel versus Egypt and Greece versus Turkey) that illustrate how the evolution of the conflict influences domestic political constraints.

In Chapter 4, I examine whether focusing on regime type alone coupled with relying on single source of data has led us to underestimate the constraining power of domestic institutions. Although the findings generally support the existing literature, they also highlight how constraint may decline in democracies and rise in autocracies. The case studies explore the lack of constraint in some democracies (India versus Pakistan in 1971, El Salvador versus Honduras in 1969, and Britain versus Russia in 1918) and the importance of constraint in some autocracies (Saudi Arabia and Jordan).

In Chapter 5, I test the relative importance of two explanations of the democratic peace: cultural norms versus institutional structures. Contrary to conventional wisdom, the quantitative findings support the structural argument more than the normative argument. In order to test the robustness of the results, I test the normative and structural arguments by using a laboratory experiment. Finally, I probe these findings, using a series of case studies in which norms and institutions failed to constrain democratic polities from initiating violence to resolve an international dispute. The cases include Britain in the Middle East during World War II and the United States in Cuba and Grenada during the Cold War.

In Chapter 6, I examine the impact of regime change (that is, democratization and autocratization) on a state's willingness to use force. I find that contrary to previous research (for example, Mansfield and Snyder [1995a, 1995b]), we need not fear democratization. I probe the quantitative findings by examining the impact of regime change in the midst of an ongoing territorial dispute (Somalia versus Ethiopia) and the emergence of a combative young democracy following World War I (Czechoslovakia during the Teschen Crisis and Hungarian War).

In Chapter 7, I explore the evolution of institutions, norms, and conflict. Using the quantitative and qualitative findings from the previous chapters, I develop an agent-based computer simulation to determine if a minimal set of assumptions about the constraining power of domestic political opposition can produce a monadic peace at the initiation stage and a dyadic peace at the war stage of conflict. The simulation allows institutions to evolve across time, norms to emerge, and conflicts to pass through stages. The results of the evolutionary model strongly support the structural version of the democratic peace.

In the concluding chapter, I synthesize the major findings and address directions for future research by comparing and contrasting the case studies and summarizing the findings for the six questions posed in this introduction.

Significance of the Project

Individually, the analyses presented in the following chapters challenge the conventional understanding of the relationship between democratic institutions and norms and the use of military force to resolve inter-state conflicts. Contrary to the dominant view, I demonstrate the importance of monadic constraints in disputes, the evolution of constraint across time, the dominance of institutions over norms in disputes, the variability of constraint in autocracies and democracies, and the pacifying effect of democratization.

Collectively, the quantitative and qualitative findings push the democratic peace literature in new directions. The synthesis of findings points to a dynamic and evolutionary model of the relationship between regime type and external conflict. The nature of the conflict, the institutional arrangements, the constraining power of norms, and the domestic opposition to the use of force all evolve over the course of time. This process implies that traditional static analyses, which view international conflicts as "snapshots in time," may obscure as much as they illuminate. For example, the findings in this book demonstrate that the rise and fall of domestic opposition to the use of force is to a large degree the product of the behavior of the opposing state. This critical and evolving variable has been neglected by the static quantitative analyses and formal models that dominate the democratic peace literature.

The project also contributes to the broader international relations literature. The evolutionary nature of international conflict implies that the impact of specific variables (including realist variables such as alliance ties and constructivist variables such as a shared sense of identity) may have very different effects at different stages of a conflict. In addition, the constraint model proposes hypotheses applicable to all states rather than the narrow subset of democratic polities that have been at the center of the dyadic-oriented democratic peace literature. Finally, the political norms discussion that focuses on the personal experiences of individual leaders is applicable to a broad range of normative and cultural explanations. The analysis demonstrates the feasibility and utility of "bringing the individual back in."

The findings have important implications for foreign policy in the post–Cold War era. First, the findings demonstrate that the monadic constraint of democracy stems more from institutional constraint than from normative constraint, implying that democratic decision makers will be tempted to avoid constraint by employing secret operations, third-party surrogates, technological solutions, and rapid and overwhelming military operations. Democratic citizens must be vigilant if the constraining power of democratic institutions is to be effective. Second, the analysis demonstrates that labeling all autocracies as "aggressive" and all democracies as "pacific" is likely to lead one astray. Given that the amount of constraint varies significantly among autocracies, foreign policy experts must open the "black box" of domestic politics to determine the extent of institutional constraint and the sources of domestic opposition. Third, the results indicate that promoting democratization will contribute to a decline in the amount of violence in the international system in the long run. This does not imply that democratic states should pursue "crusading policies" aimed at spreading democracy on the tip of a bayonet. Externally imposed democracy is rarely stable in the long run, and the analysis clearly demonstrates that the most conflictual states in the international system are transitional states possessing a mixture of democratic and autocratic features. Rather, democracies should promote policies that encourage both a peaceful external environment and the development of indigenous institutions and norms conducive with a transition to a stable democracy (such as a liberal economy, high levels of education, rule of law, and greater income equality). Democratic transitions should be welcomed rather than feared.

Notes

1. Although Gowa seeks to refute the notion that democratic institutions matter, toward the end of the book she discusses an "autocratic peace." Thus, institutions creep back into the analysis. See Owen (2000) on this point.

2. The realist school of thought contains a broad range of theoretical positions, many of which are in conflict with one another. The structural or neo-realist fac-

tion represented by the work of Waltz (1979) takes the most extreme position regarding the irrelevance of domestic institutions. Many contemporary and classical realists would disagree with Waltz's purely systemic view. See Forde (1995) and the debate between Vasquez and his critics (1997) on this point.

3. Hintze began to question this belief after Germany's failure to prevail in World War I.

4. The central claim in the Reiter and Stam argument is that democracies win because they pick fights that they can win. See Desch (2002) for a critique of the argument. Unfortunately, methodological problems blunt the force of this critique. Bueno de Mesquita and colleagues (2003) also predict and find empirical evidence for the claim that democracies try harder on the battlefield.

5. The single republic was the newly independent United States. However, due to gender, race, property, and tax restrictions, only a very small percentage of the adult population in the United States exercised their right to vote in elections. As with most of his contemporaries, Kant carefully distinguished a republic (participation of the propertied classes and legislative constraints on the executive) from a democracy (tyranny of the lower classes). The gradual expansion of the vote to all individuals has led to a reduction in this fear and a merging of the terms in everyday language. On this distinction, see Owen (1993, 1997).

6. A small number of studies, primarily qualitative in nature, have questioned the empirical support for the dyadic argument (Gowa 1999; Layne 1994, 1997; Spiro 1994; Owen 1994; Rock 1997; Elman 2000; Henderson 2002).

7. In Chapter 3, I discuss exceptions to this statement, including Dixon (1993, 1994), Huth (1996), Huth and Allee (2002), and Bennett and Stam (2004). Dixon tests propositions drawn from the democratic peace literature using the Alker and Sherman (1986) data set, which explicitly divides disputes into multiple phases as defined by Bloomfield and Leiss (1969). However, Dixon does not test a selection model. Huth and Allee focus on a single issue: territorial disputes. The massive effort of Bennett and Stam, which examines sixteen major theories using all dyads as well as conflictual subsets, provides only limited tests of the democratic peace argument. Finally, Chapter 7 addresses the evolutionary work of Cederman (2001a, 2001b, 2003).

8. Therefore, my definition of *dispute* differs from that employed in the Correlates of War Militarized Interstate Dispute (MID) data set (see Gochman and Maoz [1984]). I categorize MIDs as crises because military force is used, displayed, or threatened by at least one party in the crisis. For example, many territorial disputes never escalate to the point at which they would be captured by the MID data set. Reed (2000) examines the impact of selection on the dyadic hypothesis.

9. The one early exception is the work of Morgan and Schwebach (1992). More recently, there have been a number of studies addressing the topic: Reiter and Tillman (2002); Auerswald (2000); Ireland and Gartner (2001); Prins and Sprecher (1999); Elman (2000); and Clark (2000). In Chapter 4, I summarize these studies and explain how my research extends beyond this earlier work in important ways.

10. Constraint in the decision-making process is referred to as *ex ante* constraint whereas the ability of legislatures and publics to punish decision makers after the policy has been selected is referred to as *ex post* constraint. Elman's (1997a) case study

of the 1982 Israeli invasion of Lebanon is informative because even a coalition government appears unconstrained due to relatively homogeneous views of cabinet members and to the structure of civil-military relations. Skillful manipulation of the decision process coupled with tacit prime minister approval allowed Defense Minister Sharon to expand the war in Lebanon incrementally.

11. Morgan and Campbell (1991) and Hagan (1987, 1993) also argue that constraint can vary independent of regime type. In addition, the literature derived from Putnam's (1988) two-level game explicitly examines the role of domestic constraint on inter-state bargaining.

12. Pickering (2002) and Owen (1997) argue that the norms versus structure debate is a false dichotomy. Although conceding that there is a reciprocal relationship between norms and structures, I argue (as do Reiter and Stam [2002] and Huth and Allee [2002]) that the theories make divergent predictions in certain situations.

13. This approach may be appropriate as long as no attempt is made to distinguish the relative importance of norms and structures. Dixon's (1993) conclusion that norms are more important than structures is problematic given his reliance on structural variables.

14. Bennett and Stam (2004) argue that the directed dyad is more appropriate for theories predicting initiation. Kegley and Skinner (1976) refer to the nondirected dyad unit of analysis as the "summed dyad." In order to test a summed dyad hypothesis, data are collected at the dyad level (that is, does the crisis escalate to a war?). Kegley and Skinner question the utility of the summed dyad approach because it masks just which party in the dyad is responsible for the observed outcome.

15. This project does not address the role of shared identity in the democratic peace (Hopf 1998; Kahl 1998/99). This argument could be viewed as a variant of the normative argument discussed in Chapter 2. For an analysis of identity creation that could also explain the democratic peace, see Rousseau (2004).

16. As discussed in Chapter 6, there could be a lagged effect of regime change. A one-year lag would imply that the regime would have a medium probability of a use of force in both 1971 and 1972.

17. Using the dependent variable to select cases *for testing an argument* is generally frowned upon (King et al. 1994). However, Dion (1998) argues that selecting on the dependent variable is useful for testing necessary conditions. King and Zeng suggest that selecting on the dependent variable may be useful in situations in which the occurrence of the variable is very rare (2001, 695). This interesting debate does not apply to this project because *I am not using case studies to test arguments.*

CHAPTER 2

The Impact of Institutions and Norms in International Crises

ACCORDING TO BOTH classical and structural realism, systemic forces associated with the distribution of power among states are the primary determinants of state behavior (Morgenthau 1973; Waltz 1979; Doyle 1997). Realists assume that states resemble unitary rational actors in pursuit of a single overriding objective: survival and security in an anarchic system. The strenuous demands of the international system lead all states to behave in a similar fashion regardless of their particular political institutions, economic structure, ideological orientation, or leadership quality. This system-oriented, power-politics perspective of realism came to dominate both the study of international relations and U.S. foreign policy during the Cold War era.

The dominance of realism has been challenged from a number of perspectives.[1] Those questioning the unitary actor assumption have shown that the state is, in fact, composed of many organizations with divergent preferences, all competing for control of foreign policy (Allison 1971; Halperin 1974; Peterson 1996). Similarly, those questioning the rational actor assumption have demonstrated that foreign policy decision makers often deviate from the guidelines of purely rational choice (Jervis 1976; Jervis et al. 1985; Lebow 1981).

Perhaps the most important attack on realism, however, has centered on the relationship between domestic political structures and external behavior. Realism predicts that states, regardless of regime type, will behave in a similar manner when facing the same international situation (Waltz 1979, 68–69). Totalitarian regimes, military dictatorships, absolute monarchies, and political democracies will all behave the same because states cannot afford to

TABLE 2.1
Regime type and war involvement, 1816–1982

Regime type	Number of wars
Democracy versus democracy	0 wars
Democracy versus authoritarian	50 wars
Authoritarian versus authoritarian	68 wars

let internal factors influence decisions that are directly related to the security of the state.[2] This prediction is directly contradicted by the aggregate statistics regarding war participation and regime type presented in Table 2.1, which summarizes the relationships for all inter-state wars from 1816 to 1982.[3]

War is defined as a conflict between the regular armed forces of two independent states that results in at least 1,000 battlefield fatalities. *Regime type* simply separates political systems into two mutually exclusive categories: fully democratic states and all other nondemocratic states. Table 2.1 highlights the two empirical foundations of the rapidly growing democratic peace literature. First, democratic states rarely if ever become involved in wars with other democratic states. Indeed, the zero in the first row is the most remarkable feature of the table.[4] Second, whereas democracies may avoid war with each other, they are certainly involved in frequent conflict with nondemocracies. In fact, numerous studies have shown that democracies engage in war just as *frequently* as nondemocracies (Small and Singer 1976; Maoz and Abdolali 1989). According to Levy (1988), the two-part empirical observation now conventionally labeled the "democratic peace" is the closest thing to an empirical law found in the study of international relations. Clearly, realists have a difficult time explaining the sharp contrasts in Table 2.1.

The empirical findings shown in Table 2.1 are puzzling for idealists as well. Many idealists, such as Woodrow Wilson, have claimed that the constraining influence of a pacific public limits the use of force by foreign policy decision makers in a democratic regime (Notter 1965, 460). However, the results clearly indicate that a "pacific" public cannot be the cause of the democratic peace. If the public in democracies were pacific, then the number of democracy-authoritarian conflicts should be closer to zero. If democratic citizens abhor war and bloodshed in general, this aversion should exist regardless of the type of opposition. Thus, neither realists nor idealists can *simultaneously* explain both halves of the two-part empirical observation (that is, low democracy–democracy conflict *and* relatively high democracy–autocracy conflict).

In this chapter, I begin by reviewing two categories of explanations for the relationship between domestic institutions and international conflict: institutional structure explanations and political norms explanations. As will be shown, either type of explanation can be used to construct a monadic argument (democracies are more pacific in general) or a dyadic argument (democracies are more pacific only with other democracies). I then test the monadic and dyadic hypotheses using a data set of international crises from 1918 to 2000; testing the norms versus structures argument is deferred until Chapter 5.[5] Finally, I probe the empirical findings through two case studies: the Suez Crisis and the Ecuador-Peru territorial conflict. The statistical results indicate that only a dyad democratic peace holds at the crisis level.

Structural Explanations of the Democratic Peace

As stated above, whereas numerous studies have confirmed that democracies rarely if ever engage in large-scale conflict with each other (Babst 1972; Doyle 1983, 1986; Maoz and Abdolali 1989; Bueno de Mesquita and Lalman 1992; Bremer 1993; Maoz and Russett 1993; Russett 1993; Rousseau et al. 1996; Huth and Allee 2002; Russett and Oneal 2001; Dixon and Senese 2002; Peceny et al. 2002; Rasler and Thompson 2001; Bennett and Stam 2004; Bueno de Mesquita et al. 2003), other analyses have demonstrated that democracies are involved in war just as frequently as nondemocracies (Wright [1942] 1965; Small and Singer 1976; Chan 1984; Weede 1984; Maoz and Abdolali 1989; Dassel and Reinhardt 1999). Despite consensus on the fact that democracies do not engage in armed conflict against other democracies, there is no consensus on the process that produces this outcome. Although there are several competing explanations, most fall into either the institutional structures school or the political norms–culture school.

The institutional structures school focuses on the relationship between political structures and the domestic political costs of using force (Morgan and Campbell 1991; Morgan and Schwebach 1992). According to this school, decisions to use military force are *choices* made by political leaders based on domestic and international cost-benefit calculations. Foreign policy decisions can have costly domestic political repercussions. The expenditure of resources and loss of human life can mobilize opposition groups or fracture a ruling coalition. Relative to other political systems, democratic decision makers must be more sensitive to these potential domestic costs. This constrains their behavior in comparison with leaders of nondemocratic states. Immanuel Kant, the first proponent of the democratic peace, uses this argument to support his claim that oligarchies are more likely to initiate war than republics are (Kant [1795] 1971).[6]

Structural explanations are based, either implicitly or explicitly, on a number of underlying assumptions. Based on a review of structural arguments, I have compiled a set of assumptions that I contend are necessary for the institutional argument to operate as hypothesized. These assumptions are worth laying out in detail in order to compare structural explanations with competing normative explanations and to examine the claim that only interactions between democracies result in less conflictual relations.

STRUCTURAL ASSUMPTION I

A central goal of all state leaders is to retain their position of domestic political power.

The first assumption simply asserts that chief executives, using the information available, choose policies that maximize their probability of remaining in office. Whether they are single-minded seekers of reelection or ruthless dictators, these decision makers seek to retain their positions of power.

STRUCTURAL ASSUMPTION 2

In all political systems, domestic political opponents of a regime will attempt to mobilize political opposition when domestic and foreign policies pursued by the regime fail to achieve stated policy goals.

The second assumption is important because it implies that *all* political leaders have some basis of support, without which they would fall from power (Salamore and Salamore 1978; Hagan 1987, 1993). In very exclusive regimes, this supporting coalition may be limited to the military or the communist party. In more open political systems, this power base may be a political party or a coalition of parties. Regardless of the type of regime, all chief executives rely on constituencies whom they must reward or placate.

The second assumption also highlights the fact that domestic political opposition will exploit foreign policy failures. Although foreign policy successes may or may not help a chief executive remain in power, foreign policy failures are inevitably costly (Mueller 1973; Cotton 1987; Bueno de Mesquita and Siverson 1995). Failures can alienate members of the ruling coalition, leading to their defection from, and possibly the collapse of, the ruling coalition. In addition, a policy failure provides opposition groups with an issue useful for attacking the chief executive and ruling party. This attack can involve shifting mass opinion toward the opposition camp or mobilizing previously acquiescent groups against the regime.

STRUCTURAL ASSUMPTION 3

In democratic political systems, counterelites are better able to mobilize opposition in order to challenge incumbents for their policy failures.

The third assumption links institutional structures to opposition. Although opposition exists in all political systems, the more open the political system, the more likely it is that opposition groups will mobilize to challenge the ruling party. Moreover, the more open the system, the more likely it is that opposition groups have the power to inflict costs on the executive for making unpopular foreign policy decisions. Therefore, democratic leaders face a higher expected cost for failure because the probability that costs will be imposed is higher.

STRUCTURAL ASSUMPTION 4

In all political systems, state leaders believe that a foreign policy setback for their country, stemming from a diplomatic retreat or military defeat, could pose a threat to their domestic political position.[7]

Decisions to use military force are particularly risky since the likelihood of success and the costs to be incurred are often difficult to predict with high confidence. As a result, foreign policy leaders who face credible political opposition should be more concerned with protecting themselves from a political backlash by avoiding risky military confrontations.

The assumption also implies that using military force and failing to achieve a foreign policy goal is, on average, more costly than not using force and failing to achieve the goal. Although there are obvious historical examples to the contrary, the use of military force tends to raise the stakes for domestic leaders because it indicates they attach real importance to the issue. Moreover, whereas certain opposition groups can be expected to punish a leader for failure regardless of the actions taken by the chief executive, others can be expected to punish for either using force at all or for failing after committing resources. For example, the Suez Group in the House of Commons strongly opposed Britain's retreat from empire and the loss of British control over the Suez Canal. The Suez Group could be expected to punish Prime Minister Eden if he failed to retrieve the Canal Zone. However, having used force and failed, the opposition increased to include those who rejected the use of force to defend imperialist goals as well as those who believed Eden was responsible for a botched military operation. Similarly, it seems quite reasonable to assume that President Bush would have been punished more severely if the military operation to liberate Kuwait in 1991 had failed than if he had never committed 500,000 troops to the goal.[8]

Taken together, the four structural assumptions imply that failure is more costly in more democratic political systems.[9] If failure is more costly in open political systems, decision makers in these regimes will be less likely to initiate or escalate conflict. The structural argument in its most basic form implies that democratic polities should be less likely to use force than their counterparts in less democratic regimes *regardless* of the opponent. This is a purely *monadic* structural argument: the regime type of the state alone determines its behavior in international disputes.

However, most explanations of the democratic peace, both structural and cultural, are *dyadic* in nature. A dyadic process implies that the behavior of a state toward an adversary is conditional on the regime type of the adversary. This tendency has been driven by the second empirical observation: democracies appear to engage in conflicts with autocracies just as frequently as autocracies do with each other.

According to proponents of the institutional structures school, such as Bueno de Mesquita and Lalman, democratic states are likely to be peaceful only when dealing with other democratic states (1992, chapter 5). The logic of their dyadic argument has three steps. First, the world is filled with hawks (that is, leaders who are uncompromising and predisposed to use force to resolve disputes) and doves (that is, leaders who are compromising and predisposed to use reciprocating strategies). However, there is uncertainty surrounding which strategy will be adopted by any particular state. Second, domestic institutional structures reduce (but do not eliminate) this uncertainty by signaling a state's most likely strategy. Due to the potential domestic costs of using force, decision makers believe that democracies are more likely than nondemocracies to adopt "dovish" strategies. Third, when a democracy confronts another democracy, each expects a negotiated outcome and restraint on the use of force. However, when a hawk confronts a democracy, the hawk expects to meet a dove and is likely to exploit the situation. In such a situation, the dove adopts the strategies of its opponent and often initiates conflict in order to preempt an expected attack. The logic of the argument is purely *dyadic*: democratic states pursue compromising and nonviolent strategies only when dealing with other democratic states.

A second dyadic structural argument focuses on the difficulty of mobilizing domestic support for the use of force. According to Maoz and Russett (1993), the inclusiveness of democratic regimes hinders their ability to quickly mobilize groups in favor of military action. Authoritarian regimes, which incorporate a much narrower band of the political spectrum, can quickly reach a consensus on the use of force. When a dispute emerges between two democratic states, the slow process of mobilization in both states aids the resolution of conflicts through noncoercive means. However, when a conflict arises between a democratic state and a nondemocratic state, the rapid mobilization of the latter entity forces the democratic leaders "to find ways to circumvent the due political process" (Maoz and Russett 1993, 626). The emergency situation forces the democratic state to adopt the tactics of its opposition. Although the logic of the argument differs from that proposed by Bueno de Mesquita and Lalman, both share the belief that the democratic peace is purely a *dyadic* phenomenon.

Both the Bueno de Mesquita-Lalman and Maoz-Russett dyadic explanations require the adoption of a new "dyadic" structural assumption.

DYADIC STRUCTURAL ASSUMPTION
The expectation of democratic leaders that their nondemocratic opponents will not resolve conflict through peaceful means leads them to abandon strategies based on reciprocity and/or to circumvent institutional constraints.

Two comments about the relationship between the dyadic and monadic structural explanations are in order. First, the dominance of the dyadic perspective has led researchers to prematurely dismiss the monadic argument. As mentioned above, a large number of studies have isolated a monadic impact of institutions. Moreover, a significant amount of empirical evidence contradicts the micro-foundations of the dyadic argument.[10]

Second, the dyadic and monadic hypotheses need not be mutually exclusive propositions. It is quite possible that both forces may constrain democratic states from using force. Moreover, it is possible that the source of constraint may vary with the stage of the conflict. In fact, a major finding of this book is that whereas a monadic constraint exists at the dispute phase of the conflict (see Chapter 3), it tends to diminish as the conflict escalates into a militarized crisis (see Chapter 2). From the Bueno de Mesquita and Lalman perspective, it may be that democracies do not automatically view autocratic states as "hawks" prone to use military force. However, as the conflict escalates, democracies may interpret moves by their autocratic opponents as hostile acts indicative of a "hawkish" strategy. The perception of belligerent behavior by the adversary may in turn reduce domestic opposition to the use of force to resolve the crisis.[11]

Before concluding the discussion of structural arguments, it is important to address two recent additions to this broad category. The first is an information-signaling model proposed by Fearon (1994) and extended by Schultz (1998, 1999, 2001). The information model claims that institutions can reduce conflict by signaling the resolve of actors in a crisis. Fearon argues that in a world of complete information, decision makers can determine each side's expected value for war. In such a world, war is rare because leaders can easily determine if their threat to alter the status quo will be met with acquiescence or military force. Unfortunately, we live in a world of incomplete information. Leaders have private information on their willingness to use force, and they have an incentive to misrepresent this information (in other words, bluff) to get a better deal. Fearon argues that in this incomplete-information world, leaders facing higher domestic audience costs can signal their resolve more credibly and are less likely to bluff. Fearon contends that democratic leaders have higher audience costs because if they threaten an opponent and back down, they face higher costs than do autocratic leaders. Moreover, the transparency of debates within democracies provides information to international opponents. Schultz argues that if domestic political opposition in a democracy supports the executive, this sends a confirmatory signal that international opponents ignore at their peril (2001, 9). In sum, democratic institutions reduce uncertainty about a state's willingness to fight, which decreases the probability that a democracy initiates an attack and increases the probability that democratic opponents back down. The explanation is *monadic*: democracies should be less likely to engage in military conflict.[12]

Schultz provides the most rigorous empirical test of the signaling model to date.[13] His research design is a wonderful example of using the process underlying a theory to derive testable propositions (2001, 124). Despite this admirable effort, he concludes his statistical analysis by observing that the tests "cannot rule out the possibility that the causal mechanisms of both the informational and institutional constraints perspectives are at work" (2001, 160). Unfortunately, the new data collected for this project (for example, the institutional variables in Chapter 4 and the political norms variables in Chapter 5) cannot disentangle these processes either. However, several case studies have indicated that both the informational and the institutional causal mechanisms are at work. In particular, Schultz's claim that the domestic political opposition can play an important "confirmatory" role emerges in several case studies.

The second recent addition is the selectorate theory developed by Bueno de Mesquita, Smith, Siverson, and Morrow (2003). Although the theory has its roots in the international relations literature (for example, Bueno de Mesquita et al. 1999), the authors claim that the theory can be used to explain behaviors and outcomes in large areas of comparative and U.S. politics (such as corruption, oppression, poverty, prosperity, political inclusiveness, political survival, term limits, and distributive politics). Given that many of these issues fall well outside the bounds of the current study, I will focus on the causal logic and predictions of the selectorate theory with respect to the democratic peace.[14]

Although the formal model is complicated, the intuition behind it is rather straightforward. Bueno de Mesquita and colleagues claim that the size of the ruling coalition relative to the selectorate influences incentives for the allocation of public and private goods; the mix of these two types of goods then influences a host of dependent variables such as economic prosperity and military conflict. The model focuses on three groups in society: (1) citizens (N), (2) the subset of citizens included in selection of leaders (S), and (3) the ruling government's constituency (W). Leaders and challengers compete for loyalty from members of the selectorate by providing (or promising to provide) public and private goods through taxing and spending policies. In general, leaders with a small selectorate (typically a form of autocracy) have an incentive to reward members with private goods. These members tend to be very loyal and uncritical because if the leader falls from power, they are unlikely to be in the new winning coalition. In contrast, leaders with a large selectorate (typically a form of democracy) have an incentive to reward members with public goods because they simply lack the resources necessary to provide private benefits to each member of the huge winning coalition. Moreover, members of the winning coalition in democracies tend to be less loyal and more critical because they can more easily defect to the challenger.[15]

Bueno de Mesquita and colleagues claim that only the selectorate model can explain seven empirical regularities in the democratic peace literature: (1) democracies do not fight other democracies, (2) democracies fight non-democracies quite regularly, (3) democracies win more wars, (4) two democracies tend to peacefully resolve disputes, (5) democracies suffer fewer battle deaths and shorter wars, (6) transitional democracies are more likely to fight, and (7) major-power democracies are more constrained than minor-power democracies (2003, 219). The authors claim that the selectorate model is a marked improvement on earlier formal models because those models simply *assumed* that democracies were more constrained than autocracies.

Does the selectorate model predict a monadic or dyadic democratic peace? The authors' response in unambiguous: only a dyadic peace. However, the causal mechanisms appear to be monadic in that they constrain democratic leaders regardless of the regime type of the opponent: "Fearing public policy failure, democracies try to avoid those contests they do not think they can win" (Bueno de Mesquita et al. 2003, 226). Once they find themselves at war, democrats try harder to win because defeats are more costly than for autocracies. Thus, the central causal mechanisms are monadic in nature (in other words, less likely to start wars and more likely to fight hard regardless of the regime type of the adversary). Although war is even less likely between two democracies, it is simply the results of the interaction between two constrained states.

Given the discrepancy between the authors' claims and my interpretation of their model, what would a fair test of the selectorate model entail? I have chosen to test both a monadic and dyadic version of their argument. Bueno de Mesquita and colleagues claim that states with a large selectorate will be extremely sensitive to the balance of power. The authors predict that even within democratic dyads, stronger democracies should be willing to use force against weaker democracies (2003, 219; Dixon and Senese 2002, 550).[16] Therefore, I will test whether the monadic and dyadic constraining power of democracies declines as the balance of forces becomes more favorable. As we shall see in the empirical analysis, these predictions are not supported by the data. Moreover, the evolutionary institutional model described in subsequent chapters can explain the all the empirical puzzles tested by Bueno de Mesquita and colleagues.

Normative Explanations of the Democratic Peace

The political norms school emphasizes the socialization of political leaders within their domestic political environment (Maoz and Russett 1993; Russett 1993; Dixon 1993, 1994; Huth and Allee 2002). This argument has two parts. First, democratic political leaders are socialized within a system that emphasizes compromise and nonviolence. Leaders typically resolve political conflicts in democracies through negotiation and logrolling. Losing a political battle does not result in the loss of political rights or exclusion from future battles. Moreover, coercion and violence are not seen as legitimate means for resolving a dispute. Conversely, nondemocratic political leaders are socialized in an environment in which politics is more akin to a zero-sum game in which rivals and losers are regularly removed from the game. Coercion and violence are more widely accepted as legitimate means for resolving political conflicts. In general, political leaders are more likely to impose decisions rather than compromise when dealing with the opposition.

Second, the norms school assumes that domestic political norms are naturally externalized by decision makers when they confront international disputes. In sum, the logic of the norms argument is based on the following three assumptions:

NORMATIVE ASSUMPTION 1
Domestic political systems socialize political leaders regarding acceptable ways to resolve political conflicts.

NORMATIVE ASSUMPTION 2
Leaders socialized within democratic political systems are more likely to use compromise and nonviolent means to resolve disputes than are leaders socialized in authoritarian political systems.

NORMATIVE ASSUMPTION 3

The same norms and conflict-resolution practices employed by political leaders when they are involved in domestic disputes are used when these leaders seek to resolve international disputes and crises.[17]

From these three assumptions, I derive the central norms-based hypothesis of the study: the more firmly established the peaceful norms of conflict resolution within a society, the lower the probability of initiating or escalating the use of force in external relations.

The logic of the political norms argument described above is purely *monadic*: democratic leaders should externalize their peaceful norms regardless of the opponent's regime type. As with structural explanations, the general monadic argument has been adapted in order to fit the two-part empirical observation underlying the democratic peace. The dyadic political norms explanation adds a fourth assumption to the list.

DYADIC NORMATIVE ASSUMPTION

The expectation that a nondemocratic opponent will not rely on peaceful means of conflict resolution leads democratic states to abandon their peaceful norms.

Although all decision makers externalize their domestic norms of dispute resolution when dealing with inter-state conflicts, this externalization is *conditional* for democratic decision makers. Democratic leaders externalize their domestic norms only if they expect similar behavior from their opponent. Because democratic decision makers expect other democratic leaders to externalize norms of peaceful conflict resolution, they behave in accordance with their peaceful norms. Conversely, because democracies expect nondemocratic states to externalize "violent" norms of conflict resolution, they adopt the more coercive and uncompromising strategies of their opponents. Taken together, these assumptions imply that democratic states pursue compromising and nonviolent strategies only when dealing with other democratic states. In theory, this purely dyadic relationship can explain the two key empirical observations.

As with the institutional arguments, the monadic and dyadic impact of norms need not be mutually exclusive. Norms may decrease the likelihood that democratic leaders are the first party to resort to military force to resolve the conflict. However, this conflict-dampening effect may be accentuated when facing a state that the democracy expects to employ reciprocity-based strategies. In addition, the power of the respective explanation may relate to the stage of the conflict. The monadic constraint inhibiting initiation during the dispute phase may evaporate when the opponent's willingness to use force becomes increasingly apparent.

Testing the Arguments

There have been a number of recent works that have explored the monadic and dyadic arguments. Several of these studies have been unable to isolate a powerful impact of democratic institutions on international conflict. Gowa (1999) argues that shared interests rather than shared identity explain the dyadic democratic peace. During the Cold War, the major democratic powers faced a common enemy, which realists and liberals alike expect to reduce the probability of conflict. Gowa tests her argument against the dyadic democratic peace hypothesis by dividing her war and MID data sets into three historical eras (1816–1913, 1918–1939, and 1945–1980). The only evidence she finds of a dyadic democratic peace is during the Cold War. Gartzke (1998) also argues that interests rather than regime type determine conflict propensity. Using United Nations voting patterns as a proxy for interests, he finds the dyadic impact of democracy weakened or eliminated when controlling for interests using a MID data set from 1950 to 1985.

Dassel and Reinhardt (1999) examine diversionary war. They predict that diversionary war will take place only when major abrupt institutional change threatens the position of the military. Using a data set of all countries from 1827 and a fixed-effect duration-independent logit model, they find that abrupt institutional change is positively associated with the initiation of international violence (that is, MID use of force or war) and domestic violence (that is, coup or civil war). When focusing on international violence, they find no evidence that democracy inhibits the use of force despite a wide variety of operationalizations of the variable.

In contrast, several other recent works find strong support for the democratic peace argument. Bennett and Stam (2004) simultaneously test sixteen major competing explanations for military conflict using a directed dyad design. The tests include both the broad set of all dyads and the more narrow set of politically relevant dyads. Employing a complex set of variables that includes interactions in order to test for both a dyadic autocratic peace and democratic peace, they find mixed support for the monadic argument and strong support for the dyadic argument at various levels of conflict, including war. They also find some support for a dyadic autocratic peace, although it is not as powerful as the support they find for the dyadic democratic peace.[18]

Reiter and Stam (2002) examine democratic initiation and war fighting. Although previous research has established the fact that democracies are more likely to win wars than autocracies, the causal mechanism producing this outcome remains controversial. Reiter and Stam (2002) argue that previous explanations pointing to the greater ability of democracies to mobilize resources are incorrect.[19] Rather, democracies appear to select their conflicts with greater care because democratic leaders recognize that they will be punished for costly victories and military defeats. This is a monadic argument because democracies are inhibited from initiating regardless of the regime type of the adversary.[20]

Leeds and Davis (1999) argue that domestic political institutions should affect foreign policy decisions beyond military conflict. Drawing on both normative and structural arguments, they hypothesize that democratic states are more cooperative in general. They test the argument using a dependent variable derived from the Conflict and Peace Data Bank (COPDAB) database, which uses media publications to produce an aggregate measure of conflict and cooperation. Using a data set of political relevant states from 1953 to 1978, their regression analysis indicates democracies are more likely to display cooperative behavior and less likely to display conflictual behavior. This pattern of results is even more pronounced for pairs of democratic states. Thus, Leeds and Davis find both a monadic and a dyadic impact of democracy.

Pickering (2002) explores the relationship between regime type and foreign military intervention. Drawing on normative and structural explanations, he makes two monadic predictions: (1) democracies are less likely to initiate foreign military interventions, and (2) democracies are less likely to be targets of interventions. Using a data set of 272 military interventions involving more than 5,000 troops, Pickering finds support for the second hypothesis only.

Each of these research designs adds important information to the debate about institutions and military conflict. Bennett and Stam (2004) simultaneously test sixteen competing explanations using data sets that include both all dyads and political relevant dyads. Leeds and Davis (1999) employ a new and broader dependent variable. Dassel and Reinhardt (1999) control for periods of institutional stability. Reiter and Stam (2002) focus on the casual mechanisms explaining less initiation and more victory. Pickering (2002) focuses on the more narrow topic of intervention. Yet no individual study discussed here nor the collection of works as a whole provides a definitive answer to the question: are democracies less likely to use force? Gowa (1999) flatly rejects the dyadic argument. Dassel and Reinhardt (1999) find no evidence of monadic constraint. Pickering (2002) finds only partial support.

The quantitative analysis in this section makes four unique contributions to this ongoing debate. First, the analysis employs the International Crisis Behavior (ICB) data set updated through the year 2000. Despite its excellent documentation, this data set (much less the updated version) has not been as extensively used in the literature. Second, the dependent variables more carefully distinguish among levels of violence by examining the number of troops used in the operation. In contrast, the MID use of force variable employed in most existing studies lumps blockades and minor attacks with major uses of violence short of war. Third, the dependent variables used in this chapter (and subsequent chapters) include the use of force through third parties. The use of violence by intermediaries is neglected in many studies. It is particularly important if democracies, in order to keep casualties low, are likely to use force through third parties. It is important to note that the excellent documentation of each case in the ICB data set aids the creation of these more precise variables. Finally, the statistical analysis tests the competing institutional explanation proposed by Bueno de Mesquita and colleagues (2003).

The monadic and dyadic hypotheses are tested using the ICB data set (version 4) that contains the population of international crises involving threats of violence or the use of force between 1918 and 2001. The ICB data set has been used extensively in the quantitative international relations literature (Hewitt and Wilkenfeld 1995; Carment and James 1998; Rioux 1998; Brecher 1999). Moreover, the ICB data set has produced results very similar to those produced by the more widely used Militarized Interstate Dispute (MID) data set (Maoz and Russett 1993).

The revised ICB data set was adapted by the removal of several categories of cases, the consolidation of several multiyear cases, and the construction of a national-level data set. From the ICB data set of 434 crises, I eliminated six categories of cases. First, I removed 27 crises that occurred within the context of a full-scale war because conceptually I consider decisions to escalate the geographic scope or intensity of a major military conflict as fundamentally different from decisions to initiate an armed conflict or to escalate an existing dispute up to the large-scale use of force. For example, I removed the "Stalingrad" crisis of 1942 because the German decision to use force in the battle over Stalingrad is fundamentally different from the decision to launch the attack against the Soviet Union (Barbarossa Crisis) in 1941. Once large-scale armed conflict has occurred, the further use of force becomes largely a matter of military strategy and tactics whereas domestic political considerations become much less important.[21]

Second, I eliminated forty crises where I failed to find evidence of either verbal threats or threats of force accompanied by military deployments by the challenger. Thus, in some cases I could not find evidence in the historical record indicating that the challenger was considering the use of force even though the opponent in the crisis perceived a threat (for example, the

Bulgaria-Turkey Crisis of 1925); in other cases, the challenger was intervening on the side of the internationally recognized government (for instance, Soviet actions during the East Berlin Uprising Crisis in 1953).

Third, I removed nine crises in which states capitulated to the demands of the challenger prior to the use of force by either side. Challengers in these crises never faced a discrete decision of whether or not to use force to resolve the political conflict. For example, in the "Polish Ultimatum" crisis of 1938, Lithuania capitulated to Polish demands for the normalization of relations and the opening of the border between the two countries; thus, Poland did not face a decision of whether or not to use force in an attempt to coerce a determined adversary.

Fourth, I aggregated forty-six crises in which several conflicts erupted within the same basic dispute over a prolonged period of time. For example, the numerous cross-border-raid crises involving South West Africa People's Organization (SWAPO) guerrillas and South African defense forces from 1978 to 1987 were aggregated into a single case. After the initial crisis in 1978, all subsequent crises were treated as "intrawar" disputes because SWAPO guerrilla activity was almost continuous throughout this period.

Fifth, I removed five crises that involved a colonial power versus an indigenous independence movement. Colonial cases have been removed because one party is an internal actor lacking formal institutions and easily measured norms. For example, I removed colonial cases such as the "Indonesia Independence" crises of 1945, 1947, and 1948.

Finally, I removed seven crises because one or both actors were not internationally recognized sovereign states, as defined by Small and Singer (1982), when the conflict began. For example, the cases involving the Baltic States' struggle for independence from 1918 to 1921 were excluded because the secessionist states were not recognized members of the international system. Therefore, the conflict between Latvia and the young Soviet Union was more akin to a civil war than an international crisis.[22]

I then added several crises by disaggregating conflicts that contained multiple conflictual dyads. For example, the single case identified by the ICB data set as the "Invasion of Scandinavia" was disaggregated into two cases: Germany versus Denmark and Germany versus Norway. After removing and disaggregating crises, the final data set contains 337 conflict dyads occurring within 301 international crises. For each crisis, I collected data on both the challenger and defender states because political leaders in both countries must decide when and to what extent military force should be used.[23] As a result, the final crisis data set consists of 674 observations (337 decisions by the challenger whether to use force and 337 decisions by the defender whether to use force). A list of the crises and conflict dyads included in the analysis can be found in Appendix 2.2; a list of crises from the revised ICB data set that have been deleted or merged can be found in Appendix 2.3.

The crisis data set (as well as the dispute data set used in subsequent chapters) uses the directed dyad as the unit of analysis. A major problem with existing studies stems from the use of a "summed dyad" (or nondirected dyad) as the unit of analysis (Doyle 1983; Morgan and Schwebach 1992; Dixon 1993; Russett and Oneal 2001; Dixon and Senese 2002).[24] A summed dyad approach does not assess the actions of each actor individually; rather, codings are done at the dyad level (for example, "does the dyad escalate to war?"). For example, in a data set of international crises using a summed dyad approach, the Russo-Finnish Winter War of 1939–40 would be coded as having escalated to war whereas the Cuban Missile Crisis of 1961 would be coded as not having escalated. In contrast, a directed dyad data set contains separate codings for the behavior of each actor in the crisis (for instance, does country A escalate the crisis? Does country B escalate the crisis?). Although the summed dyad unit of analysis is useful for testing dyadic arguments, it obscures the impact of political structure on decisions to use force because the state that initiated the violence is not recorded. *Therefore, the summed dyad approach can never be used to test a monadic argument.* For instance, does participation by Finland, a democracy at the time of the Winter War, constitute evidence against the proposition that democracies are less likely to use force than nondemocracies? The answer must be no; the Soviet Union was clearly the aggressor in the conflict. The behavior and political structures of each state in the militarized crisis or dispute must be tracked individually.

One potential problem with using the directed dyad as the unit of analysis relates to dependency between the two actors in the bilateral dispute. For example, if the Soviet Union initiates violence in 1939, then by definition, Finland cannot initiate violence as well. With respect to the crisis data set, perfect dependency implies that I have "told" the statistical software that there are 674 independent observations when in fact there are only 337. In more technical terms, spatial autocorrelation could contaminate the results.

There are at least two solutions to this potential problem. First, it is possible to eliminate the problem by selecting a dependent variable that does not introduce dependency. The highest level of escalation and the aggressive use of force dependent variables used in this and subsequent chapters do not introduce dependency because both states can simultaneously be using high levels of force or aggressive force across an international border. Second, one can test for the impact of spatial autocorrelation. It is important to remember that spatial autocorrelation affects only the estimated standard errors of the coefficients and, therefore, assessments of the variables' statistical significance. The coefficients themselves are not biased (see Hanushek and Jackson [1977]). In order to assess the potential for autocorrelation to exaggerate the statistical significance of the results, consider again the worst-case scenario: perfect correlation between the error terms of the two states in a crisis. Under these circumstances, the proper statistical significance of the coefficients could be determined by multiplying their standard errors by the square root of 2. The statistical results using the initiation dependent variable presented below remain significant even in this worst-case scenario.

THE DEPENDENT VARIABLES

The hypotheses described below are tested using three dependent variables: *Initiation of Force, Highest Level of Force,* and *Aggressive Use of Force.* The first two dependent variables focus on decisions by state leaders to *initiate* the use of violence to resolve political conflicts. The most common dependent variable tested across the literature is "war involvement," the frequency of participation in armed conflict (Small and Singer 1976, 62; Rummel 1983, 44; Weede 1984, 657; Chan 1984, 633).[25] Unfortunately, the use of this variable indiscriminately mixes cases in which the state initiates conflict with those in which it is the target of conflict. In his analysis of Rummel's normative and structural propositions, Chan states:

> [T]he theory underlying Rummel's hypotheses would seem to imply that free countries are less apt to start wars. . . . On the other hand, it seems reasonable to infer that once a free country has been attacked by another country (that is, once it finds itself involuntarily in a state of war already as a result of the actions of its enemy), this restraint would be less effective in holding it back from responding militarily. (Chan 1984, 636)[26]

In order to test either normative or structural hypotheses, whether dyadic or monadic, it is crucial to distinguish between the use of force in response to force (such as defending against an invasion) and the initiation of force (such as launching an invasion in the absence of foreign military aggression). Otherwise, the purported tests of the democratic peace do not in fact test the strict logic of their arguments. Consider three kinds of foreign policies. First, a state could be a pure pacifist, unwilling to initiate or use force even in reply to the use of force. Such states are unlikely to remain independent in an anarchic system.

Second, a state could be willing to respond with force but less likely to initiate the use of force. This strategy conforms with the assumptions laid out above for both the structural and normative explanations. The structural constraints on the use of force are likely to recede if force has already been used; public opinion may be averse to using force but may recognize the necessity of it when faced with an attack. The norms against the use of force also would not constrain force as a reply to force. For example, within a democracy, police force is sanctioned as a legitimate response to criminal aggression. A foreign policy informed by this norm would permit the use of force in reply to the prior use of force.

Third, a state could be willing to both respond to a use of force and initiate the use of force. This strategy is not consistent with the monadic normative or structural explanations because force is seen as a legitimate tool of foreign policy rather than a policy undertaken as a last resort. Note that although the second and third types of foreign policies exhibit very different patterns in the use of force, both may be expected to engage in violent behavior with any kind of state under certain circumstances. The critical distinction between these patterns lies in identifying which party initiates force. Thus, in testing arguments about the norms and constraints, I focus on variables related to the initiation of force rather than simply involvement in conflict.[27]

Initiation of Force

This dependent variable measures whether a country is the first to use force at either minor or major levels of force during the crisis. The variable ranges from 0 to 2. If a state is the first to use a minor level of force (commit 1 to 1,000 troops to a combat zone) and the first to escalate the crisis to a major level of force (commit more than 1,000 troops to a combat zone), the state is coded 2. Alternatively, if one state is the first to escalate a crisis to a low level of force while the other state is the first to escalate to a high level of force, both states are coded 1. For example, in the 1969 Ussuri River confrontation between China and the former Soviet Union, both countries are coded 1. China was the first to escalate to a low level of force when it initiated a border clash at the beginning of March, but the Soviet Union was the first to escalate to a high level of force when it launched a large-scale counterattack in mid-March (Robinson 1981). In both instances, decision makers made a conscious decision to resort to military force to resolve the political dispute. Finally, if neither side uses military force, the variable is coded 0 for both actors.

The *Initiation of Force* variable includes the use of force by a state's regular armed forces *and* by nonstate actors directly supported by a state. For example, Algerian support of the Polisario rebels is considered a use of force by Algeria against Morocco. Similarly, Mozambique's support of the African National Congress guerrillas is coded as a use of force against South Africa. Algeria and Mozambique are clearly resorting to military force to resolve the conflict. Moreover, the government and public in both Morocco and Spain view their use of force as retaliation against violence initiated by their adversary. Both the normative and structural explanations imply that constrained states should not initiate the use of force directly or indirectly. This operationalization addresses, in part, Cohen's (1994) critique of the empirical tests of the democratic peace that failed to incorporate the use of surrogate forces against one's adversaries.[28]

Highest Level of Force

In order to test for the robustness of the results, a second dependent variable is included in the examination of crises. This alternative coding measures the most severe level of force used by a state during the crisis. The variable, which varies from 0 to 2, is coded for both the challenger and the defender. If the actor used more than 1,000 troops at any point during the crisis, the variable is coded 2 (reflecting a high level of force). If the actor used between 1 and 1,000 troops, the variable is coded 1 (reflecting a low level of force). If military forces were not used, the variable is coded 0 (reflecting no use of force). For example, in the Mayaguez Crisis in 1975, the United States is coded 1 because the rescue operation involved the use of approximately 300 troops (Head et al. 1978, 141). Conversely, Argentina used high levels of force in the 1982 Falkland Islands War when it captured the islands using approximately 4,000 troops. As with the initiation of force variable, the *Highest Level of Force* variable takes into account the use of force by third parties.

Any use of the *Highest Level of Force* dependent variable requires the addition of a control variable in order to separate states that initiate violence from those that retaliate with violence. Additionally, I wish to isolate disproportionate uses of force (that is, state A uses major force while state B uses only minor force or no force at all). To accomplish these tasks, I measure the highest level of force initiated by the *opposing* side as a control.

The control variable, which I label *Opponent's Initiation of Force*, is coded as the highest level of force *initiated* by the opposing state. Thus, the variable does not include uses of force by the opposing state that were a response to similar military actions of the state in question. If the opposing state *initiated* a major use of force, this variable is coded 2. If the opponent initiated a minor use of force but did not initiate a major use of force, this variable is coded 1. Finally, if the opposing state is not the first to use force at any level, this variable is coded 0. For example, in the Six Days' War in 1967, both Israel and Egypt used high levels of force. However, Israel is coded 0 because its opponent (Egypt) did not initiate a minor or major use of force.

Aggressive Use of Force

The third and final dependent variable, which I label *Aggressive Use of Force*, is defined as the use of military force on the territory of another sovereign state. The variable has three categories: (2) major use of force (more than 1,000 troops across an international border), (1) minor use of force (1–1000 troops across an international border), and (0) no use of force.[29] The variable is superior to simply measuring mere conflict involvement because defending oneself within one's own territory does not constitute a use of force. A conflict-involvement variable would code both Belgium and Germany as having used force in 1914 and 1940. However, the *Aggressive Use of Force* variable (just like an initiation of force variable) would code only Germany as having used force. Belgian troops did not enter Germany in force during either conflict.[30]

The primary drawback of the *Aggressive Use of Force* variable is the fact that states often retaliate across the border. The normative and structural explanations, which are compatible with the notion of reciprocity (that is, tit-for-tat), permit the retaliatory use of force. Thus, the *Aggressive Use of Force* is in some ways inferior to the first two dependent variables. However, given that I must use the *Aggressive Use of Force* dependent variable in subsequent chapters, I need to present baseline results in this chapter. This assures the reader that any observed changes in the estimated coefficients in subsequent chapters are not due to the introduction of a new dependent variable. As I will demonstrate in a moment, all three dependent variables produce similar results.

The three dependent variables are categorical; thus, ordinary and generalized least-squares regression techniques are not appropriate. Most of the quantitative analyses in the following chapters employ the widely used probit model, which is conventionally estimated by maximum likelihood techniques. The probit model assumes that the probability of initiating force or using aggressive force is a normally distributed but unobservable variable. What we do observe are discrete events that occur when thresholds are crossed (for example, when minor or major force is used). These observed outcomes fall into specific categories of the dependent variable. For example, during the Mayaguez Crisis there was some probability that U.S. President Ford would authorize the use of force. However, the historical record indicates only whether or not force was used—a categorical outcome. The probit model allows us to generate a curve that reflects the predicted probability of using force given the observed outcomes and the explanatory variables.

SPECIFIC HYPOTHESES AND OPERATIONALIZATIONS

The normative and structural arguments described in this chapter can be tested using two hypotheses:

HYPOTHESIS 1 (MONADIC HYPOTHESIS)
The more democratic a state, the less likely it is to initiate violence regardless of the political regime of the adversary.

HYPOTHESIS 2 (DYADIC HYPOTHESIS)
The more democratic a state, the less likely it is to initiate violence against other democracies.

An important component of the dyadic explanation is expressed in the dyadic assumption that democracies may preemptively initiate the use of force against authoritarian states because they fear exploitation. The argument posits that authoritarian leaders believe that democracies are more likely to capitulate; this belief leads the authoritarian leaders to attempt to exploit democracies by attacking first (Bueno de Mesquita and Lalman 1992, 155–60; Huth and Allee 2002).[31] If this is true, we would expect nondemocratic states to be more likely to initiate the use of force against democracies. Although I am not claiming to test the dyadic assumption directly, I can probe the underlying logic of the argument with a third hypothesis.[32]

HYPOTHESIS 3
Nondemocracies are more likely to use aggressive force or initiate a use of force against democracies than they are against nondemocracies.

The three democratic peace hypotheses are tested using aggregate-level institutional measures found in the Polity IV data set (Gurr et al. 1989). An *Actor's Democracy* variable was constructed for each state in the conflict by subtracting the Polity autocracy index from the democracy index to produce a variable that ranges from −10 to +10. To ease interpretation of the statistical results, this variable was rescaled from 0 to 20. The Polity democracy index comprises four components: openness of executive recruitment, competitiveness of executive recruitment, competitiveness of participation, and legislative constraints on the executive. The autocracy index contains all the elements in the democracy index plus a fifth component, the regulation of participation. For example, using the Polity data and this method, the United States receives a score of 20 for all years in the data set whereas the Soviet Union receives a score of 6 for all years after the death of Stalin.[33]

In order to isolate the impact of level of democracy when facing a democratic opponent, I introduce an interactive term, which I label *Actor's Democracy with Democratic Opponent*, composed of the *Actor's Democracy* score multiplied by a dummy variable indicating whether or not the opponent is a democratic state. If a state's opponent scores 17 or greater on the democracy scale, the dummy variable is coded 1. Otherwise, the variable is coded 0. Thus, when the opposing state is not democratic, this variable takes on a value of 0. When the opposing state is a democracy, however, this variable is equal to the *Actor's Democracy* score. Including this interaction as a separate variable in the analysis will allow an identification of the additional effect that the *Actor's Democracy* score has on a state's behavior because the opposing state is democratic.

The threshold of 17 identifies states as democratic if they share at least the following aspects of democratic government: (1) fully competitive political participation, which implies that "[t]here are relatively stable and enduring political groups which regularly compete for political influence at the national level" (Gurr et al. 1989, 19); (2) a popularly elected chief executive; and (3) an executive branch with at least moderate constraints on its authority. The threshold of 17 is also a salient empirical break in the data between one large group of states scoring 14 or 15 on the democracy scale and a second substantial group that scored between 18 and 20. Moreover, sensitivity analysis demonstrated that varying the threshold from 16 to 20 did not change the patterns or statistical significance of the results.

Finally, in order to test Hypothesis 3, an *Opponent's Democracy* variable is coded on the same basis as the *Actor's Democracy* score and therefore ranges from 0 to 20. The use of a dummy variable for the opponent's democracy in the interactive term and a continuous variable to test Hypothesis 3 is deliberate. The dummy operationalization does discard some information, but it aids the interpretation of the resulting coefficient. For example, a negative coefficient indicates the more democratic a state, the less likely it is to use force *when facing a democracy*. In contrast, the interaction of the two 0–20 scale variables incorporates the behavior of the state when facing *both* democracies and autocracies. A value of 20 on the new "two continuous variable" interaction term could imply a democracy facing an autocracy (20×1), an autocracy facing a democracy (1×20), or two autocracies facing each other (5×4). Thus, it is much more difficult to interpret the coefficient produced by the interaction of two continuous variables. The current interactive term provides a straightforward test of the monadic and dyadic arguments and yields readily interpretable results.[34]

In sum, three variables are used to test the democracy-initiation hypotheses: the *Actor's Democracy* score, the *Opponent's Democracy* score, and the interaction term. When the adversary is not democratic, the interaction term is coded 0, so the *Actor's Democracy* score term measures the impact of the actor's political structure on the likelihood of initiation. When the adversary is democratic, all three variables will generally be positive, so in this case the measure of the effect of an actor's political structure on the likelihood of initiation is determined by all three terms. Finally, as the actor becomes increasingly undemocratic, the *Actor's Democracy* score and interaction terms converge to 0, meaning that the effect of political structure on the likelihood of initiation is determined by the *Opponent's Democracy* score.

Three control variables are included in the analysis of both disputes and crises: the balance of forces, alliance ties, and satisfaction with the status quo. Realists hypothesize that the balance of military capabilities should be central to any decision to use force. In an anarchic world, strong states are expected to use force to resolve political-security disputes whereas weak states are not because they are unlikely to prevail.

HYPOTHESIS 4
The more favorable the balance of forces, the more likely a state is to initiate military force or use aggressive force.

The *Balance of Forces* variable measures each state's military capabilities relative to its opponent. A state's military capability is the average of two elements: number of troops and military expenditures. The variable is created in three steps. First, the raw data are converted to a percentage relative to the global total of the element (for example, actor A's troops in 1919 divided by the global total number of troops in 1919). Second, for each element, the actor's capabilities are calculated as a proportion of the combined capabilities of both actors (for example, actor A's troops divided by (actor A's troops + actor B's troops)). Finally, I average the two elements. The final variable ranges from 0 to 1. A value over 0.50 indicates that the state's military capability is superior to that of its opponent; a value approaching 1 reflects the fact that a state then enjoys an overwhelming military advantage. The source of the troop and expenditure data was the Correlates of War Project data set titled "National Capabilities of States, 1816–1993." Data for 1991–2000 were collected from the United States Arms Control and Disarmament (ACDA) data sets and the Institute for Strategic Studies' (ISS) *Military Balance*.[35]

A second control variable included in the analysis codes for the existence of alliance ties between the challenger and defender. This variable has been included because it indirectly measures the degree to which the two parties have shared interests (Bueno de Mesquita 1981; Farber and Gowa 1995a, 5; Bennett and Stam 2004). Realists would expect that common security interests, signaled by alliance ties against a common adversary, should reduce the likelihood of conflict between two states. The inclusion of this variable is important because critics of previous democratic peace analyses have argued that statistical findings are spurious if alliance ties are not explicitly included. For example, they argue that the post–World War II peace between Germany and France was a function of a common Soviet threat rather than any constraining feature of democracy.

Alliance ties between the adversaries reduce the likelihood a state will initiate military force or use aggressive force.

Alliance Ties is a dummy variable that takes a value of 1 when the two states share a defense pact; otherwise, the variable is coded 0.[36] For example, both Greece and Turkey are coded 1 during the 1967 Cyprus crisis because both were members of the North Atlantic Treaty Organization at the time of the crisis.

A third control variable included in the analyses measures whether or not a state is satisfied with the status quo. Rousseau and colleagues (1996) have demonstrated that states dissatisfied with the status quo are much more likely to initiate the use of force in crises. For example, if one state in a territorial dispute occupies the entire piece of contested territory, this state would not be expected to initiate violence. Rather, the state that is not satisfied with the status quo (in other words, does not control the territory) is much more likely to be the first to resort to violence. Controlling for this variable is important because in many cases democratic states are satisfied with the status quo. One might reasonably infer that the reason the democratic state did not initiate the use of force was due to satisfaction rather than political structure or norms.

States satisfied with the status quo will be less likely to initiate violence or use aggressive force.

The *Satisfaction with the Status Quo* control variable is coded 1 if the state is satisfied with the status quo with regard to the issue at stake in the conflict at the time that the conflict begins. Otherwise, the variable is coded 0. In general, the challenging state is coded as being dissatisfied with the status quo. However, there are a number of cases in which both states are coded as dissatisfied, such as the India-China territorial conflict.

The *Satisfaction with the Status Quo* variable is coded with respect to the issue causing the dispute (for example, territorial conflicts, antiregime conflicts, and treaty violation conflicts). Policy statements by chief executives during the conflict are used to determine if a state accepted or rejected the status quo. States that either viewed the current situation as unacceptable or were actively seeking an immediate change are coded as not satisfied. The vast majority of the years in dispute in the data set fall into two categories: territorial conflicts (60 percent) and antiregime conflicts (30 percent). In territorial crises, states are coded as satisfied with the status quo if they favored having the current borders maintained. In antiregime conflicts, states that are not actively seeking to overthrow another regime are coded as satisfied. States in which top foreign policy decision makers called for a revision of the territorial boundaries or the removal of opposing regimes are coded as dissatisfied. Other types of conflicts, such as differences over adherence to peace treaties and the treatment of nationals abroad, are coded in an analogous manner.

The final independent variables are interactions between the balance of forces and regime type. Bueno de Mesquita and associates (2003) argue that democratic polities (that is, states with a large selectorate and a large winning coalition) are constrained only when facing a strong opponent. When facing a weak opponent, democratic leaders are reasonably sure that the costs of conflict will be very low. Therefore, they feel free to use force because they no longer fear punishment from domestic challengers. Bueno de Mesquita and colleagues extend this argument to democratic dyads: strong democracies are likely to use force against weak democracies because they can do so with impunity.

HYPOTHESIS 7 (MONADIC VERSION)
Democracies are especially likely to use force when facing a militarily weak opponent regardless of the regime type of the adversary.

HYPOTHESIS 8 (DYADIC VERSION)
Democracies are especially likely to use force when facing militarily weak democracies.

Following Dixon and Senese (2002), I test this argument using interactive variables.[37] The monadic test uses a *Democracy with Weak Opponent* variable, which is created by multiplying a dummy democracy variable (greater than or equal to 17) by a dummy balance of forces variable (greater than or equal to 0.70). The dyadic test uses a *Democracy with Weak Democracy* variable created by multiplying the monadic variable by a dummy variable indicating the opponent is a democracy. Thus, if the challenger is a democracy, the defender is a democracy, and the balance of forces favors the challenger by 0.75, the dyadic variable is coded as a 1. Varying the operationalization of the variables (for example, a cutoff of 0.65) did not change the results.[38]

The term *especially* is important because the balance of forces argument predicts that everyone is more likely to use force against a weaker opponent. We expect the estimated coefficient for the balance of forces variable to be positive. Bueno de Mesquita and colleagues expect the interaction term to

TABLE 2.2
Probit analysis of the democratic peace model using the crisis data set

Independent variable	Model 1 Initiation	Model 2 Highest	Model 3 Aggressive
Actor's net democracy	−0.013	−0.006	0.004
(monadic)	0.008	0.007	0.008
Opponent's net democracy	0.018★	0.024★★	0.013
	0.009	0.008	0.008
Actor's net democracy with	−0.050★★	−0.066★★★	−0.055★★★
democratic opponent (dyadic)	0.017	0.016	0.016
Balance of forces	−0.123	−0.001	−0.120
	0.281	0.269	0.268
Shared alliance ties	0.038	−0.149	−0.202★
	0.118	0.108	0.109
Satisfaction with status quo	−1.743★★★	−1.099★★★	−1.235★★★
	0.155	0.118	0.128
Opponent's use of force	—	0.753★★★	—
		0.075	
Democracy with weak	0.252	0.512	0.583★
opponent	0.318	0.317	0.324
Democracy with weak	−0.255	−1.064	−0.815
democracy	0.871	0.749	0.823
First threshold	−0.350	−0.467	−0.481
	0.195	0.188	0.184
Second threshold	0.516	0.504	0.294
	0.193	0.187	0.184
Number of observations	674	674	674
Log likelihood function	−548.405	−638.66	−629.831

NOTE: All significance tests are one-tailed. ★p < .05, ★★p < .01, ★★★p < .001. Results were calculated using STATA version 6.0 and robust standard errors.

be positive as well, indicating that the balance of forces variable has an added impact on the use of force for democracies. Therefore, both variables must be included in the model to ensure a fair test of the two unique arguments.

ANALYSIS AND RESULTS

The dependent variables are distributed as follows: *Initiation of Force* (0 = 56%, 1 = 24%, 2 = 20%); *Highest Use of Force* (0 = 30%, 1 = 31%, and 2 = 39%); and *Aggressive Use of Force* (0 = 47%, 1 = 25%, 2 = 28%). The multi-variate results for the democratic peace model are presented in Table 2.2.[39] Hypothesis 1 (the monadic argument) predicts that the coefficient on the *Actor's Net Democracy* score will be negative and that the interaction term will be insignificant. Hypothesis 2 (the dyadic argument), on the other hand, predicts that the coefficient on the *Actor's Net Democracy* score will be insignificant and that the coefficient on the interaction term will be negative.

The results support only the dyadic hypothesis. The coefficient on the *Actor's Democracy* variable is negative as predicted with the *Initiation* dependent variable, but it falls just short of conventional thresholds of statistical significance. The coefficient is not differentiable from zero with the *Highest Use* and *Aggressive Use* dependent variables. In contrast, the coefficient for the dyadic interaction term is sharply negative and strongly statistically significant in all three models. In militarized crises, democracies are more peaceful only when interacting with other democracies. The results also provide some support for Hypothesis 3; the coefficient on the *Opponent's Democracy* variable is solidly positive in all three models and statistically significant in all but the *Aggressive Use* model (where it falls just short of the 0.10 threshold). This result implies that states are more likely to initiate force against democracies than against nondemocracies.[40] Although this result is consistent with Bueno de Mesquita and Lalman (1992), it is not consistent with the work of Bueno de Mesquita and associates (2003), who predict that the common knowledge that democracies "try harder" in war will deter others from attacking.

The substantive impact of the estimated coefficients is presented in the marginal analysis shown in Table 2.3. In an ordered probit model, the substantive significance of variables cannot be determined by simply comparing the size of coefficients in the equation. Marginal analysis is required to isolate the effect of a change in an independent variable on the probability of initiating violence. The marginal impact of each independent variable is calculated while holding constant all other independent variables at their modes (for categorical variables) or means (for continuous variables). For this data set, the baseline categories are as follows: the state is mildly autocratic, its opponent is mildly autocratic, the two antagonists are evenly matched in terms of military forces, the state is dissatisfied with the status quo, and no alliance tie exists between the two states.

Table 2.3 displays the probability of reaching the highest level of the trichotomous dependent variable for each level of the independent variable and the change in probability (shown in bold type) associated with a change in an independent variable while holding all other variables at their means or modes. Discussion of the marginal analysis is restricted to the coefficients that achieve statistical significance in the previous table. The top portion of Table 2.3 illustrates the strength of the dyadic hypotheses. When the opposing state is democratic, a shift from absolutely authoritarian (0) to fully democratic (20) decreases by 34 percentage points the probability that it will initiate high levels of force. As the table shows, the predicted probability of initiating high levels of force decreases from 42% to 8% as the *Actor's Democracy with a Democratic Opponent* score shifts from 0 to 20. Using the *Highest Use* dependent variable, a shift from 0 to 20 with a democratic opponent decreases the probability of a high use of force by 41 percentage

TABLE 2.3

Marginal effects on the democratic peace model using the crisis data set

Shift in independent variables	Probability of initiating a high level of force	Probability of highest level of force	Probability of aggressive use of force
Actor's democracy with democratic opponent			
0	42	49	47
10	20	23	28
20	8	8	14
Total change	**−34**	**−41**	**−33**
Opponent's democracy for fully autocratic state			
0	28	31	n.s.
10	35	39	n.s.
20	42	49	n.s.
Total change	**+14**	**+18**	
Alliance			
None	n.s.	n.s.	40
Allies	n.s.	n.s.	33
Total change			**−7**
Satisfaction with status quo			
No	30	35	40
Yes	1	7	7
Total change	**−29**	**−28**	**−33**
Opponent's use of force			
0	n.a.	35	n.a.
1	n.a.	64	n.a.
2	n.a.	86	n.a.
Total change		**+51**	
Democracy with weak opponent			
Weaker or same	n.s.	n.s.	40
Much stronger	n.s.	n.s.	62
Total change			**+22**

NOTE: Predicted probabilities and percentage-point change may not sum to 100 percent due to rounding. Marginal effects were calculated by generating predicted values from the probit model while changing the values of selected independent variables and holding the others at their means or modes. The predicted values were transformed into probabilities that the outcome would fall into each category by summing the area underneath the cumulative normal distribution between the predicted value and each of the category thresholds. Statistically insignificant variables in Table 2.2 are identified as "n.s." (not significant) in the marginal table. Variables that did not appear in the model are labeled "n.a." (not applicable). The marginal analyses were calculated using Clarify software (Tomz et al. 2003).

points. Using the *Aggressive Use* dependent variable, the expected change is a 33-percentage-point decline.

The *Opponent's Democracy* portion of Table 2.3 examines the behavior of nondemocratic states when facing a democratic opponent. As predicted by the Bueno de Mesquita and Lalman (1992) argument presented as Hypoth-

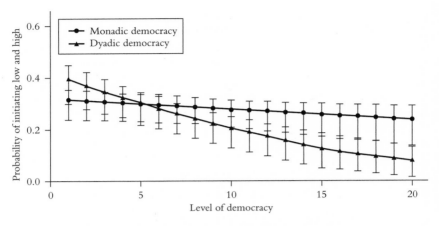

FIGURE 2.1. The effect of actor's democracy on initiation of force

esis 3, the results show that completely autocratic states are more likely to initiate force against democratic opponents. Changing the *Opponent's Democracy* score from completely authoritarian (0) to fully democratic (20) increases the predicted probability of initiating twice from 28% to 42%, or a change of 14 percentage points. Although the results cannot tell us if democratic decision makers are aware of this tendency and respond by altering their strategies, the results do support one key element of the dyadic argument: autocracies appear to view democracies as exploitable.[41]

The precise nature of the interactive relationship between regime type and a state's propensity to initiate force is illustrated in Figure 2.1. The figure presents the expected value as a line, with circles for the monadic argument and triangles for the dyadic argument. Uncertainty around the point estimates, shown in "i-bar"–like brackets, was calculated using Clarify software (Tomz et al. 2003). The relatively flat monadic line indicates that as the level of democracy increases in a state, the probability of initiation of high levels of force declines very slowly. In contrast, the steeply sloping dyadic line indicates that when facing a democratic state, the more democratic a state is has a very large impact on the probability of violence. Similar figures can be produced using either of the other dependent variables.

Moreover, the fact that the line with triangles is higher than the line with circles at the left-hand side of Figure 2.1 is consistent with Bueno de Mesquita and Lalman's claim (1992) that authoritarian leaders view democracies as weak, which leads them to initiate the use of force against democracies more often. Notice that the line with triangles remains above the dashed line until the *Actor's Democracy* score reaches 5. Thus, states with an *Actor's De-*

mocracy score of less than 5 are more likely to initiate force against a democratic opponent. Any state with an *Actor's Democracy* score greater than 5 is less likely to initiate force against a democratic state. Finally, the fact that the line with triangles reaches much lower than the line with circles captures one of the central empirical findings on the democratic peace. That is, when two states in a crisis are democratic, neither one is likely to initiate force against the other.

In addition to levels of democracy, a number of other variables appear in the three models displayed in Table 2.2. First, the coefficient for the *Balance of Forces* never achieves statistical significance. This somewhat surprising finding occurred with various operationalizations, such as using the COW capabilities index (troops, defense spending, iron, steel, total population, and urban population), discounting for distance, and including troop quality. Second, the alliance variable is statistically inconsistent and substantively weak. The *Shared Alliance Ties* coefficient is only statistically significant using the *Aggressive Use of Force* dependent variable. The marginal analysis indicates that a shift from no alliance to an alliance decreases the probability of initiating a high level of force by 7 percentage points. The weakness of the variable may seem counterintuitive but is consistent with other empirical findings (such as Bueno de Mesquita 1981).[42] Third, satisfaction with the status quo has a very large effect on a state's propensity to initiate the use of force. Table 2.3 shows that changing a state from "dissatisfied" to "satisfied" decreases the probability of initiating a high level of force by 29 percentage points. Using the other two dependent variables, the decline is 28 and 33 percentage points. Fourth, as one would expect, the opposing state's initiation of violence has a very powerful impact on a state's level of escalation in a crisis. Table 2.3 shows that as the opposing state shifts from "not initiating force" (0) to "initiating major force" (2), the probability that a state will use major force increases by 51 percentage points. Finally, the predictions of the selectorate model are not strongly supported by the data. The statistical insignificance of the dyadic interaction variable indicates that strong democracies are not likely to pick on weak democracies, as explicitly hypothesized by Bueno de Mesquita and colleagues (2003). Moreover, the monadic version of the variable is only statistically significant with the *Aggressive Use of Force* dependent variable. The substantive significance of the variable, shown in the marginal analysis table, indicates that when democracies possess more than 70 percent of the total military forces in the dyad, the predicted probability of the use of aggressive force rises by 22 percentage points. The fact that only one of six coefficients is significant coupled with the contrary findings with respect to the frequency with which states are expected to attack democracies raises important questions about the utility of the selectorate model.

In order to test the robustness of these findings, I conducted a large amount of sensitivity analysis. None of these analyses undermine the central conclusion drawn from the study of international crises: democracies are more peaceful only with other democracies. The sensitivity analysis included adding a great-power variable, using a dichotomous dependent variable, including a "years at peace" variable, adding contiguity, controlling for nuclear weapons, adding Bueno de Mesquita's alliance similarity variable (1981), including Signorino and Ritter's alliance similarity variable (1999), discounting the balance of forces for distance, adding quality to the balance of forces measure, separating the interwar and post-WWII cases, varying the cutoff for the democratic opponent variable, and expanding the alliance variable to include neutrality pacts and ententes. Only when varying the cutoff did the results change a bit. In a couple of instances the monadic variable became significant, but only with the initiation dependent variable. Thus, the central finding of a dyadic peace in crises is quite robust. Appendix 2.4 displays the coefficients and standard errors for three models, with most of the additional variables included in the equations.

Case Studies

Quantitative and qualitative methods are inextricably interconnected. Large-N statistical studies can tell us a great deal about general patterns but little about the causes of specific events. Conversely, qualitative studies are essential for explaining specific events, generating new hypotheses, exploring deviant cases, and understanding the process through which outcomes are produced. The *micro-objective* of an analysis of the 1956 Suez Crisis is to investigate the role of constraint from a monadic perspective. The statistical analysis demonstrates that democracies are more peaceful only when dealing with other democracies. Why do normative and institutional constraints break down? Why aren't the British, French, and Israelis constrained from initiating large-scale violence to resolve the international dispute? The case study demonstrates that although constraint did not prevent the initiation of violence, *it clearly shaped the actions of decision makers and the course of events in the crisis.* Constraint not captured by the quantitative model indicates that the monadic hypothesis cannot be dismissed outright.

The second case study, which explores the Ecuador-Peru territorial dispute, probes a deviant case. Although the statistical analysis provided strong support for the dyadic hypothesis, the case study demonstrates the probabilistic nature of the findings. Although democracies are less likely to use force against other democracies, decision makers can still choose to use force. Why didn't the presence of joint democracy prevent the long-simmering territorial dispute from exploding into armed conflict? The case study highlights the absence of domestic opposition to a use of force and the slow development of normative and institutional constraints in young democracies.

The *macro-objective* of the case studies is hypothesis generation. The Suez Crisis and the Ecuador-Peru territorial dispute represent four instances (three in the Suez Crisis alone) in which a democratic state chose to initiate a large-scale use of military force. Over the course of the book, we will explore eighteen cases of democratic initiation. In the concluding chapter of the book, I will present a number of testable propositions drawn from the examination of these case studies. Although the hypothesis-generation exercise requires a more extensive discussion of the cases than would be necessary for achieving the more limited micro-objective, I believe the payoff is well worth the effort.

THE SUEZ CRISIS: WHY DON'T MONADIC NORMS AND INSTITUTIONS CONSTRAIN?

The crisis grew out of the long-standing dispute between the United Kingdom and Egypt over control of the Suez Canal Zone.[43] The Canal Zone encompassed a large swath of territory stretching from the Mediterranean to the outskirts of Cairo. According to the 1936 Anglo-Egyptian Treaty, the British were to maintain control of the canal for twenty years, at which time the two parties would reexamine the agreement. Although the agreement was very unpopular with Egyptian nationalists, it was ratified by the legislature, which was controlled by the Wafd Party and approved by the newly crowned King Farouk. From the British perspective, control of the canal was absolutely essential because it was the critical communication and transport link between the island nation and its colonies in the Far East, particularly India. As Hitler and the specter of war rose in Europe, the United Kingdom increasingly planned to rely on the assets of the entire Commonwealth should violence erupt. During World War II, the protection of the canal became a central British objective because a significant portion of British wartime resources flowed through the Canal Zone.

In September 1945 the Egyptian government demanded a revision of the 1936 Anglo-Egyptian Treaty and the withdrawal of all British troops. Britain agreed to withdraw its forces to the Canal Zone and to reopen negotiations, but its desire to maintain the canal prevented any real progress. In response, Egypt broke off bilateral negotiations and attempted to resolve the issue through channels at the United Nations. However, bilateral negotiations resumed after an overwhelming Wafd Party victory in the Egyptian general election of 1950. In 1951, again frustrated by a lack of progress, the Egyptian parliament formally abrogated the 1936 treaty. Britain declared a state of emergency and reinforced the 80,000 soldiers in the Canal Zone. The Egyptian population resorted to both popular resistance and guerrilla warfare in its attempt to displace the British. The ensuing clashes resulted in hundreds of casualties. A particularly violent episode occurred on January 25, 1952, when the British attempted to disarm an auxiliary police unit in the city of Ismailia, which fell within the Canal Zone. The clash left forty-one Egyptians dead and seventy-two wounded, and triggered widespread rioting in Cairo (Clodfelter 1992, 1036). The crisis temporarily abated later that spring with the formation of a new government by King Farouk and the opening of a new round of bilateral talks.

The situation changed significantly on July 23, 1952, when King Farouk was overthrown by a group of military officers. By April 1954, Lieutenant Colonel Gamal Abdel Nasser had consolidated power within the ruling junta. Although the more autocratic regime did not drastically alter the bargaining process by resorting to direct military force, it did prove more successful than previous regimes. On October 19, 1954, the United Kingdom, led by Foreign Minister Anthony Eden, agreed to withdraw from the Canal Zone in twenty months. In return, Egypt pledged to maintain the military assets and accepted Britain's right to re-occupy the Canal Zone should the canal come under threat in time of war. This last clause would shape behavior of all parties during the Suez Crisis. The last British troops left the Canal Zone on June 13, 1956.

On July 19, 1956, the United States and the United Kingdom announced that they were withdrawing the offer to finance the Aswan high dam. In response, Nasser nationalized the Suez Canal on July 26 in the hope of using canal revenue to finance the dam project. Negotiations at both a London Conference and at the United Nations failed to produce a compromise. In October, the United Kingdom, France, and Israel secretly agreed to initiate an attack on Egypt. Fighting began when Israel launched an offensive, which would eventually encompass 45,000 troops, toward the Suez Canal on October 29. The direct threat to the canal activated the clause of the 1954 Anglo-Egyptian agreement that placed the United Kingdom in control of the zone during a militarized crisis. Britain and France issued an ultimatum to both Egypt and Israel: immediately withdraw ten miles from the canal or risk armed intervention. The next day, while vetoing U.N. Security Council resolutions aimed at halting the crisis, Britain and France began air strikes from carriers in the Mediterranean and from land bases in Cyprus. The attack completely destroyed the Egyptian air force. By November 5, the British and French landed 13,500 and 8,500 troops, respectively, in the northern

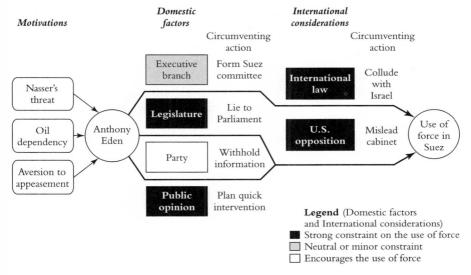

FIGURE 2.2. Suez Crisis: Why don't domestic institutions constrain British behavior?

half of the Canal Zone (Clodfelter 1992, 1038). However, severe international and domestic pressure forced the three aggressors to sign a cease-fire on November 7. Under pressure from the United States, the United Nations, and the Soviet Union, the three democracies withdrew from the occupied territory. The Egyptian armed forces lost almost 2,000 troops, but the three democracies suffered only light casualties: Israel 189, Britain 22, and France 10 (Clodfelter 1992, 1038).

Motives for British Intervention

What compelled the British to initiate violence? Why didn't the threat of punishment from domestic opposition deter the democratically elected decision makers from using force first? Finally, were the British decision makers punished for failure as predicted by the structural and normative models? Figure 2.2 provides a road map for answering these questions. A similar road map is provided for the French and Israeli cases (as well as the case studies discussed in subsequent chapters). The left-hand side of the figure identifies the motives encouraging the chief decision maker, in this case Prime Minister Anthony Eden, to use force to resolve the dispute. The center of the figure identifies key domestic factors that encouraged (or discouraged) the use of military force; the center of the figure also identifies actions, if any, taken by the chief executive to circumvent particular constraints. The right-hand side of the figure focuses on international considerations that encouraged or discouraged the chief decision maker from using military force. Although these international constraints were not developed in statistical analysis of crises, they represent important factors that often interact with the domestic constraints. As the cases demonstrate, leaders often attempt to circumvent these constraints for domestic political purposes.

Prime Minister Anthony Eden had three motives for using force to resolve his dispute with Nasser: (1) Nasser's threat to British Middle Eastern policy, (2) British dependence on Middle Eastern oil, and (3) Eden's longstanding aversion to appeasement.

The immediate impetus to the Suez Crisis can be traced to March 1956, when King Hussein of Jordan dismissed Sir John Glubb as commander of the Arab Legion following internal unrest. Eden erroneously believed the uprising had been orchestrated from Cairo (Lucas 1991, 94; Gorst and Johnman 1997, 43; Kyle 1991, 94). Prior to that point, Eden had pursued a policy of accommodation with Nasser. As foreign minister, Eden had negotiated the withdrawal from the Canal Zone despite the reservations of Churchill and the open opposition of the conservative "Suez Group" in Parliament. Following the coup attempt against Hussein and the nationalization of the canal, Eden came to believe that Nasser was an aggressive revisionist leader (Richardson 1996, 38). Eden's view of Nasser was reinforced by Egyptian support for Saudi Arabia in its territorial dispute with the British-backed Persian Gulf sheiks and by Egyptian attempts to challenge British plans to develop the anti-Soviet Baghdad Pact with Iraq. Nasser appeared determined to challenge British Middle Eastern policy on every front.

The second motive was oil. Britain was dependent on oil shipped from its Middle East holdings through the Suez Canal. Short of reserves of foreign exchange, Britain had been hit by a sterling crisis in 1947 and forced to devalue in 1949. In 1955–56 Britain once again found itself in the middle of an economic crisis that included rising inflation, declining foreign currency reserves, and the impending loss of convertibility to the dollar. Any suspension of the oil supply through the Suez Canal would raise prices by forcing tankers to round the Cape of Good Hope. The treasury calculated that the postwar merchant marine was insufficient for this operation. This shortfall would force Britain to buy higher-priced oil from the Western Hemisphere. The higher cost of imported oil threatened economic collapse. A treasury paper presented by Macmillan in the cabinet meeting of August 28 concluded that the cost of military action was small compared to the cost of the canal's closing to oil transport (Lucas 1991, 177). Although Nasser had not interfered with shipping through the canal, if he did, it would impose an enormous burden on the fragile British economy.

The third motive stemmed from Eden's aversion to appeasement. Eden's reputation was built on his expertise in foreign affairs and was particularly enhanced by his resignation as foreign secretary in 1938 to protest the appeasement of Hitler at Munich. Drawing on the Munich analogy, Eden (as well as French Prime Minister Mollet) believed that appeasement of Nasser would only encourage greater demands. Eden claimed that Nasser had pan-Arabic designs and that Nasser's canal policy was similar to Hitler's demand for the *Sudetenland*. He explicitly referred to Nasser as another Mussolini.[44] As with many decision makers in the post–World War II era, Eden and his belief in the Munich analogy required the adoption of a coercive strategy when faced with challenges to the status quo.[45]

Eden believed that the solution to his problem was the elimination of Nasser. In private, Eden clearly stated that this was his goal (Sellers 1990, 17; Richardson 1996, 38). Eden strongly supported the MI-6 plan to assassinate Nasser (Lucas 1991). Publicly, however, he claimed that nationalization of the canal violated international law and could not go unpunished. The façade was required because the prime minister believed that publicly advocating the overthrow of Nasser would trigger opposition from moderate Arabs, domestic groups, and other states. Eden also believed that a decisive military defeat would undermine Nasser's domestic support and lead to his replacement with a more malleable government. As military planning with the French and Israelis progressed, Eden rescinded his approval of the assassination program and focused on defeating and overthrowing the Nasser regime.[46]

Domestic Factors: Constraints and Opportunities for the British

Figure 2.2 highlights four domestic factors that can encourage or discourage a democratic leader from turning to military force: the executive branch, the legislature, the party, and public opinion. Throughout the crisis, Prime Minister Eden attempted to remove constraints (such as opposition from Labour in the legislature) or prevent constraint from emerging (for example, maintaining support in the Conservative Party).

In Britain, the Conservative Party was in its fifth year of rule in the House of Commons. The Conservatives had come to power with a slim majority under the guidance of Winston Churchill in October 1951. Following the April 1955 resignation of Churchill for health reasons, Anthony Eden led the party through a successful May election that resulted in a comfortable majority (Conservatives 345, Labour 277, Liberals 6, and Irish Republicans 2). Eden retained the post of prime minister, and Conservative Party members held all positions in the cabinet.

Opposition within the executive branch in Westminster parliamentary systems with a majority party is inherently limited. Ministers serve at the discretion of the prime minister (who typically serves as the party leader). Prime ministers appoint ministers who share similar preferences and remove ministers who challenge their authority. In addition, Eden took two steps to further reduce constraint on his ability to conduct foreign policy. First, he replaced the strong character of Macmillan as foreign minister with the malleable Selwyn Lloyd in order to have complete control of foreign policy decisions. Second, Eden restricted discussion of the military operation to a subcommittee of the cabinet. In fact, the entire collusion scheme was deliberately withheld from the full cabinet.

Eden's formation of a Suez "war cabinet" is illuminating. He chose to create an ad hoc Egyptian Committee to handle the crisis. Drawing on the belief that large bodies (such as the full cabinet and the legislature) cannot make decisions efficiently in crises, the Suez war cabinet comprised only five core members (Anthony Eden, Selwyn Lloyd, Harold Macmillan, A. Head, and Chief of Staff Mountbatten).[47] In setting up the ad hoc committee, Eden was obviously drawing on his experience as foreign minister in Churchill's war cabinet during World War II. However, unlike Eden's ad hoc committee, Churchill's war cabinet contained members of the chief opposition party. Labour's participation in the decision-making process during World War II made the probability of opposition emerging after the crisis, much less during the crisis itself, extremely remote. However, Eden restricted decision making to a handful of Conservative Party members with similar world views.[48] The choice increased both the probability of poor decision making and the emergence of opposition to the use of force.

Within the legislature, Eden faced the opposition of the Labour Party, which held 277 of the 630 seats in the House of Commons (versus 345 seats held by the Conservative Party). Despite the large number of seats held by Labour, the structure of the political system restricted its ability to shape policy. The strong party system in the United Kingdom inherently limits opposition because backbenchers rarely deviate from the party's program. This stands in stark contrast with the U.S. system, in which party members often vote against the administration. Given its limited ex ante power over decisions, the Labour Party focused on providing an alternative perspective on the crisis in order to punish Eden should his policy fail. In September, a majority of the Labour members opposed the use of military force to resolve the nationalization conflict (Epstein 1964, 142). Labour Party leader Hugh Gaitskill explicitly told Eden that unless Egypt interfered with canal traffic, his party would oppose the use of force (Gorst and Johnman 1997, 72).

How did Eden deal with the potential opposition in Parliament? Given that Egypt did not appear intent on giving the British a pretext for using military force by interfering with canal traffic, Eden was forced to manufacture a justification for intervention. By colluding with Israel and France, Eden believed he would shift the blame associated with the initiation of violence to Israel and Egypt. When the operation began, Eden openly lied to Parliament by denying any collusion with Israel (Gorst and Johnman 1997, 147). However, as the cover story began to unravel, opposition to the use of force by members of the Labour Party rose from 54 percent in September to 67 percent in November (Epstein 1964, 142). Unlike other crises (such as the British interventions in Russia, Iraq, and Iran) in which the opposition was brought into the decision-making process, Eden's failure to bring Labour on board became problematic as the conflict dragged out.[49] Labour offered the public an alternative frame for the intervention, and this led to the polarization of the country.[50]

Was there opposition to the use of force within the Conservative Party? Although general opposition to Eden's leadership existed (Macmillan and Butler in particular), there was no real opposition on the issue of using force. The "Suez Group," formed by Colonel Charles Waterhouse and Julian Amery in 1953, was dedicated to preserving the existing British military presence in Egypt. The Suez Group strongly favored using military force, but it represented only a minority of Conservative Party members. More influential was the strong support for action from ordinary members of the Conservative Party. The enthusiasm for Eden's pledge not to rule out force at the party conference of October 13 was so great "that the Prime Minister must have realized that any compromise solution . . . would be deeply unpopular in the Conservative Party" (Carlton 1988, 58). Although the public and opposition did not "rally around the flag" during the crisis, Conservative Party members approving the use of force rose from 47 percent in early September to 68 percent in early November to 81 percent in early December (Epstein 1964, 142). On the whole, the Conservative Party encouraged rather than discouraged the use of military force.

Public opinion in the United Kingdom was clearly divided on the issue of resorting to military force. In August 1956 a 68-percent majority believed that Nasser was not acting within his rights when he nationalized the canal (Gallup 1976b, 382). The public also strongly favored negotiation, economic sanctions, and military preparations. However, a September poll indicated that only a small minority (22 percent) favored using force immediately; most advocated exhausting other avenues first (Gallup 1976b, 382, 390). Eden believed that the public could be persuaded to support the operation if it proved to be quick and successful. Unfortunately for the British prime minister, it turned out to be neither. The opinion polls indicate that there was no pronounced "rally around the prime minister" effect in Britain; Eden's popular approval hovered around 50 percent from January 1956 through the use of force in October.

International Considerations for Britain

Internationally, two factors strongly influenced British decision making and the evolution of the crisis: (1) international law and (2) U.S. opposition. Realists have long disparaged the utility of international law. Given that international law lacks the coercive power to constrain powerful states, political leaders can ignore the law with impunity. Although international law did not *prevent* the use of military force, it certainly influenced the course of the crisis. Eden desperately wanted to appear to be within the bounds of international law. He recognized that both domestic and international (particularly U.S.) public opinion would not support a military intervention without a clear provocation (Kyle 1991, 122). Nasser's nationalization was legal as long as Egypt compensated the shareholders; Nasser clearly intended to do so in order to prevent a British retaliation. By colluding with the Israelis in order to manufacture a "threat" to the canal, Eden hoped to secure public support and satisfy international law. Contrary to the predictions of some realists, international law was very relevant for Anthony Eden, the Labour Party, the general public, and the U.S. government.

A second international constraint was U.S. opposition to the use of force. Although Britain and the United States continued to have a "special relationship" in many respects, the Eisenhower administration believed that Britain often acted as an imperialist power (Lucas 1991, 18–23). On questions relating to the colonial possessions and the newly independent states, the two countries typically had very different points of view. The special relationship was further compromised by a tense relationship between Prime Minister Eden and Secretary of State John Foster Dulles. The vast differences in philosophical beliefs and decision-making styles led to frequent condemnations of each other via press leaks.

Eden desired U.S. support for the use of military force. However, all efforts to this end were rebuffed by the United States. Eisenhower warned that military action was unjustified *unless* Egypt disrupted traffic on the canal (Eisenhower to Eden, 31 July 1956; Memo of conversation between Eden and Dulles, 1 August 1956, 12:45 pm; Eisenhower to Eden, 3 September 1956; Eisenhower to Eden, 8 September 1956, in Gorst and Johnman 1997, 65–80). Although it appears that the Central Intelligence Agency was aware of the MI-6 plan to remove Nasser by force and the plans to cooperate with Israel, the Eisenhower administration seems to have been surprised that the British actually went ahead with the project despite the repeated warn-

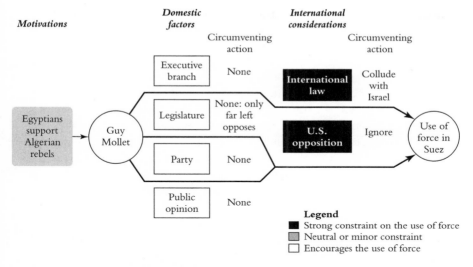

FIGURE 2.3. Suez Crisis: Why don't domestic institutions constrain French behavior?

ings (U.S. National Archives, CIA London Station to Director CIA, Cable LOND 7064, describing meeting with MI6 of April 1, 1956). Eden's attempt to circumvent U.S. opposition by colluding with France and Israel was a failure; the Eisenhower administration immediately saw through the ruse and put tremendous financial pressure on the beleaguered British pound (Kirshner 1995, 70). Facing an economic disaster, the British halted the invasion.

Motives for French Intervention

As Figure 2.3 indicates, the French decision-making environment differed significantly from the British situation. Of all the participants, the French were the strongest advocates of military intervention. The French continually pressured the British to intervene and brought the Israelis on board without first consulting the British. Prime Minister Guy Mollet was motivated by Nasser's psychological and material support for the Algerian independence movement, the FLN (*Front de Liberation Nationale*). Both Mollet and the French public believed that the Algerian situation was the most important issue facing the country. In an April 1956 national survey, 63 percent of the public identified "Algeria" as the country's most important problem (Gallup 1976b, 195). Moreover, most believed that the situation in Algeria was getting worse. Both Mollet and the public believed that Egypt was a prime cause of the troubles in Algeria and that the outcome of the Suez

Crisis would affect the rebels' behavior (Golani 1998, 43). In a September public opinion poll, 58 percent of those surveyed believed that the Suez affair would have a "very important" impact on the Algerian situation (Gallup 1976b, 206). Backing down to Nasser in Egypt became linked to capitulating to the FLN in Algeria (Golani 1998, 39).

Mollet believed, certainly incorrectly, that without Egyptian support for the Algerian rebels, the uprising would die away. The solution to Mollet's Algerian problem was the overthrow of Nasser. Just like his British counterpart, Mollet explicitly employed the Munich analogy. If Nasser was appeased in the current crisis, he would unite the Arab world against French and Western interests. Although history subsequently demonstrated that national interests and internal divisions would prevent any pan-Arab unification, the threat seemed quite real in 1956. Mollet, like Eden, appeared to believe that Nasser was an aberration rather than representative of a broad class of Egyptians socialized in an oppressive colonial society. This assumption led both leaders to advocate Nasser's overthrow based on the expectation that a stable pro-Western regime could be subsequently established.[51]

Domestic Factors: Constraints and Opportunities for the French

Although France was by almost any definition a democratic state, little in the domestic environment constrained Mollet from using force to resolve the Suez conflict. Representative institutions do not promote the peaceful resolution of conflict if the political opposition supports the use of military force. In fact, opposition support sends a strong signal (Schultz 2001). As Figure 2.3 indicates, no important forces in the executive, the legislature, the ruling party, or the public at large opposed the use of military force.

Guy Mollet rose to power as part of a center-left coalition government following the January 1956 elections. His minority ruling coalition, which included the Socialists, Radical Socialists, and the Democratic and Socialist Union of Resistance (UDSR), held only 170 of the 627 seats in the National Assembly.[52] The government was the twentieth since 1946, reflecting the notorious instability of the Fourth Republic. To De Gaulle's dismay in 1946, the Fourth Republic placed most power in a factionalized legislature rather than in the chief executive. In theory, such a weak institutional position (minority party and coalition government) should constrain leaders from undertaking risky foreign policies. However, this was not the case in 1956.

Although members of different political parties held positions in the cabinet, none were opposed to using force against Egypt. The various factions of the Socialist Party all supported the government's position. In the legislature, the parties to the right of the Socialists strongly advocated the use of force. On the left, only the Communist Party and some members of the

New Left Party opposed a military solution. Ironically, the Soviet invasion of Hungary during the middle of the Suez Crisis undermined the French Communist Party's ability to credibly protest the military intervention.[53]

The July 26 nationalization of the Suez Canal by Nasser led to a vote of "no confidence" in the French parliament. Although the Mollet government emerged with a clear majority, the debates during August 1–3 signaled to Mollet that the National Assembly supported a hard-line position against Nasser. The Munich analogy, Israeli security, and France's reputation in the Algerian conflict were all cited as reasons for taking a tough stand on Suez. Although Parliament was not involved in the decision to use force, it did approve of the military operation on October 30—the day after the commencement of joint Anglo-French air operations but before the ground assault. On that date, the legislature voted 368 to 182 in support of the use of force; most of the opposition votes came from the French Communist Party. In sum, despite the existence of opposition parties in the cabinet and legislature, the convergence of preferences supporting the use of force in the French case implied that Mollet was not constrained from using force.

Public opinion in France was much more bellicose than in Britain. In large part, this was due to the connection between the Suez affair and the conflict in Algeria (Golani 1998, 44). As mentioned, a majority of the public believed that Algeria was the most important problem facing the country and that the outcome of the Suez Crisis would influence the course of this conflict. A significant majority of the French public supported military preparations during the crisis (50 percent approve, 29 percent disapprove, and 21 percent no opinion). When it came to the use of military force, a slight majority (44 percent approve versus 37 percent disapprove) backed the initiation of violence by the French and British. Moreover, this support for military action did not wane over time despite the suspension of the military operation, the failure to secure the canal, the inability to topple Nasser, and the international outcry. In March 1957, 43 percent of the public voiced support for the military effort, and only 28 percent opposed the use of force. The public did not constrain the Mollet government from using force because a majority of French men and women supported the initiation of violence to resolve the political conflict.[54]

International Considerations for France

Internationally, the French situation was similar to the British situation in many ways. The French also felt constrained by international law and therefore sought to justify the military operation by colluding with the Israelis. The French also faced opposition from the United States. However, the French were much more willing to ignore U.S. opposition for two reasons.

First, unlike the British case, there was no "special relationship" to preserve. U.S.–French relations were close but stormy. U.S. behavior during the Suez Crisis reinforced the French view that the United States was an unreliable ally. Following the crisis, France redoubled its efforts to establish a European community that could defend French interests against the two overbearing superpowers. Second, the French economy was not nearly as vulnerable to U.S. pressure as the stumbling British economy. Simply put, the Americans did not have the necessary carrots or sticks to alter French behavior.

Motives for Israeli Intervention

For Israeli Prime Minister Ben Gurion, the decision to use force was straightforward: the use of force was supported by a majority of the cabinet, the legislature, and the public at large (see Figure 2.4). The 1948 war of independence had left the small country surrounded by hostile neighbors that openly advocated the destruction of Israel. After the war, Egypt had closed the Gulf of Aqaba and supported an increasing number of guerrilla raids from Gaza. In 1955, Egypt announced the "Czech arms deal" through which Egypt would acquire 230 tanks, 200 armored personnel carriers, 500 pieces of artillery, and 200 aircraft (Herzog 1982, 112). Nasser had always indicated a willingness to invade Israel; with the delivery of arms in 1957, he would possess the capacity to invade as well. There was virtually unanimous agreement (for example, in Israel, Egypt, the United States, Britain, and France) that the arms deal had changed the balance of power in the Middle East.[55]

Ben Gurion (first as defense minister and later as prime minister and defense minister) discussed launching a preventative attack on Egypt in late 1955. The prime minister believed that war with Egypt was inevitable; a preventative strike before Egypt absorbed the weapons would increase the odds of success. However, he was deterred by three factors. First, he recognized that preventative wars could not permanently end hostilities because Egypt would inevitably rearm. Second, the initiation of hostilities would certainly result in a suspension of arms deliveries to Israel by Western suppliers, and this would only aggravate the balance of forces problem in the long run. Finally, the British were likely to intervene on the side of the Arabs due to treaty commitments. In fact, the British-Jordanian defense treaty nearly triggered a British use of force against Israel during the Suez Crisis following Jordanian-Israeli clashes at Garandal, Husan, and Qaiqilya between September 13 and October 12, 1956.[56]

The French proposals for collusion seemed to satisfy two of these concerns. French arms would continue to flow, and the threat of British intervention would be eliminated. Moreover, the planned French and British destruction of the Egyptian air force reduced the threat from strategic

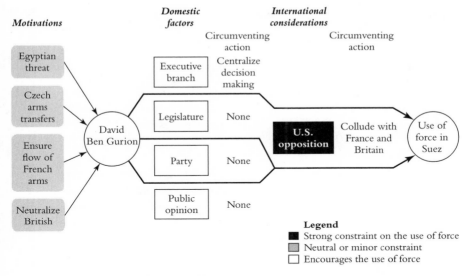

FIGURE 2.4. Suez Crisis: Why don't domestic institutions constrain Israeli behavior?

bombing to both Israeli military operations in the Sinai and civilian populations. Although Ben Gurion did not trust the British and feared being hung out to dry (given that Israel must initiate before the French and British in order to give the collusion argument a plausible façade), his belief that a French-Israeli bond was vital to the defense of Israel over the long term persuaded him to assist his closest ally.

Domestic Factors: Constraints and Opportunities for the Israelis

In Israel, David Ben Gurion's Mapai Party had ruled the country through a series of coalitional governments since independence in 1948. The most recent election on July 26, 1955, had reduced Labour's share of seats in the Knesset from forty-five to forty (Mackie and Rose 1974, 205). However, Ben Gurion's ruling coalition (Mapai, forty; Mapam, nine; Ahdut Avodah, ten; Mapai Arab affiliates, five; Religious Mizrahi, eleven; and Progressives, five) continued to hold a majority (80 of 120) in the chamber. The largest opposition parties in the Knesset at the time of the crisis were from the right of the political spectrum: the Freedom Party (fifteen seats) and the General Zionists (thirteen seats).

Within the executive branch, there was little if any constraint on the prime minister because all members of the coalition supported Ben Gurion's coercive policies. Moreover, the nature of civil-military relations in the new democracy reduced constraint on Ben Gurion (Elman 1997b). The Transition Law of 1949 placed the prime minister, defense minister, and chief of staff at the center of decisions to use force:

> When these three posts have been filled by representatives of rival political parties (or factions of the same party), each has checked the actions of the others. When the posts have been held by actors from the same party, checks to executive action were effectively removed. For example, when David Ben Gurion was both prime minister and defense minister and also had a loyal chief of staff, he was able to authorize and implement far-reaching military actions without prior cabinet approval. (Elman 1997b, 319)

Similarly, there was little or no opposition to the use of force within Ben Gurion's Mapai Party or within the legislature as a whole. In fact, the most important political opposition came from right-wing parties that strongly supported the use of force. Finally, the public opinion strongly supported the military operation after the fact:

> For the most part, the French and Israeli public identified with the goals of the war. Egypt had given Israel no end of casus belli over the past years. . . . Israel thus believed it had the moral right to decide when and where to resume hostilities—in any case, that was the way the Israeli public saw things. (Bar-On 1994, 244)

The phrase *after the fact* is important because foreign policy decision making was extremely centralized. The June 1956 arms agreement with France, which required Israel to covertly assist France in its Algerian war, was not announced to the cabinet until August 19, 1956. The Knesset was informed of the secret transfers only on October 15, a mere two weeks before the start of the Sinai war. The absence of television, state control of radio, and military censorship of the press virtually eliminated the role of public opinion in both the arms deal and the collusion with France and Britain prior to the outbreak of war.

International Considerations for Israel

Unlike the French and the British, the Israeli government was not obsessed with international law. Egyptian closure of the Straits of Tiran was an act of war; Egyptian support of *fedayeen* attacks from Jordan and Gaza was an act of war. Given the Egyptian behavior, international law did not constrain the Israeli decision makers.

The one important international constraint in the minds of Israeli leaders was the United States. Early in the crisis, U.S. support was seen as a necessary condition for Israeli action. When Ben Gurion sent Foreign Minister Golda Meir to Paris to discuss collusion, he explicitly stated that U.S. and

British support was required for any intervention. Israel needed Britain to guarantee neutrality in any Jordan-Israel clash, and Israel needed the United States for financial support (Bar-On 1994, 194). However, as the crisis wore on, concern about the U.S. reaction to the military intervention began to wane for three reasons. First, Israel had found a solid arms supplier in France. Although the Israelis repeatedly attempted to secure arms from the United States during 1956, the Eisenhower administration was unwilling to rectify the imbalance triggered by the Czech arms deal. Second, British participation reduced the probability of a hostile U.S. response. Both the French and the Israelis believed that the "special relationship" between the United States and Britain would protect them from U.S. sanctions. Third, both the French and the Israelis believed that the U.S. administration would be unlikely to punish Israel before the November elections. Despite a series of explicit warnings from Eisenhower, Israel initiated violence against Egypt.

The U.S. response was extremely hostile. Although the United States was not an important arms supplier to Israel, it threatened a variety of nonmilitary sanctions, including cutting all public and private financial aid, supporting a U.N. embargo of Israel, and even expelling Israel from the United Nations (Bar-On 1994, 274–75). Eisenhower and Dulles believed that the British, French, and Israelis should be coerced into withdrawing and that domestic elections should play no role in the crisis.

Conclusions from the Suez Crisis

The statistical models presented earlier in the chapter found that within the set of militarized crises, democracies are not generally less likely to initiate violence than are nondemocracies. *Why did the hypothesized monadic constraint fail to emerge?*[57] The examination of British, French, and Israeli behavior in the Suez Crisis provides some important clues.

First, opposition to the use of force failed to emerge within the potentially constraining institutions (that is, coalition cabinets and legislatures) for all three initiators. In fact, in some instances the opposition encouraged political leaders to use military force. The important point here is that institutions alone are not sufficient for constraint. Researchers seem to assume that there is an almost perfect correlation between institutional openness and intensity of opposition. Unfortunately, this need not be the case. The case studies indicate that in order for the democratic peace literature to move forward, researchers must put a much higher emphasis on measuring the breadth and intensity of political opposition to the specific foreign policy issue (Schultz 2001).

Second, the democratic decision makers did not expect opposition to emerge because they anticipated a rapid victory. The balance of forces strongly favored the three democracies, despite the logistical difficulties involved in projecting power at such a distance for Britain and France. In all likelihood, the military operation would have been successful had it not been halted. The prospect of a *fait accompli* proved to be very seductive, particularly for Eden. The desire to present the opposition with a *fait accompli* points to structural rather than normative constraints. Eden did not abhor violence; he simply desired to minimize any opposition to his policy.

Third, the secret collusive arrangement encouraged the intervention. Eden believed he could rally domestic and international public opinion to his position as long as he appeared to act within the confines of international law. The secret collusive arrangement with Israel provided the operation with a moral justification and façade of legitimacy. Eden's desire to keep the whole arrangement secret again points to a structural argument—as long as the opposition was not aware of a violation of international law, the transgression did not matter.[58]

Fourth, the restricted number of decision makers involved in the decision to intervene may have encouraged a breakdown in institutional constraints. In the British case, a mere five decision makers were involved in the collusive agreement and the decision to issue an ultimatum. Even in theoretically open societies, foreign policy decisions, particularly those that involve highly secret operations such as the initiation of violence, are typically made by a handful of individuals. This narrowness can lead to inefficient decision making by restricting the range of alternatives proposed and by encouraging a quick consensus. Ironically, more decision makers were involved in the Soviet decision to invade Afghanistan than in the British decision to use force against Egypt (Seymour-Ure 1984; Mendelson 1993).

Finally, the *assumption* in the structural model that decision makers are punished for foreign policy failures is not supported by the Suez cases.[59] In general, the case points to two reasons for this lack of punishment. First, the military operations resulted in very low numbers of casualties and lasted only eight days. As Mueller (1973) demonstrated in the Vietnam case, there is an inverse relationship between body bags returning home and public support for the use of force.[60] Second, in the Suez Crisis a third party could be blamed for the failure (scapegoating). Most observers in Britain and France believed that without U.S. interference, the Canal Zone would have been occupied quite easily. In particular, the French blamed the United States for the failure, which led it toward a more independent and European-focused foreign policy.[61]

More specifically, were any of the decision makers punished for failure? The answer appears to be "somewhat." Eden was clearly punished as an individual; the pressure of the crisis triggered a physical breakdown that resulted in his departure for Jamaica shortly after the November 7 cease-fire. By January 1957, he had resigned his post for reasons of health. Although many have speculated that Eden would have been required to resign following the failure, a December 1956 opinion poll indicated that 56 percent of the public reported that they were satisfied with Eden (Gallup 1976b, 398). This figure was actually a slight improvement over his precrisis numbers. Moreover, as has been previously shown, the vast majority of Conservatives rallied to the government's side following the use of force. A British opinion poll taken a year later indicated a continuing split on the use of force, with 48 percent supporting, 32 percent opposing, and 20 percent undecided (Gallup 1976b, 432). However, when asked how the Conservative Party actions during the crisis would affect their voting behavior in subsequent elections, the subjects responded: more inclined—10 percent, less inclined—26 percent, no difference—52 percent, and don't know—12 percent. Clearly, the salience and impact of the event had diminished greatly over one year's time. By the 1959 elections, the Suez Crisis was a nonissue. In part, this was due to the Labour Party's fear of being labeled unpatriotic were it to use the Suez failure against the Conservatives.

In the French and Israeli cases, the absence of punishment is more clear-cut. In a December 20, 1956, vote of "no confidence," Mollet's government easily survived with a 325 to 210 majority. Moreover, French public opinion polls demonstrated that of those respondents with an opinion on the crisis, a majority continued to support the prior use of force (Vaisse 1989, 339). In Israel, the operation was considered a military success. Ben Gurion was rewarded rather than punished for using force successfully.

In sum, the assumption that decision makers are punished for foreign policy failures is conditional on the presence of significant domestic opposition to the use of force generated either prior to the crisis or during the crisis.

Do the cases support the statistical conclusion that monadic constraint is not important? Clearly, the monadic normative and structural explanations predict that democracies should be less likely to initiate violence. In the Suez Crisis, these predictions failed. However, the cases demonstrate that constraint can play an important role in the evolution of a crisis in ways not captured by the operationalization of the dependent variable (for example, initiation of force).

First, to a large degree the obsession with conforming to international law shaped the form of the military intervention and the evolution of the entire crisis. Clearly, Eden was not constrained from within. Violating international law did not lead to a sense of guilt or a loss of self-esteem. Yet Eden clearly realized that others (such as members of the House of Commons, the British public, and the U.S. government) believed that conforming with international law was absolutely essential. Therefore, constraint shaped the type of intervention.

Second, the scope of the planned military operation was very conservative in the hope of avoiding *both* British military and Egyptian civilian casualties. Civilian and military planners feared that casualties would undermine support for the operation. The original military plan, "Operation Musketeer," was abandoned after planners became concerned about casualties. In "Operation Musketeer Revised," British and French forces planned a two-week interval for forces to reach and secure the canal. Whereas the slow movement was partially due to an overestimation of the capability of the British-trained Egyptian army, it was also designed to allow the allies to bring overwhelming force in the hopes of minimizing casualties. Given that bombing began two days before the landing of troops, the drawn-out operation allowed political opposition forces to mobilize (Richardson 1996, 70). The cease-fire was reached just as the ground forces had begun their march southward. Fear of potential domestic and international opposition helped shape the development of war plans, which in turn shaped the course of political events.

Third, the emergence of opposition within the cabinet and Conservative Party, in addition to opposition from Labour, clearly unnerved Eden and led to the halting of the operation. To a large degree, this opposition occurred because Eden consciously chose to keep the cabinet ill-informed. The result was a divided government in which two ministers, albeit junior ministers, resigned in protest of Eden's actions. External pressure in the form of U.S. pressure on the British pound, coupled with internal opposition, led to the halting of hostilities long before the goals of the operation were achieved. Whereas constraint did not prevent the start of conflict, it clearly influenced the ending of conflict.

These three observations indicate that the impact of the monadic variables should be tested at several points in the evolution of conflict. Although the variables might not constrain states from initiating violence during a militarized crisis, they could influence the manner of escalation, the opportunity for settlement, and the duration of hostilities (Huth and Allee 2002).

THE ECUADOR–PERU DISPUTE:
CONFLICT IN A DEMOCRATIC DYAD

In both January 1981 and January 1995, Ecuador and Peru clashed over disputed territory in the Cordilla del Condor region.[62] In both cases, fighting broke out after Peruvian military forces discovered Ecuadorian military posts on the east side of the Cordilla del Condor. The 1981 clash involved hundreds of troops, but the 1995 incident escalated to the extent that thousands of troops from both sides were involved in the fighting in the remote jungles. The Peruvian-Ecuadorian clashes raise several interesting questions. First, were both states really democratic? If not, the outbreak of war hardly constitutes a deviant case for the democratic peace. Second, why didn't norms and structures prevent the emergence of violence? In particular, how did opposition parties within each state react to the use of force? Third, was the Ecuador-Peru case an example of diversionary war? Fourth, did civilian authorities in the Ecuadorian government control the military? Finally, how did the regime change in Peru between the 1981 and 1995 clashes influence the emergence and escalation of the 1995 military clash?

Background

The source of the Ecuador-Peru territorial dispute dates back to the era of Spanish rule. The Audiencia of Quito originally fell within the jurisdiction of the Viceroyalty of Peru. In 1739 control of the territory was shifted to the Viceroyalty of Nueva Granada, which encompassed most of what is present-day Colombia and Venezuela. The province of Maynas, which is the focus of the dispute in question, was transferred from Nueva Granada back to Peru by Spanish royal decree in 1802. Therefore, Peruvians claim that Maynas was part of Peru at the time of its independence from Spain in 1821. However, Ecuadorians claim that the royal decree merely transferred specific military and ecclesiastical functions rather than administrative control.

The first international conflict with respect to the disputed territory occurred in 1828 between the newly independent Peru and the Gran Colombia Federation (formally the Viceroyalty of Nueva Granada), which included present-day Ecuador. The defeat of the Peruvian forces led to the Treaty of Guayaquil on September 22, 1829. In 1830, just prior to the breakup of Gran Colombia and the independence of Ecuador, Peru and Gran Colombia signed a protocol which stipulated that the left bank of the Maranon River belonged to Gran Colombia and the right bank to Peru. Finally, in 1832 Peru and newly independent Ecuador signed a treaty of alliance and friendship that stated that existing borders should be recognized until a boundary convention could establish a definitive border. However, Peru subsequently claimed that the 1829 treaty was void because Gran Colombia no longer existed and that the 1830 protocol was irrelevant because Ecuador had never exhibited an original of the document. Therefore, Peru claimed that the 1832 document defined the boundaries.

Conflict erupted over the territory throughout the nineteenth and twentieth centuries. In 1857 Peru broke off diplomatic relations and blockaded Ecuadorian ports the following year. Although both sides mobilized for war, tensions subsided with the signing of the Mapasingue Convention in 1860, after which Ecuador agreed to annul a plan to transfer some of the disputed territory to British creditors, and both parties accepted the legal principle of *uti possidetis juris*, in which former colonies accept borders established under colonial rule. However, the Peruvian congress and the new constitutional government in Ecuador rejected the proposal.

Both sides accepted arbitration by the king of Spain in 1904, but when the king was about to rule in Peru's favor, the Ecuadorian government refused to continue the process. Conflict erupted again in July 1941, as both countries began stationing troops in the disputed region. During the month-long battle, the Peruvian force of 15,000 soundly defeated an overmatched Ecuadorian force of 3,000. Estimates of wartime casualties vary. Clodfelter (1992, 705) claims that the war resulted in between 80 and 100 Peruvian deaths and 500 to 600 Ecuadorian deaths. The war ended on January 29, 1942, with the signing of the Protocol of Rio de Janeiro, which was subsequently ratified by the legislatures of both countries.

The Rio Protocol "provided for guarantor responsibilities that appeared to be rather modest at the time: i.e., (a) to help the parties to the conflict lay out, and mark a boundary, and (b) to assist in addressing any disputes that might arise, if that was deemed necessary" (Palmer 1997, 111). The protocol also specified navigation rights on the Amazon and its northern tributaries for Ecuador. The Ecuador-Peru Boundary Commission definitively demarcated over 95 percent of the border during the period 1942–48. However, disagreement emerged over a seventy-eight-kilometer stretch of the border in the Cordillera del Condor and Cenepa River area. The U.S Army Air Corps' mapping of the area had revealed that "the height of the land that was to determine the border was not where the agreement had stipulated in one small section because of the presence of a previously uncharted river and mountain spur" (Palmer 1997, 113). The Ecuadorian government ordered a cessation of its demarcation team's activities, and from 1960 to the present Ecuadorian presidents have declared the 1942 protocol null and void. Ecuadorian officials claimed that "Ecuador always has been, is and will be an Amazonian country." Official maps continued to show the disputed territory as part of Ecuador, and children were taught in school that Ecuador had been denied its historical right to the region (Avery 1984, 68; see also B. Wood 1978). In sum, Ecuador rejected the status quo imposed by the Peruvian military in 1941.

Recent Crises

The 1981 conflict began on January 22, when a Peruvian helicopter, which Ecuador claimed had crossed the border, was fired upon in the disputed territory. Fighting erupted five days later, when ground forces clashed over control of three military outposts within the disputed zone. Both countries declared states of emergency (thus suspending many political rights at home) and mobilized large number of troops until a cease-fire was declared on February 2.[63] The remote locations of the conflict and its short duration limited the scope of the conflict. The Ecuadorian forces engaged numbered fewer than 600; relatively few Peruvian troops were deployed on the front. Official combat deaths were light (Peru admitted one; Ecuador admitted eight), "but casualties for both sides were probably considerably heavier" (Clodfelter 1992, 1190).[64] Although the clash does not represent a case of full-scale war between democracies, the question remains: did the fact that both states were democratic influence the emergence, the course, and/or the settlement of the dispute?

Although disagreement remains over who fired the first shot during the incident (Peruvians claimed that an unarmed helicopter on a supply mission had been shot at by Ecuadorian troops, whereas Ecuadorians claimed the helicopter had attacked its outpost), the event that precipitated the incident was the establishment of three military outposts by the Ecuadorian army on the east side of the Cordillera de Condor. All three bases were given the names of established Ecuadorian towns that lay on the west side of the mountain range, leading to the quite reasonable claim by Peru that Ecuador had resorted to deception in an attempt to mislead world opinion (Krieg 1986, 268). Given that Ecuador was not satisfied with the status quo settled on by the Rio Protocol and wished to keep the issue of the disputed territory on the agenda (and, if possible, push the issue into the wider forum of the Organization of American States [OAS]), it seems quite reasonable to argue that Ecuador initiated the incident.

The three military outposts had been established by September 1980 and provided permanent housing for the troops stationed there, with fields sown with corn and an area cleared for helicopter landings. The shooting began on January 22, when Peru apparently accidentally stumbled upon the military outposts. Peruvians claimed that an unarmed supply helicopter had chanced upon the Ecuadorian post named Paquisha and had been shot at by the Ecuadorian troops. The helicopter then returned to its base with a bullet hole in its fuselage. According to Peruvian sources, this was the first they were aware of the existence of the military post. Further reconnaissance revealed the existence of the two other Ecuadorian posts. According to the Ecuadorian version, the Peruvians had been aware of the posts since September 1980, and the military had planned an attack to undermine the position of Peru's civilian leader, President Belaunde. The Peruvian helicopter carried six armed soldiers, who opened fire on the encampment, seriously wounding one man. The foreign offices of both governments exchanged letters of protest, but there was a tendency on behalf of both to play down the incident, at least publicly. However, two days after the first incident, sixty-four Ecuadorian troops were brought to the outposts as reinforcement, while the Peruvians were preparing their aircraft and infantry for an all-out attack. On January 28, eight waves of Peruvian aircraft attacked the Ecuadorian encampments, using bombs, rockets, and machine-gun fire. The Peruvian air force easily overpowered the poorly equipped Ecuadorian forces. Paquisha and the other two posts were virtually destroyed, two Ecuadorians were killed, and the remainder of the forces scattered into the jungle. Within a couple of days, all three outposts were occupied by the Peruvian forces.

The Ecuadorian government quickly looked to the OAS to step in and broker a cease-fire. Such a move was important because it was an attempt to neutralize the Rio Protocol and the role of the guarantor countries. Peru initially blocked such moves by claiming that the OAS had no jurisdiction because the boundary dispute had been settled by the Rio Protocol and that Peru's actions had been those of a defender of its own territory. However, the OAS agreed to a meeting of its foreign ministers on February 2 and to immediately set up a commission of inquiry to ascertain the actual events. Meanwhile, the Peruvian government, facing calls within the hard line of the military to invade Ecuador, appealed to the guarantors of the Rio Protocol. It was through such a mechanism that Peru agreed to a cease-fire. With such a cease-fire in place, it appeared that there was little for the meeting of foreign ministers to do. However, the meeting did examine the events that led to the outbreak of hostilities and attempted to draft a resolution on the affair. Initially, Ecuador refused any resolution that explicitly mentioned the four guarantors of the Rio Protocol, whereas Peru would not accept any resolution that did not mention them. Peru agreed to a resolution that referred to the "four friendly nations" but that clearly left the four countries as arbitrators of the dispute. Ecuador finally agreed to such a resolution, claiming, however, that it had won a victory in eliminating all references to the guarantor countries. Breaches of the cease-fire occurred throughout February, when fighting broke out between the Ecuadorian troops who remained in the jungle on the eastern side of the Cordilla del Condor and Peruvian forces. It was unclear who initiated these incidents. However, by the end of the month, Ecuadorian troops had returned to the western side of the Cordilla del Condor, no nearer the Maranon River than before the outbreak of hostilities.

Whereas Ecuador had been successful in bringing its case to the OAS and removing mention of guarantors in the resolution, the "four friendly nations" had agreed and made statements to the effect that their agreement with the resolution in no way affected the responsibilities that they had as-

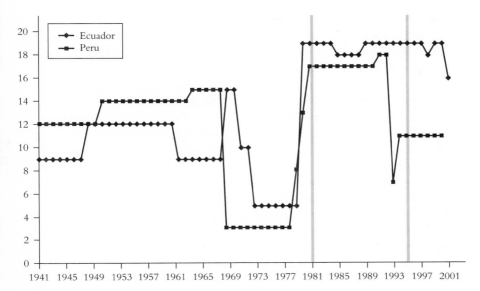

FIGURE 2.5. Democracy scores from the Polity IV data set

sumed under the Rio Protocol. Furthermore, Ecuador had failed to force the Peruvians to renegotiate the border, and the efforts of both the OAS and the "four friendly nations" were directed towards avoidance of open conflict rather than settlement of the border dispute.

Were both states democratic? The democratic credentials of both states for the recent period are shown in Figure 2.5. The measure of democracy employs the same operationalization used in the statistical analysis (in other words, Democracy Index minus Autocracy Index plus 10). Therefore, the level of democracy ranges from 0 to 20.[65] The figure highlights three factors. First, both states had experienced several regime changes over the last two decades. Second, both states were democratic when fighting broke out in 1981. Third, Peru no longer qualified as a democracy when fighting broke out again in 1995 due to President Alberto K. Fujimori's suspension of the constitution and closing of the national legislature in 1992.[66]

Ecuador has a long history of autocratic rule by both soldiers and civilians. In 1970 the popularly elected President Jose Maria Velasco Ibarra seized dictatorial powers by suspending Parliament and the Supreme Court. In 1972 the Army Chief of Staff Guillermo Rodriguez Lara seized power just months before scheduled elections. Rodriguez Lara, who envisioned long-term rule by the military, quickly consolidated power and led an extremely personalistic regime (Isaacs 1993). Opposition within the military led to Rodriguez Lara's replacement by a more collegial three-member military junta in 1976. A gradual transition to civilian rule was planned, and on January 15, 1978, a national referendum approved a new constitution. Much to the military's dismay, the left-leaning ticket of presidential candidate Jaime Roldos (Concentration of Popular Forces) and vice-presidential candidate Osvaldo Hurtado (Christian Democratic Party) soundly defeated the conservative candidate by amassing 69 percent of the vote in a runoff election. However, the military did not exit empty-handed, for it possessed the right to (1) name the board of directors of major state corporations, (2) participate in the selection of the defense minister, and (3) prevent any investigations into human rights abuses occurring under military rule.

As part of the price of military withdrawal, the military insisted that Asaad Bucaram, the controversial leader of the populist party *Concentración de Fuerzas Populares* (CFP), be barred from running for election. Bucaram nonetheless remained in the center of things by handpicking his nephew-in-law, Jamie Roldos, as his stand-in. Throughout the campaign it was implied by the CFP that a vote for Roldos would ensure power for Bucaram. However, in choosing Osvaldo Hurtado of the center-left *Democracia Popular* (DP) as his vice-presidential running mate, Roldos distanced himself from Bucaram (Conaghan 1994, 442). Roldos's cabinet was made up of members of the CFP and the DP, and a number of independent figures.

Elections for the unicameral legislature were held in April 1979. As Table 2.4 indicates, President Roldos's Concentration of Popular Forces party emerged with thirty of the seventy-one seats in the chamber. Bucaram's skill in coalition building secured himself election as the president of Congress with the support of the Conservative Party (PC), the Radical Liberal Party (PLR), and the National Velasquita Party (PNV). Controlling only 42 percent of the seats in Congress forced Roldos to form coalitions to pass key legislation.

Although Roldos appeared to have a strong mandate from the people following his election with nearly 70 percent of the presidential vote, the coalition backing him crumbled almost immediately upon his taking office. Even prior to inauguration, rival groups clashed in the streets. After the inauguration of Roldos, bitter tensions over party leadership and patronage erupted, with Bucaram using his position as president of Congress to block Roldos. This internal party fighting turned into a paralyzing executive-legislative conflict, which saw the disintegration of the majority CFP-led coalition. The process deteriorated to such an extent that Roldos began forming his own party, separate from the CFP, called People, Change and Democracy (PCD). Bucaram, who had become increasingly conservative, "had no apparent agenda other than blocking the reformist agenda of the president,

TABLE 2.4

Ecuadorian elections for the unicameral legislature, April 1979

Political parties	SEATS	
	Number	Percentage
Concentration of Popular Forces	30	42
Democratic Left	14	20
Conservative party	10	14
Radical Liberal party	4	6
Social Christian party	3	4
Democratic Institutional Coalition	3	4
Others	7	10
Total	71	100

NOTE: Three representatives were expelled in August and replaced with representatives from the Concentration of Popular Forces.

who was thus forced to spend most of his first year in office scratching together his own political base, independent of the CFP, in order to achieve a legislative majority" (Hudson 1991, 46). He managed to do so by shuffling and reshuffling a menagerie of small parties in Congress, and by August 10, 1980, he had gone some way towards consolidating his position by successfully placing his candidate for president of Congress, Raul Baca Carbo from the ID (Democratic Left) Party, into office. The new leader of Congress agreed to cooperate with the government.

In sum, the emerging democratic institutional structures constrained the chief executive.[67] The president faced opposition within his own party and the legislature. However, from a norms perspective, the very young democratic state had little time to socialize either rulers or followers. Ecuadorians were socialized in either a weakly autocratic civilian system or under military rule; proponents of norms-based explanations claim that it takes at least a generation before democratic norms can be deeply entrenched in any society. Opinion polls taken in 1989, a decade after the transition to democratic rule, highlight the difficulties associated with transitioning to and consolidating a democracy. Most Ecuadorians were either not affiliated with a political party or not interested in political parties. A vast majority believed that political parties did not care about their problems. More ominously, between a third and a half of the population preferred a dictatorship to a democracy.[68]

Democracy is also a recent creation in Peru. The long-running conflict between the conservative oligarchy, the military, and the leftist APRA (*Alianza Popular Revolucionaria Americana*) defined political competition until the emergence of middle-class parties (such as Popular Action and the Christian Democratic Party) in the 1950s and 1960s, following the industrialization of

TABLE 2.5
Peruvian legislative elections, May 1980

Political parties	SEATS	
	Number	Percentage
Senate		
Popular Action	26	43
American Popular Revolutionary Alliance	18	30
Popular Christian party	6	10
Others	10	17
Total	60	100
Chamber of Deputies		
Popular Action	98	54
American Popular Revolutionary Alliance	58	32
Popular Christian party	10	6
National Front of Workers and Peasants	4	2
Others	10	6
Total	180	100

SOURCE: *Political Handbook of the World* (1981, 390).

the economy. Democratic competition peaked in the 1960s under the rule of reformer Fernando Belaunde (Popular Action). However, economic instability led to a military intervention in 1968 under General Velasco. The reform-oriented military replaced the foreign-dominated, export-oriented, laissez-faire economy with an import-substitution industrialization program that encouraged state ownership and state intervention. The return to civilian rule began in 1978 with the election of a constituent assembly whose mission was to draft a new constitution. In 1980 Popular Action Party candidate and former president Fernando Belaunde was elected president with 45 percent of the vote. As Table 2.5 indicates, the president's party controlled 43 percent of the seats in the Senate and 54 percent of the seats in the Chamber of Deputies. Economic crisis, triggered by oil crises and rapid borrowing during military rule; commodity price collapse; and high unemployment under the new administration dominated Peruvian politics during the 1980s. The economic distress led to the emergence of military guerrillas belonging to the Shining Path and the MRTA (*Movimiento Revolucionario Tupac Amaru*).

As with Ecuador, Peru was institutionally a democracy with an elected chief executive who was constrained by the institutionalized opposition. However, once again the political leaders and masses supporting and opposing the ruling party had been socialized in a decidedly autocratic environment. Although both sides recognized the other as democratic, this bond did not prevent the emergence of conflict in 1981.

Why didn't norms and structures prevent the emergence of violence? The dyadic version of the democratic peace hypothesizes that political norms and/or institutional structures should reduce the probability that a democratic state initiates violence against another democracy. The failure of the constraining power of norms and structures in the Peru–Ecuador dispute can be traced to four factors.

First, there was no domestic opposition to the use of military force. Ecuadorian governments, whether democratic or autocratic, have rejected the status quo that was imposed on them after a military defeat in 1941. Successive governments have socialized the public through school texts and political speeches to demand territorial changes. No political party or significant political actor advocated giving up the claims; no political platform explicitly denounced the use of force to change the status quo. Without domestic opposition to the use of force, institutional constraints are irrelevant. Opposition groups in Ecuador did not oppose the use of force; therefore, Roldos did not have a great deal to fear from a minor military probe designed to jump-start negotiations. The highly charged nationalist issue meant that opposition leaders would gain little from seizing the issue to criticize the Roldos administration.

The case study also demonstrates that existence of opposition varies with the issue at hand. Roldos was highly constrained with respect to domestic economic issues; the clash between the executive and legislative branches virtually paralyzed the government. However, the conflict did not exist in the foreign policy issue area. Typical measures of institutionalized opposition, whether they are based on structural features such as those found in the Polity data sets or more variable measures such as the number of seats held by the ruling party in the legislature, neglect the fact that opposition varies across issue areas.

Second, the outbreak of violence appears to be tied to the limited nature of the military probe. Ecuador, which on aggregate measures of military power is distinctly weaker than Peru, did not initiate a large-scale war against its neighbor.[69] Rather, it placed three small military outposts in territory it claimed it already owned. The objective was to force negotiations back to the forefront and to shift the burden of "initiating hostilities" back onto the Peruvians. The institutional explanation of the democratic peace emphasizes that domestic leaders avoid the use of military force because a defeat can be politically costly. However, the Ecuadorian deployment in the extremely remote area was unlikely to lead to a large-scale conflict. This raises an interesting question that will be explored in greater detail in Chapter 5: Are democracies less likely to use only large-scale violence?

Third, the Ecuadorian case emphasizes the importance of consolidation of democratic institutions and norms. The transition to democracy had taken place only in 1979 with the election of a new legislature—fewer than three years before the outbreak of violence. Ecuadorian chief executives faced weak, factionalized parties and an unenthusiastic public. The personal and charismatic nature of leadership in the country severely undermined the development of groups that could constrain the chief executive (Isaacs 1993). Opinion polls indicated that very little consolidation had taken place even after more than a decade of democratic rule.

Are new democracies more conflictual than old democracies? This question will be addressed more extensively in Chapter 6. If new democracies were found to be more violence prone, it would provide some support for the normative argument because it typically takes years for norms to develop. In contrast, the structural argument implies that constraint is likely to emerge with the establishment of the institutional structure.

Although the preceding factors undermined the pacifying effect of jointly democratic institutions, it is important to remember that the conflict did not escalate to full war. As previously mentioned, Ecuador chose to implement a minor probe rather than a full-scale invasion. Moreover, both leaders sought mediation to quickly resolve the conflict. Dixon (1993) has shown that democracies are more likely to turn to mediation to manage a dispute. In this particular case, the problem was that Peru wanted mediation within the context of the Rio Protocol whereas Ecuador wanted it outside of the protocol, which it considered null and void. Finally, Ecuador and Peru were able to negotiate a settlement to the crisis before it escalated to war. Huth found that democracies are less likely to escalate conflict and more likely to settle a conflict than nondemocracies (1996, 107, 135). Whereas in this case the parties did not settle the entire territorial dispute, they were able to agree on a cease-fire and a framework for avoiding future conflict. Therefore, in some respects the behavior of the two states did conform with the expectations of the democratic peace model.

Was the Ecuador-Peru conflict an example of diversionary war?   Scholars have long debated the extent to which political leaders engage in foreign policy adventures in order to divert attention from domestic troubles (Wright [1942] 1965; Mayer 1971; Levy 1989; Gelpi 1997; Dassel 1998). Within the context of democratic regimes, this debate has focused on the "electoral cycle of war," which predicts that democratic leaders will use force prior to elections in order to provoke a "rally around the flag" effect (Gaubatz 1999).

Was this a case of diversionary war? Roldos faced significant opposition both within Congress and among the population over plans to implement controversial economic measures to deal with the failing Ecuadorian economy. Business sectors were strongly opposed to these measures, and student rioting occurred in January 1981, just days before the outbreak of hostilities. The outbreak of hostilities consolidated support behind the government, at least in the short run, via the "rally around the flag" effect (Mueller 1973, 1994). On February 10, Vice President Osvaldo Hurtado highlighted the need for financial retrenchment in other areas of government spending in order to ensure the territorial integrity of Ecuador. Within one week of that announcement the Roldos government announced and passed an austerity program.

However, three factors undermine the diversionary war hypothesis. First, the new outposts were secretly constructed and operated for months without being discovered. In diversionary war, timing is typically crucial. The goal is to create a public incident to divert attention when the government's popularity is at its nadir. The construction of secret outposts is more akin to laying a mine; no one knows when (or if) it will be stumbled upon. Second, the Ecuadorian military was poorly prepared for the conflict. Diversionary conflict tends to be a well-planned strike or limited operation that results in the quick victory and pronounced rally effect.[70] Third, Roldos initially appeared to play down the early incidents. He refrained from making the customary speech on January 29, the anniversary of the signing of the Rio Protocol. Even the announcing of a state of emergency, the closing of schools, and the imposed censorship of the press was relatively subdued. Roldos became more vitriolic only after it was clear that Peru had scored a military victory. In sum, although there is little evidence that Roldos initiated the conflict as a diversionary tactic, he did benefit from the surge in nationalist feelings as a result of the hostilities (Krieg 1986, 296–98).

Did civilian authorities in the Ecuadorian government control the military? One of the key questions in the Ecuador-Peru dispute is the role of the Ecuadorian military. The military had demanded and received a number of concessions in exchange for relinquishing power, which insulated the military from civilian oversight and allowed it to function with great autonomy. This raises the interesting point: is this case more about the nature of civil-military relations than the impact of regime type? Did weak civilian control of the military undermine the constraining impact of democratic institutions?

Although the Ecuadorian military possessed tremendous power, such as direct involvement in the choice of the minister for defense, it appears that the construction of new outposts was a political decision made by civilian authorities. Krieg argues that the establishment of the outpost was carried out at least with the consent, if not at the initiative, of the civilian authorities and quotes Foreign Minister Barrera as saying that it was not a case of the military acting behind the back of the constitutionally elected government (Krieg 1986, 268–69). Moreover, the military does not appear to have attempted to escalate the scope of the conflict once the "probe" was proposed by civilian authorities. Ecuadorian forces in the region were limited in number and offensive capability; the lack of preparation was a prime reason the Peruvian military was able to deliver such a stinging rebuff. The limited nature of the probe seems to imply that it was more of a political than a military maneuver. It was designed to force the Peruvians to negotiate in earnest rather than to seize a large portion of the disputed territory. When the probe resulted in an unexpectedly quick defeat, the Roldos government scrambled to find a solution "designed to 'save face' for Ecuador and avoid a public reaction which might result in the overthrow of the Roldos government" (Krieg 1986, 271). Had Roldos attempted to escalate the conflict and lost, he would have faced tremendous pressure from the public (via democratic channels) and perhaps from the military (via a coup).

How did the regime change in Peru influence the 1995 military clash?   Military skirmishes erupted again in 1995. The situation was similar to the Paquisha incident fourteen years earlier in that Ecuador remained committed to overturning the status quo. Once again, Ecuador initiated the crisis by placing military outposts in the disputed territory. However, the more recent clashes differed from the 1981 situation because Peru was no longer a democracy. President Alberto Fujimori suspended the constitution and dissolved the elected legislature in 1992. Moreover, the 1995 clashes were much more serious in terms of the number of troops engaged and the casualties inflicted. Marcella (1995) claims that 3,000 Ecuadorians and 2,000 Peruvians were deployed to the region. The fighting resulted in the death of 27 Ecuadorian soldiers, 46 Peruvian soldiers, and more than 300 Peruvian noncombatants.

Did the interaction of regime types (democratic-democratic in 1981 but democratic-autocratic in 1995) contribute to the escalation of the conflict? The answer seems to be no. The key difference appears to be the history of the dispute itself. Huth (1996, 107) has shown that prior militarized conflict increases the probability of escalation in subsequent crises. Ecuador had been humiliated in 1981 and had used the intervening fourteen years to develop the military capability required to ensure that this never happened again. When Peru attempted to dislodge the encroaching Ecuadorians, it found to its dismay that it could not do so without a much more extensive mobilization and costly use of force. In the end, both sides compromised. Ecuador, in a radical shift from the policy position established in 1960, accepted the framework of the Rio Protocol for negotiation.[71] Simultaneously, Peru retreated from its position that the Rio Protocol had definitively solved the conflict. Negotiation within the Rio Protocol framework continued until a final settlement was reached in October 1998 with the assistance of the four guarantors (Marcella and Downes 1999).

Conclusions from the Ecuador-Peru Case Study

Does the Ecuador-Peru conflict of 1981 refute the dyadic hypothesis and quantitative findings from earlier in the chapter? The answer is no. The dyadic hypothesis is probabilistic rather than deterministic. It predicts that when both states are democratic, the dispute or crisis is less likely to escalate. It does not imply that democratic states will never engage in armed conflict. Whereas the quantitative analysis identifies general trends, it tells us little about any particular case. The case study allows us to identify several factors that help explain why this case deviates from the general trends. The absence of domestic opposition to the use of force, the limited nature of the initiation, and the newness of the democratic regimes all contributed to the weakening of constraint on key foreign policy decision makers.

Conclusions

This chapter began by laying out the assumptions built into the normative and structural explanations of the democratic peace. Either approach can be used to create both a monadic and dyadic explanation for the relationship between regime type and conflict. The quantitative analysis of militarized crises supports only the dyadic explanation: democracies are less likely to use force only when facing other democracies. However, the Suez Crisis indicates that whereas constraining democratic institutions may not prevent conflict in mixed dyads, it can influence decision making by democratic leaders within crises. Democratic institutions had a profound impact on the course and conclusion of the Suez Crisis. In contrast, the Ecuador-Peru conflict highlights the fact that joint democracy is not a panacea. A history of military conflict coupled with an intense nationalist outpouring can undermine the emergence of opposition to the use of force even when the potential for constraint theoretically exists.

The quantitative analysis and case studies also highlight four issues that demand further examination. First, *does the stage of the conflict matter?* The analysis in this chapter has focused on militarized crises (that is, situations in which one or both parties are actively considering using military force). Fortunately, militarized crises are rare events; most international disputes simmer at a much lower level of conflict. Before we can dismiss the monadic explanation entirely, we must explore the more general subject of disputes.

If democracies are less likely to trigger militarized conflicts, then there could still be a monadic impact of norms or institutions. This issue is explored in the following chapter.

Second, *would more precise and discriminating measures of constraint lead to different conclusions for the monadic hypothesis?* The Suez Crisis case studies clearly demonstrate that constraint can exist in the executive, the legislature, the political party, or the public at large. Aggregate measures, whether they are dummy democracy variables or measures based on the Polity indices, cannot disaggregate constraint into more precise components. In Chapter 4 I develop measures of constraint for each of these channels to determine if disaggregation leads to more nuanced findings.

Third, *can we determine the relative explanatory power of norms versus structures?* Conventional wisdom points to the power of norms (for example, Maoz and Russett 1993). However, the cases examined here provide little evidence of normative constraints among the key decision makers in each country. In contrast to behavior predicted by the normative model, British leaders supported assassination, resisted negotiation, violated international law, issued ultimatums, and initiated violence.[72] Although there is some evidence of normative constraints (for instance, the Labour Party's and the British public's demands for the exhaustion of all other means of conflict resolution prior to the use of force), most of the evidence points toward a structural explanation. This evidence includes restricting information, reducing participants, conducting secret operations, lying to the legislature, and attempting to minimize casualties. The issue of norms versus structures is addressed more systematically in Chapter 5.

Finally, *do recent regime transitions alter the probability that a state uses military force?* Both Ecuador and Peru were young democracies at the time of their military conflict in January 1981. Are young democracies more likely to use military force because of weakly consolidated institutional constraints or because of weakly reinforced peaceful norms of conflict resolution? These issues are explored in Chapter 6, which focuses on democratization and military conflict.

APPENDIX 2.1

Dropping the Aggressive Leader Assumption

Many researchers add a fifth assumption to the structural explanation: the public is relatively *less* inclined to use force to solve political disputes than are foreign policy decision makers (see Morgan and Campbell 1991, 187; Owen 1993; Layne 1994).[73]

Chief executive preferences

	Antiwar	Prowar
Antiwar	Choose peace	If constrained: choose peace If unconstrained: choose war
Prowar	If constrained: choose war If unconstrained: choose peace	Choose war

Opposition preferences

FIGURE 2.6. The potential indeterminacy of structure

Although the public may strongly support the use of force, this level of support is always less than that of the foreign policy elite. According to this assumption, which I will refer to as the "aggressive leader" assumption, increasing the inclusiveness of the political system will always result in a decline in the use of force by a state. I contend that structural explanations need not make such a strong assumption.

The aggressive leader assumption implies that the public is always pulling bellicose leaders back from the edge of crises. However, historically we know that during many crises the public has been more willing to use force than the chief executive (for example, the U.S. public during the Spanish-American War and the French and British publics during the Crimean War). As Figure 2.6 demonstrates, if the public is not on average less willing to use force, then the structural argument becomes indeterminate.

Can we simply assume that the public is more peaceful than elites? Probably not. However, from a theoretical perspective, this rather significant assumption may not be necessary. The solution involves shifting the focus away from simply measuring the relative militancy of various groups. In his analysis of U.S. elite versus mass public opinion using Chicago Council on Foreign Relations data, Wittkopf has isolated two separate dimensions that characterize foreign policy beliefs: (1) an internationalist versus isolationist dimension and (2) a militarist versus nonmilitarist dimension (Wittkopf 1986, 1987, 1994). An internationalist supports an active role of the United States in world affairs. A militarist supports the use of military means (among others) to solve disputes. An isolationist rejects involvement abroad, and a nonmilitarist rejects the use of military force. The two-factor model implies that decision makers and citizens fall into one of four categories: internationalist-militarist, internationalist-nonmilitarist, isolationist-militarist, and isolationist-nonmilitarist. For example, an internationalist-nonmilitarist would support U.S. involvement abroad if it focused on the application of economic instruments and participation in international institutions.

In general, the probability of supporting a military intervention is a function of an individual's internationalist and militarist beliefs. Suppose we could measure the internationalist-isolationist dimension with a variable ranging from "very isolation-

TABLE 2.6
Combining militarism and internationalism

	(A) Militarist	(B) Internationalist	HYPOTHETICAL PROBABILITY OF SUPPORTING INTERVENTION	
			Multiply (A • B)	Minimum of two elements
Decision makers	0.50	0.75	0.375	0.50
General public	0.50	0.25	0.125	0.25

ist" to "very internationalist." We would expect that the probability of supporting a foreign involvement would increase as one moved up the scale. For simplicity, we can assume that this increases in a linear manner (although it does not matter for the overall argument). We could develop a similar scale for support of military means. Wittkopf develops such scales using questions about the willingness to use force from the Chicago Council on Foreign Relations surveys.

The implication of this argument is shown in Table 2.6. Even though there is no difference in the propensity to use force between the elite and the masses, the elites will in general be more willing to support military interventions simply because they are more internationalist. Although there are countless ways to combine the probabilities, the most intuitive methods produce patterns similar to those shown in Table 2.6. For demonstrative purposes, Table 2.6 combines the probabilities in two alternative ways: a multiplicative function and a "minimum of the two elements" function.

The logic of this argument implies that structural theories need to assume only that relative to the public, decision makers are not less willing to use force and they are more internationalist in general.[74] If these assumptions are true, then the number of cases falling in the upper-right-hand quadrant in Figure 2.6 should be larger than the number falling in the lower-left-hand quadrant. Obviously, assuming that national decision makers are more concerned about international affairs than the average citizen requires much less of a leap of faith than assuming that leaders are more willing to use force.

Ideally, there would be some empirical information that would free us from having to assume anything at all. The most extensive study of elite versus mass opinion in the area of foreign affairs comes from a series of surveys by the Chicago Council on Foreign Relations. This organization has conducted parallel surveys of elite and public opinion every four years since 1974. These surveys have repeatedly demonstrated that foreign policy decision makers are far more internationalist than the general public. Moreover, the foreign policy decision makers show a significantly greater willingness to use force across a broad range of situations.[75] Therefore, in the U.S. case the data clearly support both the stronger "elites are more willing to use force" assumption and the weaker "elites are more internationalist" assumption. If these data were available across more countries and for a longer period of time, they would be ideal for substantiating these important structural assumptions. Unfortunately, the data are simply not available for the countries and time periods needed for my analysis. Therefore, the structural model presented here incorporates the rather innocuous implicit assumption that decision makers are simply more internationalist than the general public.

APPENDIX 2.2

Crisis Data Set: 337 Conflict Dyads in 301 International Crises (Challenger Versus Defender)

Year			
1918	United Kingdom v. Soviet Union	Nicaragua v. Costa Rica	Japan v. Soviet Union
	Russian Civil War I	*Costa Rica coup*	*Russian Civil War II*
1919	Poland v. Czechoslovakia	Czechoslovakia v. Hungary	Soviet Union v. Finland
	Teschen	*Hungarian War*	*Russo-Finnish War*
	Afghanistan v. United Kingdom	Soviet Union v. Romania	
	Third Afghan War	*Bessarabia*	
1920	Poland v. Lithuania	Poland v. Soviet Union	Soviet Union v. Iran
	Vilna I	*Russo-Polish War*	*Persian border*
	Greece v. Turkey		
	Greece-Turkey War I		
1921	Panama v. Costa Rica	France v. Germany	Czechoslovakia v. Hungary
	Costa Rica–Panama border	*German reparations*	*Karl's Return to Hungary I*
	Yugoslavia v. Albania	Hungary v. Austria	Czechoslovakia v. Hungary
	Albanian border	*Burgenland dispute*	*Karl's return to Hungary II*
	Greece v. Turkey		
	Greece-Turkey War II		
1923	France v. Germany	Italy v. Greece	
	Ruhr I	*Corfu incident*	
1924	Turkey v. United Kingdom		
	Mosul land dispute		
1925	Greece v. Bulgaria		
	Greece-Bulgaria front		
1926	Mexico v. Nicaragua	Yugoslavia v. Albania	
	Nicaragua Civil War I	*Albania*	
1927	Japan v. China		
	Shantung I		
1928	Japan v. China	Paraguay v. Bolivia	
	Shantung II	*Chaco I*	
1929	China v. Soviet Union		
	Chinese E. railway		
1931	Japan v. China		
	Mukden incident		
1932	Bolivia v. Paraguay	Ecuador v. Colombia	
	Chaco II	*Leticia*	

(continued)

APPENDIX 2.2 *(continued)*

Year			
1933	Yemen v. Saudi Arabia *Saudi-Yemen War*		
1934	Germany v. Austria *Austria putsch*		
1935	Germany v. Lithuania *Kaunas trials*	Ethiopia v. Italy *Ethiopian War*	Ecuador v. Peru *Maranon I*
1936	Germany v. France *Remilitarization of Rhineland* Turkey v. France *Alexandretta II*	Germany v. Spain; Italy v. Spain *Spanish Civil War* Turkey v. France *Alexandretta III*	Turkey v. France *Alexandretta I*
1937	Soviet Union v. Japan *Amur River incident* Dominican Republic v. Haiti *Haiti–Dominican Republic*	China v. Japan *Marco Polo Bridge*	Honduras v. Nicaragua *Postage stamp crisis*
1938	Soviet Union v. Japan *Changkufeng*	Germany v. Czechoslovakia *Munich*	Italy v. France *Italy threatens France*
1939	Germany v. Czechoslovakia *Czech annexation* Japan v. Mongolia	Germany v. Lithuania *Memel* Japan v. United Kingdom	Italy v. Albania *Invasion of Albania* Germany v. Poland; Soviet Union v. Poland; Germany v. France; Germany v. United Kingdom
	Nomonhan Soviet Union v. Lithuania; Soviet Union v. Latvia; Soviet Union v. Estonia *Soviet occupation of Baltics*	*Tientsin* Soviet Union v. Finland *Finnish War*	*Entry into World War II* Turkey v. France *Alexandretta IV*
1940	Germany v. Denmark; Germany v. Norway	Germany v. Belgium; Germany v. Netherlands; Germany v. Germany v. Luxembourg	Japan v. United Kingdom
	Invasion of Scandinavia Soviet Union v. Romania; Hungary v. Romania; Bulgaria v. Romania *Rumanian Territory*	*Fall of Western Europe* Italy v. Greece; Germany v. Yugoslavia *Balkan invasions*	*Closure of Burma Road*
1941	United Kingdom v. Iraq *Middle-East campaign* United Kingdom v. Iran; Soviet Union v. Iran	Germany v. Soviet Union *Barbarossa* Japan v. United States; Japan v. Netherlands; Japan v. United Kingdom; Japan v. Thailand	Peru v. Ecuador *Maranon II*
	Occupation of Iran	*Pearl Harbor*	
1944	Germany v. Hungary *Occupation of Hungary* France v. Syria *Syria-French forces* Soviet Union v. Iran *Azerbaijan*	Soviet Union v. Iran *Iran* Soviet Union v. Turkey *Kars Ardahan*	Yugoslavia v. United Kingdom *Trieste I* Soviet Union v. Japan *End of World War II*

APPENDIX 2.2 (*continued*)

Year			
1946	Soviet Union v. Turkey	Yugoslavia v. Greece	
	Turkish Straits	*Greek Civil War II*	
1947	Cuba v. Dominican Republic	India v. Pakistan	Pakistan v. India
	Dominican Republic–Cuba	*Junagadh*	*Kashmir I*
1948	Jordan v. Israel; Syria v. Israel; Egypt v. Israel; Iraq v. Israel; Lebanon v. Israel	Soviet Union v. United States	Nicaragua v. Costa Rica
	Israel independence	*Berlin Blockade*	*Costa Rica–Nicaragua I*
1949	Afghanistan v. Pakistan	Guatemala v. Dominican Republic	Soviet Union v. Yugoslavia
	Pushtunistan I	*Luperon*	*Soviet Bloc–Yugoslavia*
1950	North Korea v. South Korea		
	Korean War I		
1951	Syria v. Israel	Pakistan v. India	Egypt v. United Kingdom
	Tel Mutilah	*Punjab War*	*Suez Canal*
1952	Soviet Union v. Sweden		
	Catalina Affair		
1953	Taiwan v. Burma	Yugoslavia v. Italy	Jordan v. Israel
	Burma	*Trieste II*	*Quibya*
	United States v. Guatemala		
	Guatemala		
1954	China v. Taiwan		
	Taiwan Straits I		
1955	Nicaragua v. Costa Rica	Egypt v. Israel	Afghanistan v. Pakistan
	Costa Rica–Nicaragua II	*Gaza raid*	*Pushtunistan II*
1956	United Kingdom v. Egypt; France v. Egypt; Israel v. Egypt	Soviet Union v. Hungary	Soviet Union v. Poland
	Suez nationalization	*Hungarian uprising*	*Poland liberalization*
1957	Nicaragua v. Honduras	Tunisia v. France	Turkey v. Syria
	Nicaragua-Honduras	*Tunisia-France I*	*Syria-Turkey border*
	Morocco v. Spain	Soviet Union v. United States	
	Ifni	*Berlin deadline*	
1958	Tunisia v. France	Egypt v. Sudan	China v. Taiwan
	Tunisia-France II	*Sudan-Egypt border*	*Taiwan Straits II*
	Thailand v. Cambodia	Guatemala v. Mexico	
	Cambodia-Thailand	*Mexico fishing rights*	
1959	Cuba v. Haiti; Cuba v. Dominican Republic; Cuba v. Nicaragua; Cuba v. Panama	China v. India	Iran v. Iraq
	Cuba–Central America I	*India-China border I*	*Shatt Al Arab I*
1960	United Arab Republic v. Israel	Togo v. Ghana	Dominican Republic v. Venezuela
	Rottem	*Ghana-Togo border*	*Assassination attempt-Venezuela*
	Zaire v. Belgium	Cuba v. Guatemala; Cuba v. Nicaragua	Somalia v. Ethiopia
	Congo I-Katanga	*Cuba–Central America II*	*Ethiopia-Somalia*

(*continued*)

86   *Chapter 2*

APPENDIX 2.2 *(continued)*

Year			
1961	North Vietnam v. Laos *Pathet Lao offensive I* Soviet Union v. United States *Berlin Wall* Indonesia v. Netherlands *West Irian II* N. Vietnam v. S. Vietnam *Vietcong attack*	United States v. Cuba *Bay of Pigs* Iraq v. Kuwait *Kuwait independence* Egypt v. Syria *Breakup of UAR*	Afghanistan v. Pakistan *Pushtunistan III* Tunisia v. France *Bizerta* India v. Portugal *Goa II*

1962	Mali v. Mauritania
	Mauritania-Mali
	India v. China
	
	India-China border II
		Taiwan v. China
		Taiwan Straits III
		Saudi Arabia v.
		   North Yemen
		Yemen War— Cluster I
			North Vietnam v. Laos
			Pathet Lao offensive II
			United States v.
			   Soviet Union
			Cuban Missile Crisis

1963	Indonesia v. Malaysia *Malaysia federation* Somalia v. Kenya *Kenya-Somalia* Dahomey v. Niger *Niger-Dahomey*	Haiti v. Dominican Republic *Haiti–Dominican Republic* Greece v. Turkey *Cyprus I* Burundi v. Rwanda *Rwanda-Burundi*	Morocco v. Algeria *Morocco-Algeria border* Jordan v. Israel *Jordan waters*

1964	Somalia v. Ethiopia
	
	Ogaden I
		North Vietnam v.
		   United States
		Gulf of Tonkin
			Saudi Arabia v.
			   North Yemen
			Yemen War— Cluster III

1965	N. Vietnam v. S. Vietnam *Pleiku* Rhodesia v. Zambia *Rhodesia's UDI*	Pakistan v. India *Rann of Kutch*	Pakistan v. India *Kashmir II*
1966	North Yemen v. Saudi Arabia *Yemen War— Cluster IV*	Jordan v. Israel *El Samu*	
1967	Cuba v. Bolivia *Che Guevara/Bolivia*	Egypt v. Israel; Syria v. Israel; Jordan v. Israel *Six Days' War*	Greece v. Turkey *Cyprus II*
1968	North Korea v. United States *Pueblo* Venezuela v. Guyana *Essequibo Territory*	Jordan v. Israel *Karameh* Egypt v. Israel *Pre-War of Attrition*	Soviet Union v. Czechoslovakia *Prague spring* Israel v. Lebanon *Beirut Airport*
1969	China v. Soviet Union *Ussuri River* Iraq v. Iran *Shatt Al Arab II*	Egypt v. Israel *War of Attrition I* El Salvador v. Honduras *Football War*	North Korea v. United States *EC-121 spy plane* Syria v. Lebanon *Cairo Agreement-PLO*
1970	North Vietnam v. Cambodia *Invasion of Cambodia*	Syria v. Jordan *Black September*	Guinea v. Portugal *Portuguese invasion of* *Guinea*
1971	India v. Pakistan *Bangladesh* Tanzania v. Uganda *Uganda/Tanzania I*	Libya v. Chad *Chad-Libya*	Zambia v. South Africa *Caprivi Strip*
1972	Tanzania v. Uganda *Uganda/Tanzania II*	North Yemen v. South Yemen *North-South Yemen I*	

APPENDIX 2.2 (*continued*)

Year			
1973	Zambia v. Rhodesia	Iraq v. Kuwait	Egypt v. Israel
	Zambia	*Iraq invasion of Kuwait*	*Israel mobilization*
	Iceland v. United Kingdom	Egypt v. Israel; Syria v. Israel	South Yemen v. Oman
	Cod War	*Yom Kippur War*	*South Yemen–Oman*
1974	Greece v. Cyprus; Turkey v. Cyprus		
	Cyprus III		
1975	Cambodia v. United States	Zaire v. Angola	Morocco v. Spain
	Mayaguez	*War in Angola*	*Moroccan march*
	Guatemala v. United Kingdom	Algeria v. Morocco; Algeria v. Mauritania	Iceland v. United Kingdom
	Belize I	*Sahara*	*Cod War II*
	Indonesia v. Portugal		
	East Timor		
1976	Syria v. Lebanon	Uganda v. Kenya	Mozambique v. Rhodesia
	Lebanon Civil War I	*Uganda claims*	*Operation Thrasher*
	Iraq v. Syria	Israel v. Uganda	Libya v. Sudan
	Iraqi threat	*Entebbe raid*	*Sudan coup attempt*
	Turkey v. Greece	Syria v. Israel	Botswana v. Rhodesia
	Aegean Sea	*Syria mobilization*	*Operation Tangent*
1977	Angola v. Zaire	Guatemala v. United Kingdom	Egypt v. Libya
	Shaba I	*Belize II*	*Egypt-Libya border*
	Somalia v. Ethiopia	Zambia v. Rhodesia	Vietnam v. Cambodia
	Ogaden II	*Rhodesia raids*	*Vietnam invasion of Cambodia*
	Algeria v. France	Argentina v. Chile	
	French hostages	*Beagle Channel I*	
1978	Libya v. Chad	Syria v. Lebanon	Cambodia v. Thailand; China v. Vietnam
	Chad-Libya II	*Lebanon Civil War II*	*Sino-Vietnam War*
	Lebanon v. Israel	Angola v. South Africa	Angola v. Zaire
	Litani operation	*Cassinga incident*	*Shaba II*
	Costa Rica v. Nicaragua	Argentina v. Chile	Uganda v. Tanzania
	Nicaraguan Civil War	*Beagle Channel II*	*Fall of Amin*
1979	South v. North Yemen	Soviet Union v. Afghanistan	Iran v. United States
	North-South Yemen II	*Afghanistan invasion*	*U.S. hostages-Iran*
1980	Libya v. Tunisia	Soviet Union v. Poland	Libya v. Malta
	Raid on Gafsa	*Solidarity*	*Malta-Libya oil dispute*
	Iraq v. Iran	Libya v. Gambia	Syria v. Jordan
	Iran-Iraq War	*Libya intervention in Gambia*	*Jordan-Syria confrontation*
	Somalia v. Ethiopia		
	East Africa confrontation		
1981	Libya v. Chad	Ecuador v. Peru	Mozambique v. South Africa
	Chad-Libya merger	*Peru-Ecuador*	*Mozambique raid*
	Venezuela v. Guyana	Israel v. Syria	Cameroon v. Nigeria
	Essequibo II	*Al-Biqua missiles*	*Nigeria-Cameroon border*
	Israel v. Iraq	Libya v. United States	Iran v. Bahrain
	Iraq nuclear reactor	*Gulf of Syrte II*	*Coup attempt-Bahrain*
1982	Argentina v. United Kingdom	Israel v. Lebanon	Ethiopia v. Somalia
	Falklands-Malvinas	*Lebanon War*	*Ogaden III*
	Lesotho v. South Africa		
	Lesotho raid		

(*continued*)

APPENDIX 2.2 *(continued)*

Year			
1983	Libya v. Sudan *Libya Threat-Sudan* United States v. Grenada *Invasion of Grenada*	Chad v. Nigeria *Chad-Nigeria clashes* Botswana v. Zimbabwe *Botswana-Zimbabwe border*	Libya v. Chad *Chad-Libya VI* Ethiopia v. Sudan *Sudan-Ethiopia border*
1984	Thailand v. Vietnam *Thai border incident* Laos v. Thailand *Village border crisis I*	Libya v. Sudan *Omduran bombing* United States v. Nicaragua *Nicaragua Mig-21s*	China v. Vietnam *Sino-Vietnam clashes*
1985	Botswana v. South Africa *Botswana raid*	Libya v. Tunisia *Expulsion of Tunisians*	Burkina Faso v. Mali *Burkina Faso—Mali border*
1986	Libya v. United States *Gulf of Syrte II* Sudan v. Uganda *Rebel attack-Uganda* Honduras v. Nicaragua *Honduras-Nicaragua border*	Qatar v. Bahrain *Bahrain-Qatar dispute* Malawi v. Mozambique *Mozambique ultimatum*	Zimbabwe v. South Africa *South Africa cross border raid* Ghana v. Togo *Attempted coup-Togo*
1987	China v. Vietnam *China-Vietnam border* Turkey v. Greece *Aegean Sea II* Iran v. Saudi Arabia *Mecca pilgrimage*	India v. Pakistan *Punjab war scare II* Cameroon v. Nigeria *Nigeria-Cameroon border* Laos v. Thailand *Village border crisis II*	Ethiopia v. Somalia *Somalia-Ethiopia border* India v. Sri Lanka *India intervention in Sri Lanka* Kenya v. Uganda *Kenya-Uganda border*
1988	China v. Vietnam *Spratly Islands*	Libya v. U.S. *Libyan jets*	
1989	Mauritania v. Senegal *Mauritania-Senegal*	U.S. v. Panama *Invasion of Panama*	
1990	Pakistan v. India *Kashmire III: nuclear crisis*	Iraq v. Kuwait *Gulf War*	Uganda v. Rwanda *Rwanda-Uganda*
1991	Burkina Faso v. Sierra Leone *Liberian Civil War* Ecuador v. Peru *Ecuador/Peru border IV*	Togo v. Ghana *Ghana-Togo border II* Armenia v. Azerbaijan *Nagornyy-Karabakh*	France v. Zaire; Belgium v. Zaire *Foreign intervention in Zaire*
1992	Egypt v. Sudan (both) *Egypt/Sudan border*	Papua New Guinea v. Solomon *Papua New Guinea v. Solomon*	Myanmar v. Thailand *Sleeping Dog Hill*
1993	North Korea v. U.S. (both) *North Korea nuclear crisis*	Lebanon v. Israel *Operation Accountability*	Nigeria v. Cameroon *Nigeria/Cameroon*
1994	U.S. v. Haiti *Haiti Military Regime*		
1995	Ecuador v. Peru *Ecuador/Peru border V* Eritrea v. Yemen *Red Sea Islands*	China v. Philippines *Spratly Islands*	China v. Taiwan *Taiwan Strait IV*
1996	Turkey v. Greece (both) *Aegean Sea IV* Zaire v. Rwanda (both) *Zaire Civil War*	Lebanon v. Israel *Operation Grapes of Wrath*	North Korea v. South Korea *North Korean submarine*
1998	Turkey v. Cyprus *Cyprus-Turkey missile crisis*	Ethiopia v. Eritrea (both) *Ethiopia-Eritrea*	India v. Pakistan (both) *Nuclear tests*

APPENDIX 2.2 *(continued)*

Year			
1998	Rwanda v. Congo; Uganda v. Congo *Democratic Republic of Congo War*	Afghanistan v. U.S.; Sudan v. U.S. *U.S. Embassy bombings*	
1999	U.S. vs. Kosovo *Kosovo*	Pakistan v. India (both) *Kargil (Kashmir IV)*	
2001	Iran v. Azerbaijan (both) *Caspian Sea*	Afghanistan v. U.S. *U.S.-Afghanistan*	Pakistan v. India *Indian Parliament attack*

APPENDIX 2.3

Crises from the ICB Data Set That Have Been Deleted or Merged

Intrawar crises (27)

Smyrna 1919	Fall of Saipan 1944	Vietnam Spring Offensive
Cilician War 1920	Leyte and Luzan 1944	1969
Battle of Britain 1940	Final Soviet Offensive	War of Attrition II 1970
East African Campaign 1940	1945	Invasion of Laos II 1971
El Alamein 1942	Iwo Jima 1945	Vietnam ports mining 1972
Stalingrad 1942	Okinawa 1945	Christmas bombing 1972
Fall of Italy 1943	Sinai Incursion 1948	Final Vietnam offensive 1974
Soviets in Eastern Europe	Korean War II 1950	Khorramshahr 1982
1944	Korean War III 1953	Basra-Kharg Island 1984
D-Day 1944	Tet Offensive 1968	Iraq Recapture-Fao 1988

No threat A: no strong evidence that the challenger seriously considered using force (26)

Aaland Islands 1919	West Irian I 1957	Libyan Plane 1973
Rhenish Rebellions 1920	Jordan regime 1957	Soviet threat—Pakistan 1979
Austrian Separatists 1921	Aborted coup—	Nicaragua-Colombia 1979
Ruhr II 1924	Indonesia 1958	Libyan threat—Sadat 1980
Haiti Unrest 1929	Formation of UAR 1958	Coup attempt—Gambia
Bulgaria-Turkey I 1935	Mali Federation 1960	1981
Bulgaria-Turkey II 1935	Cuba-Venezuela 1963	Aegean Naval Crisis 1984
Panay Incident 1937	Guinea regime 1965	Al Biqua missiles 1985
Czech May Crisis 1938	Cienfuegos sub base	Egypt-Libya tensions 1985
Baghdad Pact 1955	1970	

No threat B: no government to government threat (14)

Assassination of King	Goa I 1955	East Africa rebellions 1964
Alexander 1934	Lebanon-Iraq Upheaval	Congo II 1964
Greek Civil War I 1944	1958	Dominican Republic 1965
Truman Doctrine 1947	Jordan internal challenge	Syria in Lebanon 1987
China Civil War 1948	1963	Cambodia peace 1989
East Berlin Uprising 1953	Panama Canal 1964	

(continued)

APPENDIX 2.3 (*continued*)

Capitulation crises (9)

Anschluss 1938
Polish ultimatum 1938
Communism in Rumania
1945
Communism in Poland 1946

Communism in Hungary
1947
Marshall Plan 1947
Communism in
Czechoslovaki 1948

Soviet note to Finland I
1948
Soviet note to Finland II
1961

Merged crises (46)

Transcaucasia 1917
with Russian Civil
War I 1918
Vilna II 1920
with Vilna I 1920
Greece-Turkey War III
1922
with Greece-Turkey
War II 1921
Chanak 1922
with Greece-Turkey II
1921
Shanghai 1932
with Mukden 1931
Jehol Campaign 1933
with Mukden 1931
Walwal 1934
with Ethiopian War
1935
Danzig 1939
with Entry WWII 1939
Palestine Partition 1947
with Israel independence
1948
Qalqilya 1956
with Quibya 1953
Suez-Sinai Campaign 1956
with Suez
nationalization 1955
Yemen War—Cluster II
1964
with Yemen War I 1962
Nouakchott I 1976
with Sahara 1975
Nagomia raid 1976
with Operation
Thrasher 1976

Chimolo Tembue raids
1977
with Operation
Thrasher 1976
Mapai seizure 1977
with Operation
Thrasher 1976
Nouakchott II 1977
with Sahara 1975
Chad-Libya III 1978
with Chad-Libya II
1978
Air Rhodesia incident 1978
with Rhodesia raids 1977
Angola invasion scare 1978
with Cassinga 1978
Tan Tan 1979
with Sahara 1976
Raids on Zipra 1979
with Rhodesia raids
1977
Raids on Swapo 1979
with Cassinga 1978
Chad-Libya IV 1979
with Chad-Libya II
1978
Goulimime Tarfaya Road
1979
with Sahara 1975
Rhodesia settlement 1979
with Operation Tangent
1976,
and Operation Thrasher
1976,
and Rhodesia raids 1977
Raid on Angola 1979
with Cassinga 1978

Operation Iman 1980
with Sahara 1975
Operation Smokeshell
1980
with Cassinga 1978
Operation Protea–Angola
1981
with Cassinga 1978
Polisario attack 1981
with Sahara 1975
Operation Askari 1983
with Cassinga 1978
South Africa raid on Lesotho
1985
with Lesotho raid 1982
Chad-Libya VII 1986
with Chad-Libya VI 1979
Chad-Libya VIII 1986
with Chad-Libya VI 1979
Western Sahara 1987
with Sahara 1975
S. Africa intervention Angola
1987
with Cassinga 1978
Sandanista border crossing
1988
with Honduras-Nicaragua
1986
with Contras IV 1989
Gulf War 1990
with Bubiyan 1991
with Iraq no fly zone 1992
with Iraq troop deployment
1994
with Desert Strike 1996
with UNSCOM I 1997
with UNSCOM II 1998

Colonial crises (5)

Indonesia independence I
1945
Indonesia independence II
1947

Indonesia independence II
1948
Invasion of Laos I 1953

Dien Bien Phu 1954

APPENDIX 2.3 *(continued)*

One or both parties are not recognized members of the international system (7)

Baltic independence 1918	East Timor 1999	Hyderabad 1948
Yugoslavia I: Croatia/	Nejd-Hijaz War 1924	Georgia-Abkhazia 1992
Slovenia 1991	Yugoslavia II: Bosnia 1992	

APPENDIX 2.4

Sensitivity Analysis

Independent variable	Initiation Model 1	Highest Model 2	Aggressive Model 3
Actor's net democracy	−0.012	−0.002	−0.003
(monadic)	0.010	0.008	0.009
Opponent's net democracy	0.013	0.022★★	0.015
	0.009	0.009	0.009
Actor's net democracy with	−0.051★★	−0.067★★★	−0.060★★★
democratic opponent (dyadic)	0.020	0.018	0.018
Balance of forces	−0.210	−0.082	−0.120
	0.301	0.279	0.285
Shared alliance ties	0.047	−0.259★	−0.205
	0.179	0.151	0.153
Satisfaction with status quo	−1.926★★★	−1.174★★★	−1.312★★★
	0.179	0.121	0.139
Opponent's use of force	—	0.723★★★	—
		0.079	
Democracy with weak opponent	0.246	0.450	0.541
	0.353	0.330	0.338
Democracy with weak	0.475	−0.607	−0.209
democracy	1.039	0.832	0.913
Great power	0.221★	0.174	−0.154
	0.129	0.126	0.120
Nuclear weapons	−0.165	−0.131	0.089
	0.192	0.178	0.184
Years at peace	0.006★	−0.001	0.002
	0.003	0.003	0.003
Contiguous	−0.021	−0.018	−0.059★
	0.028	0.027	0.026
Alliance similarity (Tau-B)	−0.124	0.151	−0.035
	0.182	0.159	0.166
First threshold	−0.415	−0.524	−0.628
	0.214	0.200	0.199
Second threshold	0.441	0.457	0.160
	0.214	0.200	0.199
Number of observations	618	618	618
Log likelihood function	−492.16	−585.19	569.14

NOTE: All significance tests are one-tailed. ★p < .05, ★★p < .01, ★★★p < .001. Estimated using STATA 6.0 and robust standard errors.

Notes

1. For an interesting debate on the realist research program, see the exchanges between Vasquez, Waltz, Christensen, Snyder, Elman, Elman, Schweller, and Walt in the December 1997 issue of the *American Political Science Review* (Vasquez 1997).

2. Waltz argues that his systemic neorealist theory does not make predictions about foreign policy (Waltz 1997, 916; 1996). However, many realists such as Walt (1997) and Elman (1996; Elman and Elman 1997) believe that neorealism does make predictions at the state level. My view falls closer to Walt and Elman because Waltz makes state-level predictions (e.g., states balance against more powerful states) in order to derive his systemic-level predictions (e.g., bipolarity is more peaceful than multipolarity).

3. The table is adapted from Doyle (1986). Doyle draws on Small and Singer (1982) for his list of wars and develops a unique dichotomous measure of democracy. The difference between sixty-eight wars and fifty wars is due to the fact that democracies are quite rare prior to World War II.

4. In terms of "never" engaging in war, the results are somewhat dependent on the operationalization of both "democracy" and "war" (Russett 1993; Ray 1995). However, if we assume that the level of democracy is a continuous rather than dichotomous variable, then the level of democracy–war hypothesis can be stated in probabilistic terms. The more democratic a country, the less likely it is to engage in armed conflict with another democracy. This study, along with most in the literature, focuses on probabilistic hypotheses. To my knowledge, only Rummel (1983) explicitly argues a deterministic position.

5. The first half of this chapter is a revision of Rousseau, Gelpi, Reiter, and Huth (1996). I have updated the data set from 1988 to 2000 and have added several new variables of interest, but the arguments and analyses are drawn from that article. I wish to thank my coauthors and the *American Political Science Review* for their permission to include this material. Of course, any errors are my sole responsibility.

6. It should be noted that Kant's explanation combines both normative and structural elements.

7. Empirical support for the relationship between failure in war and the loss of political power for wartime leaders is presented in Bueno de Mesquita and Siverson (1995), Bueno de Mesquita, Siverson, and Woller (1992), and Russett and Graham (1989).

8. If this assumption is not true (e.g., autocratic leaders actually face higher costs for failure), then subsequent statistical tests should demonstrate that autocracies are less likely to initiate conflict than democracies are. The empirical results in chapters 2 through 6 demonstrate that this is not the case.

9. Many researchers add a fifth assumption to the structural explanation: the public is relatively *less* inclined to support the use of force to solve political disputes than foreign policy decision makers are (e.g., Morgan and Campbell 1991, 187; Owen 1993; Layne 1994). Appendix 2.1 argues that this strong assumption is not necessary.

10. Bueno de Mesquita and Lalman propose that in anticipation of potential exploitation, democracies are prone to initiate preemptive attacks (1992, 158). However, an examination of the list of democratically initiated wars by Small and Singer

(1976) and Chan (1984) reveals that preemption rarely plays an important role. More broadly, Reiter (1995) has shown that preemption is an extremely rare cause of war. Schweller (1992) argues that democracies do not engage in preventative war either (but see Levy and Gochal's [2002] analysis of Israeli behavior in the Suez Crisis).

Similarly, Maoz and Russett assume that autocracies have less trouble extracting resources from society and that democratic leaders circumvent democratic processes when dealing with authoritarian states. However, D'Lugo and Rogowski (1993) have argued that many authoritarian states have been severely constrained from extracting resources by both societal groups and institutional structures. Similarly, the historical record does not seem to support the argument that the democratic process was short-circuited by manipulative elites in the Korean War (Paige 1968), the Vietnam War (Gelb and Betts 1979), or the Persian Gulf War (Mueller 1994). Although the completeness of the process may vary from crisis to crisis due to time constraints, the process does not appear to systematically change in response to the regime type of the opponent. In sum, the empirical evidence supporting the micro-foundations of the dyadic institutional argument is not as strong as the evidence supporting the macro-level dyadic peace argument.

11. Two forces may be at work here. First, democracies might be less likely to initiate coercive policies. Leng (1993) has shown that democracies favor reciprocity-based strategies (e.g., tit-for-tat) that frown upon unilateral defections. Second, democratic leaders may be more likely to interpret the same policy as less threatening when initiated by a democracy. In the survey experiments by Herrmann and colleagues (1999), U.S. subjects reading identical hypothetical scenarios save for the identity of the attacker were less likely to intervene when the attacker was democratic (Israel) than when it was autocratic (Iran). Although the use of real countries rather than abstract labels (e.g., democratic) makes interpreting the result difficult, it raises the possibility that regime type influences the filtering of information.

12. Fearon (1994, 587) implies that his model can explain the dyadic democratic peace. However, Schultz correctly points out that Fearon's argument is strictly monadic (1999, 243). Although Schultz clearly builds on Fearon, he also departs from this earlier work in important ways (2001, 18). Kinsella and Russett (2002, 1047) also point out that Schultz presents a monadic argument.

13. Other tests include the case studies by Auerswald (2000) and the statistical analysis by Eyerman and Hart (1996).

14. The selectorate "theory" consists of a set of closely related models that are tailored for specific issue areas (Bueno de Mesquita et al. 2003, 39).

15. Although Bueno de Mesquita and colleagues (2003, 219) deny that a large winning coalition or a large selectorate defines democracy, the combination of a large S and large W should be highly correlated with measures of democracy such as the Polity or Freedom House indices (2003, 219).

16. Dixon and Senese do not find any support for the preponderance exception to the dyadic democratic peace (2002, 561).

17. Several studies of foreign policy in the former Soviet Union have examined the link between internal patterns of political competition among elites and foreign policy behavior. See Roeder (1984), Goldgeier (1994), and Ritcher (1994).

18. Gowa (1999) also finds some evidence for an autocratic peace.

19. Lake (1992) argues that democracies will devote more resources to security, and Bueno de Mesquita and associates (2003, 226) argue that "democrats try hard[er]."

20. See Desch (2002) for a critique of Reiter and Stam. Also, see Reiter and Stam's reply (2003b).

21. See, for example, decision making within Britain during wartime crises (chapters 4 and 5).

22. British intervention in the Baltics is coded as part of the Russian Civil War I case.

23. For each crisis, I have paired the primary challenger(s) and defender(s); the original ICB data set simply listed the actors involved in the conflict. The challenger is seeking to overturn the status quo. Although the challenger typically initiates the use of force, this need not be the case. In the 1967 Six Days' War, I code Egypt as the challenger and Israel as the initiator of armed conflict. In some cases, such as the India–China territorial dispute, both states are coded as challengers because both reject the status quo.

24. Kegley and Skinner (1976) contrast a "summed dyad" hypothesis with a "directed dyad" or a "monadic" hypothesis. They question the utility of the summed dyad hypothesis. Bennett and Stam (2000) discuss directed versus nondirected dyads and argue that the directed dyad is more appropriate for testing theories that predict initiation of conflict.

25. Some studies use only inappropriate dependent variables such as severity of conflict or war involvement (Weede 1984). Other studies combine both appropriate (e.g., conflict initiation) and inappropriate (e.g., war involvement) dependent variables (Small and Singer 1976; Chan 1984). Small and Singer (1976, 66) find that of the nineteen wars involving bourgeois democracies, eleven were initiated by the democratic state. Similarly, Chan (1984, 637) finds that democracies are *more* likely to initiate war than nondemocracies. However, these two tests only focus on wars, thus obscuring the impact of structure.

26. Rummel (1985, 438), in a response to Chan, continues to claim that involvement rather than initiation is the best way to assess the conflict proneness of polities.

27. The inappropriate dependent variable problem is related to the unit of analysis problem discussed above. The use of a summed dyad (or conflict) data set encourages the use of a conflict involvement variable (i.e., does the conflict escalate to a war). However, the problems are independent in that even after selecting the proper unit of analysis, a researcher could choose an inappropriate dependent variable, making testing the monadic argument impossible.

28. A political norms explanation clearly implies that both direct and indirect uses of force should be less likely in more democratic regimes. Whereas the structural barriers to the use of force may be reduced somewhat in the indirect cases through the elimination of certain types of costs (e.g., combat fatalities), potential monetary and prestige costs should make constrained regimes more reluctant to use force even indirectly. In the extreme case of covert action, we would expect the structural constraints to be eliminated because opposition cannot emerge if it lacks knowledge of the event. Interestingly, the political norms explanation implies that even in the case of covert action, leaders socialized with more peaceful norms of conflict resolution should be less willing to use force to resolve disputes. For a dis-

cussion of covert action, see James and Mitchell (1995), Forsythe (1992), Russett (1993, 120), Johnson (1989), and Reiter and Stam (2002). Chapter 5 tests the covert action argument using a laboratory experiment. It should be noted that the current operationalization would not completely satisfy Cohen because I do not code for covert actions. For a critique of Cohen's other criticisms, see Russett and Ray (1995).

29. The use of four- or two-category versions of this dependent variable produces similar results. The four-category version contains the following scale: (4) massive (more than 10,000 troops), (3) major (1,001–10,000 troops), (2) minor (1–1,000 troops), and (1) no use of force. The two-category version combines the two highest levels.

30. Troops entering a state immediately following a conflict in accordance with armistices and treaties are not coded as aggressive force.

31. Bueno de Mesquita and Lalman (1992) have an existence proof that identifies the possibility of defensive preemption by democratic states in this situation. However, Reiter (1995) finds that preemptive strikes rarely happen.

32. If democratic leaders can be shown to fear exploitation, even if no empirical evidence exists to support this belief, the logic of the dyadic argument remains intact.

33. I have revised the Polity codings in two ways. First, I have used the "Polity2" variable in the data set to code cases in transition (for example, −66, −77, and −88) as recommended at the Polity Web site. Second, I have examined the subcomponent level data to ensure that codings corresponded to conventional historical accounts. The only cases in which I found the codings to be extremely questionable involved Japan during the interwar period. According to the Polity data set, the Japanese legislature had authority equal to or greater than the executive from 1885 to 1945. This places the Japanese legislature in the most constraining category, making it equivalent to the British house of commons or the U.S. congress. The historical record indicates that only slight to moderate limitations on executive authority existed after the assassination of Prime Minister Inukai Tsuyoshi and the demise of the party system in 1932 (Beasley 1990, 181; Berger 1988). There are eleven disputes involving Japan after 1932. I have recoded the 7-point legislative constraints on the executive component of the Polity indices from "Executive Parity or Subordination" (level 7) to "Slight to Moderate Limitations on Executive Authority" (level 3).

34. Sensitivity analysis using an interaction between two 0–20 terms did not change the findings.

35. See the COW2 Web site for a discussion of missing data in the National Capabilities data set. Shifting to the use of ACDA and ISS should not be problematic because they were used as sources for the COW codings.

36. In sensitivity analysis, the alliance variable is coded as 1 if the two states shared a defense pact, a neutrality pact, or an entente. This change had no impact on the findings.

37. Dixon and Senese test only the dyadic version of the argument (2002, 561). They employ a different operationalization for both the balance of forces and democracy variables. I highlight their work because their straightforward test stands in marked contrast to the extremely complex operationalization proposed by Bueno de Mesquita and colleagues (2003, chapter 6).

38. The only exception was when the cutoff was set so high that only a handful of the almost 700 observations were coded as a 1. As one would expect, in this situation the addition or subtraction of a single observation can swing a coefficient wildly from positive to negative.

39. An ordered probit model employing a three-category dependent variable requires the estimation of two thresholds that separate the categories (i.e., a threshold between no initiation of force and initiating once and a threshold between initiating once and initiating twice).

40. The marginal analysis indicates that this result is the product of nondemocratic states initiating against democracies.

41. Although the research design was not developed to test the relative power of the constraint and signaling structural explanations, the results clearly do not support the predictions of the signaling model. If a democratic structure increased information on preferences and resolve, autocratic states should be *less* likely to attack democracies.

42. Auxiliary regressions performed for the democratic peace equations revealed that none of the variables that failed to achieve statistical significance had auxiliary r-squares of more than 0.49. Thus, multicollinearity cannot explain the insignificant results in any of these analyses. There is no evidence to support the Farber and Gowa (1995a; Gowa 1999) claim that shared alliances ties between democracies are the real cause of the democratic peace. Moreover, in contrast to the predictions of Farber and Gowa, the coefficients are stable across both the interwar and postwar periods.

43. The Suez Crisis case studies in this chapter were developed using the following sources: Motti Golani, *Israel in Search of a War: The Sinai Campaign, 1955–56* (Brighton, UK: Sussex Academic Press, 1998); Leon D. Epstein, *British Politics in the Suez Crisis* (Urbana: University of Illinois Press, 1964); Chaim Herzog, *The Arab-Israeli Wars: War and Peace in the Middle East from the War of Independence to Lebanon* (London: Arms and Armour Press, 1982); William Roger Louis and Roger Owen (eds.), *Suez 1956: The Crisis and Its Consequences* (Oxford: Clarendon, 1989); Selwyn Ilan Trowen and Moshe Shemesh (eds.), *The Suez-Sinai Crisis 1956: Retrospective and Reappraisal* (New York: Columbia University Press, 1990); Thomas Risse-Kappen, *Cooperation Among Democracies: The European Influence on U.S. Foreign Policy* (Princeton, NJ: Princeton University Press, 1995); Louise Richardson, *When Allies Differ: Anglo-American Relations During the Suez and Falklands Crises* (New York: St. Martin's, 1996); Jonathan Kirshner, *Currency and Coercion: The Political Economy of International Monetary Power* (Princeton, NJ: Princeton University Press, 1995); David P. Auerswald, *Disarmed Democracies: Domestic Institutions and the Use of Force* (Ann Arbor: University of Michigan Press, 2000).

44. The Mussolini reference was apparently first used in March after the removal of Glubb (Lucas 1991, 95–96). In a letter to President Eisenhower dated August 5, 1956, Eden rejected the idea that Nasser was another Hitler because Egyptians were not a "warlike people" (Gorst and Johnman 1997, 68–69).

45. See Jervis (1978) for a discussion of the shortcomings of such a policy.

46. Given that Nasser was openly anti-imperialist and anti-Zionist, it is unclear why a military setback at the hands of France, the United Kingdom, and Israel would cause such furious domestic opposition. Nor is it clear, even from the British records released to date, exactly who Eden thought would replace Nasser.

47. This discussion draws on Seymour-Ure's (1984) comparison of the British cabinets during militarized crises. In addition to the core members, fourteen other ministers attended Egyptian Committee meetings during the July–November crisis. However, only the core members were responsible for the decision to issue the ultimatum.

48. Obviously, secrecy was a factor in Eden's decision. As Seymour-Ure points out, the similar world views and dominance of Eden created a perfect environment for what Irving Janis (1982) has labeled "groupthink."

49. The British intervention in the Russian Civil War is examined in Chapter 4, and the Middle Eastern interventions are explored in Chapter 5.

50. See Zaller (1992) and Rousseau (2004) for the effects of framing and elite divisions on the emergence of opposition to government policy.

51. In contrast, Eisenhower believed Nasser was a nationalist rather than a Hitler-like expansionist. Therefore, he felt analogies to Munich were inappropriate.

52. The cabinet posts and legislative seats were as follows: Socialists, two cabinet seats and ninety-four chamber seats; Radical Socialists, four and fifty-seven respectively; UDSR, two and nineteen respectively; and one nonparty cabinet seat.

53. This seems to be the only important link between the two crises. Although many have speculated that Soviet actions were encouraged by the tough stance taken by the United States against its NATO allies, Soviet decision making as to the timing and scope of the Hungarian intervention seems to have proceeded independently of the Suez Crisis (Campbell 1989; Valenta 1984b). U.S. officials expressed anger that the Suez Crisis prevented them from condemning the Soviets as strongly as they had wished (Richardson 1996, 83).

54. The public opinion data is from Gallup (1976a, 202, 203, 206).

55. Golani (1998) argues that the shift in the balance of power was only temporary. The flow of French weapons in 1956 shifted the balance of power back toward Israel. However, Levy and Gochal (2002) claim that Egypt continued to hold both a quantitative and qualitative advantage. They contend that Israel's 1956 war was a preventative strike aimed at destroying the new hardware before it could be effectively integrated into the Egyptian military.

56. British plans to use force against Israel highlight the fact that similarity in political structure does not guarantee pacific relations.

57. Risse-Kappen (1995) and Richardson (1996) focus on norms and behavior among the democratic allies. In contrast, my case study focuses on the behavior of democracies toward an autocracy. Whereas there was no serious consideration of using military force among the democratic allies, Richardson (1996, 97) argues that harassment (with the possibility of inadvertent escalation) did take place.

58. A colleague of Eden's once remarked that although the decision to intervene did not call Eden's judgment into question, his belief that the collusive arrangement could be kept secret did raise doubts.

59. Only the British and French interventions are considered failures from a military perspective; Israel succeeded in its goals despite its subsequent withdrawal from the Sinai.

60. For a more recent analysis of this issue, see Gartner, Segura, and Wilkening (1997). They find that early in a conflict, casualties and partisanship have a powerful impact on public opinion.

61. Whereas these observers are probably correct in their view that the United States contributed to the failure, they erroneously assume that if the Canal Zone had been occupied, the policy would have been a success. A successful policy would also have required the fall of Nasser and the creation of a stable pro-West Egyptian government.

62. The Ecuador-Peru dispute case study was developed using the following sources: William P. Avery, "Origins and Consequences of the Border Dispute Between Ecuador and Peru." *Inter-American Economic Affairs* 38 (Summer 1984): 65–77; Fernando Bustamante, "Ecuador: Putting an End to the Ghosts of the Past." *Journal of Interamerican Studies and World Affairs* 34:4 (Winter 1992–93): 195–225; Jack Child, *Geopolitics and Conflict in South America: Quarrels Among Neighbors* (New York: Praeger, 1985); Catherine M. Conaghan, "Politicians Against Parties: Discord and Disconnection in Ecuador's Party System." In Scott Mainwarin and Timothy R. Scully (eds.), *Building Democratic Institutions: Party Systems in Latin America* (Stanford, CA: Stanford University Press, 1985): 434–58; Dennis Hanratty (ed.), *Ecuador: A Country Study* (Washington, DC: Federal Research Division, Library of Congress, 1991); Jeanne A. K. Hey, "Ecuadorean Foreign Policy Since 1979: Ideological Cycles or a Trend Towards Neoliberalism." *Journal of Interamerican Studies and World Affairs* 37:4 (Winter 1995): 57–88; Rex A. Hudson, "Government and Politics." In Dennis Hanratty (ed.), *Ecuador: A Country Study* (Washington, DC: Federal Research Division, Library of Congress, 1991): 153–207; Anita Isaacs, *Military Rule and Transition in Ecuador, 1972–92* (Pittsburgh, PA: University of Pittsburgh Press, 1993); William L. Krieg, *Ecuadorean-Peruvian Rivalry in the Upper Amazon* (2nd ed., enlarged to include the Paquisha incident, 1981) (Washington, DC: U.S. Department of State, 1986); John D. Martz, "Ecuador: The Fragility of Dependent Democracy." In Howard J. Wiarda and Harvey F. Kline (eds.), *Latin American Politics and Government* (Boulder, CO: Westview, 1996): 326–42; David Scott Palmer, "Peru-Ecuador Conflict: Missed Opportunities, Misplaced Nationalism, and Multilateral Peacekeeping." *Journal of Interamerican Studies and World Affairs* 39 (Fall 1997): 109–148; Ronald Bruce St. John, "The Ecuador-Peru Dispute: A Reconsideration." In Pascal O. Girot (ed.), *World Boundaries, Vol. 4: The Americas* (London: Routledge, 1994): 113–32; Bryce Wood, *Aggression and History: The Case of Ecuador and Peru* (New York: Columbia Press, 1978).

63. Emergency power can be declared in situations involving imminent foreign aggression, international war, or serious internal strife. Under these powers, the president may divert revenue from other sources to defense, move the seat of government, enforce press censorship, suspend observance of constitutional guarantees, and declare a security zone in the national territory. Such constitutional provisions obviously undermine the constraining power of democratic institutions, particularly with respect to the escalation of the conflict after its onset.

64. According to Krieg, the casualty figures were even lower, with two Ecuadorians dead and twelve wounded and two Peruvians dead and sixteen wounded (Krieg 1986, 319).

65. For comparative purposes, the annual Freedom House publication scores Ecuador as Partly Free (1972–73), Not Free (1973–76), Partly Free (1976–79), Free (1979–96), Partly Free (1996–98), Free (1998–2000), and Partly Free (2000–2002).

Freedom House codes Peru as Not Free (1972–75), Partly Free (1975–80), Free (1980–89), Partly Free (1989–2001), and Free (2001–2002). For a description of the methodology employed and changes in the methodology across time, see www .freedomhouse.org. The final Freedom House typology has three categories: Free (F), Partly Free (PF), and Not Free (NF). The categorization is based on a complex scoring system that is distilled into two dimensions: political rights (1–7) and civil rights (1–7), where 1 is most free and 7 is least free. Countries with numbers between 1 and 2.5 are considered "free," 3–5.5 "partly free," and 5.5–7 "not free."

66. Mares (1996–97) assumes that Peru reverted to a full democracy in 1992. Therefore, he treats both the 1981 and 1995 crises as joint democracy violence. Most sources agree with the Polity codings.

67. For a discussion of the weakness of presidentialism in Ecuador and Peru, see Conaghan (1994) and McClintock (1994). Although they emphasize attempts by the chief executive to circumvent the legislature, the clash between the executive and legislature is clearly evident.

68. Public opinion data from Isaacs (1993).

69. According to *The Military Balance*, Ecuador had 38,800 military personnel, 120 tanks, and 55 combat aircraft. In contrast, Peru had 130,000 military personnel, 620 tanks, and 115 combat aircraft (International Institute for Strategic Studies 1981).

70. Diversionary war is not always well planned and executed. A classic example of diversionary war, the Russo-Japanese War of 1904–1905, resulted in a stinging defeat for Russia.

71. Palmer (1997) explains that Ecuador "recognizes the existence (vigencia) of the Protocol without accepting its validity (validez), due to the inability to execute (inejecutibilidad) one of its provisions."

72. Although Eden pursued negotiation, he clung to an extremely hard-line position that he knew Nasser would be unwilling to accept (and perhaps unable to accept due to heightened domestic awareness). Eden did not pursue bilateral and third-party negotiations because he accepted democratic norms advocating compromise and logrolling. He pursued negotiation in order to placate potential domestic and international opposition.

73. In their conclusion, Morgan and Campbell question the validity of this assumption (1991, 208).

74. The argument also assumes that internationalism is not negatively correlated with militarism. In fact, Wittkopf (1986, 1987, 1994) and Holsti and Rosenau (1990) find the two dimensions are positively correlated.

75. To see this, compare the response of political leaders with those of the general public in any Chicago Council on Foreign Relations survey. For example, when asked whether they favored the use of U.S. troops to defend Western Europe, 75 percent of U.S. leaders approved of the use of troops compared to just 40 percent of the general public (Chicago Council on Foreign Relations 1977, 50, 127). Divergence is the norm rather than the exception over a host of hypothetical situations and across all years of the survey (Wittkopf 1994, 380).

CHAPTER 3

International Disputes and the Evolution of Conflict

THE EARLIEST EMPIRICAL tests of the relationship between regime type and international conflict focused on the population of international wars (Wright [1942] 1965; Babst 1972; Small and Singer 1976; Doyle 1986). Although the precise definition of a *war* is still a topic of debate, researchers armed with a clear set of criteria were generally able to develop an easily replicable list of wars. The second phase of empirical tests moved beyond wars into militarized crises (Morgan and Campbell 1991; Maoz and Russett 1993; Hewitt and Wilkenfeld 1995; Senese 1997a, 1997b). Both the Militarized Interstate Dispute (MID) data set and the International Crisis Behavior (ICB) data set include cases in which one or both parties contemplate or threaten to use military force.[1] Therefore, the crisis data sets capture a broader range of international conflicts. Whereas some of these crises escalated to war, most did not.

This chapter represents the next logical step in this cumulative process: the identification and analysis of the population of international disputes. This data set captures conflicts that never escalated into a militarized crisis or full-scale war. As shown in Figure 3.1, by definition the crisis data set is a subset of the dispute data set.[2] Take, for instance, the conflict between the United States and Cuba during the Cold War. A crisis data set, such as the ICB used in the previous chapter, would record a single instance in which one state contemplated and used military force against the other—the U.S.-supported Bay of Pigs landing in 1961. In the crisis data set, all variables are coded for the year 1961, at which time the U.S. government initiated large-scale violence through its support of the rebel movement.[3] In contrast, a dispute data set is much broader. It includes all years in which the United States

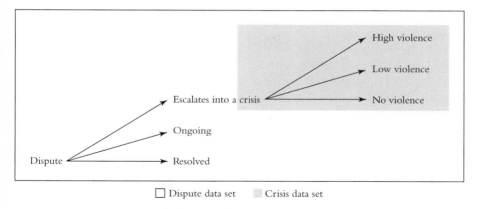

Dispute data set Crisis data set

FIGURE 3.1. Evolution of disputes and crises

and Cuba had an ongoing conflict. Since the rise of Castro in 1959, there has been an ideological conflict as well as a territorial conflict between the two states. During this entire period of dispute, Castro had to decide whether or not to use military means to force the United States out of Guantanamo Bay. Simultaneously, U.S. presidents from Kennedy to Reagan had to decide if military force was appropriate for resolving the ideological conflict.[4]

Why is expanding the scope of analysis from wars to crises to disputes important? What can we learn from a data set of disputes that we could not have learned from an examination of crises or wars? The answer is that the total impact of institutions cannot be assessed using the more restricted data sets. If one were to find that institutional constraints or democratic norms did not lessen the probability of using force in crises, one could not make the *general statement* that constraints and norms play no role in international conflict. That is, we cannot generalize from the specific (crises) to the general (disputes). The fact that I do not like Oreo cookies sheds little light on my preferences for cookies in general. As described in Rousseau and colleagues (1996), the use of a crisis data set to test the relationship between political structure and the use of force to resolve political disputes neglects a potential selection effect. If more democratic or constrained states systematically choose not to escalate disputes to the crisis stage, then the influence of political structure will be underestimated in any analysis focusing solely on crises. For example, norms could encourage states to accept mediation and arbitration that could help resolve the dispute entirely, or at least prevent an aggrieved party from resorting to force. Therefore, any complete test of the relationship between institutional and normative constraints and the use of force to resolve an international conflict must include an examination of both disputes and crises.

Why not simply expand the data set to include all dyads, as do Bennett and Stam (2004), or politically relevant dyads, as does Reed (2000)? Obviously, Figure 3.1 could be expanded one step backward to include the set of peaceful dyads. Some of these dyads would transition into disputes; others would not. Although this would be a useful endeavor, we would still need a data set of disputes in order to analyze this initial transition (or selection process) (Huth and Allee 2002, 22). Moreover, the field has long acknowledged that using all dyads to examine military conflict is problematic because the vast majority of dyads (for example, Uruguay versus Ghana) have little incentive and opportunity to use military force against each other. The most common solution to this problem is the use of "politically relevant dyads," which include any contiguous states and dyads with great powers. The problem with this restricted set is that it includes many states that have no disputes and excludes many states that do in fact have a dispute. About 25 percent of my dispute data set is not captured by the politically relevant dyad definition. Whereas researchers use "all dyads" or "politically relevant dyads" because they are easily definable data sets, they cannot shed light on transitions to disputes and from disputes to crises.

Finally, Huth and Allee argue that regime type is unlikely to explain why disputes arise in the first place because all types of states get into disputes (2002, 23). Rather, regime type is likely to influence how states go about resolving these disputes. This implies that the big impact of democratic institutions will be in the link between disputes and crises, which is the focus of this chapter.[5]

A handful of studies have attempted to examine the broader set of international disputes. Leeds and Davis (1999) use the COPDAB data set to examine all cooperative and conflictual interactions within dyads. Evidence of the behavior in the form of statements or actions is drawn from media outlets such as the *New York Times* and Facts on File. COPDAB captures a wide range of interactions, from a Belgian official complaining about the death penalty in the United States to a Ghanian diplomat chiding the United States for its textile policy. Thus, the data set captures many interactions that do not correspond to "disputes" in the traditional sense (for example, Butterworth with Scranton 1976).

Perhaps the most successful attempts to create data sets of both disputes and crises fall within the area of territorial conflicts. Huth (1996) and Huth and Allee (2002) examine all territorial disputes in the twentieth century. Whereas some of these disputes escalate to crises and wars, others do not. Therefore, Huth and Allee can study the escalation of conflict from mere disputes, to militarized crises, and to war. Similarly, Hensel (2001) analyzes a set of all territorial disputes in the Western Hemisphere since 1816. Hensel and McLaughlin Mitchell's ambitious ICOW ("issue correlates of war") hopes to expand this data set to include all issues and across all continents. If completed, this data set would become a standard in the field analogous to the MID or ICB data sets of crises. Unfortunately, it will be literally years before a complete data set of all issues is developed for all continents from the end of the Napoleonic area to the present.

Finally, the enduring rivalries literature also addresses the evolution of conflicts. This literature focuses on pairs of states engaged in an intense, longer-term competition. Although early enduring rival works often focused on great powers, the more recent works have used definitions such as that employed by Hensel, Goertz, and Diehl (2000, 1177): "An enduring rival is defined as a competition between states that involves six or more militarized disputes between the same two states over a period lasting at least 20 years." Given that these dyads enter and exit particular militarized crises, the dyads include both dispute years and crisis years.

Although all this work represents a significant advancement in the literature, none of it can substitute for the analysis in this chapter. Huth and Allee (2002) can tell us if there is a monadic impact of democracy in the area of territorial disputes, but they cannot generalize to the broad set of international disputes. Similarly, although the Hensel and McLaughlin Mitchell project may someday define the set of international disputes, it currently does not have a data set that tracks all disputes across all countries. Finally, the enduring rival literature as it stands includes only a narrow set of disputes because many international national disputes never escalate to a militarized crisis—much less the six crises needed to define the dyad as an enduring rivalry. In sum, the dispute data set examined in this chapter fills an important gap in the literature.

The Dispute Data Set

The primary source for the identification of international disputes is a data set developed by Sherman (1994) that identifies all domestic quarrels and international disputes from 1945 to 1988.[6] The roots of SHERFACs can be traced to Ernst Haas's work on the collective management of conflict by international organizations. Over time, a number of dispute and conflict management data sets were merged and expanded, including Nye (1971), Hass, Butterworth, and Nye (1972), and Butterworth with Scranton (1976). Sherman and Alker incorporated the phases into the data set by drawing on the work of Bloomfield and Leiss (1969). Finally, Sherman expanded the list of the primary and secondary actors involved in the conflict-management process and coded their actions in each phase of the dispute.

The purpose of the SHERFACs data set is to provide a comprehensive list of all international disputes (such as territorial disputes and antiregime disputes) and domestic quarrels (such as civil wars and ethnic cleansing). The division of the data set into phases allowed Sherman to study the utility of conflict-management techniques at different stages of conflict (1987). Although the SHERFACs data set is not as widely used as the MID or ICB, it has been employed in a number of studies (for example, Dixon 1993, 1994; Eyerman and Hart 1996). After the death of Frank Sherman, the data set has been made publicly available by Hayward Alker through the University of Southern California.

I have adapted the Sherman data set in a number of ways. First, due to the scope of the effort involved, I have restricted the analysis of disputes to the 1960–88 period. As I will discuss, even with this restriction the final dispute data set contains 223 disputes and almost 6,000 country-dispute years.

Second, I removed all domestic quarrels because my theoretical framework is designed to examine the impact of institutions and norms on the use of force externally (as opposed to governmental force against one's own citizens). Any domestic quarrel that escalates into an international dispute due to third-party intervention is included in my data set. For example, Indonesia's repression of its ethnic Chinese citizens during the 1960s triggered a China-Indonesia international dispute that is included in the dispute data set.

Third, I have eliminated several categories of cases, including human rights cases, maritime boundary cases, purely economic conflicts, colonial cases, and non-state-sponsored terrorism. In essence, I hope to focus on political-security conflicts that have some probability of escalating to military conflict between internationally recognized sovereign states. Although the U.S.-China conflict springing from Chinese human rights violations at Tiananmen Square constitutes an international dispute in a broad sense, no decision maker in the United States seriously contemplated using military force to resolve the dispute. The vast number of maritime boundary cases, unlike territorial disputes, very rarely escalate to the point in which one or both parties contemplate using force. Most of these cases are, in fact, tied to economic conflicts (such as fishing disputes and undersea mineral rights disputes). Economic conflicts, though important, are qualitatively different from political-security disputes because threats and the use of military force rarely play a central role.[7] Colonial cases have been removed because the theoretical framework for this study applies to the bargaining norms and political structures of independent state actors. Independence movements typically lack formal political institutional structures. In addition, the conflict-resolution norms established under colonial rule are rarely clear. Finally, although state-sponsored terrorism is clearly a use of force by one government versus another and therefore included in the data set, general terrorist attacks by internal groups aimed at altering governmental policies are not incorporated into the data set.

Fourth, I have aggregated disputes into "country conflicts," resulting in a pooled time-series data set. For example, rather than treat the U.S. opposition to Castro and the Cuban challenge to the U.S. control of Guantanamo as independent events as Sherman does, I have created a single U.S.-Cuba dispute from 1960 to 1988 that tracks the number and types of issues under dispute in any given year. Another example comes from India and Pakistan. Rather than treating each disputed piece of territory as an independent conflict, I have consolidated the disputes into a single India-Pakistan dispute that has multiple territorial disputes, as well as conflicts over other issues such as nuclear weapons.

The net result of the effort has produced a dispute data set consisting of 223 international disputes from 1960 to 1988. A list of the disputes and conflict dyads included in the analysis can be found in Appendix 3.1. The disputes range in length from a single year to twenty-nine years (that is, all years under investigation); the average territorial dispute is twenty-one years, and the average antiregime dispute is just over ten years. The 223 international disputes correspond to 2,880 dispute years. For example, India and Pakistan were in a dispute from 1960 to 1988, which corresponds to 29 dispute years in the data set.[8] As with the crisis data set, I collected data on both the challenger and defender states because political leaders in both countries face decisions regarding the timing and extent of military force. As a result, the final directed dyad dispute data set consists of 5,760 country-dispute observations (in other words, 2,880 decisions by the challenger whether to use force and 2,880 decisions by the defender whether to use force).[9]

Hypotheses and Analysis

As discussed in the previous chapter, from a theoretical standpoint the initiation of violence represents the ideal dependent variable for measuring the impact of regime type on external conflict. However, using initiation of force as a dependent variable for the dispute data set is difficult because the use of force is a relatively rare event; in the full dispute data set of 5,760 country-years, only about 12 percent of the cases involved a use of military force. If one were to examine only years in which force was initiated, only about 1 percent of cases would be coded above zero for the dependent variable. The skewness of the dependent variable makes estimating a probit or logit model relatively uninformative. In order to estimate the model, I employ the dichotomous *Aggressive Use of Force* dependent variable briefly introduced in the last chapter (1 = use of military force on the territory of the opponent; 0 = no use of force).[10] While being relatively frequent, this variable has closer ties to the initiation of force than does mere involvement in a dispute. Moreover, in the minds of decision makers the crossing of international borders represents a salient threshold in terms of the use of force. In the Korean War, the United States and the United Nations wrestled with the decision of whether or not to cross the 38th parallel into North Korea (Foot 1985). Although the North Koreans had clearly initiated the large-scale attack in June 1950, crossing the border into North Korea in the hopes of toppling the Communist regime and reuniting the peninsula was clearly seen by all parties as a more aggressive use of force than merely defending South Korea.

In sum, although the *Aggressive Use of Force* dependent variable is in some respects inferior to an initiation variable, its relative frequency coupled with its superiority to traditional measures, such as conflict involvement, makes it the best choice for the pooled time-series analysis of international disputes. As with the crisis model, the use of a categorical dependent variable requires the use of a probit model.

The definition and operationalization of the independent variables used in this chapter were presented in the preceding chapter. In order to summarize, the normative and structural variants of the democratic peace model can be used to derive the three central hypotheses of the democratic peace model:

HYPOTHESIS 1 (MONADIC)
In a dispute, the more democratic a state, the less likely it is to use aggressive force regardless of the regime type of the adversary.

HYPOTHESIS 2 (DYADIC)
In a dispute, the more democratic a state, the less likely it is to use aggressive force against other democracies.

HYPOTHESIS 3
In a dispute, nondemocracies are more likely to use aggressive force against democracies than they are against nondemocracies.

In addition to the analysis of the democratic peace, the model includes the five important control variables that were discussed at length in the previous chapter:

HYPOTHESIS 4
In a dispute, if a state is challenging the status quo, it is more likely to use aggressive force.

TABLE 3.1
Probit analysis with aggressive use of force dependent variable and dispute data set

Independent variable	Coefficient	Standard error	T-ratio
Actor's net democracy (monadic)	−0.018★★★	0.004	4.301
Actor's net democracy with a democratic opponent (dyadic)	−0.071★★★	0.014	4.932
Opponent's net democracy	0.014★★★	0.004	3.386
Balance of forces	0.166★★	0.071	2.343
Shared alliance ties	−0.112★	0.060	1.871
Satisfaction with the status quo	−0.694★★★	0.057	12.236
Democracy with weak opponent	−0.010	0.109	0.092
Democracy with weak democracy	0.309	0.488	0.634
Constant	−1.699★★★	0.083	22.270

NOTE: Number of observations = 5,600. Log likelihood at convergence = −1832.28. All significance tests are one-tailed. ★p < .05, ★★p < .01, ★★★p < .001.

HYPOTHESIS 5

In a dispute, the more the balance of military forces tends to favor a state, the more likely it will use aggressive force.

HYPOTHESIS 6

In a dispute, if a state has any military alliance ties with its adversary, it is less likely to use aggressive force.

HYPOTHESIS 7 (MONADIC VERSION)

Democracies are especially likely to use force when facing a militarily weak opponent regardless of the regime type of the adversary.

HYPOTHESIS 8 (DYADIC VERSION)

Democracies are especially likely to use force when facing militarily weak democracies.

The multivariate results for the democratic peace model are presented in Table 3.1. The hypotheses are tested using an ordered probit model and the *Aggressive Use of Force* dependent variable (N = 5,600, 1 = 12%, 0 = 88%). Hypothesis 1 (a purely monadic argument) predicts that the coefficient on the *Actor's Net Democracy* score will be negative and that the interaction term which isolates the effect of the actor's democracy when facing a democratic opponent will be insignificant. On the other hand, hypothesis 2 (a purely dyadic argument) predicts that the coefficient on the *Actor's Net Democracy* score will be insignificant and that the coefficient on the interaction term will be negative and significant.

Table 3.1 indicates both a monadic and dyadic effect of democracy. Both the *Actor's Net Democracy* variable and the interaction term (*Actor's Democracy with a Democratic Opponent*) are negative and statistically significant at better than the .001 level. The more democratic a state, the less likely it is to initiate a military conflict; when the opponent is a democratic state, this conflict-dampening effect of institutions is even stronger. In addition, three of the five control variables have a powerful influence on the probability of using force aggressively. States that share an alliance tie are less likely to use aggressive force. In addition, the more the balance of forces favors a state, the more likely it is to use force to resolve an international dispute. Finally, Table 3.1 indicates that states that are satisfied with the status quo are less likely to use violence. The only estimated coefficients that fail to achieve standard thresholds of statistical significance are the interactive balance of forces and regime type variables used to test the selectorate model of Bueno de Mesquita and colleagues (2003). Strong democracies are neither more likely to pick on weak states (monadic) nor more likely to pick on weak democracies (dyadic).

The marginal impacts of the coefficients estimated in the model are shown in Table 3.2.[11] The table displays the probability of the use of aggressive force and the change in probability (shown in bold type) associated with a change in an independent variable while holding all other variables constant. The *Actor's Democracy* portion of the table indicates that shifting from a totally autocratic state (0) to a totally democratic state (20) decreases the probability of aggressive force from 20% to 12%, or a net decrease of 8 percentage points.[12] The marginal impact of the *Actor's Democracy with a Democratic Opponent* is even more powerful. A shift in the independent variable from the minimum of 0 to a maximum of 20 results in a 27-percentage-point decline in the probability of using aggressive force. The probability of using aggressive force, shown as 0 in the table due to rounding, falls to a mere 0.01 percent. Although there is a substantive monadic effect of democratic institutions and norms, the marginal analysis clearly indicates a powerful dyadic effect above and beyond the monadic effect. Finally, increasing the level of democracy in the opponent from 0 to 20 increases the probability of being attacked by 8 percentage points. Contrary to the predictions of Bueno de Mesquita and colleagues (2003), autocratic states appear to find democracies inviting targets.

Table 3.2 also displays the substantive impact of the statistically significant control variables in the equation. The marginal analysis indicates that increasing the *Balance of Forces* from a very unfavorable 1 : 9 ratio to a very favorable 9 : 1 ratio increases the probability of aggressive force by 3 percentage points. Thus, although the variable is statistically significant, its substantive impact is minor. The alliance variable also has a weak effect on the use of force. A shift from no alliance to alliance decreases the probability of aggressive force by only 2 percentage points. Finally, states that reject the status quo in a dispute are, as expected, much more likely to use aggressive force. A

TABLE 3.2

Marginal effects with aggressive use of force dependent variable and dispute data set

Shift in independent variables	Probability of using aggressive force	Shift in independent variables	Probability of using aggressive force
Actor's democracy		Balance of forces	
0	20	1:9	17
10	15	1:3	17
20	12	1:1	18
Total	**−8**	3:1	20
		9:1	20
Actor's democracy with a democratic opponent		**Total**	**+3**
0	27	Alliance	
10	7	No	18
20	0	Yes	16
Total	**−27**	**Total**	**−2**
Opponent's democracy for fully autocratic state		Satisfaction with status quo	
		No	18
0	19	Yes	6
10	23	**Total**	**−12**
20	27		
Total	**+8**		

NOTES: See Table 2.3 for methodology. Only statistically significant coefficients in Table 3.1 are presented in the table. Clarify software was used to calculate the marginal impacts (Tomz et al. 2003).

shift from "dissatisfied" to "satisfied" decreases the probability of using aggressive force by 12 percentage points.

Figure 3.2 displays the impact of the monadic and dyadic variables on the use of aggressive force. The figure presents the expected value as a line, with circles for the monadic argument and triangles for the dyadic argument. Uncertainty around these point estimates, shown in "i-bar"−like brackets, was calculated using Clarify software (Tomz et al. 2003). The slowly descending monadic line indicates that as the level of democracy in a state increases, the probability of aggressive force declines slowly. In contrast, the steeply sloping dyadic line indicates that when facing a democratic state, the more democratic a state is has a very large effect on the probability of violence.

In order to test the robustness of these findings, I conducted a large amount of sensitivity analysis. None of these analyses undermine the central conclusion drawn from the study of international disputes: democracies are less likely to use aggressive force with both autocracies and democracies. The sensitivity analysis included adding a great-power variable, using a trichotomous dependent variable, including a "years at peace" variable, adding interdependence and trade variables, inserting gross domestic product per

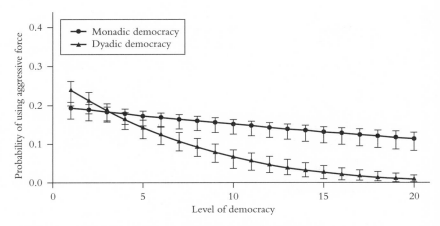

FIGURE 3.2. Comparing the monadic and dyadic explanations

capita, adding contiguity, controlling for nuclear weapons, adding Bueno de Mesquita's alliance similarity variable (1981), including Signorino and Ritter's alliance similarity variable (1999), adding Gartzke's similarity in U.N. voting measure (1998), using the COW balance of forces variable (troops, defense spending, iron and steel production, energy, urban population, and total population), varying the cutoff for the democratic opponent variable, and expanding the alliance variable to include neutrality pacts and ententes. None of these changes had an important impact on the monadic and dyadic democracy variables. Appendix 3.2 displays the coefficients and standard errors for a model that includes the additional variables for each issue area.[13]

Finally, I conducted sensitivity analysis by altering the specification of the model in order to explore the impact of the rareness of the dependent variable and the use of the pooled cross-sectional time-series data. The results of all these tests appear in Table 3.3. First, only 12 percent of the values on the dichotomous *Aggressive Use of Force* dependent variable are 1. Gates and McLaughlin argue that probit and logit models assume an underlying symmetric distribution: "With a substantially skewed distribution, any symmetric statistical model can produce inefficient and biased results" (1996, 4). Gates and McLaughlin suggest using a gompertz curve as an alternative link function to the cumulative normal density function used in traditional probit analysis. Reestimating with the gompertz curve did not produce any significant changes in the model.

Second, King and Zeng (2001) suggest using a "relogit" model when the dependent variable rarely occurs. Although researchers have long understood that logit coefficients are biased in small samples (under 200 observations), King and Zeng claim that researchers have neglected the bias resulting from rare events in big data sets (such as coups and wars in time-series data sets). The reestimating of the model using their relogit command in STATA reveals that this potential problem does not affect the dispute data set. As column 2 of the table indicates, the coefficients for the monadic and dyadic democracy variables remain statistically significant.

Third, the model was reestimated using cross-sectional pooled time-series methods recommended by Beck, Katz, and Tucker (1997).[14] They argue that researchers using ordinary logit or probit to analyze time-series cross-sectional data with a binary dependent variable are likely to violate a key assumption in the model: independence of observations. The authors use their methodology to reassess Oneal and Russett's (1997) finding that economic interdependence decreases the probability of conflict. They conclude that the statistically significant interdependence coefficient is an artifact of Oneal and Russett's failure to address temporal dependence in the pooled times-series data set. Therefore, I reestimated the model using a generalized linear model that employs a "complementary log–log link" (in place of the traditional probit link function) and incorporates temporal dummy variables for each year of the data set. In addition, I reestimated the dispute data set using a cubic spline model. This revised equation, shown in column 5 of Table 3.3, addresses temporal dependence by including the number of years of peace between the states in the dispute as an independent variable as well as estimates of the three spine segments.[15] Neither model produced results that significantly differed from those reported earlier.[16]

Finally, I explored the impact of using a pooled time series by compressing the time series into a "regime" data set. If the democracy index for both states in the dispute remains constant for the entire time period, the multiyear dispute is compressed into a single observation. The dependent and independent variables are calculated by simply averaging values across the years that have been compressed. In cases in which either country experienced a change of at least two points on the 0–20 democracy index, a new observation was created.[17] For instance, the Chile-Argentina dispute contains six observations in the regime data set, reflecting the numerous regime changes experienced by both countries between 1960 and 1988. The time period from 1976 until 1982, for example, represents a single observation because both states are highly autocratic. The fall of the military government in Argentina after the disastrous Falklands War triggers the creation of a new observation that pits a fairly democratic Argentinean regime against Pinochet's autocratic Chilean state. The creation of a regime data set reduces the number of observations from 5,600 to 1,076 and virtually eliminates any chance that the results are the by-product of the pooled cross-sectional time-series

TABLE 3.3
Sensitivity analysis with the dispute data set, 1960–88

Independent variable	Probit model[a]	Gompertz model	Relogit model	Cloglog model[b]	Cubic spline model[c]	Regime model
Actor's democracy (monadic)	-0.018***	-0.013***	-0.036***	-0.028**	-0.012*	-0.004**
	(0.004)	(0.003)	(0.008)	(0.009)	(0.006)	(0.002)
Actor's democracy with democratic opponent (dyadic)	-0.071***	-0.047***	-0.166***	-0.107***	-0.058***	-0.006*
	(0.014)	(0.009)	(0.040)	(0.025)	(0.016)	(0.003)
Opponent's net democracy	0.014***	0.011***	0.027***	0.017**	0.011*	0.003
	(0.004)	(0.003)	(0.008)	(0.007)	(0.005)	(0.002)
Balance of forces	0.165***	0.134**	0.305**	0.108	0.136	0.027
	(0.071)	(0.057)	(0.130)	(0.130)	(0.086)	(0.031)
Shared alliance ties	-0.112*	-0.055	-0.280**	-0.173	-0.081	-0.004
	(0.060)	(0.046)	(0.115)	(0.106)	(0.074)	(0.021)
Satisfaction with the status quo	-0.694***	-0.513***	-1.399***	-1.115***	-0.681***	-0.099***
	(0.057)	(0.041)	(0.121)	(0.120)	(0.078)	(0.020)
Democracy with weaker opponent	-0.010	-0.024	0.026	0.043	-0.057	0.051
	(0.109)	(0.082)	(0.213)	(0.223)	(0.155)	(0.046)
Democracy with weaker democracy	0.309	0.216	1.179	-0.093	0.186	-0.064
	(0.488)	(0.299)	(1.264)	(1.116)	(0.672)	(0.102)
Constant	-1.661***	-1.112***	2.974***	-1.036***	0.790***	0.083**
	(0.075)	(0.057)	(0.148)	(0.155)	(0.072)	(0.029)

	(1)	(2)	(3)	(4)	(5)	(6)
Peace years	—	—	—	—	−1.269*** (0.072)	—
Spline(1)c	—	—	—	—	−0.125*** (0.011)	—
Spline(1)c	—	—	—	—	0.028*** (0.003)	—
Spline(1)c	—	—	—	—	−0.002** (0.001)	—
Number of observations	5,600	5,600	5,600	5,600	5,600	1,076
Log likelihood at convergence	−1832	−1837	n.a.	n.a.	−1135	n.a.
Deviance	n.a.	n.a.	n.a.	2153	n.a.	n.a.
F-statistic	—	—	—	—	—	6.27, p < .000

NOTE: Robust standard errors appear in parentheses below the coefficient estimates. All significance tests are one-tailed. *p < .05, **p < .01, ***p < .001. STATA 6.0 used to produce the results.

[a]Thresholds not shown.

[b]Temporal dummies not shown.

[c]Coefficients of peace years cubic spline segments.

design. As the results from column 6 of the table indicate, the results from the regime analysis are very similar to the baseline findings.

In sum, the analysis indicates that in the broader set of international disputes, democracies are less likely to use aggressive force than nondemocracies. This finding stands in sharp contrast to the exclusively dyadic finding found in Chapter 2 and most of the democratic peace literature. However, it is consistent with a growing body of literature in which new research designs and data sets have found evidence of a monadic peace (for example, Bennett and Stam 2004; Schultz 2001; Huth and Allee 2002). The findings presented here are also quite robust. The addition of numerous control variables and the alternation of the model specification did not alter the central findings.

The findings in chapters 2 and 3 raise an interesting question: would a selection model that formally links the dispute phase with the crisis phase be the most appropriate model? Perhaps the most common selection model used in the literature is the Heckman two-stage selection model. The Heckman model consists of two equations: the selection equation and the outcome equation. The probit selection equation, which employs a dichotomous dependent variable (1 = enters crisis; 0 = does not), models the likelihood that a state becomes involved in a militarized crisis. The probit outcome equation, which employs a dichotomous dependent variable (1 = uses aggressive force; 0 = does not), models the likelihood that a state uses military force once a crisis is under way. The results from this chapter and the last chapter would lead us to expect a monadic impact of democracy in the selection equation and a dyadic impact of democracy in both equations.

Unfortunately, use of a Heckman model with my data sets produces extremely unstable results. Slight alterations in the content of the selection and outcome equations cause tremendous shifts in the substantive impact and statistical significance of the variables. This unexpected instability appears to be the product of two factors: (1) the structure of this particular data set and (2) the nature of Heckman models in general.

First, the data sets as currently configured cannot be easily combined to test a selection model. The crisis data set is an *event* data set derived from the ICB data; the data set includes observations from 1918 to 2000. In contrast, the dispute data set is a *time-series* data set derived from the Sherman data; this data set includes annual observations from 1960 to 1988. Given the differences in years and structure, only 163 crises are selected from the almost 6,000 observations in the dispute data. Stolzenberg and Relles argue that in cases of severe censoring the application of the Heckman model can "easily do more harm than good" (1990, 408). The obvious solution to the problem is to expand the dispute data set back to 1918 and to transform the crisis data set into a time series. Although I certainly endorse this expansion and transformation, completing these tasks would involve literally years of work (as the team of researchers working on the ICOW project can attest).

Second, Heckman models are notoriously unstable (Lillard et al. 1986). This implies that although there may be a selection process at work, it simply may be very difficult to model empirically. Slight changes in model specification can cause coefficient signs to flip, marginal impacts to change abruptly, and the sudden failure of models to converge. Which version of the model is correct? The Monte Carlo analysis by Stolzenberg and Relles (1990) demonstrates that in many cases it is difficult, if not impossible, to tell. The implications of this instability can be highlighted by examining one of the few selection models found in the democratic peace literature—Reed (2000).[18] Reed concludes that "joint democracy" decreases the probability a state becomes involved in a militarized crisis but has no impact on whether or not the crisis escalates to a use of force (in other words, "joint democracy" was significant in the selection equation but not in the outcome equation). However, exploratory analysis with the original data set indicates that slight changes in the model can lead the analyst to draw very different conclusions. If a "peace years" variable (identical to that used in Table 3.3) is added to the outcome equation, the joint democracy coefficient becomes negative and statistically significant. Similarly, if you delete the "power parity" variable from the outcome equation and insert "joint satisfaction" and "interdependence" variables, you find that the joint democracy is once again negative and statistically significant. Does joint democracy decrease the probability of escalation? Given the instability of the model, it is very difficult to draw a firm conclusion.

A second method available to explore temporal dependence is survival analysis (also known as event history analysis or duration analysis). Survival analysis has been used to analyze a wide variety of "events," including onset of disease, stock market crashes, bouts of unemployment, arrests, and revolutions. Survival analysis is designed for longitudinal data on the occurrence of events (such as a qualitative change from one discrete state to another [Allison 1995, 2]). An event could be a shift from "healthy" to "sick" or from a "peaceful dyad" to a "conflictual dyad" in which force is employed by one or both parties. Although biostatisticians are often concerned with events that can occur only once (such as death), most political scientists focus on repeated events (for example, coups). The fact that early coups can influence later coups implies that the data are heterogeneous rather than homogeneous. Disregarding the unobserved heterogeneity can result in biased coefficient estimates.

Box-Steffensmeier and Zorn (2002) use the Oneal and Russett (1997) data set of 20,990 annual observations of "politically relevant" dyads. The dependent variable is the use of military force (including war) derived from the MID data set. The independent variables are the level of *democracy* (low score in pair), the level of *interdependence* (low score in pair), *economic growth* (low score in pair), ratio of *military capabilities, geographic contiguity*, and the presence of an *alliance tie*. All the variables are defined by Oneal and Russett (1997).

Oneal and Russett find that as the level of democracy in a dyad rises (measured by the least democratic member), the less likely a state is to use force. Box-Steffensmeier and Zorn demonstrate that this conflict-dampening effect occurs only for the onset of the first militarized conflict. Once an MID has occurred between two states, the institutional constraint evaporates. As Box-Steffensmeier and Zorn conclude, "For democracy, . . . we find that the widely-supported findings of a negative effect is driven entirely by its effect on the dyads' first conflict; in second and subsequent conflicts, this effect largely disappears" (2002, 1088). Although the Box-Steffensmeier analysis differs in many ways from the research design employed in this study (for example, dyadic unit of analysis, conflict involvement dependent variable, politically relevant dyads), their conclusion that the constraining power of institutions depends on the behavior of the states in an ongoing dispute is an important insight that correlates with my findings. The following case studies illustrate the process through which this situation can occur.

Case Studies

The quantitative analysis in the last two chapters has shown a selection process. Democratic institutions constrain states from behaving aggressively in international disputes. However, once the dispute escalates to the point in which military force is under consideration by one or both states, the proverbial "gloves" come off. At this point, democracies are less likely to use force only when facing another democracy. It appears that during the dispute phase of the conflict (and perhaps the early crisis phase of the conflict), the behavior of the opponent can strongly influence domestic opposition to the use of force. This dynamic process has been uncovered in other works in the literature. In her qualitative analysis of the Crimean War, Peterson (1996) finds that the belligerent attitude of Russia early in the crisis shifted the balance of opinion in the British cabinet and the public at large. Foreign Secretary Clarendon, originally allied with the more pacific Prime Minister Aberdeen, shifted into the hard-line camp led by Home Secretary Palmerston after Russia demonstrated it was not a status quo state in the search of a compromise.

In order to explore how constraint can melt away without any change in institutional structure, I present two cases: Israel versus Egypt and Turkey versus Greece. In each case, we see a democratic state launch a major war against its opponent (Israel in the 1967 Six Days' War and Turkey in the 1974 invasion of Cyprus). In both cases, the history of the dispute and the behavior of the opponent led to the evaporation of domestic opposition to the use of force.

ISRAEL AND EGYPT IN THE 1967 SIX DAYS' WAR

The Six Days' War in 1967 was the third major conflict between Israel and its Arab neighbors since Israel's independence in 1948.[19] The Israeli attack on Egypt on June 5, 1967, represents the only clear case of a democratic state preemptively attacking an adversary in my data sets.[20] Convinced that Egypt intended to initiate hostilities, Israel chose to gain a military advantage by striking first.[21]

The dispute continued to revolve around the Arab states' refusal to recognize the existence of Israel, their territorial claims against Israel, and their support of guerrilla action against the Jewish state. In 1966 and 1967, increasing Palestinian guerrilla raids from Jordan and Syria had heightened tensions considerably. In November 1966, an Israeli retaliatory raid against Jordan at El Samu escalated into heavy fighting. In April 1967, an air battle over the Israeli–Syrian border resulted in the destruction of several Syrian aircraft. The following month, Nasser's Egyptian government undertook a series of actions designed to threaten Israel and signal support for its Arab allies:

May 14: Egypt began reinforcing the Sinai with 35,000 troops.

May 16: Egypt requested the withdrawal of U.N. peacekeepers.

May 17: Aircraft flew over Israel's nuclear research station.

May 23: Egypt closed the Straits of Tiran.

May 30: Jordan placed its forces under Egyptian control.

The Israeli prime minister during the crisis was Levi Eshkol. Eshkol was a long-time Mapai Party member who had served in Ben Gurion's cabinet, first as minister of agriculture and later as minister of finance. When Ben Gurion resigned in June 1963 during an internal scandal, Eshkol became prime minister. Eshkol's coalition was reelected in 1965, despite Ben Gurion's formation of the Workers List (popularly known as Rafi) splinter party.

As shown in Table 3.4, following the 1965 elections, Eshkol's ruling coalition was composed of five major parties that together controlled 69 of the 120 seats in the Knesset. Since its founding, the Israeli political system had encouraged a proliferation of political parties in the parliament, which had

TABLE 3.4

Distribution of seats in the Israeli Knesset in 1967

Political parties	Knesset seats	Cabinet posts
Ruling coalition	**69**	**18**
Labour Alignment		
(Mapai and Ahdut Ha'avoda)	45	12
National Religious Party	11	3
United Workers Party	8	2
Independent Liberals	5	1
Gahal	26	0
Workers List	10	0
Orthodox Religion Party	4	0
New Communist List	3	0
Orthodox Workers Party	2	0
Other parties	6	0
Total	**120**	**18**

resulted in a series of coalition governments. Although the Labor Alignment of Mapai (itself a coalition of two parties) had by far the largest number of seats of any single party, it possessed only 45 seats (or 37.5 percent) in the legislature. From a purely structural perspective, the Eshkol government was apparently constrained by a factional ruling party, a coalitional cabinet, and a bare majority in the legislature. However, as the discussion will demonstrate, the lack of opposition to the use of force in each of these channels translated into limited constraint on the decision to use violence.

The Eshkol government responded to each aggressive step taken by Egypt in May 1967.[22] The day after the introduction of Egyptian troops into the Sinai, Eshkol authorized Chief of Staff Rabin to reinforce the southern border. The cabinet retroactively approved the measure. When the government informed the Knesset Foreign Affairs and Security Committee, the largest opposition party (Gahal, with twenty-six seats) demanded *stronger* action. This pattern was repeated throughout the crisis: the main opposition parties consistently took a more hard-line position than Eshkol. Rather than restraining the chief executive, the opposition encouraged a military confrontation (Oren 2002, 88–89).

On May 16 Nasser requested the removal of the 3,400 U.N. peacekeeping troops in the Sinai who had separated Egypt and Israel since the 1956 Suez Crisis. Secretary General U Thant replied that there could be no partial withdrawal—either all peacekeepers must go or none. On May 18 Egypt requested the complete removal of the U.N. Emergency Force (UNEF), and within three days Egyptian forces occupied positions vacated by the United Nations in the Sinai and in Sharm el-Sheikh, which overlooked the Straits of Tiran. Nasser closed the straits on May 23.

Eshkol and the general staff ordered a partial mobilization on May 16 and ordered an iterated progressive mobilization every day from May 16 through May 19 (Parker 1996, 7). This decision required the calling up of reserves, putting considerable stress on the Israeli economy and society as the dispute dragged on. Once again, the cabinet retroactively approved the decision.[23] When Nasser closed the Straits of Tiran the following day, the Israeli cabinet began discussing the feasibility of a preemptive strike. Foreign Minister Meir of Israel had categorically stated in 1957 that any closing would be viewed as an act of war. Clearly, the hard-line tactics adopted by Nasser were uniting Israeli officials behind an aggressive foreign policy.

From the closing of the straits on May 23 until the Israeli decision to attack on June 4, the cabinet struggled with the decision whether or not to initiate violence against Egypt. Although hard-liners claimed Egyptian actions displayed hostile intentions and justified an immediate attack, most members of the cabinet sought to exhaust all peaceful measures. Norms of peaceful conflict resolution still dominated the cabinet even at this late date (Oren 2002, 99, 121, 124).

The cabinet's aversion to initiating hostility was demonstrated by its plan to force Egypt to fire the first shot. The cabinet ordered an Israeli boat crew to be flown to Massawa, Ethiopia, in order to sail a ship through the Egyptian blockade of the Straits of Tiran (Brecher 1980, 139). However, the Israeli military halted the plan because of fears that it would jeopardize the surprise attack. Other democratic leaders, such as President Lyndon Johnson and President Charles De Gaulle, also stressed the importance of not being the state to initiate hostility. When Israel protested, quite correctly, that a blockade was an act of war according to international law, De Gaulle responded that initiation meant firing the first shot. At that point France instituted an arms embargo against all parties in the hopes of dampening the escalation of conflict. Ironically, De Gaulle's arms embargo actually encouraged Israel to initiate violence; the expected lack of spare parts for its mostly French-built air force meant Israel was capable of fighting only a very short war. The need for a short war immensely increased the benefit of going first.[24] De Gaulle's policy encouraged the exact outcome he sought to avoid.

By May 30, it became clear that international efforts to rectify the situation were doomed to failure; despite Israeli pleas, no great power naval flotilla was forcibly going to open the straits. On the same day, King Hussein of Jordan signed a defense agreement with Egypt, placing Jordan's forces under Egyptian command. Simultaneously, Jordan invited the Iraqi government to send a combat division into Jordan. Facing tremendous pressure to act, Eshkol formed a National Unity government on June 1, 1967. The cabinet was enlarged with the appointment of Moshe Dayan (Rafi) as defense

minister and Begin (Gahal) and Y. Saphir (Gahal) as ministers at large. The
unity government shifted the balance in the cabinet toward the hard-line
camp and removed the more moderate Eshkol from the position of minister of defense. Moreover, by bringing the opposition camp into the government, all parties would be responsible for any subsequent failure. Without
an opposition group to promote an antigovernment frame, the likelihood
that the ruling elite would be punished declined precipitously.

On June 4, 1967, the Israeli cabinet voted in favor (eighteen to two) of a
preemptive strike against Egypt the following day. Two United Workers
Party (Mapam) members reserved the right to consult party members; their
parties' subsequent approvals meant that the vote to use force was unanimous.
On June 5, Israel destroyed the Egyptian air force and launched a ground attack in the Sinai. However, Israel did not strike preemptively against Jordan
and Syria. Israel indicated to Jordan through U.N. intermediaries that if Jordan did not initiate hostilities, no Israeli action would be forthcoming. Nevertheless, both Jordan and Syria initiated hostilities, and Israel immediately
responded with force. In the course of six days, the Israeli victory was complete. Israel captured Gaza and the Sinai from Egypt, the West Bank and East
Jerusalem from Jordan, and the Golan Heights from Syria.[25]

In summary, the monadic argument leads one to predict that Israel would
not have been the first to use force during the 1967 crisis. In theory, its prime
minister was constrained by factions within his ruling party, a coalitional
government with five parties, and a bare majority in the Knesset. However,
Israel chose to fire the first shot. The case study reveals why Israel was not
constrained in a manner predicted by the model.

First, the Israeli case clearly demonstrates that democratic or constraining institutions do not bind decision makers if opposition does not exist at
the termini of the institutional channel (for example, in the legislature or
cabinet). The fact that the opposition parties of Gahal and Rafi were more
aggressive than the ruling coalition implied that the democratic system actually made conflict more likely rather than less likely. Eshkol was forced toward a more militant stance by the aggressive opposition position.

Second, Israel faced adversaries that had previously used force against it
and openly called for its elimination. Therefore, the history of the dispute
shaped perceptions. Egyptian actions in May 1967 were, quite reasonably,
interpreted as movement toward an Egyptian surprise attack. Although the
U.S. military did not believe Egypt was planning a surprise attack, the concentration of forces and removal of peacekeeping troops clearly made this a
possibility. Moreover, Egyptian support of Palestinian raids from Jordan and
Syria indicated that force was being used against Israel just prior to the crisis in May. Given this situation, Israel's behavior does not seem radically at

odds with the reciprocity-oriented strategy upon which the monadic democracy peace proposition is built.

Although the case deviated from predictions, Israel's behavior was consistent with the monadic argument in several ways. First, Israel attempted to negotiate a settlement prior to the use of force. Although the mobilization of the Israeli military limited the duration over which negotiations could be held, moderate members of the cabinet demanded that Israel exhaust all noncoercive strategies before using force. These attempts appear to have been sincere, despite the fact that some members of the unity government openly stated they would come to naught.

Second, the formation of a unity government appears to conform with the logic of the constraint argument. Just as with the war cabinets in the United Kingdom during the world wars, the unity government brought the opposition into the decision-making process. This technique reduces the costs of being the first to use force because the opposition is unlikely to exploit a failure when it too is accountable for the decision. The action also sends a clear signal to the adversary about the seriousness of the issue for the democratic polity (Schultz 2001).

TURKEY, GREECE, AND CYPRUS AND THE 1974 INVASION OF CYPRUS

The island of Cyprus has long been a source of conflict between Greece and Turkey. The 3,572-square-mile island located in the eastern Mediterranean is inhabited by a Greek-Cypriot majority (80 percent) and a Turkish-Cypriot minority (18 percent).[26] The heterogeneous population and the competing historical claims of ownership by Greece and Turkey have led to both domestic ethnic clashes and international crises in the post–World War II period. Both before and after independence, a majority of Greek-Cypriots desired unification with Greece, or "enosis." Turkish-Cypriots, fearing that unification would result in the destruction of Turkish culture and/or the expulsion of the Turkish community, responded with demands for partition of the island and unification of the Turkish sector with Turkey proper, or "taksim." However, the fact that the Turkish minority was spread throughout the island at independence made implementing this option very difficult. Finally, a third segment supported an independent republic with strong guarantees for the political and economic rights of the Turkish minorities. This domestic-international conflict exploded into violence four times in the postwar period: 1954 through 1959, 1963 through 1964, 1967, and 1974. For the purposes of this study, the final episode is the most important. In 1974 a democratic regime in Turkey initiated a massive use of military force to resolve the international conflict.[27]

From 1571 to 1878, Cyprus was a province in the Ottoman Empire.[28] In 1878 the sultan leased the island to the United Kingdom in exchange for British support against Russian encroachment on the declining empire. In 1914, when the Ottoman Empire joined the Central Powers, Britain annexed Cyprus. British repression of the island's traditional authority, the Orthodox Church of Cyprus, fueled opposition to colonial rule and increased demands for enosis (Markides 1977, 8). Calls for some form of independence accelerated after World War II as the decolonization movement gathered force around the globe. Although Britain approved institutional changes designed to provide greater local control, it consistently opposed enosis, which was favored by an overwhelming majority of the Greek-Cypriot community. In 1955 a pro-enosis terrorist group led by Colonel George Grivas initiated a campaign of violence against British rule. Over the next four years, EOKA (National Organization of Cypriot Fighters) activities claimed the lives of 104 British servicemen (Clodfelter 1992, 979) and led to a series of negotiations that for the first time opened the delicate subject of independence. Although the 1955–59 rebellion was primarily a Greek-Cypriot versus British affair, the realization that the departure of the British was imminent triggered the rise of a more militant Turkish-Cypriot community and focused Turkish attention on the fate of the island. In 1960, with the independence of Cyprus, the scope of the dispute(s) shifted as the United Kingdom receded from the scene. Over the next fourteen years, growing internal ethnic conflict triggered an external Greece-Cyprus conflict. This conflict, in turn, contributed to the Turkey-Cyprus dispute. Finally, together the disputes fueled the ongoing and purely external Greek-Turkish conflict.

The Zurich-London agreements, which formed the basis of the post-independence political system, were composed of three primary elements: the Basic Structure of the Republic of Cyprus, the Treaty of Guarantee, and the Treaty of Alliance.[29] The Basic Structure agreement laid the foundation for the 1960 constitution, which institutionalized power sharing between the two ethnic groups in all three branches of government. The executive was composed of a Greek-Cypriot president and a Turkish-Cypriot vice president, both of whom possessed veto powers; the council of ministers was to have a ratio of seven Greek to three Turks. The unicameral legislature was to be composed of 70 percent Greek-Cypriots and 30 percent Turkish-Cypriots, elected by universal suffrage within each communal group. The federal system also provided each community with a communal chamber that controlled issues relating to religion, culture, and education. The supreme constitutional court was to be composed of one Greek-Cypriot, one Turkish-Cypriot, and a chief justice chosen from a neutral country.[30] Finally, the civil service was to be composed of 70 percent Greek-Cypriots and 30 percent Turkish-Cypriots. Turkish-Cypriots welcomed the new arrangement, but the Greek-Cypriots openly rejected the accord, which was imposed on the majority group by outside powers (Britain, Turkey, and Greece) and gave the minority power disproportionate to its population (that is, 30 percent of legislative seats for a group that made up 18 percent of the population).

The Treaty of Guarantee made the United Kingdom, Greece, and Turkey responsible for the territorial and constitutional integrity of the island. The Treaty of Alliance gave Greece and Turkey the right to station 950 and 650 troops, respectively, on the island. The forces were distinct from the 2,000-troop national Cypriot army (composed of 1,200 Greek-Cypriots and 800 Turkish-Cypriots). The treaties of guarantee and alliance provided the mechanism with which Turkey justified its intervention in 1974.

The constitution, which was designed to ensure the rights of the minority, proved to be unworkable; governmental gridlock between 1960 and 1963 prevented the government from acting on the most pressing issues. In November 1963, President Makarios proposed thirteen constitutional amendments designed to end the impasse. The Turkish government and the Turkish-Cypriots protested the move, claiming the proposal violated the London–Zurich accords. In December 1963, communal violence flared after Greek-Cypriot police clashed with Turkish-Cypriots. The violence, which continued throughout 1964 and led to Turkish invasion threats, triggered four important changes on the island.[31] First, 6,500 U.N. peacekeeping troops were dispatched to Cyprus in May 1964; U.N. troops have remained there to this day. Second, the ethnic violence led to the migration of the Turkish minority into heavily armed enclaves located throughout the island. The Greek-Cypriot–controlled national government, which was unable to extend its authority into the enclaves, instituted an economic embargo against them. Third, the Turkish-Cypriots refused to participate in the government. Although the Greek-Cypriots left the boycotted seats open, the walkout signaled a complete breakdown of the 1960 constitution and left the Greek-Cypriots in complete control of all national legislation. Fourth, the legislature passed a bill creating a Cypriot national guard composed of conscripted soldiers. Although intended as a compromise measure designed to aid in the control of irregular Greek-Cypriot forces, the National Guard quickly became linked to enosis and the Greek military. Grivas, the leader of the EOKA movement in the 1950s, became commander of the new military force. More important, between 1964 and 1967 approximately 10,000 Greek soldiers were secretly seconded to the National Guard.

A new wave of communal violence engulfed the island in 1967, after Turkish-Cypriots refused the Greek-Cypriot police passage through an enclave. Turkey once again threatened to invade if the Turkish minority was not protected and the excess Greek soldiers were not removed from the island. The return of Grivas to Greece on November 19 failed to diffuse the crisis. The reply of the military government in Greece to the Turkish demands was publicly rejected by the government of Turkey on November 22, 1967. The growing probability of conflict between the two NATO allies led to a round of shuttle diplomacy by U.S. diplomat Cyrus Vance. Vance's skillful negotiating, together with the realization that Turkey was not bluffing about invading, led to an agreement on December 3 that called for (1) the removal of excess Greek troops; (2) Turkish demobilization; (3) mutual pledges to respect Cypriot independence; (4) an increase in the power of peacekeeping forces; and (5) a demobilization of local forces, including the National Guard (Wiener 1980, 157). Although the Turkish government hailed the accord as a complete victory, no firm guarantees were put in place to prevent the Greek government or the Greek-Cypriots from returning to an enosis strategy. Moreover, even the specific terms of the agreement were not upheld because the National Guard was never demobilized.

In the post–1967 period, militant supporters of enosis began to increasingly clash with moderates such as President Makarios, who believed the hard-line policy would lead to a Turkish invasion and permanent partition of the island. The elections of 1970 indicated that the majority of the Greek-Cypriot electorate adhered to the Makarios position rather than the militant line. In the early 1970s, the militants began a guerrilla campaign against both moderates and the Turkish-Cypriot community. The military government in Greece increasingly supported the EOKA-B guerrilla group, which was, like its predecessor in the 1950s, led by Grivas. On July 2, 1974, Cypriot President Makarios demanded the removal of Greek officers assigned to the National Guard, accusing them (correctly) of encouraging the EOKA-B movement and plotting to overthrow his government (Ertekun 1981). The Greek military junta replied to the letter with military force—ordering the National Guard to overthrow the constitutionally elected Makarios government.[32] The coup occurred on July 15, 1974; Makarios fled to Malta aboard a British air force plane. The following day Nicos Sampson, a former member of the EOKA-B organization, was installed as president of Cyprus. The seizure of power by an obviously pro-enosis individual supported by the military junta in Greece immediately triggered a crisis for Turkey.

Turkish Prime Minister Bulent Ecevit immediately flew to London to discuss implementing the Treaty of Guarantee. The British declined to participate in any military operation, hoping to resolve the conflict through diplomatic means. Despite U.S. attempts to peacefully resolve the dispute between the two members of NATO, Turkey invaded Cyprus on July 20 with a force that eventually reached close to 40,000 troops. Although the Greek actions violated both the Zurich–London agreements and the U.N. Charter, which prohibits the interference in the domestic affairs of other states, the unilateral resort to force by Turkey against the newly installed Sampson regime represented a first use of force by a democratic government.[33]

The application of the monadic model requires specifying if Turkey was a democracy in 1974. The answer appears to be a qualified yes; the qualification stems from the active role played by the military throughout the country's modern history. The modern state of Turkey was founded by Mustafa Kemal (also known as Attaturk) after the disintegration and partition of the Ottoman Empire following World War I. Kemal ruled the state through a single political party (Republican People's Party [RPP]), which was dominated by the charismatic leader. The democratization process began after Kemal's death in 1938. The first multi-party elections, which took place in 1946, led to the emergence of the first opposition party in modern Turkish history; the Democratic Party captured 61 of the 465 seats in the Turkish Grand National Assembly. In 1950 the Democratic Party secured an overwhelming majority in the legislature, and Turkey experienced its first peaceful transition of power under democratic institutions. However, growing domestic unrest coupled with increased repression by the ruling party triggered a coup by the armed forces in 1960. The military, which had been designated guardians of the constitution under Attaturk, ruled through the thirty-eight-member Committee of National Unity until civilian politics could be reestablished. General Gursel became president, prime minister, and defense minister during the transitional regime.

After several political reforms, including a new constitution and the barring of several former party leaders from politics, elections were held in 1961. The indecisive results, shown in Table 3.5, led to a series of unstable coalition governments. However, the elections of 1965 and 1969 produced a strong majority for the right-of-center Justice Party, led by Suleyman Demirel. By 1971, growing domestic violence, economic turmoil, and legislative gridlock led to a second military intervention on March 12, 1971 (the so-called "coup by memorandum"). Demirel was forced to resign (although permitted to remain in the legislature), and a government of technocrats was established under the leadership of Nihat Erim. Although the military did not actively run the government, it was able to dictate the formation of governments and the passage of politically repressive policies. The continual threat of military intervention began to recede only in 1973, when a compromise candidate was elected president in March and when the general elections were held in October.[34]

The election of 1973 failed to produce a majority government as the mil-

TABLE 3.5

Seats in the lower house of the Turkish Grand National Assembly, 1961–73

Political parties	1961 election	1965 election	1969 election	1973 election
Republican People's Party	173	134	143	185
Justice Party	158	240	256	149
(new) Democratic Party	★	★	★	45
New Turkey Party	65	19	6	★
Republican Peasant Nation Party	54	★	★	★
National Party	★	31	6	0
National Salvation Party	★	★	★	48
Other parties	0	26	39	23
Total	450	450	450	450

S O U R C E : Nyrop (1979, 216).

N O T E : The military intervened in domestic politics in 1960–61 and 1971–72. The Justice Party was originally composed of members of the banned (old) Democratic Party. The Republican Peasant Nation Party became the National Party in 1962. The (new) Democratic Party was a splinter group from the Justice Party. An asterisk (★) indicates that the party did not compete in the election.

itary had hoped. Moreover, the ideological and personality differences between the parties made forming a coalition government extremely difficult. A caretaker government was forced to rule from October 1973 to January 1974, when a Republican People's Party–National Salvation Party coalition government was finally formed. The unusual coalition teamed the secularist party of Attaturk with the pro-Islamic National Salvation Party. Republican People's Party leader Bulent Ecevit became prime minister, and National Salvation Party leader Erbakan became deputy prime minister; the coalitional cabinet was composed of eighteen representatives of the Republican People's Party and seven representatives of the National Salvation Party. The ideologically ill-suited coalition was in power for six months when the 1974 Cyprus crisis broke out.

According to the monadic version of the democratic peace model, the existence of democratic institutions and opposition within the executive and legislative branches should have deterred Ecevit from being the first to resort to force. The model fails to predict events in Turkey during the 1974 crisis for four reasons: (1) opposition parties not objecting to the use of force, (2) the history of Greek and Greek-Cypriot violations of accords, (3) the belief that the intervention was in compliance with international law; and (4) U.S. indecision.

A coalitional executive and large legislative opposition did not constrain Ecevit from using force because all major groups, from the left to the right of the political spectrum, favored the use of military force. After a two-hour party meeting, the deputy chairman of the largest opposition party, the right-of-center Justice Party, reported:

> The Justice Party believes that in view of the current conditions Turkey is more than ever before in need of national unity and solidarity. Those who doubt our nation's full unity [in the face of] national problems are mistaken. The Justice Party Parliamentary Group has unanimously decided to vote in favor of giving the government special powers on the Cyprus questions [should] the government seek such powers. (Foreign Broadcast Information Service, hereafter FBIS 1974, Q6)

The leftist Confederation of Revolutionary Workers Unions also issued a statement supporting the government's policy: "Our confederation supports the firm stand taken by the government in connection with recent developments. We fully approve of the government's desire for a peaceful solution and its reservation of military intervention as a last resort" (FBIS 1974, Q6). Upon news of the invasion on July 20, the leader of the Democratic Party, Ferruh Bozbeyli, stated: "Today marks the beginning of another page in the glorious history of our beloved nation. We applaud the firm and determined attitude of our republican government and armed forces against those who completely ignored the rights of neighborliness, peace and humanity" (FBIS 1974, Q8). Finally, Deputy Prime Minister Erbakan, leader of the junior partner in the ruling coalition, stated on the day of the invasion:

> We see in the hearts of the cheering crowd in front of the prime minister's office now that we have taken the most appropriate decision in regard to Cyprus. We are greatly satisfied by this. As the Council of Ministers, all we did was to reflect the feelings of the people. We do not have the least doubt that the same decision would have [been] taken if 40 million—the whole population of Turkey—were in the same hall. (FBIS 1974, Q8)

On the day before the invasion, the Turkish parliament formally gave the executive the power to resolve the crisis, including initiating military force. Shortly after the announcement of the intervention on July 20, the Grand National Assembly unanimously approved the use of force to occupy northern Cyprus. In sum, there was no opposition from within the executive or the legislature.[35]

As in the Israeli case, the decision to intervene in 1974 cannot be understood without regard for the history of the dispute. From Turkey's perspective, it had pursued diplomatic rather than military solutions to the dispute in the previous two crises. However, in each case the agreements were subsequently violated by both the Greeks and the Greek-Cypriots. In 1963–64 and 1967, both the public and opposition parties called for a use of force to "permanently resolve" the issue. Yet the prime ministers at the time (Inonu and Demirel) opposed resorting to force until all other options had been exhausted. In 1964 Inonu resorted to minor uses of force (air strikes) only after seven months of negotiation and delay; the use of force proved to be quite effective, for a settlement was reached within days. In 1967 Demirel decided to mobilize an invasion force, which proved enough to force Greece to withdraw its military contingent from Cyprus. In contrast, in 1974 Ecevit, believing that temporary cease-fires would only be violated by the Greek/Greek-Cypriot opposition, almost immediately resolved to use force; upon his return from a day trip outside of Ankara and before meeting with his cabinet, Ecevit ordered the military to begin planning for an invasion (Wiener 1980, 269).[36] Ecevit was not more prone to violent solutions than previous leaders; he simply believed that given history, Turkish-Cypriot rights would continue to be violated until Turkey established a strong military presence on the island.[37]

The government of Turkey also believed that the military intervention was justifiable according to international law. As Ecevit stated in his public address on the morning of the invasion,

> Turkey is fulfilling its legal responsibility through this operation. The Turkish Government has resorted to armed action after all other ways failed to produce a result. This is not an invasion. This is an operation against the invasion. This is not an aggression but it is an operation to terminate aggression. (FBIS 1974, Q16)

The Greek-backed overthrow of Makarios was a violation of international law, the London-Zurich agreements, the 1960 Cypriot constitution, and the 1967 Vance Accord. The pre-independence treaties gave Turkey (as well as Greece and the United Kingdom) the right to ensure that no outside entity overthrew the constitutional framework of the new republic: "[E]ach of the three guaranteeing powers reserves the right to take action with the sole aim of re-establishing the state of affairs established by the present Treaty." Although U.N. Resolution 353 called for the removal of all foreign troops, the international community in general blamed Greece for triggering the crisis. Greek complicity in the coup and British aversion to military action led the Turkish government to act unilaterally to restore the status quo.[38]

Finally, U.S. indecision encouraged the Turkish government to act immediately. The Nixon administration, nearing the end of the Watergate scandal, failed to warn Turkey against invasion as previous administrations had in 1964 and 1967. Moreover, the Nixon administration appeared to be debating whether the deposed Makarios government or the new Nikos Sampson government was the legitimate government of Cyprus. Hints that the U.S. government was preparing to recognize the Sampson government appear to have been the final stimulus for Turkey's decision (Couloumbis 1983, 88–91; Bahcheli 1990, 97–99; Laipson 1986, 68–69).[39]

Conclusions

The analysis in Chapter 2 demonstrates that within the context of *militarized crises*, democracies are more peaceful only with other democracies. In contrast, the analysis in this chapter demonstrates that within the broader context of *international disputes*, democracies are generally less likely to use aggressive force to resolve conflicts. Many disputes involving democracies never escalate to the point in which military force is threatened or thought about. By focusing on the more restricted set of war and militarized crises, previous research has neglected the selection effect and underestimated the constraining powers of institutions.

Although this pacifying effect of institutions is powerful, it is not all encompassing. The balance of military forces, which is traditionally used by realists to explain state behavior, remains a significant predictor of the use of force. However, the monadic and dyadic impact of democracy does not disappear when democratic polities have a significant military advantage, as predicted by Bueno de Mesquita and colleagues. Given that Reiter and Stam (1998) find that democracies are much more likely to win conflicts because they are very careful about picking their opponents, why aren't they more likely to initiate against the weak? I believe the answer has three causal elements. First, within democratic dyads, using force against other democracies may be viewed as a failure in foreign policy even if the weak democracy is quickly vanquished (Mintz and Geva 1993). Second, domestic political opposition plays a more powerful role than the balance of military power. That is, although opposition support will allow a democracy to enter an evenly matched battle, strong domestic opposition will reduce the probability of initiation even when in a position of strength. Third, the calculation of the probability of victory includes more than just raw military power. National morale, government unity, alliance support, international permission, and so on all play a role in how quickly a democracy can win on the battlefield.

Although democratic institutions dampen aggressiveness generally, the Israeli and Turkish cases demonstrate that institutions alone are not sufficient for constraint. Belligerent behavior by an adversary can undermine the power of soft-liners and strengthen the hand of hard-liners at home. The evaporation of opposition to the use of force decreases the costs of employing military power. Whereas democracies are less likely to use force initially, once force has been used in the dyad, democracies appear to behave no differently from nondemocracies. The results cannot be viewed as conclusive given the instability of the selection model using my data sets, but they strongly suggest that constraint evolves over the course of the conflict.

What are the implications of the analysis for research on the relationship between regime type and war? First and foremost, the field needs to place much greater emphasis on models that allow coefficients to vary over the life of the conflict. Selection models and survival models should become commonly used in the democratic peace literature. Second, research needs to place domestic opposition at the center of the analysis. In particular, quantitative and formal models must incorporate domestic opposition in a more sophisticated fashion. The quantitative analysis in the following chapter and the simulation model in Chapter 7 take the first steps in this direction. Finally, the field needs to explore all stages of the selection process simultaneously (peaceful dyad to dispute to crisis to war).

APPENDIX 3.1

Dispute Data Set—223 International Conflicts

Europe

Albania v. Yugoslavia 1960–88	Soviet Union v. Poland 1979–82
Austria v. Italy 1960–71	Soviet Union v. Sweden 1980–85
East Germany v. West Germany 1960–88	Soviet Union v. U.S. 1960–72
Greece v. Albania 1960–71	Spain v. U.K. 1960–88
Greece v. Cyprus 1971–74	Turkey v. Bulgaria 1960–72
Greece v. Turkey 1960–88	Turkey v. Cyprus 1974–88
Hungary v. Romania 1960–88	West Germany v. Netherlands 1962
Ireland v. U.K. 1960–88	Yugoslavia v. Austria 1974–78
Soviet Union v. Czechoslovakia 1968–69	Yugoslavia v. Italy 1960–75
Soviet Union v. Norway 1960–88	

Africa

Algeria v. France 1977	Mauritius v. U.K. 1980–88
Algeria v. Mauritania 1975–79	Morocco v. Algeria 1962–88
Algeria v. Spain 1964–88	Morocco v. Mauritania 1960–70
Angola v. Rhodesia 1975–79	Morocco v. Spain 1960–88
Belgium v. Zaire 1960–70	Mozambique v. Rhodesia 1975–79
Botswana v. Rhodesia 1969–79	Mozambique v. South Africa 1975–88
Botswana v. South Africa 1969–88	Portugal v. Zaire 1966–68
Burundi v. Rwanda 1962–88	Senegal v. Portugal 1965–75
Cameroon v. Nigeria 1981–88	Somalia v. Ethiopia 1960–88
Cameroon v. U.K. 1960–64	Somalia v. France 1960–77
Chad v. Nigeria 1960–88	Somalia v. U.K. 1960–62
Chad v. Sudan 1965–68	— Somalia v. Kenya 1963–81
Comoros v. France 1975–88	South Africa v. Angola 1975–88
Dahomey v. Nigeria 1960–65	South Africa v. Swaziland 1977–88

APPENDIX 3 . 1 *(continued)*

Ethiopia v. U.K. 1960 – 62
— Ethiopia v. Kenya 1963 – 70
Ethiopia v. France 1960 – 77
Ethiopia v. Sudan 1983
Gabon v. Congo 1960 – 64
Gabon v. Equatorial Guinea 1972 – 75
Gabon v. Nigeria 1967 – 69
Ghana v. Nigeria 1965 – 67
Ghana v. Upper Volta 1963 – 67
Guinea v. Portugal 1965 – 75
Italy v. Ethiopia 1960
Ivory Coast v. Ghana 1981 – 82
Ivory Coast v. Guinea 1965 – 67
Lesotho v. South Africa 1966 – 88
Liberia v. Sierra Leone 1983
Liberia v. U.K. 1960 – 61
Libya v. Gambia 1980
Libya v. Senegal 1981 – 83
Madagascar v. France 1960 – 88
Malawi v. Mozambique 1982 – 86
Malawi v. Portugal 1964 – 75
Mali v. Mauritania 1960 – 65
Mali v. Upper Volta 1960 – 88
Mauritania v. Spain 1960 – 76

South Yemen v. Saudi Arabia 1969 – 78
Spain v. Equatorial Guinea 1968 – 79
Sudan v. Uganda 1979 – 86
Tanzania v. Kenya 1977 – 83
Tanzania v. Malawi 1964 – 69
Tanzania v. Portugal 1965 – 75
Togo v. Benin 1975 – 78
Togo v. Ghana 1960 – 88
Tunisia v. Algeria 1962 – 70
Tunisia v. France 1960 – 63
Uganda v. Israel 1976
Uganda v. Kenya 1976, 1987
Uganda v. Tanzania 1971 – 79
Zaire v. Angola 1975 – 88
Zaire v. Burundi 1964 – 66
Zaire v. Congo 1964 – 66
Zaire v. Rwanda 1967 – 68
Zaire v. Zambia 1979 – 88
Zambia v. Malawi 1981 – 88
Zambia v. Portugal 1965 – 75
Zambia v. Rhodesia 1964 – 79
Zambia v. South Africa 1972 – 88
Zimbabwe v. Botswana 1980 – 88
Zimbabwe v. South Africa 1979 – 88

America

Argentina v. Chile 1960 – 88
Argentina v. Paraguay 1960 – 62
Argentina v. U.K. 1960 – 88
Brazil v. Paraguay 1973 – 79
Canada v. Denmark 1973 – 88
Chile v. Bolivia 1962 – 88
Colombia v. Panama 1962
Costa Rica v. Nicaragua 1960, 1978 – 81
Cuba v. Bolivia 1966 – 70
Cuba v. Dominican Republic 1960, 1973 – 75
Cuba v. Guatemala 1960 – 66
Cuba v. Haiti 1960
Cuba v. Mexico 1961 – 62
Cuba v. Venezuela 1960 – 69
Dominican Republic v. Peru 1962 – 63
Dominican Republic v. Venezuela 1960
Ecuador v. Peru 1960 – 88
El Salvador v. Honduras 1960 – 80
Guatemala v. U.K. 1960 – 81
— Guatemala v. Belize 1982 – 88

Guatemala v. Mexico 1961 – 62
Haiti v. Dominican Republic 1963
Honduras v. U.S. 1960 – 71
Mexico v. U.S. 1962 – 70
Nicaragua v. Colombia 1979 – 88
Nicaragua v. El Salvador 1980 – 88
Nicaragua v. Honduras 1960 – 61, 1980 – 88
Panama v. U.S. 1960 – 77
U.K. v. Netherlands 1960 – 65
— Guyana v. Netherlands 1966 – 75
— Guyana v. Surinam 1976 – 79
U.S. v. Chile 1971 – 74
U.S. v. Cuba 1960 – 88
U.S. v. Grenada 1981 – 83
U.S. v. Haiti 1967 – 68
U.S. v. Jamaica 1973 – 81
U.S. v. Nicaragua 1980 – 88
Uruguay v. Argentina 1960 – 73
Venezuela v. U.K. 1960 – 66
— Venezuela v. Guyana 1967 – 88

Asia

Afghanistan v. Pakistan 1960 – 88
Australia v. Indonesia 1973 – 74
Burma v. Pakistan 1960 – 66

Indonesia v. Portugal 1974 – 88
Japan v. China 1960 – 88
Japan v. Soviet Union 1960 – 88

(continued)

APPENDIX 3.1 (*continued*)

Asia	
China v. Afghanistan 1960–63, 1980–88	Malaysia v. China 1975–88
China v. Burma 1960, 1967–71	Malaysia v. Singapore 1965–66
China v. India 1960–88	Malaysia v. Thailand 1979–88
China v. Indonesia 1960–65	North Korea v. South Korea 1960–88
China v. Mongolia 1960–87	North Vietnam v. Cambodia 1960–74
China v. Nepal 1960–61	— Vietnam v. Cambodia 1975–88
China v. Pakistan 1960–63	North Vietnam v. Laos 1960–75
China v. Philippines 1960–88	North Vietnam v. South Vietnam 1960–75
China v. Portugal 1960–88	North Vietnam v. Thailand 1961–88
China v. South Vietnam 1960–75	Papau New Guinea. v. Indonesia 1983–88
China v. Soviet Union 1960–88	Philippines v. Malaysia 1961–88
China v. Taiwan 1960–88	Soviet Union v. Afghanistan 1978–88
China v. U.K. 1960–88	Taiwan v. Burma 1960–61
China v. Vietnam 1976–88	Thailand v. Cambodia 1960–82
India v. Bangladesh 1973–88	Thailand v. Laos 1975–88
India v. France 1960–62	Vietnam v. Malaysia 1979–88
India v. Nepal 1960–64	U.S. v. Afghanistan 1980–88
India v. Pakistan 1960–88	U.S. v. Cambodia 1975
India v. Portugal 1960–74	U.S. v. New Zealand 1979–81
India v. Sri Lanka 1983–84, 1988	U.S. v. North Korea 1960–88
Indonesia v. Malaysia 1960–66, 1979–82	U.S. v. North Vietnam 1962–75
Indonesia v. Netherlands 1960–62	

Middle East	
Egypt v. Israel 1960–88	Libya v. Sudan 1972–85
Egypt v. Jordan 1960–65	Libya v. Tunisia 1970–88
Egypt v. Sudan 1960–88	North Yemen v. U.K. 1960–66
Egypt v. Syria 1961	— North Yemen v. South Yemen 1967–88
Iran v. Bahrain 1979–88	Oman v. United Arab Emirates 1974–88
Iran v. Kuwait 1980–88	Qatar v. Bahrain 1971–88
Iran v. Saudi Arabia 1980–88	Saudi Arabia v. Israel 1960–88
Iran v. U.K. 1960–70	Saudi Arabia v. United Arab Emirates 1971–85
Iran v. U.S. 1979–81	Saudi Arabia v. U.K. 1960–70
Iraq v. Iran 1960–88	— Saudi Arabia v. Oman 1971–75
Iraq v. Israel 1978–88	Saudi Arabia v. North Yemen 1962–68
Iraq v. U.K. 1960	South Yemen v. U.K. 1969–70
— Iraq v. Kuwait 1961–88	— South Yemen v. Oman 1971–80
Israel v. Lebanon 1969–88	Syria v. Jordan 1966–73, 1980–88
Jordan v. Israel 1960–88	Syria v. Iraq 1961–63, 1975–80
Jordan v. Saudi Arabia 1960–65	Syria v. Israel 1961–88
Libya v. Chad 1969–88	Syria v. Lebanon 1969–88
Libya v. Egypt 1974–88	Syria v. Saudi Arabia 1970–71
Libya v. Israel 1969–88	Turkey v. Iraq 1960–74
Libya v. Jordan 1984–88	U.S. v. Libya 1973–88

Sensitivity Analysis Displaying Results with the Inclusion of Additional Control Variables

The monadic and dyadic democratic peace variables remain statistically significant even after including these control variables. On the dangers of including too many variables in a model, see Achen (2002).

Independent variable	Coefficient	Standard error	T-ratio
Actor's net democracy (monadic)	−0.029★★★	0.008	3.58
Actor's net democracy with			
democratic opponent (dyadic)	−0.030★	0.017	1.77
Opponent's net democracy	0.009	0.006	1.54
Balance of forces	−0.101	0.120	0.85
Shared alliance ties	0.014	0.083	0.17
Satisfaction with the status quo	−0.740★★★	0.095	7.78
Democracy with weak opponent	0.062	0.217	0.28
Democracy with weak democracy	−0.072	0.668	0.11
Great power	−0.489★★	0.157	3.122
Interdependence	−1.161	1.384	0.839
GDP per capita	0.0000003★★★	0.00000009	3.83
International trade	−0.000	0.000	0.46
Contiguity	−0.217★	0.090	2.41
Nuclear weapons	0.113	0.195	0.58
Similarity of UN voting	−0.072	0.077	0.93
Peace years	−1.176★★★	0.083	14.12
Spline 1	−0.119★★★	0.120	9.90
Spline 2	0.027★★★	0.003	8.18
Spline 3	−0.001★★	0.001	3.00
Constant	0.963★★★	0.181	5.31

NOTE: Number of observations = 4,265. Log likelihood at convergence = −778.003. Results calculated with STATA 6.0 and robust standard errors. Some coefficients appear as 0.000 or −0.000 in the table due to rounding. All significance tests are one-tailed. ★p < .05, ★★p < .01, ★★★p < .001.

Notes

1. I refer to the MID data set as a "crisis" data set, despite its official name, because force is threatened by at least one party in every instance. I use the term *dispute* to include all cases of conflict, even those that never escalate into a crisis.

2. The two data sets do not overlap perfectly because the dispute data set includes only the years 1960–88 whereas the crisis data set stretches from 1918 to 2000. Were the temporal domain of the dispute data set expanded back in time to 1918, there would be extensive overlap between the data sets. The scope of the effort involved in creating the dispute data set makes such an expansion impossible at this time.

3. The Cuban Missile Crisis is coded as a U.S.-Soviet dispute, with Cuba supporting the Soviet Union.

4. The natural unit of analysis for a crisis data set is the crisis itself (e.g., the Bay of Pigs or the Suez Crisis). In contrast, the natural unit of analysis for the dispute data set is a cross-sectional time series (e.g., the United States and Cuba from 1960 to the present). The different units of analysis make linking the two data sets inherently difficult.

5. Although I find Huth and Allee's argument persuasive, some researchers do not accept this position. Kacowicz (1995) argues that democracies are more satisfied than other states and therefore less likely to become involved in disputes. Also see Werner (2000).

6. Due to the death of Frank Sherman, this data set has not been widely used in the literature. Although Sherman completed his identification of disputes, he did not complete the codings for all the variables in his study. I am able to use his data set because I am relying only on his list of international disputes; all variables used in the following analysis were developed by me or drawn from a third source.

7. The crisis data set used in the last chapter contains only three purely economic or maritime boundary disputes: the 1980 Libyan threat to Malta and the 1973 and 1975 cod wars between Iceland and the United Kingdom. The Libya-Malta case involved Libyan naval forces boarding a commercial oil exploration platform. The Iceland-U.K. cases, mislabeled wars, involved a fishing dispute triggered by the British failure to recognize Iceland's unilateral extension of its territorial waters. In this case, both sides made a show of force by sending warships to patrol the waters; Iceland technically initiated violence when one of its patrol boats fired over the bow of a British fishing boat.

8. Although the dispute runs from independence in 1947 to the present, only the years 1960 to 1988 fall within the scope of this study.

9. In any particular test in subsequent chapters, the number of observations will be slightly below this total due to missing data.

10. The use of four- or three-category versions of this dependent variable produces similar results. The four-category version contains the following scale: (4) massive (more than 10,000 troops), (3) major (1,001–10,000 troops), (2) minor (1–1,000 troops), and (1) no use of force. The three-category version combines the two highest levels.

11. As discussed in the preceding chapter, the substantive significance of variables in an ordered probit model cannot be determined by simply comparing the size of coefficients in the equation. Marginal analysis is required to isolate the effect of a change in an independent variable on the probability of using aggressive force. The marginal impact of each independent variable is calculated while holding constant all other independent variables at either their modes (for categorical variables) or means (for continuous variables). For this data set, the baseline categories are as follows: the state is mildly autocratic, its opponent is mildly autocratic, the two antagonists are evenly matched in terms of military forces, the state is dissatisfied with the status quo, and no alliance tie exists between the two states.

12. For the sake of clarity, predicted probabilities will be referred to using a per-

cent sign (%) while a change in the predicted probability from X to Y will be referred to as a "Z-percentage-point change."

13. In the cases where there were many operationalizations for the same variable (e.g., alliance similarity), only one has been included in order to minimize multicolinearity. The statistically insignificant variables were also insignificant when added individually.

14. I have chosen to present the temporal controls in the sensitivity analysis rather than the main tables because the creators of the technique warn that their method is not appropriate in all circumstances. In my dispute data set, the mean length of the time series is ten years, and the range is from one year to twenty-nine years. The skewed nature of the distribution implies that a majority of my panels are less than ten years. Beck, Katz, and Tucker (1998, 1262–63) state that the panels should be about twenty years and that "our proposed method would not work with datasets with very small T's." Other corrections, such as the latent dependent-variable model proposed by Jackman (2000; Beck et al. 2001), also require panels that are longer than those in my data set.

15. For a complete treatment of both approaches, see Beck, Katz, and Tucker (1997).

16. Although the use of the cubic spline correction has become common, it is not without its critics (e.g., Gowa 1999, 58).

17. Using a five-point change rather than a two-point change in the democracy index produces similar results.

18. I want to thank Will Reed for providing me the data set and command files used in his paper. Kinsella and Russett (2002) also examine a selection model using event count data (e.g., COPDAB, WEIS, and PANDA) for the dependent variable in the selection equation and MID involvement as the dependent variable in the outcome equation. As with much of the work by Russett and his colleagues, the authors employ a dyadic unit of analysis with an involvement dependent variable. Whereas the event count data come closest to identifying a set of "disputes," the uneven coverage of the data sets is problematic. In 120 of 745 cases, the authors observe the impossible: a 0 on the selection equation and a 1 on the outcome equation. Kinsella and Russett simply recode the selection dependent variable for these 120 cases (2002, 1058). Although they find a modest selection effect, it does not alter the impact of the dyadic democracy variable, which is negative and statistically significant in both equations. Huth (1996) examines a selection model with three stages of conflict (initiation, escalation, and settlement) using a set of territorial disputes.

19. The Six Days' War case study was developed using the following sources: Michael Brecher, *Decisions in Crises: Israel, 1967 and 1973* (Berkeley: University of California Press, 1980); Michael B. Oren, *Six Days of War: June 1967 and the Making of the Modern Middle East* (New York: Oxford University Press, 2002); Chaim Herzog, *The Arab-Israeli Wars: War and Peace in the Middle East from the War of Independence to Lebanon* (London: Arms and Armour Press, 1982); Walter Laquer, *The Road to War 1967: The Origins of the Arab Israel Conflict* (London: Weidenfeld and Nicolson, 1968); Howard M. Sachar, *A History of Israel: From the Rise of Zionism to Our Time* (New York: Knopf, 1979).

20. As discussed in Chapter 2, Bueno de Mesquita and Lalman contend that preemption could in theory explain the historically large number of democracy-autocracy conflicts.

21. In contrast, the 1956 war was more of a preventative war in which Israel initiated action to destroy Egyptian military power. The 1967 war differed from Israeli attacks on Lebanon in 1978 and 1982 because in the latter cases Israel was responding to a first use of force by guerrillas. Prior to the 1967 war, Egypt was not supporting guerrilla activity from its territory.

22. The following discussion draws heavily on Brecher (1980). Brecher's detailed case study provides a wealth of information concerning political opposition and the decision to use force.

23. The term *retroactively* should not be taken to imply that Eshkol dictated decisions to the cabinet. Eshkol's decision-making style emphasized consensus building. He appears to have communicated with cabinet members individually, ensuring a strong majority, before making decisions. However, the rapidly moving crisis demonstrates how collective bodies, even small cabinets, have a difficult time managing decision making.

24. The majority of Israel's 286 first-line aircraft were French-built Mystere and Mirage Mark III planes (Clodfelter 1992, 1041). For similar, but not identical figures, see Young (1967, 44).

25. Although I have not considered Lebanon a war participant in the Six Days' War, its behavior in relation to the democratic peace arguments is interesting. According to some observers and measures, Lebanon had a democratic government until at least the outbreak of the civil war in 1976. Although the distribution of seats was determined by religious sect (e.g., Maronite Catholic thirty, Sunni Muslim twenty, Shia Muslim nineteen), political competition for votes within the sects was often intense. In 1967, Lebanon sent a single plane into combat, and it was shot down by the Israelis. The constraint model would postulate that the factionalized government was incapable of action despite the fact that many, if not a majority, supported the use of force by the Arab states.

26. Figures are according to the 1960 census. Although no censuses have been taken since that date, most observers estimate that the split remains roughly the same today.

27. The Cyprus case study was developed using the following sources: Feroz Ahmad, *The Turkish Experiment in Democracy, 1950–1975* (London: Royal Institute of International Affairs, 1977); Kyriacos C. Markides, *The Rise and Fall of the Cyprus Republic* (New Haven, CT: Yale University Press, 1977); Sharon A. Wiener, *Turkish Foreign Policy Decision-Making on the Cyprus Issue: A Comparative Analysis of Three Crises* (Ph.D. dissertation, Duke University, 1980); Eric Solsten (ed.), *Cyprus: A Country Study* (Washington, DC: U.S. Government Printing Office, 1993); Henry Kissinger, *Years of Renewal* (New York: Simon & Schuster, 1999).

28. Greece was also part of the Ottoman Empire until its rebellion, beginning in 1821, resulted in independence in 1828. Greek historical claims date from the Mycenaean migrations and the Byzantine age (300–1192 A.D.). Frankish and Venetian rulers occupied the island between the Byzantine and Ottoman periods (Markides 1977, 3).

29. The texts of the conference agreements and subsequent accords can be found in Ertekun (1981).

30. The original agreement called for a four-member high court; this was revised to a three-member court in the 1960 constitution (Ertekun 1981, 149; Solsten 1993, 166). The first neutral judge was a German.

31. The democratic Turkish government used minor levels of force in the crisis when it ordered the air force to strike Greek-Cypriot forces attacking Turkish-Cypriot villages. The democratic leader of Greece in 1964, George Papandreou, a longtime supporter of enosis, also wanted to use military force by fulfilling Makarios's request for air support. However, the limited range of Greek aircraft was insufficient to sustain combat time over Cyprus (Bahcheli 1990, 64).

32. The coup was led by Grivas's successors because the general had died of natural causes earlier in the year.

33. The coding of the case is complex due to the trilateral nature of the dispute. I have coded Greece as using minor levels of force to overthrow Makarios, and Turkey as having used major levels of force to overthrow Sampson. The Treaty of Guarantee states that Greece, Turkey, and the United Kingdom agreed to respect the Basic Articles of the Constitution and "undertake to prohibit, so far as concerns them, any activity aimed at promoting, directly or indirectly, either union of Cyprus with another State or partition of the Island." Moreover, should a crisis arise and consultations fail to resolve the conflict, "each of the three guaranteeing Powers reserves the right to take action with the sole aim of re-establishing the state of affairs created by the present Treaty" (Ertekun 1981, 159–60).

34. The last two presidents (Gursel and Sunay) had been former chiefs of the General Staff. The military candidate for president in 1973 was Chief of the General Staff Faruk Gurler. However, party leaders rejected Gurler, and a compromise candidate, retired Admiral Fahri Koruturk, was elected president. Although the president's power is limited (e.g., restricted veto power and chair of the National Security Council), the military's control of the position sent a clear message to all parties that the military was willing to safeguard the constitution.

35. Wiener (1980) argues that some cabinet members initially expressed opposition to the use of force. However, the opposition parties' public statements prior to and during the crisis supported intervention and partition. Moreover, other sources (Ahmad 1977) state that some of the supposedly "reluctant" ministers supported intervention wholeheartedly.

36. The exact position of the military during the crisis is somewhat unclear. Institutionally, the president is commander and chief of the armed forces and chairman of the National Security Council. In 1974 President Koruturk headed the National Security Council, which was composed of Prime Minister Ecevit, Chief of the General Staff Semih Sancar, the service commanders, and other cabinet ministers. By all accounts, both the prime minister and the military leaders agreed that an invasion was necessary. However, I have found no source that examines policy debates within the National Security Council prior to the use of force.

37. Unlike previous crises, Turkish-Cypriots were not under attack when the prime minister and his cabinet discussed using force to resolve the crisis. However,

Ecevit believed that the coup made enosis inevitable in the long run and that this policy would come at the expense of the Turkish community.

38. Legal support for the Turkish position seriously eroded in August 1974, when a second Turkish offensive in response to failed negotiations led to its control of over 30 percent of the island and the de facto partition of Cyprus. The treaties allowed intervention to restore the status quo; the second offensive was not aimed at this objective.

39. Kissinger (1999, 239) rejects this argument. He contends that preserving NATO's eastern flank was the most important consideration for the United States. Therefore, the U.S. policy was largely successful because it prevented a war between two NATO allies.

CHAPTER 4

Institutional Constraint Versus Regime Type

THE PRIOR TWO CHAPTERS, as well as the democratic peace literature in general, have focused on the relationship between regime type and international conflict. The objective has been to determine if democracies are less likely to use military force in general or less likely only when facing other democracies. Whereas earlier works tended to use simpler dichotomous measures of regime type (in other words, a state is either a democracy or it is not), more recent analyses have employed a continuum ranging from extremely autocratic to fully democratic. Most of these continuums or indices relied on the Polity databases developed by Gurr and his colleagues.

This latest line of research can be challenged from two perspectives. First, the heavy reliance on the Polity data sets calls into question the robustness of the results. The accessibility of the Polity data sets coupled with the difficulty associated with independently creating alternative measures for a similar time period has led to this overdependence.[1] Just as engineers at the National Aeronautics and Space Administration (NASA) build redundant systems in which all critical systems have one or more independent backup systems, social scientists must focus on redundancy and independence in order to ensure robustness.[2] The overreliance on the Polity data sets raises an important question: is the convergence in findings in the democratic peace literature due to the use of the same (and perhaps idiosyncratic) data source?[3]

Second, the democratic peace literature implicitly (or explicitly) assumes a perfect correlation between institutional constraint and regime type.[4] That is, all democratic leaders face institutional constraint whereas all autocratic leaders do not. Several authors have attacked this assumption (Peterson 1996; Elman 1997b; and Hagan 1993), arguing that the imperfect correlation between constraint and regime type opens the door for democratic hawks and autocratic doves. By erroneously grouping diverse regimes within a single category, whether it be "democracy" or "autocracy," we run the risk of underestimating the impact of institutions on external behavior.

This chapter addresses both the overreliance on the Polity data sets and the assumption that constraint and regime type are perfectly correlated by developing an alternative framework: the institutional constraint model. The new constraint variables have been constructed completely independent of standard inventories such as the Polity data sets; the theoretical framework and the operationalization of the variables are based on the premise that constraint can emerge in certain autocracies and wane in certain democracies.

The Institutional Constraint Model

The institutional constraint model assumes that domestic political opposition exists in all political systems. However, the extent to which this opposition is allowed to express itself varies significantly across political systems. Whereas democratic institutions allow the emergence of opposition, many autocratic rulers also face political opposition that has the power to punish, or even remove, the decision maker (Peterson 1996; Gowa 1995; Hagan 1993; Morgan and Campbell 1991; Salamore and Salamore 1978). King Hussein of Jordan has long confronted both latent and actual opposition from his Palestinian subjects. Siad Barre, the military dictator of Somalia after 1969, was initially confronted by opposition within the military junta and continually forced to balance competing clan interests. Even within a more institutionalized regime, Nikita Khrushchev faced intense opposition at least until his purge of the Politburo in 1957. In much of the democratic peace literature, the great variation among autocratic regimes is obscured by the use of dichotomous variables, which compels researchers to group many very different types of regimes into a single category. In order to more fully comprehend the relationship between external violence and regime type, a more careful disaggregation of the broad categories of democracy and authoritarianism is needed.

The predictions of the institutional constraint model are derived from four basic assumptions.

ASSUMPTION 1
A central goal of state leaders is to retain their position of domestic political power. In order to remain in power, state leaders must rely on a supporting constituency.

ASSUMPTION 2
Domestic political opposition operates, to various degrees, in all political systems. Domestic opponents of a regime will attempt to mobilize political

opposition when domestic and foreign policies pursued by the regime have failed to achieve stated policy goals.

ASSUMPTION 3
Leaders of states with institutional structures that encourage the emergence and expression of domestic opposition in the executive, legislature, ruling party, and/or society at large are more likely to be punished for foreign policy failures.

ASSUMPTION 4
In all political systems, state leaders believe that a foreign policy setback for their country that stems from a diplomatic retreat or military defeat could pose a threat to their domestic political position.

The assumptions lead to the central hypothesis of the institutional constraint model: leaders of constrained states will be less likely to initiate armed violence to resolve international conflicts. The logic directly parallels that of the structural explanation of the democratic peace, with one important exception: the level of domestic opposition can vary across both democracies and autocracies. Although some democracies have a great deal of political opposition throughout the executive and legislature (Elman 1997b), some autocratic leaders are also very constrained from initiating violence on a large scale (Peterson 1996). The strength of the constraint model is twofold. First, the model allows a differentiation of the broad and diverse category of states traditionally lumped in a "nondemocracy" category. Second, the framework aids the identification of situations in which we can expect to find relatively unconstrained and belligerent democracies.

How does one define *constraint*? Given that foreign policy decisions are primarily made by the executive branch, this chapter focuses on how other groups and institutions in society influence executive decisions. For the purposes of this study, executives are considered constrained to the degree that they must take the preferences of other groups into account during the decision-making process. This position implies that constraint occurs only if there are differences in preferences between key groups. If all groups in society have the same preferences and the executive acts according to those preferences, the idea of constraint has no real meaning. Decision makers are considered unconstrained if they are able to act without any regard for the preferences of other societal actors. For example, suppose that society consists of two actors: an executive decision maker with preferences of A $>$ B $>$ C (in other words, A is preferred to B, etc.) and a legislature with preferences C $>$ B $>$ A. If the decision maker is able to choose policy A without any costs, he or she is considered unconstrained. The higher the costs imposed on the decision maker for choosing a policy that deviates from the

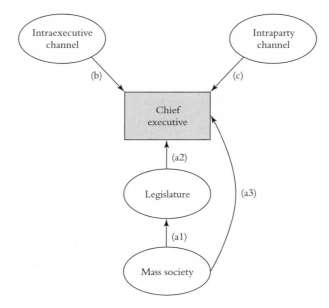

FIGURE 4.1. Potential constraint channels

preferences of other actors, the greater the constraints on the decision maker. Institutional structures play a vital role in this process because structures create *channels* through which other actors impose costs on decision makers; that is, institutions influence the probability that the decision maker will be punished for failure.[5]

Figure 4.1 displays how institutional structures create channels that can be used by opposition groups to impose costs on decision makers. The figure identifies three institutions through which societal groups can potentially have important influences on foreign policy decision making: the legislature, the executive, and the ruling party. In a fully constrained regime, all channels are open. In less constrained regimes, the institutional channels either do not exist or fail to function properly. For example, in an unconstrained regime, the legislature cannot impose costs on the executive for choosing policies that deviate from its preferences—in other words, channel (a2) does not exist. Similarly, if political parties are so weak that populist leaders can ignore them with impunity, the chief executive is not constrained through this channel—in other words, channel (c) does not exist.

The legislative institutional channels connect mass society directly to the chief executive through the legislature. The openness of these channels determines the degree of inclusiveness of the political system. Inclusiveness measures the extent to which societal groups are included in the political process (Dahl 1971). In a completely inclusive regime, all societal groups are incorporated into the political process. A partially inclusive regime may incorporate some economic classes but exclude the working class, or incorporate some ideological groups but exclude communists. A totally exclusive regime has no links from mass society to the chief executive or the legislature. The degree of inclusiveness varies across democracies and authoritarian regimes as well as over time within any particular regime. In the United Kingdom, the expansion of the vote in 1832, 1867, 1884, and 1918 increased the inclusiveness of the regime as the properted middle class, and then the working class, were incorporated into the political process. The addition of these groups into the process constrained the executive because the preferences of the newly included groups had to be considered in any foreign policy decision. After 1884, a portion of the working class had a channel to impose costs on decision makers who acted contrary to its interests.

The legislative channel can be regulated through a variety of institutional mechanisms that allow political systems to escape an "included versus excluded" dichotomy. In some regimes, votes are openly weighted in the aggregation process. These regimes explicitly reject the one-person-one-vote philosophy. A historical example of weighted voting is the three-tiered voting system used in Prussia before 1918. All voters were divided into three classes based on taxes paid to the government. Each group then elected one-third of the legislature. The system resulted in the wealthiest segment of the population having much larger voting weights (Koch 1984). Another common technique for weighting votes is multiple or plural voting rights. Obviously, the more votes one is given, the greater the weight of that voter in the aggregation process. For example, in the United Kingdom the landed aristocracy (and university professors) maintained the right to multiple votes. Plural voting rights in Britain were very important through 1918 and were not completely eliminated until 1948 (Therborn 1977, 8). Similarly, in Belgium from 1893 until 1918, middle-aged males of properted families received three votes whereas others received only a single vote (Therborn 1977, 12). In all three examples, institutional rules regulated the openness of the channels from mass society to the government.

The legislative channel also runs from the legislature to the chief executive (that is, link a2). This link is the cornerstone of democratic theory. The greater the power of the legislature, the easier it is to punish the executive for selecting policies that diverge from the preferences of the legislature. It is clear that both society-legislature and legislature-executive links are required for the legislature to be a highly constraining institution. If the legislature has no ability to regulate executive behavior, then universal suffrage in legislative elections will have no political impact. Conversely, political systems that severely restrict participation are unlikely to elect a legislature that has preferences radically different from those of the chief executive.

Historically, the openness of channel (a2) has varied greatly across both authoritarian and weakly democratic regimes. A historical example of a weak legislature in the area of foreign policy is Imperial Germany. The kaiser, an unelected executive, was only weakly constrained in the area of foreign policy and possessed almost total control over the military. Imperial Germany is especially interesting because legislative power varied greatly across issue areas, from relatively strong for domestic political issues to almost nonexistent for foreign policy issues. A second example comes from Japan in the 1930s. The strength of the legislature rose after World War I with the emergence of the truly competitive two-party system. However, following the assassination of the prime minister in 1932, the legislature lost the power to appoint both the prime minister and the cabinet (Beasley 1990).

Link (a3) connects mass society directly to the chief executive. Although this link does not exist in most parliamentary systems, the channel typically exists in presidential systems in the form of direct voting for the president. Presidential systems strengthen mass control, but they tend to weaken the power of the legislature over the executive by eliminating votes of no confidence. A number of countries have hybrid structures (such as the French fifth republic) that mix elements of presidential and majoritarian systems (Lijphart 1984).

The second major institutional channel focuses on intraexecutive competition, a dimension along which political systems differ enormously. Some political systems, such as presidential systems, severely curtail or eliminate competition within the executive. U.S. presidents are very unlikely to confront individuals or coalitions with sharply divergent preferences actively competing for control of foreign policy. Unlike the situation found in many parliamentary systems, U.S. presidents are not forced to confront opposition parties in the cabinet. Although the president's cabinet appointments are approved by the Senate, the candidates must be nominated by the president. Moreover, should opposition emerge over time, the president is free to remove the individual.[6]

In contrast to the case of extremely weak intraexecutive competition found in presidential systems stands the very constrained chief executive found in Switzerland. According to the Swiss model, the chief executive position is rotated among the seven members of the Federal Council on a yearly basis. In this collegial system, the current chief executive has no ability to dictate policy over the wishes of the remaining six members of the council. Falling between these extremes are systems that allow factions to compete for authority within the executive. An informal case would be the Politburo in the Soviet Union after the death of Stalin. Leaders such as Nikita Khrushchev were very conscious of the ability of opposition factions in the Politburo to inflict costs following policy failures. A more formal system of intraexecutive competition can be found in Lebanon. According to the 1943 unwritten "national pact," a Christian Maronite always serves as president while a Sunni Muslim always serves as prime minister. Although the president appoints the prime minister, the fact that the two individuals represent societal groups with very divergent preferences implies that all presidents can expect competition from within the Lebanese cabinet.[7]

The third major institutional channel focuses on the relationship between the ruling party and the chief executive. Strong political parties limit the probability that opposition to the chief executive policies will emerge. In contrast, political parties that have formal or informal factions aid the development of opposition. The formal split in the Afghanistan Communist Party, which included the Khalq and Parcham wings, increased the probability of opposition to the chief executive. Similarly, the coalitional National Opposition Party (UNO) headed by Violeta Chamorro in Nicaragua lacked the political power to constrain virtually independent parties within the umbrella organization. The variance in party power also occurs within more consolidated democratic political systems. The strong party system in the United Kingdom severely constrains party members from openly opposing party leaders. Renegade members of the Tory Party face a number of potential sanctions, including removal from ministerial positions, loss of access to parliamentary order papers, limited committee assignments, and ultimately expulsion from the party (Garner and Kelly 1998; Budge et al. 1998).[8] Conversely, in the United States, political parties have very few instruments that can be used against deviant members. The existence of weak parties implies that within a party, opposition can easily develop.

In summary, the institutional constraint model hypothesizes that the presence of domestic opposition within the executive, legislature, or ruling party raises the potential costs of using force for decision makers, therefore reducing the probability that the leader will initiate violence to resolve an international dispute.

RECENT RESEARCH

There have been a handful of recent studies in the international relations literature that have attempted to move beyond the Polity data sets for measuring institutional constraint. Reiter and Tillman (2002) examine public, legislative, and executive constraint on the initiation of violence by democracies. After examining the behavior of thirty-seven democratic states from 1919 to 1992 using a regression model, they conclude that (1) democracies with inclusive electoral systems are less likely to initiate in a crisis, (2) democracies with strong legislative control over treaty ratification are less likely to initiate, and (3) democracies with various types of semi-presidential systems are less likely to initiate. The Reiter and Tillman work is an important contribution to the literature, but it examines only democracies and the crisis stage of conflict. In contrast, the institutional constraint model examines domestic opposition within all types of states, explores the issue using a new data set of disputes, and employs a new *Aggressive Use of Force* dependent variable.

Auerswald (2000) also examines institutional constraint within democratic polities. Using two dichotomous dimensions of constraint (accountability and agenda control), he divides presidential and parliamentary democracies into one of four categories. Auerswald predicts that coalitional parliamentary democracies, which face severe accountability and possess only partial agenda control, will be the most constrained type of democracy. He examines his hypotheses using two historical case studies, Suez (1956) and Bosnia (1995). Unlike the work of Schultz (2001) or the institutional constraint model presented below, Auerswald's theoretic framework neglects the variation of domestic opposition within a single structural type. Thus, the United States is coded as moderately constrained (minimal accountability and partial agenda control) due to constitutional checks on whether or not the president's party controls Congress.[9] The institutional constraint model discussed in this chapter measures opposition to the chief executive on a yearly basis using more diverse measures of intraexecutive and legislative constraint.

Ireland and Gartner (2001) employ a hazard model to explore the conflict propensity of various types of democracies. Assuming that all democracies share similar norms, their decision to focus only on democracies allows them to isolate the impact of structures. They predict that minority governments should have longer durations of peace compared to single-party majority or coalition cabinets. Ireland and Gartner find that minority governments are less likely to initiate a use of force in an MID (that is, level 4 or 5 on the five-point MID scale). Contrary to expectations, coalitional governments were no more violence prone than single-party majority governments.

Ireland and Gartner restrict their focus to a particular type of democracy: parliamentary. Thus, presidential systems such as the United States are consciously excluded from their analysis. Although there are legitimate reasons for these decisions, it is impossible to generalize from an examination of eighteen parliamentary democracies to other types of states. In contrast, the model developed in this chapter examines institutional constraint within the executive across both autocracies and democracies.

Prins and Sprecher (1999) also reject the standard practice of lumping all democracies into a single, all-encompassing category. They argue that institutional variation among democracies should influence their foreign policy behavior. Moreover, the authors claim, as do Reiter and Tillman (2002), that norms cannot explain variation among democracies. Prins and Sprecher examine differences in reciprocation among three types of democracies: single-party majority, coalition, and minority governments. As was found in chapters 2 and 3, Prins and Sprecher find that nondemocracies tend to target democratic polities. They also find that democracies are more likely to reciprocate when they are targeted by nondemocracies. Surprisingly, they find that coalitional democracies are more likely to reciprocate than are single-party majority democracies. They argue that the absence of a unitary actor can actually reduce accountability, which traditionally restrains executives. The findings are not consistent with those of Ireland and Gartner (2001).

The institutional constraint test differs from the Prins and Sprecher study in several ways. First, it examines constraint within both democracy and autocracy. Second, it focuses on initiation rather than reciprocation. In Chapter 2 the results demonstrated that virtually all states reciprocate high levels of force. Finally, whereas Prins and Sprecher use the MID data set of militarized crises, the analysis below employs the broader set of international disputes.

Elman (2000) "unpacks" the democratic peace by exploring differences between presidential and parliamentary democracy using case studies of U.S. behavior in 1812 and Finnish behavior in 1940.[10] According to Elman, "The cases show that institutional constraints make war more likely when the legislature is the hawkish side (the U.S. case), while fewer institutional constraints make war more likely when the executive is more hard-line (the Finnish case)" (2000, 94). Elman's account stresses the variance in the preferences of actors and the role of ideological beliefs in the decision-making process. Although the case studies are well executed and important for theory building, her flat rejection of the monadic version of the democratic peace seems unwarranted given her nonrandom selection of a couple of cases and the probabilistic nature of monadic proposition. Moreover, if the legislature is typically more domestically oriented than the executive, we should see institutional constraint on average (see Appendix 2.1).

Finally, Clark (2000) predicts that a convergence in policy preferences between the executive and legislative branch will increase the frequency and duration of military disputes. He tests this hypothesis using event count and hazard models of the United States in the Cold War era and the MID data set. Convergence in preferences is measured in three ways: (1) a dummy unity government variable, (2) the average percentage of votes in favor of the president's position on domestic and foreign legislation, and (3) a dummy variable identifying severe incongruence (such as a Republican president and a Democratic House and Senate). Regardless of the measure employed, increasing convergence in preferences increases dispute involvement.

Although Clark's research design is innovative, the generalizability of the argument is limited for three reasons. First, he studies a single democratic country. Second, the measures he has developed are not useful for unicameral states (or countries such as Britain, in which the vast majority of power now resides in a single lower house). Third, the voting data include a wide variety of issues unrelated to the international conflict. As we saw in the case study of Ecuador and Peru in Chapter 2, opposition to domestic politics does not necessarily extend to the realm of international politics.

In summary, although the institutional constraint model discussed in this chapter examines many of the issues raised in these articles, it is unique in several respects. First, it examines institutional constraint such as coalitional governments across both autocracies and democracies. None of the studies discussed here take on this broader issue. Second, it employs a new data set of disputes, rather than the MID data set, which is used in *all* of the quantitative studies. Finally, the measurement of political opposition—such as the number of seats by the ruling party in the legislature—is both a more precise and more variable measure of opposition than those used in most of these studies.

VARIABLES AND SPECIFIC HYPOTHESES

The dependent variable used to test the following hypotheses is the *Aggressive Use of Force*. An *Aggressive Use of Force* involves the use of force, either by the regular military or proxy forces, across an international boundary. As explained in Chapter 3, this dependent variable is closely related to the ideal dependent variable (initiation of violence) while at the same time occurring relatively frequently in the pooled time-series data set. Given that sensitivity analysis has indicated that using the four-category version of the dependent variable (no use, minor use, major use, and massive use) produces virtually identical results to the dichotomous version of the variable (no use and use), the following analysis relies on the dichotomous variable, which is easier to calculate and present.

The institutional constraint argument is tested using four hypotheses:[11]

HYPOTHESIS I
States with coalitional executives are less likely to use aggressive force.

HYPOTHESIS 2

States with collective decision-making bodies within the executive are less likely to use aggressive force.

HYPOTHESIS 3

The larger the size of the ruling coalition, the more likely a state is to use aggressive force.

HYPOTHESIS 4

States with factional or coalitional ruling parties are less likely to use aggressive force.

The dichotomous *Coalitional Executives* for hypothesis 1 is coded 1 if the chief executive depends on the support of formally independent parties to remain in office and these parties are officially represented within the cabinet. Representation in the cabinet allows the opposition forces, in theory, to directly participate in major foreign policy decisions. Although political parties often declare that they support the prime minister, unless the party in question holds cabinet seats, it is not considered a member of the ruling coalition. An example of a coalition government is Belgium during the Eyskens administration (Christian Socialists and Liberal Party), which held office during the "Congo I: Katanga Crisis" in 1961. States without coalitional executives include the United States (all years), parliamentary systems such as the United Kingdom when a single party controls the cabinet, and a military regime under a single ruler such as Pinochet in Chile from 1974 to 1988.

Hypothesis 2 is tested using a dichotomous *Collective Decision-Making Executive* variable. Many states possess institutions that allow multiple individuals to participate in executive decision making. The constraint model hypothesizes that the inclusion of multiple actors in the decision-making process creates an institutional channel that allows for the punishment of decision makers for policy failures. Collective decision-making institutions typically take one of two forms: collective decision-making bodies or factions within the executive branch. In regimes with collective leadership, executive power is formally or informally dispersed among individuals. No single executive can dominate proceedings; all executives have some veto power over proposals. An example of formal collective leadership is Switzerland's rotating presidency. An example of informal collective leadership is Argentina under the military junta from 1976 to 1982. In regimes with factional divisions, the executive is formally or informally divided into competing factions. The decision maker must secure approval of the competing factions before implementing a policy. The factions tend to be fluid, and the chief executive faces the threat of removal at any time. An example of informal factional divisions is the Khrushchev administration in the Soviet

Union. An example of a more formal factional division is the People's Democratic Party of Afghanistan (PDPA) government in Afghanistan after the 1978 coup and before the purging of the Parcham members in 1979.

Decision makers can also be constrained by the presence of opposition groups in the legislature. In theory, legislatures in which chief executives are supported by only a minority of members should be more constraining than legislatures dominated or completely controlled by a single party. The *Size of the Ruling Coalition* variable used to test Hypothesis 3 is calculated by dividing the number of seats held by the ruling party and its supporters by the total number of elective seats in the legislature. Once again, the supporting parties must be formally represented in the cabinet in order to be added to the seats controlled by the ruling party. In cases in which the legislature is divided into two chambers, the lower chamber, which is typically the more powerful of the two, was selected for coding. In instances in which the chief executive did not belong to a political party, I estimated the size of the consistently "pro-government" forces. If the chamber contained nonelective seats (such as tribal chiefs or functional representation of societal groups such as "professionals"), these seats were excluded from the total number of seats unless it was clear whether the representatives were pro-government or anti-government.

Two examples illustrate coding of this variable. In Israel in 1960, although Ben Gurion's Mapai Party possessed only 47 of the 120 seats in the Knesset, the ruling coalition held a slight majority in the chamber with 69 seats. A second example comes from the United States in 1970, when President Nixon's ruling Republican Party controlled only 192 of the 435 seats in the House of Representatives; no ruling coalition existed.

Ruling parties vary in terms of cohesion. The constraint model predicts that the degree of cohesion influences decisions to use force. The more cohesive the ruling party, the less likely opposition is to develop from within the party itself. In cases of coalitional or factionalized parties, much of the opposition to the chief executive's policy emerges from within the party itself. The presence of opposition should reduce the likelihood that a chief executive will initiate a risky foreign policy. Regimes in which the chief executive leads a coalitional party or a factional party are coded as 1 on the *Factional Ruling Party* variable. A coalitional party implies that the regime is actually composed of a coalition of independent parties. These parties have independent headquarters, membership lists, and organizational hierarchies. An example of a coalitional party is the National Opposition Party (UNO), headed by Violeta Chamorro, which came to power in Nicaragua in 1990. Conversely, a factional party is one with formal or clearly recognized divisions. Factionalized parties can exist in both democratic and authoritarian

TABLE 4.1
Correlations between institutional constraint and Polity IV measures

	Polity IV actor's democracy index	Coalitional executive	Collective decision making	Size of ruling coalition	Factional ruling party
Polity IV actor's democracy index	1.00	—	—	—	—
Coalitional executive	0.44	1.00	—	—	—
Collective decision making	−0.25	−0.25	1.00	—	—
Size of ruling coalition	−0.76	−0.30	0.38	1.00	—
Factional ruling party	0.23	0.34	−0.07	−0.21	1.00

regimes. The Liberal Democratic Party in Japan and the Congress Party in India are coded as factionalized parties, as is the communist PDPA party in Afghanistan prior to 1979, with its Khalq and Parcham wings.

In addition to the institutional constraint variables, the model includes the three control variables that were operationalized in Chapter 2 and employed in chapters 2 and 3:

HYPOTHESIS 5
The more the balance of military forces tends to favor a state, the more likely it will use aggressive force.

HYPOTHESIS 6
States that share a military alliance tie with their opponent are less likely to use aggressive force.

HYPOTHESIS 7
States challenging the status quo are more likely to use aggressive force.

How much do the institutional measures developed in this project differ from the Polity democracy and autocracy indices used in the democratic peace literature? Table 4.1 displays the correlations between the 0–20 scale *Actor's Level of Democracy* index used in the previous two chapters with the institutional variables just described. The only strong relationship is between the *Size of the Ruling Coalition* constraint variable and the Polity IV *Actor's Level of Democracy* variable. Intuitively, this makes sense because the most heavily weighted component of the Polity democracy and autocracy indices is legislative constraint on the executive.

ANALYSES AND RESULTS

The multivariate results for the institutional constraint model using the set of international disputes from 1960 to 1988 are presented in Table 4.2. The hypotheses are tested using a probit model and the *Aggressive Use of Force*

TABLE 4.2

*Probit analysis using the aggressive use of force dependent
variable and the international dispute data set, 1960–88*

Independent variable	Coefficients and standard errors
Coalitional executive	−0.276**
	(0.096)
Collective decision making	−0.049
	(0.054)
Size of ruling coalition	0.669***
	(0.153)
No legislature	−0.247***
	(0.061)
Factional ruling party	−0.131*
	(0.066)
Balance of forces	0.396***
	(0.087)
Shared alliance ties	−0.052
	(0.058)
Satisfaction with the status quo	−0.727***
	(0.058)
Democracy with weak opponent	−0.102
	(0.103)
Democracy with weak democracy	−0.666*
	(0.314)
Constant	−2.345***
	(0.145)
Number of observations	5,509
Log likelihood at convergence	−1828.31

NOTE: Robust standard errors appear in parentheses below the coefficient estimates. All significance tests are one-tailed. *p < .05, **p < .01, ***p < .001. Estimated with STATA 6.0.

dependent variable; the dichotomous dependent variable is distributed as follows: (1) no use of force in 88 percent of the cases and (2) use of force in 12 percent of the cases (N = 5,509). The marginal impacts of the estimated coefficients are shown in Table 4.3.

In a probit model, the substantive significance of variables cannot be determined by simply comparing the size of coefficients in the equation. Marginal analysis is required to isolate the effect of a change in an independent variable on the probability of using aggressive force. The marginal impact of each independent variable is calculated while holding constant all other independent variables at either their modes (for categorical variables) or means (for continuous variables). For the institutional constraint model, the baseline categories are as follows: the chief executive does not rule through a coalition or collective body, the ruling coalition controls 82 percent of the seats in the legislature, the ruling party is unified, the two antagonists are

TABLE 4.3

Marginal effects of the estimated coefficients from the institutional constraint model

Shift in independent variables	Probability of using aggressive force	Shift in independent variables	Probability of using aggressive force
Coalitional executive		Balance of forces	
No	20	1:9	17
Yes	13	1:3	18
Total change	**−7**	1:1	20
		3:1	22
Size of ruling coalition		9:1	23
0%	8	**Total change**	**+6**
20%	10		
45%	13	Satisfaction with status quo	
60%	16	No	20
80%	19	Yes	6
100%	23	**Total change**	**−14**
Total change	**+15**		
		Balance of forces for democracies	
No legislature		Weaker or same	20
No	20	Much stronger	8
Yes	14	**Total change**	**−12**
Total change	**−6**		
Factional ruling party			
No	20		
Yes	16		
Total change	**−4**		

NOTE: See Table 2.3 for discussion of methodology. All statistically significant variables from Table 4.2 appear in this table. The marginal analyses were calculated using Clarify software (Tomz et al. 2003).

evenly matched in terms of military forces, the state is dissatisfied with the status quo, and no alliance tie exists between the two states.

As discussed in Chapter 3, the reader should keep in mind the skewed distribution of the dependent variable in the dispute data set: the aggressive use of force by any state is a relatively rare event. This rareness depresses the marginal impact of the variables. Although a shift in an independent variable may double the probability of using force, the associated shift in the predicted probability may be only from 10 to 20 percent. However, while a 10-percentage-point shift may appear slight in other contexts, I believe that given the rareness of the use of force, the doubling in the probability of using force implies a substantively important finding.

The first two variables in the institutional constraint model shown in Table 4.2 measure the amount of opposition found within the executive branch. The dichotomous *Coalitional Executive* variable identifies regimes with coalitional governments in which multiple parties are represented in the cabinet. The second variable identifies regimes that have some form of joint or collective decision-making body within the executive (for example, a politburo or multimember junta). Although the model predicts that both variables will be negative and significant, the results indicate that only the *Coalitional Executive* variable conforms to expectations.

The marginal analysis for the estimated coefficients in Table 4.3 indicates that shifting from a noncoalitional government to a coalitional government decreases the probability of using force by 7 percentage points. Specifically, the predicted probability of using force falls from 20% to 13%.[12] In contrast, the existence of joint decision-making bodies in the executive has virtually no effect on the probability of using aggressive force. Although the variable is negative as expected, it is not statistically or substantively significant.

The third variable in Table 4.2, *Size of Ruling Coalition*, examines legislative constraint on the executive. As predicted, the larger the size of the ruling coalition, the more likely a state is to use force. The statistically significant variable also has an important substantive effect. A shift in the size of the ruling party from 60 percent (a typical democracy) to 100 percent (a typical autocracy) increases the probability of using force by 7 percentage points (3 + 4). A shift from the lowest to the highest category increases the predicted probability of using force from 8% to 23%.

The fourth variable in the constraint model identifies states that have no legislatures during the year of dispute or at the moment in which violence is initiated by the state. The *No Legislature* variable implies that either no legislature has ever existed in the polity (such as Saudi Arabia all years) or the legislature was currently suspended during the year (for example, Argentina 1976–82). The variable must be included in the model to distinguish between two types of states in the data set: those countries in which the legislative exists but does not constrain chief executives and those countries that place no legislative constraint on the executive precisely because no legislature exists. States without legislatures cannot be coded as 0 for the *Size of Ruling Coalition* variable because this would imply that they are more constrained than democratic regimes. Therefore, this distinction is made by introducing an interactive term that multiplies the *Size of Ruling Party* variable by the *No Legislature* variable. An example is given in Table 4.4. Given that the interactive term is perfectly correlated with the *No Legislature* term, I simply refer to this variable as the *No Legislature* term. Although the operationalization is somewhat awkward, it allows estimating the model with all available observations; the model can be used to simultaneously compare autocratic regimes that have a legislature with those that lack such an institution.

The logic of the constraint argument would predict that those states without a parliament should be less constrained than those with a parlia-

TABLE 4.4
Example of interactive "no legislature" term

Country	Year	Ruling coalition	No legislature	Interactive term
Soviet Union	1960	1.00	0	0
Saudi Arabia	1960	1.00	1	1
United States	1960	0.55	0	0

ment. However, the results in Table 4.2 clearly indicate the opposite; the *No Legislature* variable is negative and strongly significant. The marginal analysis shown in Table 4.3 indicates that the lack of a legislature decreases the probability of using force by 6 percentage points.

An examination of the data provides some insight into this unexpected finding. In general, there are two types of regimes that do not possess legislatures: monarchies and military regimes. Of the 1,205 country-dispute years in the data set in which no parliament exists, monarchies account for 287 observations whereas military regimes account for another 758 observations. Typically, these military regimes have seized power in times of instability. Such regimes are unlikely to possess the capacity or the will to extract the resources from society required for a prolonged conflict (Andreski 1980). Similarly, it appears that monarchies are either small, weak states (such as Qatar and Bahrain) or lack the capability to mobilize resources (for example, Libya during King Idris's reign). Although there are obvious exceptions, such as the military regimes in Turkey and the monarchy in Saudi Arabia, instability and lack of capacity appear to explain the unexpected finding.

The fifth variable in the constraint model is *Factional Ruling Party*. The framework predicts that factional parties encourage within-regime opposition, which in turn should lower the probability of using aggressive force. Although the estimated coefficient is negative and statistically significant at better than the 0.05 level, the marginal impact of the variable is the weakest of the institutional constraint variables. The predicted probability of using any force falls from 20% to 16% with a shift from unified to factional.

Table 4.2 indicates that the *Balance of Forces* variable is positive and strongly significant. Consistent with prediction of realists, the more the military balance favors a state, the more likely it is to use force. A change from the most unfavorable to the most favorable balance of forces results in a 6-percentage-point increase in the probability of using force aggressively. What is interesting to note here is that contrary to the expectations of some realists, domestic political institutions such as the size of the ruling coalition play just as an important a role as a traditional realist power-oriented variable. Clearly, both external and internal factors shape decisions to use military force.

The *Shared Alliance Ties* variable, another realist variable incorporated to control for the existence of shared interests, is not statistically significant (B = −0.052; SE = 0.058). Sensitivity analysis indicates that including non-aggression pacts and ententes along with defense pacts has no impact on the results.

The next variable in the constraint model shown in Table 4.2 is *Satisfaction with the Status Quo*. The hypothesis predicts that the state challenging the status quo is more likely to use military force. The results strongly support this contention: the *Satisfaction with the Status Quo* variable is negative and statistically significant at better than the .001 level. The marginal impact analysis shows that the predicted probability of using force falls from 20% for a dissatisfied state to 6% for a satisfied state.

The final variables in the model in Table 4.2 are the interactive variables linking balance of forces and regime type. Although the selectorate model developed by Bueno de Mesquita and colleagues (2003) predicts positive coefficients for both variables, we find that the monadic variable is statistically indistinguishable from zero and the dyadic variable is negative. Contrary to the selectorate model, strong democracies do not pick on weak democracies.

In order to test the robustness of these findings, I conducted a large amount of sensitivity analysis. None of these analyses undermine the central conclusion drawn from the study of international disputes: constrained states are less likely to use aggressive force. The sensitivity analysis included adding a great-power variable, using a trichotomous dependent variable, including an economic interdependence variable, adding a GDP per capita variable, controlling for total international trade, controlling for geographic contiguity, including nuclear weapons, adding Bueno de Mesquita's alliance similarity variable (1981), including Signorino and Ritter's alliance similarity variable (1999), including a United Nations voting similarity variable (Gartzke 1998), using the COW balance of forces variable (troops, defense spending, iron and steel production, energy, urban population, and total population), adding quality to the balance of forces measure, using a cubic spline function for years at peace (Beck et al. 1997), and employing King and Zeng's (2001) relogit model for rare dependent variables.

The final sensitivity analysis involves including in a single probit model both the institutional constraint model and the democratic peace model from the previous chapter.[13] From a robustness perspective, this test is unnecessary. The results of the institutional constraint model demonstrate that the monadic findings from the previous chapter are not due to the use of the Polity data set. Using unique measures developed explicitly for this project, we find that institutional constraints reduce the likelihood of aggressive uses of force. However, from a competing model perspective, one might want to test one model versus the other. Although an examination of the estimated coefficients in the full model (shown in Appendix 4.1) indicates that the Polity variables are more stable, a nested test of the models reveals the full model is superior to either model by itself. Moreover, given that a nested test may be inappropriate in this situation (we might not expect variables such as the size of the ruling coalition to vary independent of the Polity IV level of democracy variable), a nonnested "J-test" was executed. This test also revealed that each model contributes uniquely to an explanation of the use of aggressive force. Thus, although the institutional constraint model should not be seen as a substitute for the democracy model, it does add some important information.

In summary, the quantitative analyses in this chapter clearly demonstrate that the findings in the democratic peace literature are not the product of overreliance on a single data source. The institutional constraint model reduces the likelihood of violence regardless of the regime type of the adversary. The case studies in this book, including the three democratic initiations discussed in the following section, indicate that the institutional constraint model does a much better job at capturing the *process* leading to decisions to use military force (that is, prospective constraint). In contrast, the less precise components of the polity democracy index (such as openness of executive recruitment) may adequately capture the power of democratic publics to punish decision makers for foreign policy mistakes (for example, retrospective constraints). By shifting the focus to the decision-making process, the institutional constraint model could fill an important gap between the quantitative and qualitative findings in the democratic peace literature.

Case Studies

The findings from the institutional constraint model are probed using three case studies. In the India versus Pakistan case involving the 1971 Bangladesh War of Independence, the analysis confirms the assertion that the degree of constraint varies considerably among democracies. The size of the ruling coalition, together with the structure of civil-military relations in India, insulated Prime Minister Gandhi from the public and the legislature to a far greater extent than the polity democracy model would lead one to expect. The El Salvador–Honduras conflict of 1969 represents a deviant case for both the constraint and the democracy model; as the opposition parties gained power in the political system, the territorial dispute exploded into war. Finally, the British intervention in the Russian Civil War sheds light on the weakness of the "coalitional" executive variable. Why, despite the existence of a coalition government, was the British government capable of initiating a large-scale use of force?

INDIA VERSUS PAKISTAN IN THE 1971 BANGLADESH INDEPENDENCE WAR

The Bangladesh War in 1971 was the third major India-Pakistan confrontation since both countries achieved independence from the United Kingdom in August 1947.[14] The immediate cause of the war was the ongoing civil war in East Pakistan (which was geographically separated from West Pakistan by 1,000 miles of Indian territory). Indian support of rebel forces led to numerous border clashes and ultimately the Pakistani attack on India on December 3, 1971. The subsequent fourteen-day war, fought on both eastern and western fronts, left 8,000 Pakistani and 1,500 Indian soldiers dead on the battlefield (Clodfelter 1992, 1104). The Indian-supported secession of Bangladesh from Pakistan forever changed the balance of power on the continent; Pakistan's population dropped from 125 million to 50 million, and India no longer had to continuously plan for a two-front war.

Motives for Indian Intervention

The former British colony of India encompassed the present-day states of India, Pakistan, and Bangladesh. The colony was extremely heterogeneous, containing a vast number of ethnic, religious, and language groups. The anti-British movement, which had united all these groups during the early struggle for independence, began to break up as independence approached following World War II. In particular, Muslims under the leadership of Mohammad Ali Jinnah's Muslim League increasingly feared becoming a permanent minority in a Hindu-dominated state. The Hindu-Muslim split led to the partition of the subcontinent; the predominantly Muslim areas became Pakistan (West and East) while the truncated state became India. Communal violence during and after partition resulted in the flight of twelve million individuals and the deaths of one million people.

Whereas border disputes led to the first two wars between India and Pakistan, in 1947–48 and 1965, the cause of the third conflict was primarily internal unrest in East Pakistan.[15] Although the vast majority of Muslims had supported Jinnah and the Muslim League during the partition phase, conflicts between East and West Pakistan quickly emerged. The more populous eastern state, which was inhabited by Bengalis (20 percent of whom were Hindu), chaffed under the political and economic dominance of West Pakistan. The language riots of 1952, which resulted from an attempt to make Urdu the sole official language of the entire country, highlight the conflict between the two parts. The inability of decision makers to resolve conflicts within a democratic structure led to the military coup in 1958 by Ayub Khan.

Ayub Khan's political program, which limited participation by all groups, temporarily suppressed demands for more autonomy in East Pakistan. However, the economic development program, which favored the West, widened the gap between the two regions—by 1970, average income in West Pakistan was 61 percent higher than in East Pakistan.[16] In the eyes of the Bengali inhabitants of East Pakistan, the Western-dominated political elite channeled export earnings from the East and virtually all foreign aid toward development projects in the West (Jackson 1975). The Awami League, led by Sheik Mujibur (Mujib) Rahman, claimed that East Pakistan had become an exploited colony of the West; the six-point Awami League manifesto, declared in 1966, demanded almost complete autonomy (except for defense and foreign affairs).[17]

Increasing unrest, particularly in Eastern Pakistan, led to Ayub Khan's replacement by fellow general Yahya Khan in March 1969. Later that year the new president declared that elections would be held as part of a transition to civilian rule. Interestingly, the elections were to be held under universal adult suffrage rather than by communal groups (that is, Muslims vote for a set number of Muslim seats, Hindus vote for a set number of Hindu seats, etc.). Although the number of western Muslims outnumbered the number of eastern Muslims, the total population of the East was higher due to the fact that 20 percent of the population in the East was non-Muslim. Voting by universal adult suffrage implied that Eastern leaders could conceivably capture power for the first time.

In the 1970 elections, Mujib's Awami League captured 167 of the 313 seats in the new parliament, including all but two of the eastern seats and none of the western seats. Zulfika Ali Bhutto's Pakistan People's party dominated results in the West. The results placed Yahya Khan in a quandary because both Bhutto and the military rejected Mujib becoming prime minister; Bhutto demanded constitutional agreements before the opening of Parliament. After several delays and extensive negotiation, on March 1, 1971, Yahya Khan postponed the meeting of Parliament indefinitely. Two days later, Mujib declared a general strike. Facing unexpectedly violent opposition, Yahya Khan backtracked and stated that the legislature would meet in late March. Mujib responded with a declaration of independence.

This open defiance by Mujib led to a massive crackdown on March 25, 1971, and to Mujib's arrest the following day. Although most military resistance was crushed by April, the operation triggered a massive flow of refugees into India. Over the course of several months, internal unrest resulted in the flight of millions of refugees (see Table 4.5). The number of refugees

TABLE 4.5
Refugees from East Pakistan living in India, 1971

Date	Number
April 21	250,000
May 6	1,480,000
May 21	3,400,000
June 15	5,800,000
October 31	10,000,000

SOURCES: Jackson (1975, 45); Gaan (1992, 93).

NOTE: International organizations generally agreed with these figures; Pakistani estimates were significantly lower.

and the scope of reported human rights violations triggered demands by the Indian legislature and the Indian public for decisive action.

Figure 4.2 summarizes the Indian motivations for intervention. The most immediate causes stemmed from the ongoing civil war in Pakistan. The conflict led to massive refugee flows and human rights violations. At a deeper level, the intervention was triggered by the hostile relationship with Pakistan since independence. Indian and Pakistan had several ongoing territorial disputes, including the conflict over Kashmir, which could erupt into full-scale war at any time. The partition of Pakistan would reduce Pakistani power, would eliminate the need to plan for a two-front war, and could advance the spread of democracy on the subcontinent.

Domestic Factors

Since Indian independence in 1947, the ruling Congress Party had dominated both houses of Parliament—the House of the People (Lok Sabha) and the Council of States (Rajya Sabha). The role played by the Congress Party in India's independence, together with Nehru's charismatic leadership, made the party virtually invulnerable. In the 1952 elections, Nehru's Congress Party captured 364 of 489 contested seats while the largest opposition party, the Communists, captured a mere 16. This pattern of domination continued through the next two elections (1957 and 1962). Only in the fourth general election, the first since Nehru's death in 1964, did the ruling Congress Party begin to appear vulnerable.

Indira Gandhi, who became prime minister following Lal Bahadur Shastri's death in 1966, led the Congress Party during the February 1967 elections.[18] As Table 4.6 shows, the Congress Party captured only 54 percent of the seats in the lower house. The party also lost control of nine of the seventeen state houses following these elections. Gandhi was further constrained by internal divisions within the party, which led to a formal split in

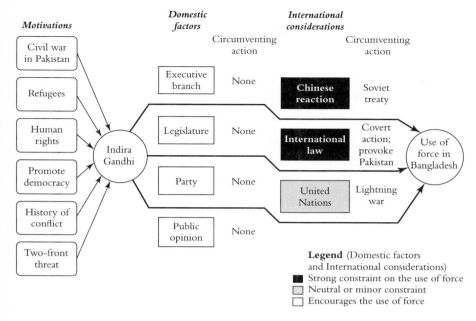

FIGURE 4.2. Institutional constraint on India in the Bangladesh War (1971)

late 1969; for the first time in history, the Congress Party required support of other political parties to pass legislation.[19]

The March 1–10, 1971, elections were a major test of the party split; for the first time, the voters were asked which faction best reflected their views. Quite unexpectedly, Gandhi scored a tremendous victory. The ruling Congress Party captured 350, or almost 68 percent, of the seats in the Lok Sabha. The added seats came at the expense of the opposition faction as well as socialist parties whose views closely paralleled Gandhi's. Just a week after naming a new cabinet, Gandhi was forced to deal with the East Pakistan crisis that escalated on March 25, 1971, with Yahya Khan's crackdown.

The immediate reaction of members of Parliament and the general public to the crackdown was a call to arms; a military intervention would have been strongly supported by the democratic public. However, Gandhi took a more cautious route. As her biographer stated, "With her massive majority in Parliament, Mrs. Gandhi could afford to ignore public pressure and tackle the problem in a cool and level-headed way" (Masani 1975, 237).

On March 31, 1971, both houses of Parliament unanimously passed a resolution condemning the military government of Pakistan for human rights violations and nullifying democratic elections. The resolution, which stated that India could not "remain indifferent to the macabre tragedy" occurring

TABLE 4.6

Seats held in the Indian parliament (Lok Sabha), 1967–71

Political parties	1967 Election	1970 at dissolution	1971 Election
Congress Party	283	—	—
Ruling Congress	—	228	350
Opposition Congress	—	65	16
Communist party (Marxist)	19	19	25
Communist Party	23	24	23
Dravida Munnetra Kazhagam	25	24	23
Jan Sangh	35	33	22
Telengana Praja Samithi	—	—	10
Swatantra Party	44	35	8
Moslem League	3	3	4
Samyukta Socialist Party	23	17	3
Praja Socialist Party	13	15	2
Bharatiya Kranti Dal	—	10	1
Other parties and vacancies	52	46	31
Total	520	519	518

SOURCE: *Keesing's Contemporary Archives* (1971, 24582).

across its borders, concluded: "This House records its profound conviction that the historic upsurge of the 75 million people of East Bengal will triumph. The House wishes to assure them that their struggle and sacrifices will receive the wholehearted sympathy and support of the people of India" (Gandhi 1972, 14). The government-sponsored resolution clearly reflected Gandhi's moderate position—the resolution did not endorse an armed struggle, nor did it recognize the independence of Bangladesh.

International Considerations

Although no domestic constraints on the use of force inhibited the prime minister, three important international factors had to be taken into consideration (see Figure 4.2). The most important factor was the reaction of the Chinese. India and China had fought a war over disputed mountainous territory along a common border in 1962. Although China had decisively triumphed in that conflict, the prospect of a major shift in the balance of power on the subcontinent toward India made future Chinese victories far less certain. China had long supported Pakistan, and Indian officials feared a Chinese intervention should India begin to rout the Pakistani forces. India sought to reduce the probability of a Chinese intervention by commencing the operation in the winter (when large-scale operations in the mountains were almost impossible) and, most important, by the signing of the Indian-Soviet Treaty of Peace, Friendship, and Cooperation in August 1971. Given the intense hostility between China and the Soviet Union at the time and the recent military clashes between the former allies, the treaty drastically altered Chinese calculations. The Chinese intervention could lead to a Soviet intervention.

A second international consideration was international law. An overt and direct Indian intervention was clearly in violation of international law. In order to circumvent this obstacle, the Indian government used covert action to support the rebel forces. When the Pakistani reaction to this use of force triggered a military clash between regular forces, India had its legal justification for using large-scale force.

A final international constraint was the reaction of the United Nations. India feared that Pakistan would rally international opposition (including U.S. opposition) to the use of force. India sought to minimize this problem by planning for a short and decisive military campaign. India sought to present the international community with a *fait accompli*. By the time the international community mobilized its political forces, the intervention would be both completed and irreversible.

Decisions to Intervene

The first major decision made by Gandhi involved refugees: they would be allowed to enter India but only as temporary political refugees. For Gandhi, the decision was simple: sealing the border was both impractical and inhumane. However, the decision would have a profound impact on the evolution of the dispute. As the total number of refugees grew into the millions and drained Indian coffers, the demand to eradicate the source of the migration became increasingly intense.

Perhaps more important, the presence of refugee camps, which contained many defectors from the Pakistani army, made Gandhi's second major decision relatively easy; in April, the government began supplying the rebels with arms and training. Whereas this activity was initially managed by the Indian Border Security Forces, the Indian army took control of all operations after April 30 as the scope of the project steadily increased.[20] The Mukti Bahini, as the rebel group was called, gradually increased in size until it possessed 30,000 volunteers organized in three brigades. The rebels began their "monsoon offensive" in June and launched operations continuously until the full-scale Indian intervention in December. The 90,000-strong government of Pakistan force, including almost five army divisions from West Pakistan, was unable to suppress the uprising.

The guerrilla conflict directly led to both India and Pakistan redeploying their conventional forces to the borders along the eastern and western fronts. The forward deployment led to numerous border clashes that escalated during October and November. India claimed 600 land and air space violations during the March–December period. As Pakistani forces pursued the rebels across the Indian border, they increasingly became entangled with Indian security forces. By November 1971, India was launching large-scale retaliatory raids into Pakistan and providing covering fire for rebels entering and leaving East Pakistan. Clearly, India was not simply responding to Pakistani provocations at this point in time.

On December 3, 1971, the military government of Pakistan launched an air and ground assault from West Pakistan. Yahya Khan hoped that a surprise air assault modeled on the Israeli attack on Egypt at the start of the Six Days' War in 1967, coupled with a successful ground invasion of the Kashmir, would give Pakistan either territory with which to bargain or bring the country's most important great-power allies, the United States and/or China, into the war. Both hopes proved illusory. India was prepared for the attack and quickly neutralized both the Pakistani air force and the ground offensive in West Pakistan. Moreover, the massive Indian invasion into East Pakistan was astonishingly successful due to excellent execution by the Indian armed services and to strategic errors by the Pakistan military leadership (Singh 1980; Gaan 1992, 226).[21] By the December 17 cease-fire, Bangladesh was completely occupied by Indian forces, and almost 90,000 Pakistani troops had been captured.

Was India, the initiator of large-scale violence, a democracy?[22] Clearly, the answer must be yes. India possessed all the structural features of a democracy (for example, its leaders were elected in free and fair elections via universal suffrage). Moreover, the democratic system had functioned without interruption for twenty-four years—a duration arguably long enough for the establishment of peaceful norms of conflict resolution. However, the Indian democratic system at the time of the crisis was relatively unique in two respects: the dominance of the Congress Party and the dominance of the prime minister in foreign affairs.

According to the legislative constraint hypothesis, the greater the legislative majority of the ruling party, the more likely a decision maker is to use force because the probability of punishment is expected to decline. In theory, the Congress Party's overwhelming majority reduced constraint on the prime minister. Moreover, the lack of a formidable opposition party further reduced constraints on India's leadership. The largest opposition party in the Lok Sabha was the Communist party (Marxist) with a mere twenty-five seats (or 5 percent) in the House. Any sustained opposition would have been a hodgepodge of Congress defectors, right-wing nationalist parties, and left-wing socialist or communist parties. Clearly, such a diverse group could not have sustained a united opposition for any extended period of time.

The case study supports the "size of the ruling coalition" hypothesis: Gandhi's overwhelming majority freed her from having to worry about opposition. However, in this case the size of the ruling party allowed Gandhi, at least initially, to pursue a *more moderate policy* against the wishes of Parliament and the public. When Gandhi chose to use force via the rebels, she knew her decision was supported by a vast majority of the population; when she later chose to commit conventional forces to the struggle, she knew that the resulting conventional war would be supported by Parliament and the public. Her strategy was also one of relatively low risk. The initial support of rebels was inexpensive and unlikely to fail completely; the conventional operation was very likely to succeed because the Indian concentration of forces in the East gave it a very favorable balance of forces position with respect to Pakistani units in East Pakistan.[23]

The dominance of the prime minister in foreign affairs also profoundly influenced the course of events. In virtually every democratic political system, the executive and legislative branches clash over control of foreign policy. In the United States, the balance between the two branches has shifted back and forth over time (Fisher 1995). In India, the executive dominance has been more extreme and stable. During the Bangladesh crisis, from March to December, the parliament played virtually no role in the decision-making process (Gaan 1992, 258). Moreover, the cabinet played a very limited role as well; all key decisions were made by Gandhi and a handful of close advisors (D. P. Dhar, P. N. Haksar, T. N. Kaul, and P. N. Dhar) (Gaan 1992, 259, 265).

Gandhi's dominance of foreign policy was the product of historical tradition, institutional design, and decision-making style. Nehru, considered an expert on foreign affairs, established a tradition of unilateral decision making by the prime minister. For instance, Nehru ordered the occupation of the Portuguese enclave of Goa in 1961 without notifying the cabinet or Parliament (Brecher 1968).[24] Institutionally, the executive had tremendous powers to conduct foreign policy; Parliament, for example, had no power to approve or repeal treaties signed by the executive. Finally, Gandhi's autocratic decision-making style led to decision making among a very narrow group of individuals. The August 1971 Indian-Soviet treaty, explicitly designed to balance against the possibility of a Chinese intervention, was negotiated in secret by D. P. Dhar. Two senior members of the cabinet (Y. B. Chanvan and Jagjivan) were informed after the treaty was finalized; the rest of the cabinet was notified a mere thirty minutes before the press conference announcing the historic event (Gaan 1992, 259).

In sum, the Indian democracy concentrated power in the foreign policy arena within the prime minister's office. This situation limited the extent of discussion within the Indian government even before the selection of a policy. After the fact, the dominant position of the Congress Party made decisively punishing the executive extremely difficult. Also, whereas factional fighting opened the door for some domestic opposition, the inherent weakness of the opposition made any severe punishment in the near term unlikely. Finally, in the Bangladesh crisis, the overwhelming legislative and popular support for coercive policies greatly reduced the probability of punishment; no one opposed the use of force.

The Bangladesh case also highlights three additional points about institutional constraint. First, the case clearly demonstrates that authoritarian leaders, just like their democratic counterparts, can be held accountable for their actions: General Yahya Khan was quickly removed from power following his failure to defend East Pakistan. Similarly, Pakistan's failure in 1965 triggered the Awami League manifesto; domestic opposition groups seized upon the foreign policy failure and pursued antiregime policies. Second, the case also points to the constraining power of international institutions. Although there has been much discussion about the ineffectiveness of the United Nations, Indian decision makers acted as if the body was an important source of constraint. India explicitly planned for a lightning strike in the hope of avoiding a U.N. intervention, which it believed would prevent a final solution to the East Pakistan problem. Finally, the case highlights how the words and deeds of democratic decision makers often diverge. In March, Gandhi had cautioned members of the Indian parliament against using military force to resolve the crisis: "The House is aware that we have to act within international norms" (Gandhi 1972, 11). One norm to which she referred is sovereignty; states do not have the right to intervene in the domestic affairs of other states. However, within a matter of days Gandhi began training and supplying rebels dedicated to breaking away from the central government. Later in the conflict she stated that India would not be the first to resort to force; in her eyes, she kept her word, for the Pakistani air attack on December 3 was used to justify the retaliatory invasion. Despite the rhetoric, the use of surrogate forces constituted a violation of Pakistan's sovereignty and a first use of force by the democratic polity.

EL SALVADOR VERSUS HONDURAS
IN THE 1969 FOOTBALL WAR

The El Salvador–Honduras dispute, which culminated in the Football War of 1969, stemmed from two sources of conflict: the treatment of Salvadorans residing in Honduras and a territorial dispute involving the unclear demarcation of boundaries between the two Central American neighbors.[25]

Both sources of conflict contributed to spiraling levels of hostility in the late 1960s. On July 14, 1969, El Salvador invaded Honduras after a series of border clashes following the forceful expulsion of Salvadorans from Honduras and the confiscation of their land. The war left 1,900 Salvadorans and 700 Hondurans dead (Small and Singer 1982).[26]

El Salvador contrasts sharply with Honduras on geographic, demographic, and economic dimensions. Historically, El Salvador has been a small, densely populated country with a significant industrial base. In contrast, the much larger country of Honduras has been sparsely populated and agriculturally oriented. The population density differential has contributed to outward migration of Salvadorans beginning as far back as the early 1900s. Although many Salvadorans migrated to work in the large-scale agricultural operations in Honduras (bananas, coffee, and later cotton), many others settled on the sparsely populated land just across the border. By the 1960s, between 100,000 and 300,000 Salvadorans lived in Honduras. Honduran concerns about this large concentration of foreign workers periodically rose and fell; periods of extreme xenophobia and physical attacks on foreigners were typically followed by long stretches of relatively peaceful cohabitation. The Football War occurred during a peak in this antiforeigner cycle, when the reported mistreatment of Salvadorans prompted the military action by the El Salvadoran government.

Institutional Structures in El Salvador

Was El Salvador a democracy in 1969? Were its leaders constrained from within the executive, the legislature, or a factional ruling party? Unlike the Suez Crisis or the Six Days' War, the democratic credentials of the aggressor state in the Football War are more uncertain. Although the Salvadoran regime possessed many of the structural features of a democratic state, the role of the military in politics, coupled with the lack of institutionalization of the democratic process, makes the situation less than clear. An examination of this crisis demonstrates that the Salvadoran leadership was sensitive to public opposition. Moreover, the case shows that the prowar sentiments of both the public and the largest opposition parties led to an aggressive foreign policy that resulted in the use of high levels of force. Ironically, the inclusion of opposition groups in the government encouraged conflict.

Historically, El Salvador has been governed by military regimes punctuated by brief spells of unstable democratic rule. The latest in a series of post–World War II coups brought Colonel Anibal Portillo and Colonel Julio Adalberto Rivera to power on January 25, 1961. In April of the following year, Rivera was elected president unopposed. The new government began a liberalization program designed to loosen political control incrementally.

TABLE 4.7
Legislative elections in El Salvador

Political parties	1962	1964	1966	1968	1970	1972	1974	1976
National Conciliation Party (PCN)	54	32	32	27	34	39	32	52
Christian Democratic Party (PDC)	0	14	15	19	15	—	—	0
Authentic Revolutionary Party (PAR)	0	6	3	—	—	—	—	—
National Revolution Movement (MNR)	—	—	—	2	0	—	—	—
National Opposition Union (NOU)	—	—	—	—	—	8	14	—
Popular Socialist Party (PPS)	0	0	1	4	1	4	4	0
Other	0	0	1	0	2	1	2	0
Total	54	52	52	52	52	52	52	52

N O T E : All elections were held in March. Presidential and legislative elections do not necessarily coincide.

Much to the dismay of the newly elected president, however, all opposition parties boycotted the March 1962 legislative elections. Rivera's dismay stemmed from his grand political vision for El Salvador. Rivera believed that the military and his Party of National Conciliation (PCN) would lead the political and economic development of the country by serving as impartial mediators between competing societal interest groups. He envisioned leading a one-party state modeled on Mexico's Partido Revolucionario Institucional (PRI) (Webre 1979, 74). Although he recognized that competing interests would inevitably exist in any society, Rivera believed that the party could equitably resolve conflict under a quasi-corporatist system. Rivera believed the opposition boycott of the 1962 legislative elections undermined the party's legitimacy and ability to function as an impartial mediator.

Therefore, Rivera took great strides to encourage participation in the political system. The 1964 legislative elections were reported to have been relatively free and fair. Although minor disturbances occurred during the campaign, these appear to have been the product of local decisions rather than policies set by Rivera and the PCN. The Christian Democratic Party (PDC) won fourteen seats in the 1964 election, formally ending PCN's monopoly of power in the legislature. Table 4.7, which displays the results of the biannual legislative elections in El Salvador, demonstrates that the power of the chief opposition party grew steadily during the 1964 to 1968 period just prior to the outbreak of war. El Salvador was clearly becoming more democratic. The leftist parties, such as the Authentic Revolutionary Party (PAR) and the Salvadorian Popular Party (PPS), which had been traditionally banned since the communist revolt of 1932, openly competed for seats in the 1964, 1966, and 1968 elections.[27]

The March 1967 presidential election was won by the minister of the interior, Colonel Fidel Sanchez Hernandez.[28] Sanchez won 54 percent of the vote while his chief rival, PDC candidate Rodriguez, managed only 22 percent of the popular vote. The lack of protest by opposition groups attested to the relative fairness of the election. An analysis of the results also indicates that the PCN was broadly supported by both conservative peasants and conservative landowners. The PDC, on the other hand, drew its support from the more urbanized greater San Salvador area. Rodriguez's lack of charisma, a growing fear of communism, and the PDC's weakness among peasants led to its weak showing in the presidential elections.

In the 1968 legislative elections, PDC increased its share of the legislature to nineteen seats. Although the election permit of the most leftist party (PAR) was revoked after the 1967 presidential election, other leftist parties such as National Revolution Movement (MNR) quickly filled the void and participated in the 1968 legislative elections. The fact that the government no longer possessed the two-thirds majority needed for legislation on international loans and treaties implied that the opposition had a powerful means for influencing the government (Webre 1979).

Although a two-party democratic system appeared to be developing in El Salvador, several factors make the degree of constraint on top foreign policy leaders difficult to estimate. First, all of the presidential candidates of the PCN were former military officers. The military clearly believed that it was to play a central role in the development of El Salvador. Second, as the government party, PCN had access to considerable resources that were not available to its chief competitors. Although this advantage was not used to the extent that elections had become a farce, as had previously been the case, it did tip the scales in favor of the PCN. Third, although Rivera allowed the leftist parties to compete, it was common knowledge that the military would intervene if PAR or any of its successors won the office of the president (Webre 1979, 105). Subsequent events proved this to be so. In 1972, when PDC candidate Duarte appeared to win the presidential election, the government resorted to fraud to ensure that its candidate took office.[29] Moreover, a case could be made that low turnout, particularly in the 1964 elections, in which only one-quarter of eligible voters went to the polls, signaled a lack of a real choice.

Nevertheless, it is quite clear that Rivera and Sanchez were popular leaders. Sanchez's overwhelming victory and PCN's continued dominance indicated broad popular support for the government's policies. Although the idea of popularly elected military officers sounds foreign to many Americans and Europeans, there was certainly a strong democratic flavor to the Salvadoran political system.[30]

As Oren (1995) argues, retrospectively evaluating the democratic credentials of states could introduce systematic bias because the definition of terms such as *democracy* evolves over time. For example, Oren argues that labeling Imperial Germany as "authoritarian," which is a standard practice in quantitative studies of the democratic peace, would have seemed inappropriate to social scientists in the early twentieth century.[31] The logic of Oren's argument leads us to ask this: how did El Salvador's peers in the 1960s judge the country's democratic credentials? The United States openly embraced El Salvador and Rivera as democratic. El Salvador, in fact, was held up as the model for the Alliance for Progress program: democratic, stable, growing, and anticommunist (Webre 1979, 74). According to his biographer,

> [President Kennedy] often wondered how he could strengthen the governments most deeply pledged to these objectives. For a time he even mused about the possibility of a "club" of democratic presidents—Bentancourt [of Venezuela], Lleras [of Colombia], Jorge Alessandri of Chile, Jose Orlich Balmarcich of Costa Rica, and Jose Rivera of El Salvador. . . . (Schlesinger 1965, 768)

In sum, although the Salvadoran political system was not perfectly democratic, most observers would categorize it as "democratic."

Motives for Salvadoran Intervention

Having identified both the democratic and undemocratic aspects of the Salvadoran political system, we can turn to the evolution of the dispute itself. Figure 4.3 identifies key motivations, potential domestic constraints, and international considerations. An immediate cause of the conflict was the border dispute between the two countries. The border area between Honduras and El Salvador was a haven for cattle rustlers and other criminals; both governments had difficulty projecting authority into this remote area, and criminals exploited their ability to disappear across inter-state borders.[32] Equally problematic was the undemarcated and disputed boundary itself.

El Salvador was often accused of pursuing alleged criminals across the ill-defined border into Honduran territory. On May 25, 1967, El Salvador raided a hacienda it disingenuously stated was in Salvadoran territory, arrested Antonio Martinez Argueta, and charged him with a six-year-old murder. Martinez Argueta was a close friend of Lopez Arellano, the military dictator of Honduras at the time. Honduras took its own captives on June 5, 1967, when two truckloads of Salvadoran soldiers inexplicably wandered into Honduras.[33] The capture led to a series of border clashes that lasted for two years. The captives themselves were not released until June 1968, under pressure from U.S. President Lyndon Johnson, who was scheduled to attend a Central American summit at the time. A harbinger of things to come, the chief opposition party in El Salvador, the Christian Democrats, protested the exchange of prisoners as a sign of government weakness in the conflict with Honduras. The opposition parties, in fact, boycotted the Central American summit and President Johnson's visit.

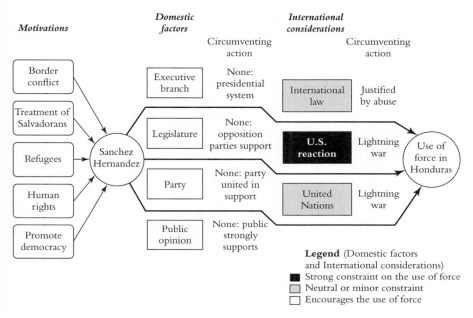

FIGURE 4.3. Institutional constraint on El Salvador in the Football War (1969)

The reason for the intensity of the opposition's position was the alleged human rights abuses by the Honduran government during the period. The immediate conflicts, the disputed borders and prisoners, took place within a context of increasingly hostile relations. The Honduran government and landowners consciously sought to exploit the growing anti-Salvadoran sentiments in their country. Rather than seriously consider land reform (such as breaking up the huge tracts of unused land owned by United Fruit), the government sought to evict Salvadoran squatters on Honduran soil. At the end of 1968, the Honduran government began enforcing a long-standing provision of the 1962 land reform measure: all redistributed land must go to Hondurans by birth. The Salvadoran farmers, unable to provide proof of ownership and citizenship, were evicted.

With the expulsions came stories of total confiscation of property, rape, mutilation, and murder. Papers on both sides of the borders fueled the flames. While the Honduran papers strongly supported further ethnic cleansing, the Salvadoran papers published undocumented cases of abuse. Although the role of the Lopez Arellano government in promoting the anti-Salvadoran outpouring is unclear, "it would be hard to imagine that this campaign did not have his blessing" (Anderson 1981, 94). Clearly, the government that benefited from the diversionary issue made no effort to halt the abuse.

Tensions were heightened in June 1969 by the mistreatment of fans attending a three-game qualifying series between the two nations for the World Cup. Crowds in Honduras apparently kept the visiting Salvadoran team up all night with noise outside their hotel; the Hondurans won the match the next day. The Salvadorans responded with similar treatment in the second match in El Salvador; once again, the team deprived of sleep lost the match. Although two visiting fans required hospitalization for their injuries, the reports of widespread beatings were fabrications. In order to defuse tensions, the third game was moved to Mexico City.

During the prewar period, approximately 20,000 Salvadorans either fled or were expelled from Honduras. Officials in El Salvador documented many cases of murder and mutilation of men, women, and children. However, the extent of the abuse was certainly exaggerated (Duarte with Page 1986, 62). For example, the Red Cross, which handled the incoming refugees, did not find mass evidence of physical abuse or torture (Anderson 1981, 102). Despite this fact, the El Salvadoran population was agitated to the point of frenzy; leaders from across the political spectrum demanded that action be taken.

Domestic Factors

On June 19, PDC leader Jose Napoleon Duarte requested a meeting with President Sanchez Hernandez that would include all opposition groups. The goal was to create a unity government to deal with the crisis. All parties, from the extreme left to the extreme right, agreed to form a council of national unity. Only one official dissented from the aggressive position (the minister of the economy). The communists, who were not invited to the meeting, also rejected the coercive approach.

On June 23, the National Unity Front was created; the coalition included all major parties. The united and bellicose legislature sent a clear message to all at home and abroad: the abuse must stop regardless of the cost (Webre 1979, 115). The Sanchez Hernandez government, which had initially responded with calls for calm and patience, was pushed toward a military solution (Webre 1979, 112).

> What finally pushed Sanchez Hernandez into a surprise attack on Honduras was his fellow officers. The people were saying that the military were cowards, that they couldn't even defend the country. The officers reacted, confident about going to war. They had been impressed by Israel's recent success in the Six-Day War and thought they could match Moshe Dayan. (Duarte with Page 1986, 63)

In a later interview with Anderson (1981, 111), Sanchez Hernandez stated that given the intensity of public opinion and the position of the military, there would have been a coup had he not initiated war. Clearly, the inclusive political system did not constrain the foreign policy elite.

International Considerations

Domestic factors did not inhibit the use of force, but three international considerations were important. First, international law clearly restricts military intervention. By focusing the debate on human rights violations, El Salvador sought to justify its use of force in the eyes of the international community. Second, El Salvador feared a U.S. intervention. The solution to this was the execution of a "lightning" war in order to achieve victory before the United States could come to the aid of the Hondurans. Finally, the United Nations was a possible obstacle to intervention. Again, the solution was a large-scale operation and quick victory. Both the United States and United Nations were to be presented with a *fait accompli*.

The War and Its Consequences

The war began on July 14 with an air and ground attack by El Salvador. Virtually the entire El Salvadoran army of 5,000 was involved in the attack. Although El Salvador made some initial progress on the ground, it was unable to duplicate the success of the Israelis two years earlier. Logistical problems and Honduran air superiority quickly stalled the offensive. Under pressure from the Organization of American States, Central American leaders, and the United States, both sides agreed to a cease-fire on June 19.[34]

Was the government punished for the unsuccessful military operation? The answer is clearly no. Despite the fact that the operation was a military failure, it was a domestic political success. The public strongly backed action to halt the human rights abuses. Despite the quick stalemate on the ground and the destruction of the Salvadoran air force, an estimated 500,000 Salvadorans welcomed the military home in a parade in the capital. More important, the opposition parties' deep involvement in the conflict precluded their exploitation of the "military" failure. Although the war proved costly in economic terms in the long run (large government deficits, the expulsion of Salvadorans from Honduras, the closing of the border for a decade, and the lack of access to southern points on the Pan-American highway), the military defeat did not politically hurt the ruling regime.

In conclusion, the El Salvador–Honduran case highlights three important points with respect to the constraint model. First, institutional constraints are effective only if the opposition opposes the use of force. In this case, the use of force was widely popular; indeed, the opposition parties demanded that force be used in response to Honduran actions. Ironically, in the case of El Salvador a more inclusive political system increased the probability of a clash. The fact that a legislature existed and the media were independent allowed opposition groups to pressure the government into taking a more aggressive position than it had originally deemed necessary. The case points out that *assuming* opposition to the use of force will exist if the institutional channels exist is incorrect. Although inclusive institutions may be a necessary condition, they are not sufficient in and of themselves for constraining leaders.

Second, norms of peaceful conflict resolution, if they are to develop within democratic states, take years to solidify. In the Salvadoran system, where leaders were socialized under repressive military regimes, peaceful norms were embryonic if they existed at all. I will return to this topic in the next chapter.

Third, the issue at stake can affect the evolution of conflict and the constraining power of institutions. Territorial disputes, while often enduring for decades, are more conducive to third-party mediation and arbitration because the "pie" can be divided a number of ways.[35] In contrast, the alleged human rights abuses were much more difficult to deal with peacefully because, as the Salvadoran government explicitly stated, human rights cannot be negotiated. Given that the treatment of minorities is an increasingly important issue as heterogeneous empires dissolve (for example, Yugoslavia and the Soviet Union), a greater focus needs to be placed on the role of international institutions in diffusing these types of conflicts before they spiral out of control as in the case of the Football War.[36]

THE UNITED KINGDOM VERSUS THE SOVIET UNION DURING THE RUSSIAN CIVIL WAR

The Allied intervention in the Russian Civil War marks one of the most complex, indeed confusing, military interventions in modern history.[37] The number of interveners was large (Britain, the United States, France, Canada, Serbia, Italy, Japan, and independent Czecho-Slovak forces). The geographic scope of the intervention was immense—Allied troops landed from Vladivostok in the Pacific to the Baltic States in Europe and from the Transcaucasus in Asia to Murmansk/Archangel near the Arctic. The range of actors and the broad geographic scope led to bizarre occurrences such as Czecho-Slovak legions fighting in Siberia and Serbian units fighting near the Arctic Circle. The motives for intervention varied from country to country. Moreover, the motives changed over the course of the intervention as the war with Germany ended and fear of the spread of Bolshevism grew. A list of interveners, together with an estimate of the scope and duration of their intervention, is shown in Table 4.8.

The following case study focuses primarily on the behavior of Great Britain—the democratic state that forcefully pursued an interventionist policy and most actively participated in the intervention itself (Ullman 1968, vii).

TABLE 4.8
Allied interventions in the Russian Civil War

Locations of intervention	State intervening
Murmansk	British (7,400: June 1918–October 1919) French (1,000: June 1918–October 1919) Canadian (n/a: June 1918–October 1919) Italian (1,350: June 1918–October 1919) Serb (1,200: June 1918–October 1919)
Archangel	British (2,420: April 1918–September 1919) French (900: April 1918–September 1919) Canadian (n/a: June 1918–September 1919) U.S. (4,800: May 1918–August 1919) Italian (n/a: June 1918–September 1919) Serb (350: June 1918–September 1919)
Baltics	British (material and naval support: June 1918–July 1920) French (material and naval support: June 1918–July 1920)
Ukraine/Odessa/ Transcaucasus	British (22,000: December 1918–August 1919) French (30,000: December 1918–April 1919) Greek (30,000: December 1918–April 1919)
Siberia and Far East	Czecho-Slovak (50,000: June 1918–1920) Japanese (70,000: December 1917–October 1922) U.S. (8,358: August 1918–April 1920) Canadian (4,000: 1918–1920) French (3,000: 1918–1920) British (2,000: 1918–1920) Polish (small numbers) Italian (small numbers)

SOURCES: Ullman (1961, 243, 252; 1968, 47, 50); Clodfelter (1992, 615–18); Langer (1968, 1031).
NOTE: Dates and troop numbers are approximate.

Another democracy, France, was also an enthusiastic supporter of intervention. However, the secondary literature on decision making within France is much more limited. Conversely, while the United States intervened with thousands of troops, it remained a reluctant participant. At no time did President Wilson support the British-French policy aimed at overthrowing the Bolshevik regime.[38] The U.S. intervention, addressed tangentially below, is a secondary concern in the case study.

Motives for British Intervention

Figure 4.4 highlights British motivations, domestic constraints, and international considerations influencing the decision to use military force in Russia. The Allied intervention was the by-product of World War I, which pitted the Central Powers (Germany, Austria-Hungary, and the Ottoman Empire) against the Allied Powers (Great Britain, France, Russia, Italy, the United States, and Japan). The huge cost of the war put tremendous pres-

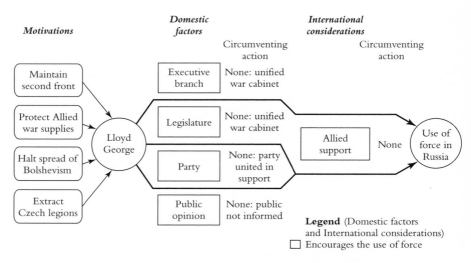

FIGURE 4.4. Institutional constraint on Britain in the Russian Civil War (1918–20)

sure on all participants, for their political leaders attempted to extract vast resources from society in order to support the war effort. The first "total" war resulted in massive social and economic disruptions as societies struggled to meet the demands of the war. The first state to collapse under this pressure was Russia, in March 1917. Continued military defeats, coupled with a second revolution in November 1917, ended the Russian war effort; the Bolshevik-controlled state immediately sued for peace and signed an armistice with the Central Powers in early December 1917. On March 3, 1918, the Bolsheviks signed the Treaty of Brest Litovsk, in which they formally abandoned Poland, Lithuania, Estonia, Latvia, the Ukraine, Finland, and Transcaucasia. German and Austro-Hungarian forces quickly occupied these regions and established pro–Central Power governments.

The collapse of the eastern front jeopardized the Allied war effort; Allied military leaders believed that the movement of German troops to the western front before the arrival of U.S. troops would tip the balance of the war. The Allies were also concerned that war materials supplied to the Russian tsar through the ports of Murmansk and Archangel would fall into German hands. The movement of 12,000 German troops into Finland in support of the White forces in the 1918 Finnish Civil War exacerbated this concern.[39] Finally, the Allies feared the rapid spread of Bolshevism throughout war-torn central and western Europe. Starvation, economic collapse, and a breakdown in civil order created a volatile atmosphere that could readily have been exploited by revolutionary forces. Reopening the Russian front, protecting war supplies, and halting the spread of communism became important motives for the Allied intervention.

A final motive for the intervention was the protection of Czecho-Slovak troops trapped within revolutionary Russia. This rationale, in fact, proved decisive in the U.S. decision to intervene (Kennan 1956; Unterberger 1989). Prior to World War I, the Czechs and Slovaks were inhabitants in the multi-ethnic Austro-Hungarian Empire. For the most part, Czech and Slovak males of draft age responded to conscription calls by Emperor Franz Joseph at the start of the war. Over the course of the war, however, Czech leaders in exile such as Tomas Masaryk and Edward Benes developed a strong independence movement. Masaryk believed that if Czecho-Slovak units could be formed from entente prisoners of war and contribute to the war effort against the Central Powers, the Allies would be compelled to support Czecho-Slovak demands for full independence.[40] Beginning in 1916, Czecho-Slovak units were formed in Italy, France, and Russia.

The Bolshevik withdrawal from the war placed the Czecho-Slovak legions in Russia, which numbered over 50,000 troops, in a very awkward position. The troops could not have been repatriated to Austria-Hungary because they would have been tried and executed as deserters. Nor was it a simple matter to send the forces to the French and Italian battlefields—these fronts were located on the far side of the Central Powers. Therefore, Masaryk requested that the Allied powers transport the Czecho-Slovak troops from Russia to the Allied fronts. Thus, the Czech and Slovak troops began a long trek across Siberia to Vladivostok; from this Pacific port, the troops were to be shipped by boat to France and Italy. The journey turned hostile in March 1918, when the Bolsheviks began disarming the Czecho-Slovak units, which were on several different trains across the Trans-Siberian Railroad. By May 1918, full-scale fighting had erupted as the Czecho-Slovak forces seized several towns on the railway in response to the use of force by Bolshevik forces. Ensuring the safe withdrawal of the Czecho-Slovak troops, which were technically Allied units under French command, was an important fourth motive for intervention.

The British intervention can be divided into two phases. Phase 1 ran from March 1918 to the German armistice on November 11, 1918. Phase 2 extended from the armistice until the British withdrawal in 1920. The first objective of Phase 1 was to secure the Allied war materials at Murmansk, Archangel, and Vladivostok. The port cities had been supply routes for the tsar's army and contained Allied war materials. The stockpiles existed because Allied freighters could deposit material (coal, food, and war supplies) faster than the primitive Russian rail system could transport it to the front.

Small numbers of British and U.S. troops arrived in Murmansk and Archangel just after the signing of the Brest Litovsk treaties in March 1918. These units were reinforced with a small contingent in June and a large contingent in August. By October, the Allies had 15,000 troops in North Russia.

As forces were deployed for the protection of supplies, British Prime Minister David Lloyd George pushed for a second objective: the reopening of the Russian front. Since becoming prime minister, Lloyd George had consistently supported an "eastern strategy" that involved creating a strong second front to reduce the need to mount costly offensives in Flanders and France.[41] The British cabinet and War Office believed that a combination of Czecho-Slovak and Japanese forces could rally the Russian people into re-entering the war, thereby relieving pressure on the western front. However, this scheme was flawed for several reasons. The Japanese had openly rejected extending operations deep into Siberia; the Bolshevik regime was not inclined to welcome thousands of Allied forces deep in its territory; and Russian people, Red and White alike, had no intention of rallying for the Allied cause.

The consistency with which the British pursued the policy in the face of an abundance of information questioning the scheme can be attributed only to desperation. Unlike the outcome of World War II, in which the Allied powers slowly wore down Germany and Japan, the British believed that the war could be lost well into its final year. The British War Office clearly stated its position in June: "Unless Allied intervention is undertaken in Siberia forthwith we have no chance of being ultimately victorious and shall incur serious risks of defeat in the meantime" (Ullman 1961, 211). The latest German offensive, begun in March 1918, had driven the British back by forty miles. By May, the Germans had reached the Marne, a mere thirty-seven miles from Paris. The cabinet felt an increasingly desperate need to re-open a second front. A small British force, together with U.S. assistance, was seen as the first step in this direction.[42]

Phase 2 of the British intervention began with the laying down of German arms in November 1918. After the armistice, the Allied powers could no longer claim the intervention was simply to support the war effort against Germany. The British were now clearly pursuing an antiregime policy. It should be emphasized that the shift to an antiregime policy was gradual and almost imperceptible (Ullman 1968, 9). Moreover, despite claims to the contrary, many in the British camp had always seen the intervention as both an anti–German and anti–Bolshevik policy. However, a strong case can be made that Lloyd George was primarily focusing on the German threat until late in 1918. For example, the immense amount of time Lloyd George spent attempting to secure Bolshevik approval for the proposed Allied operation makes sense only if his primary goal was winning the war against Germany. However, by November 1918, Lloyd George and the war cabinet consciously shifted to an antiregime policy. Four days after the German armistice, the war cabinet approved the following actions: (1) provide financial and material support for White Russian forces in the Ukraine, (2) maintain Allied troops in the Soviet Union, (3) recognize the rebellious Omsk government, (4) encourage the Czecho-Slovak troops to remain in Siberia, (5) occupy the Batum-Baku railroad in the Transcaucasus oil region, and (6) aid the separatist Baltic republics (Ullman 1968, 14).

Domestic Factors

Was the United Kingdom a democratic state in 1918? If so, how can we explain the decision to initiate military force on a large scale? Why didn't the existence of opposition forces constrain the British decision makers from using force as predicted by the theoretical framework described earlier? As the following discussion will demonstrate, the mere existence of institutional channels (such as coalitional cabinets and opposition in the legislature) is not sufficient to produce constraint. Opposition to the foreign policy must exist within the channels.

In the conceptual framework of Dahl (1971), the evolution of the British political system can be described as slow growth of competition between political groups followed by the gradual expansion of political participation (in other words, competition followed by inclusiveness). The Reform Bill of 1832 introduced true competition and triggered the slow evolution of the party system. Intense party competition between the Tories and Liberals in the second half of the nineteenth century was followed by the gradual expansion of suffrage, which led to the incorporation of the middle and working classes in the nineteenth and twentieth centuries: "The male franchise was considerably extended in 1867 and 1884, but it was only during the war, in 1918, that more or less equal and universal suffrage was legislated by a Liberal government" (Therborn 1977, 16). According to Anthony Wood (1978, 145), the Representation of the People Act of 1918 expanded suffrage from 7 million to 20 million. The act allowed the majority of working class and women over the age of thirty to vote for the first time in British history.

The British decision to intervene in Russia took place before the first election (December 1918) based on the expanded suffrage. However, at the time of the decision the Prime Minister was accountable to a large percentage of the public through the legislature; thus, Britain was relatively (but certainly not perfectly) democratic. Although the model would predict that constraint would increase following the expansion of suffrage, the existence of opposition should have affected decision making prior to the election.

The British situation is, in fact, not qualitatively much different from that found in the United States in 1918. The denial of voting rights to blacks and poor whites in the South, together with the denial of suffrage for women, implied that a large proportion of the population in the United States was excluded from politics.[43] Given that the democracy model is designed to be a continuum, the United Kingdom can be viewed as a highly constrained regime resorting to the first use of force.

The British decision to intervene was made by a coalition government led by Liberal Prime Minister David Lloyd George. The Liberal Party had risen to power in 1905 and had been led by Herbert Asquith since 1908. In the last elections before the war in December 1910, the Liberals retained power (272 Liberal, 272 Conservative, 42 Labour, and 84 Irish Nationalist out of 670 total seats in the House of Commons) but had to rely on the support of John Redmond's Irish Nationalists for a working majority. Asquith had led the country into war in 1914 and formed a coalitional government in 1915 to support the war effort. Following the resignation of the Asquith cabinet on December 4, 1916, Lloyd George formed a coalitional government directed by a "war cabinet" that included members of all leading parties. The war cabinet, which consisted of between five and seven members, was a significant departure from much larger peacetime cabinets because it concentrated power in the hands of a very small number of officials. At the time of the crisis the war cabinet included Lloyd George (Liberal), Earl Curzon (Conservative), A. Bonar Law (Conservative), G. Barnes (Labour), A. Chamberlain (Conservative), and Jan Smuts (president of South Africa).

The initial decision to intervene was made by the war cabinet on May 23, 1918. The intervention continued after the defeat of Germany and the general elections in December 1918. The new coalition government, promising tough policies toward the defeated Germans (such as war criminal trials and full reparations), won an overwhelming majority on December 14, 1918, capturing 478 of the 707 seats in the House of Commons.[44] The upcoming peace negotiation in Paris, rather than the ongoing Russian intervention, was the primary issue raised in the two-week campaign period leading to the first postwar elections (Mowat 1955, 6). Neither Lloyd George nor the Coalition Manifesto even mentioned the Russian intervention (Ullman 1968, 64).

The series of decisions leading to the intervention in Russia did not elicit opposition for several reasons. First, no opposition existed to the use of force designed to defeat Germany. The constraint model predicts that caution occurs because the opposition can exploit foreign policy failures. However, Britain was in the midst of World War I; it had already suffered nearly a million killed and two million wounded. If the protection of war material and opening of a second front would end the hostilities, no one in Britain would question the action.

Moreover, the existence of a "war cabinet" greatly reduced the likelihood of opposition emerging. In a war cabinet, opposition parties are brought into the government in order to expedite decision making and eliminate post-decision criticism. The rationale behind centralizing power is the belief that traditional democratic processes can be dangerous during wartime because they slow mobilization, endanger execution, and/or lower morale. A war cabinet, which is a conscious symbol of unity, is unlikely to encourage open opposition to government policy. Moreover, if the political elite have achieved a consensus, public opposition is very unlikely to emerge (Zaller 1992; Rousseau 2004; Schultz 2001).

As members of the ruling coalition and war cabinet, Labour could not criticize policy. In fact, Labour leader Arthur Henderson had been removed from government for supporting a call for an international socialist conference on war aims in 1917. The Labour Party, which left the coalition just prior to elections and just as the intervention explicitly transitioned into an anti-Bolshevik policy, increasingly criticized the government. The *New Statesman*, a major leftist publication, feared a drift into another war and stated on December 21, 1918: "We feel that the time has come to break the self-imposed silence which we have observed with regard to the British Government's attitude toward Russia" (1918, 231). However, Labour criticism was muted by Labour's complicity in the decision to intervene and its electoral weakness (only 63 seats in Commons).

Second, a lack of information stifled opposition. Voters at the December 1918 elections could not have punished the government because they simply did not know the scope of the government's actions or the motive behind the government's policy. When the government was asked in the House of Commons about the purpose of its Russian policy just after the armistice, it responded that it was not in the national interest to discuss the topic. From the armistice until the spring of 1919, the government made only one public statement about the intervention. Clearly, most members of Parliament and the public were unaware that thousands of British troops were being deployed with the explicit purpose of overthrowing the Bolshevik government.

Third, the British government's decision to intervene was based on the belief that it would be a relatively cheap operation. The success of the Czechs encouraged the British belief that the Bolshevik regime could be easily toppled due to its limited popularity and inefficiency. As the British realized that this belief was incorrect over the course of 1918 and 1919, it withdrew its troops from vulnerable areas. The British suffered fewer than 500 battlefield fatalities during the entire multi-theater operation. Moreover, the British increasingly relied on naval power (for example, in the Baltics), which greatly limited the probability of casualties.[45] Finally, the British increasingly relied on support of third parties to obtain their objectives. By transferring guns and ammunition to White Russian forces such as Denikin in the Ukraine, Britain believed it could achieve its policy goals without British casualties or by slowing the domestically popular demobilization process.

Fourth, Lloyd George did not believe the intervention was contrary to democratic norms: "I am interventionist just as much because I am a democrat as because I want to win the war" (Ullman 1961, 222). The effort was designed to preserve and promote democracy in the face of an assault by the autocratic regimes of Germany, Austria-Hungary, and the Ottoman Empire. Nor did the transition into an antiregime policy following the German defeat conflict with Lloyd George's democratic ideology, given that the Bolshevik regime had seized power via force. Whereas few of the White Russian forces supported by Britain were "democratic" freedom fighters, they were not pledged to the spread of a workers' revolution dedicated to overthrowing the bourgeois democracies.

Overall, the Allied intervention proposed by the British and French was a dismal failure. The Americans and Canadians refused to join in any antiregime operations. Japan, solely intent on exploiting an opportunity to extend its influence on the mainland, did not significantly aid the anti-Bolshevik forces. The British and French withdrew their forces after only minor engagements. Despite the failure, the military intervention did not play a large role in subsequent British domestic politics. Economic troubles plus the failure of Versailles were the topics of the next election.

CONSTRAINT AND TWO MONARCHIES: SAUDI ARABIA AND JORDAN

The democratic peace literature assumes, for the most part, that constrained regimes and autocratic regimes are mutually exclusive categories. This is particularly true for monarchies, which are coded as extremely autocratic in traditional data sets such as Polity. Even the more inclusive constraint model, which probes for legislative-executive divisions, intraexecutive conflict, and party factionalism, places traditional monarchies at the "unconstrained" end of the spectrum. However, the quantitative analysis demonstrates that certain types of very autocratic regimes, such as monarchies and military dictatorships, are *less* likely to use force. Nor is this finding extremely unusual. Gowa (1999) and Bennett and Stam (2004) find some evidence of an autocratic peace. Similarly, Peceny, Beer, and Sanchez-Terry (2002) differentiate three types of autocratic regimes: personalist, military, and single-party dictatorships. Using MID involvement as a dependent variable, they find no cases of either personalist dictatorship dyads or military regime dyads fighting a war in the post–World War II period. In addition, they find that single-party dictatorships were less likely to be involved in military conflict compared to mixed dyads.[46]

Why do we find some evidence of an autocratic peace? Does the model examined in this chapter fail to capture constraint, or do monarchies share some other attribute that makes them less violence prone? In order to probe this unexpected finding, I examine two cases in which monarchies were involved in a militarized crisis: Saudi Arabia (versus Egypt in the Yemen War) and Jordan (versus Israel during the Yom Kippur War).[47]

Saudi Arabia

The modern state of Saudi Arabia was created by Abd al-Aziz ibn Abd ar Rahman Al Saud during the first decades of the twentieth century, when his tribal supporters expanded their control from the Riyadh in the interior of the Arabian peninsula to the coastal regions. The territorial consolidation was completed in 1927, and Abd al-Aziz was declared king of the dual monarchy of Hejaz and Najd. In 1932 the two kingdoms were combined into Saudi Arabia.

Saudi Arabia is a monarchy based on the tenets of Islam. Law (*sharia*) is derived directly from the Islamic holy book, the Quran. Whereas the Quran identifies rules (do not steal) and remedies (removal of a hand—see chapter 5, verse 38), it does not dictate a particular institutional structure for government as a whole. For this reason, the Saudi monarchy rules through royal decree in accordance with its interpretation of Islamic law.

Saudi Arabia has no constitution, no legislature, and no elections.[48] There are neither active political parties nor formal collective decision-making mechanisms. For these reasons, Saudi Arabia is coded as 0 for all years of its existence on the 0–20 democracy scale developed using the Gurr Polity IV data. Saudi Arabia is considered more autocratic than Stalin's communist regime (+1) or Hitler's fascist state (+1). Indeed, all legislation is enacted by the king through decree, and all political appointments ultimately rest with the king.

However, since the foundation of Saudi Arabia under King Abd al-Aziz, Saudi monarchs have carefully adhered to the golden principles of *shura* (consultation) and *ijma'* (consensus) within the ruling class. According to Abir (1993, 6), the ruling class is made up of leading members of the royal family, the *ulama* (the religious leaders), and the *umara* (the tribal leaders). Although the *ulama* and *umara* had been crucial to the consolidation of the Saudi kingdom, their role diminished after the 1930s. The commercial exploitation of oil during the 1940s provided the king not only with the opportunity to develop his armed forces without relying on the military services of the tribal leaders but also the opportunity to buy off, rather than fight, opposition. Likewise, the *ulama* declined in importance from the 1940s, and the king was in a position to be able to disregard *ulama* objections to the limited modernization process then under way. However, the king continued to show respect for the *ulama* and offer them certain privileges, for their support remained important for the legitimization of the regime, internal stability, and national integration.

The leading figures of both the *ulama* and the *umara*, combined with the leading figures in the royal family, play an extremely important part in Saudi political life. As such, the Saudi political system more closely resembles an oligarchy than an absolute monarchy. Although the monarch may veto all the decisions of the royal consultative council (the *majlis al-shura*, created in 1992) and the appointed council of ministers (*majlis al-wuzara*, created in 1953), in certain circumstances the "unofficial leadership" (the *ahl al-hal wa'l-'aqd*, which literally means those who loosen and bind) may overrule the king, limit his authority, or even depose him, as happened in the case of King Saud in 1964. Thus, as Abir argues, "if the policies of the king were to threaten the kingdom's stability and the regime's power," a coalition against the king could emerge and replace him (1993, 7).

The decision-making process is Saudi Arabia is extremely difficult to document. It appears that informal consultation prior to making a major decision is the norm. Royal family members and religious leaders loosely define the boundaries of acceptable behavior beyond which a prudent leader should not go. King Saud's attempt to assassinate Nasser in the late 1950s is a prime example of the repercussions of exceeding these loosely defined bounds. The informal nature of this constraint is not captured in either the Polity data sets or the constraint model developed in this chapter.

At the time of King Saud's succession to the throne in November 1953, relations between Saudi Arabia and Egypt were cordial. Even after the coup d'etat in Egypt and Nasser's assumption of power in 1954, Saud continued close and fruitful relations with Egypt. Indeed, in 1955 Egypt sent a military mission to train the Saudi army and thousands of advisors, teachers, and health workers to build up the Saudi civil service and to staff the kingdom's schools and hospitals (Badeeb 1986, 12). As Wilson and Graham point out, "Saud soon became one of Nasser's greatest backers, willingly bankrolling many of the Egyptian's schemes" (1994, 95). They both refused to join the Baghdad Pact and pressured Jordan not to join. Saud supported Egypt's claims to the Suez Canal and backed Nasser's Czech (Soviet) arms deal. Furthermore, Saud agreed to finance a tripartite alliance with Egypt and Syria, although he refused to countenance a full-scale union (Badeeb 1986, 12). Such a stance distanced Saud from his U.S. allies—always a potential source of opposition from the nationalist elements in the Arab world—and indeed alarmed Washington (Wilson and Graham 1994, 95).

However, relations began to sour in the late 1950s. Nasser's popularity in Saudi Arabia led to the establishment of radical pro-Nasser groups in the military and among oil-field workers. The conservative monarchy began to view the Nasserist political and economic messages as threatening. Saudi Arabia openly opposed the unification of Egypt with Syria in 1958. In March 1958, King Saud's plot to assassinate Nasser was uncovered and publicized. In response to the domestic and international uproar as well as deteriorating economic conditions, Prince Faysal was given full executive power (domestic and foreign). Conflict with Saud led Faysal to step down in 1961, only to resume control over foreign policy in 1962, when Saud left the country for medical treatment. Faysal remained in charge of foreign policy during the early phases of the Yemeni crisis until the royal family removed Saud permanently from power in 1964, after Faysal gathered the *ulama* and chiefs and asked them to intervene (Bligh 1984, 79). During the entire 1958–64 period, divisions within the royal family (the Saud faction versus the Faysal faction versus the Talal faction) prevented the development of consistent domestic and foreign policies.

The Yemeni crisis began in September 1961, with the fall of the conservative monarchy in Yemen, and continued until shortly after the 1967 Six Days' War, when a bruised and battered Egyptian government conceded the long-stalemated conflict. Although Egypt bombed Saudi Arabia territory on a number of occasions and supported subversive movements in Saudi Arabia throughout this period, Saudi Arabia's forces were never directly engaged with their Egyptian counterparts. Rather, Saudi Arabia extended political, financial, and moral support to the royalist forces, which allowed them to stalemate (but not win) the conflict with the numerically superior republican-Egyptian forces. According to Sullivan (1970), Saudi Arabia's policy reflected first and foremost its desire to maintain a balance of power between the conservative (allied with Western powers) and the radical (linked to the USSR) states in the Arab world.

Egypt not only had foreknowledge of the coup that overthrew Imam Muhammad al-Badr but actively supported it as well. Nasser decided to intervene militarily in support of the Yemeni revolution on September 27, the day after the coup, and the first contingent of Egyptian forces arrived in Yemen on October 5. By the end of the month, the number of troops exceeded 1,000. With the growth in royalist opposition to the new republican regime, Egypt increased its forces to roughly 20,000 by February 1963

(Gause 1990, 59). The Egyptian presence in Yemen "bolstered a weak republican regime which promised to convert North Yemen from a relatively harmless neighbor into an enemy professing a hostile ideology and harboring irredentist ambitions" (Gause 1990, 59). Given the large number of Yemenis working in Saudi Arabia and the affinity among the population of Asir for Yemen, this constituted a definite internal threat.[49] Furthermore, Egypt could now use Yemen as a base from which to "extend material support to opposition forces throughout the Peninsula, particularly in South Yemen and Saudi Arabia itself" (Gause 1990, 59). Also, should direct confrontation between Egyptian and Saudi forces occur, which would in all likelihood lead to Saudi defeat, "all the centrifugal forces in the Kingdom, ideological and regional, could have broken loose" (Gause 1990, 60).

The Yemen civil war dragged on for seven years. As early as 1963, a United Nations–sponsored peace plan was approved by all parties, but the plan broke down during implementation. A second cease-fire was established in 1964 after mediation by Algeria and Iraq; within a month, this effort broke down as well. Negotiation continued in 1965 and 1966, but agreements reached between Nasser and Faysal could never be implemented due to conflict between the Yemeni republicans and royalists. At the peak of its involvement, Egypt had committed 70,000 troops to the campaign. The long conflict ended only with the Egyptian defeat at the hands of the Israelis in the Six Days' War in June 1967. The defeat forced Nasser to refocus his remaining military power and to reestablish a united Arab front against Israel.

The most critical decision Saudi Arabia faced during the Yemeni crisis was how to balance the growing Nasserist threat. Realists claim that states balance against (rather than bandwagon with) rising threats in order to ensure their security and survival.[50] However, should states balance threats internally (that is, military buildups) or externally (that is, alliances)? Although most realists focus on alliances, the internal/external ratio depends on the size of the threat relative to available domestic resources, the reliability of potential allies, and the political costs associated with mobilizing domestic resources (Downing 1992; Conybeare 1994).

It is this last factor that stands out in the case of Saudi Arabia. Stein (1980) has shown that rising external threats can increase domestic cohesion and governmental support, but the act of mobilization leads to rising opposition. Historically, rulers have dealt with this rising opposition by exchanging political rights for cooperation in the crisis (Rousseau and Blauvelt 1998; Rousseau and Newsome 2004; Downing 1992). Such a process is unthinkable in Saudi Arabia; there is no conception of citizenship in the Western sense there. Napoleon's tactic of convincing French peasants to die for the state (without pay!) because they were defending a polity they owned could not work in the case of Saudi Arabia because a family (rather than people) owns the state.[51]

A critic might argue that the Yemen conflict was not a severe military threat, but Saudi behavior is consistent even in the case of the Persian Gulf War. Even when facing a threat of invasion from a vastly superior military force, the Saudi government chose to ally rather than mobilize. Despite much talk of expanding the military during the war, this avenue was largely rejected after the crisis abated. The use of mercenaries (U.S., British, French, Egyptian, etc.) rather than citizens minimized a potential long-run challenge to the regime.

In sum, monarchies traditionally have a narrow basis of support and are, therefore, less able to mobilize vast resources to achieve foreign policy objectives. Saudi Arabia, blessed with extensive oil revenues, can use its wealth to coerce neighbors through intermediaries (such as the Yemeni royalists). However, monarchies without such resources seem to be less likely to resort to force to resolve an international dispute.

Jordan

The modern state of Transjordan was created in 1921 in the wake of World War I. Jordan had been part of the Ottoman Empire until the empire's disintegration at the closing stages of the war. At the Conference of San Remo in 1920, Britain was awarded mandates for both Palestine and Transjordan; these mandates were confirmed by the League of Nations in 1922. In 1928 Britain formally handed over control of all government affairs to the government of Emir Abdullah, with the exceptions of finance and foreign policy. The 1946 Treaty of Rome established the Kingdom of Transjordan as a sovereign state.[52] In 1949 a new constitution renamed the country the Hashemite Kingdom of Jordan.

The declaration of Israeli independence in 1948 triggered the first Arab-Israeli war. Jordanian forces, along with those from Egypt, Syria, Iraq, and Lebanon, entered the conflict in an attempt to eradicate Israel. Although the Arab military assault failed to achieve its objectives, Jordan took control of the territory of the West Bank. Suddenly, the population of Jordan doubled with the addition of 400,000 Palestinian residents of the West Bank and refugees.

Abdullah was assassinated in 1951 by a Palestinian extremist. Although his son Talal replaced him briefly, mental illness forced him to resign the office. In 1953, Talal's eighteen-year-old son Hussein became king of Jordan. Hussein struggled with both domestic divisions (West Bank Palestinians versus East Bank Jordanians) and international divisions (conservatives led by Saudi

Arabia versus radicals led by Egypt). The internal-external conflict peaked in 1957, when units from the National Guard, manned primarily by soldiers drawn from the West Bank, attempted a coup. Hussein survived the attempt in large part due to the loyalty of the Bedouin soldiers from the East Bank. In response to the coup, Hussein purged Parliament and centralized power in the crown.

By 1967, King Hussein faced few, if any, meaningful constitutional or institutional constraints upon his power, and the main feature of the Hashemite leadership was "its highly centralized character and the monarch's role as the nation's chief executive" (Mutawi 1987, 2). Under the 1952 constitution, "Jordan is a hereditary monarchy, with control of the executive, legislative, and judicial branches of Government reserved to the King" (Yorke 1988, 16). The king had the power to summon, suspend, and dissolve the parliament; to rule by decree; and to appoint the prime minister, cabinet, government officials, and the thirty-member senate. Although the prime minister and his cabinet were responsible to the parliament, and the parliament had the power to conduct votes of confidence in them and to impeach ministers, the system was parliamentary in form only (Yorke 1988, 16–17). Political parties were banned during the political crisis in 1957 and remained so until the late 1980s. As a result, members of the House of Deputies were elected primarily on the basis of tribal, family, or ethnic allegiances or because of their prominent socioeconomic position. As such, they were already members of the establishment who supported the status quo. Parliament's role in the formulation and implementation of policy was severely limited, and it operated rather "as a platform for the discussion of important issues," presenting opinions that tended to reflect public feeling, thus influencing the nation's leaders indirectly (Mutawi 1987, 17–18).

As described in the preceding chapter, tension along the Jordan-Israel border mounted steadily during 1966–67. Although Hussein possessed tremendous power in the formal governmental institutions, he did not control the Palestinian Liberation Organization (PLO). Supported by Syria and Egypt, the PLO became a state within a state, with the ability to tax and arm supporters in its refugee camps. The PLO launched a series of attacks on Israel from Jordanian territory, inviting retaliation that brought the Israeli and Jordanian armies into conflict. The retaliatory attack on El Samu in November 1966 triggered rioting in Jordan—threatening the legitimacy of the regime.

In May 1967, Arab-Israeli tension grew as Egypt began reinforcing the Sinai, requested the withdrawal of U.N. peacekeepers, flew over the Israeli nuclear research station, and closed the Straits of Tiran. Finally, on May 30 the Jordanian military was placed under the command of Egypt. Israel responded to the buildup with a preemptive strike against Egypt on the morning of June 5. Although Israel offered to remain at peace with Jordan as long as it did not become involved in the dispute, Jordanian military forces under Egyptian command immediately engaged the Israeli army. The Six Days' War lasted only three days for Jordan; it lost not only control of the historically important city of Jerusalem but the entire West Bank as well. The 58,000-strong Bedouin-dominated army fought better than the Syrian or Egyptian forces, but it took heavy casualties (3,000 killed or wounded and 179 of 286 tanks destroyed) (Clodfelter 1992, 1044).

What factors lay behind Hussein's decision to participate in the Six Days' War? Does the Kantian story about autocratic rulers initiating conflicts "without any significant reason, as a kind of amusement" ring true in the case of Hussein? In fact, the case study shows that Hussein faced tremendous informal constraint that thrust him into a dilemma: choose to fight a war that he knew he was going to lose versus abstain from conflict and risk being removed from power by domestic opposition. The interaction between external conflicts (Jordan versus Syria/Egypt and Arabs versus Israelis) and internal conflicts (Palestinians versus Jordanians) created a situation in which war represented the most palatable of all options.

From its inception, the Jordanian monarchy struggled to create a "national identity." Prior to 1920, no independent Jordanian state had ever existed. Moreover, the Hashemite ruling family had no roots in the immediate region—the powerful family originally controlled Mecca and Hejaz prior to territorial consolidation of Saudi Arabia. Furthermore, the native population of Jordan was quite heterogeneous, and subnational or tribal loyalties were often more significant than national loyalties. The monarchy had the difficult task of forging a "Jordanian" national identity while at the same time controlling the Palestinian groups that formed a majority of the population after 1948 (Salloukh 1996, 3).

The monarchy's desire to create a national identity was undermined by external factors. New radical regimes such as Nasser's in Egypt attacked the conservative monarchy, hoping to replace it with a more progressive domestic regime or to amalgamate it into an Egyptian-led Pan-Arab state. Moreover, as long as the dream of an independent Palestinian homeland in the West Bank remained alive, a distinct Palestinian identity would compete with the drive to create a Jordanian identity.

In January 1964 at the Cairo conference, the deeply divided Arab leaders announced two important provisions designed to foster unity in the fight against Israel. First, the United Arab Command (UAC) was created to consolidate Arab military forces in the hopes of creating offensive capacity in the long run. Second, the umbrella PLO organization was created to unite various Palestinian factions and to begin guerilla attacks on Israel. On December 31, 1964, Yasir Arafat's al-Fatah launched its first strike against the Jewish state. Nasser hoped the two provisions would increase Arab cohesion and deflect criticism from Syria, which had been pushing Egypt for a more aggressive stance toward Israel.

Although Hussein supported the UAC and the PLO, both possessed a clear threat to his regime. Hussein refused to allow Egyptian troops into his country and attempted to prevent PLO raids from Jordanian territory in order to prevent conflict with Israel. However, the Syrian-supported al-Fatah proved difficult for the monarchy to control. With Arab financial backing, the autonomous PLO-controlled camps became a threat to the regime. When Nasser deserted the PLO in September 1966, Hussein ordered a crackdown on the movement.

Ironically, from 1966 to May 1967, Arabs rather than Jews were the primary security concern for Hussein. Syrian and Palestinian supported guerrilla activity threatened to provoke the militarily superior Israeli forces. The crackdown on the PLO threatened to turn Palestinians against the Jordanian government. By this point, Syria had become even more bellicose and joined with the PLO in calling for the destruction of the Hashemite regime. Although Nasser had some sympathy for Hussein's position, he could not ignore public opinion and moved toward an alliance with Syria and the PLO. Having failed to win the war in Yemen and in an attempt to regain his hegemony in the Arab world, Nasser turned toward attacking the conservative monarchies and supporting the hard-line Syrian position against Israel.

Given his situation, Hussein was forced to soften his repression of the Palestinian organizations, and as a result the number of attacks on Israel carried out by them greatly increased. A serious threat to the regime occurred in November 1966, with the Israeli attack on Samu as retaliation for earlier Fatah attacks. Eighteen Jordanians were killed and a further 134 wounded (Bailey 1984, 25; Mutawi 1987, 77). Serious rioting occurred throughout the West Bank, and criticism of Hussein became intense as he failed to take retaliatory measures. The twelve days of rioting, spurred on by Egyptian, Syrian, and Iraqi radio broadcasts, increased in both intensity and scope. Unlike previous demonstrations, the rioters explicitly called for the abdication of the king and the establishment of a PLO government (Bailey 1984, 25). Hussein attempted to quell the riots by agreeing to issue arms to villages on the Israeli border, but the concession failed to bring peace. He then responded by dissolving Parliament, imposing martial law, and using Jordanian troops against the Palestinians. The use of troops created a massive gulf between the government and the Palestinians. Moreover, it further deepened the rift between Jordan and the other Arab states. The Arab League passed a number of anti-Jordanian resolutions, and the propaganda war against it was increased. Nasser openly accused Hussein of selling out the Arab cause. In February 1967 Hussein recalled his ambassador from Egypt and, just prior to the outbreak of war in June, broke off relations with Syria.

Hussein's decision to participate in the Six Days' War was based on four assumptions. First, he assumed that war with Israel was inevitable. He simply did not believe the Israeli statement that it would reciprocate but not initiate violence. Second, contrary to his Arab peers, he assumed that the Arabs would lose a military conflict with Israel. Third, unless the Arab states created a three-front war, the outcome would be a disaster. Without a united military effort, the Arab states would lose considerable territory, including the West Bank (Mutawi 1987, 87). Fourth, he believed the failure to participate in an Arab war would trigger domestic unrest and increase Arab support for rebellion. With these four assumptions, war was the most preferred option. In May 1967, Hussein aligned his troops with Egypt and Syria, two states that had been calling for his overthrow just weeks before.

The Jordanian experience is informative for two reasons. First, it demonstrates that informal constraint is not captured by standard data sets or institutional models that focus on formal decision-making structures. Although Hussein appears to be an absolute monarch in the Polity data, he is severely constrained by both domestic and international factors. Second, the model demonstrates that constraint coupled with aggressive domestic audiences can force a leader into conflict that he or she might have wished to avoid. Therefore, the Jordanian case closely parallels the El Salvadoran case discussed earlier in the chapter.

Conclusions

In this chapter, I developed an institutional constraint model in place of the standard democratic peace model based on the Polity data sets. The goal was to explore the traditional assumption that constraint and democracy are perfectly correlated and to probe the impact of an overreliance on the Polity data sets in the democratic peace literature. The constraint model, when examined in isolation, performs very well. As predicted, coalitional executives, small ruling coalitions, and factional ruling parties were all less likely to use aggressive force. The analysis conclusively demonstrates that the major findings of the democratic peace are not the product of overreliance on the Polity data sets. The analysis is less definitive with respect to the power of the constraint model to the democratic peace model. Although the quantitative tests (for example, nested and J-test) were somewhat inconclusive, the case studies presented in the first four chapters of this book clearly demonstrate that the institutional constraint variables capture the *process* of deciding to use force better than the more aggregate and abstract democracy variables.

The case studies probe these quantitative findings by exploring why constraint breaks down in some democracies (India, El Salvador, and Britain) and emerges in some autocracies (Saudi Arabia and Jordan). The Indian case highlights that the centralization of foreign policy varies from democracy to democracy and can have important implications on the use of force. Moreover, the case highlights that leaders with overwhelming coalitions, even democratic leaders, may feel less constrained because the threat of punishment is reduced. The El Salvadoran case indicates that aggressive domestic opposition can force constrained leaders toward war. Finally, the British case highlights the importance of encompassing coalitions in democracies. Broad-based coalitions developed during times of national emergency are more likely to use force because the threat of punishment declines.

The quantitative results also indicate that, contrary to the predictions of the democratic peace model, monarchies and military regimes are less likely to use aggressive force. The Saudi case study demonstrates that an unwillingness (or inability) to mobilize human resources restricts a monarch's options when dealing with an international crisis. In contrast, the Jordanian case highlights the fact that informal constraints, not captured by either the democratic peace or the constraint model, can force leaders into war when war is widely supported by domestic groups.

Overall, the qualitative and quantitative analysis points to a weakness found in both the constraint and the democracy models: the failure to address institutional channels *and* active opposition within these channels simultaneously. For example, all members of a coalition cabinet may support a use of force despite their differing party affiliations. Similarly, although opposition parties may exist in the legislature, they may be more willing to forcibly resolve the dispute than the ruling party. Finally, whereas factions within a party may vehemently disagree on the best approach to economic development, they may have similar preferences with respect to the territorial dispute with the neighbor to the north. Ideally, a measure of constraint would consist of two elements: the existence of institutional channels and the presence of active opposition. Although measuring opposition to the use of force on an annual basis (which would be required for any time-series analysis) is extremely difficult, the coupling of institutions and opposition could make the constraint model a much better predictor of the use of force.

Nested Versus Nonnested Models of the Democratic Peace

This appendix examines nested and nonnested tests of the democratic peace and institutional constraint models. The results are presented in Table 4.9. The formula used to determine significance levels of the log-likelihood ratio test is as follows:

$v = -2$[log-likelihood function value x_1 − log-likelihood function value x_2], with $x_2 - x_1$ degrees of freedom and where x_1 represents the restricted model and x_2 represents the full model.

TABLE 4.9

Nested comparison of democracy and institutional constraint models using the aggressive use of force dependent variable and the dispute data set, 1960−88

Independent variable	Model 1	Model 2	Model 3
Institutional constraint model			
Coalitional executive	−0.276**	—	−0.167
	(0.096)		(0.105)
Collective decision making	−0.049	—	−0.061
	(0.054)		(0.056)
Size of ruling coalition	0.669***	—	−0.024
	(0.153)		(0.186)
No legislature	−0.247***	—	−0.230***
	(0.061)		(0.062)
Factional ruling party	−0.131*	—	−0.146*
	(0.066)		(0.068)
Democratic peace model			
Actor's net democracy (monadic)	—	−0.017***	−0.015**
		(0.004)	(0.006)
Actor's net democracy with	—	−0.073***	−0.081***
democratic opponent (dyadic)		(0.015)	(0.016)
Opponent's net democracy	—	0.017***	0.017***
		(0.004)	(0.004)
Balance of forces	0.396***	0.359***	0.344***
	(0.087)	(0.087)	(0.093)
Shared alliance ties	−0.052	−0.073	−0.063
	(0.058)	(0.060)	(0.061)
Satisfaction with the status quo	−0.727***	−0.686***	−0.705***
	(0.058)	(0.057)	(0.059)
Democracy with weak opponent	−0.102	−0.076	−0.125
	(0.103)	(0.109)	(0.114)
Democracy with weak democracy	−0.666*	0.313	0.410
	(0.314)	(0.487)	(0.505)
Constant	−2.345***	−1.784***	−1.705***
	(0.145)	(0.082)	(0.190)
Number of observations	5509	5596	5444
Log likelihood at convergence	−1828	−1826	−1765

NOTE: Robust standard errors appear in parentheses below the coefficient estimates. All significance tests are one-tailed. *p < .05, **p < .01, ***p < .001.

The significance level is calculated using a chi-square distribution. The log-likelihood ratio test demonstrates that the full model provides a significantly better fit to the data than either the democratic peace model ($v = 120$, df $= 3$, $p < .001$) or the constraint model ($v = 124$, df $= 5$, $p < .001$) alone. For a full explanation of the log-likelihood test, see Greene (1990, 356).

The nonnested "J-test" involves four regressions. First, the constraint model is run, and the predicted values are saved. Second, the democratic peace model is run with the predicted values from the constraint model inserted as independent variables. If the estimated coefficient of the predicted values is not statistically significant, we can conclude that the constraint model does not add any information above and beyond that provided by the democratic peace model. The process is then reversed and repeated (that is, the predicted values from the democratic peace model are placed in the constraint model). The results of the J-test indicate that neither model can be discarded. In both cases the estimated coefficients of the predicted values are positive and statistically significant (t-ratios of 4.555 and 8.11 for the constraint and democratic peace predicted values, respectively). See Greene (1990, 231) for a discussion of the test.

Notes

1. Many quantitative studies of the democratic peace have tens of thousands of observations; Bremer (1992), for instance, begins his analysis with 202,778 dyad years (e.g., U.S.–Soviet Union 1950). An international relations scholar would be forced to don a "comparative politics cap" and wade hip deep into country studies for literally years to assemble a data set with the scope of the Polity data sets.

2. Many social scientists have emphasized the importance of redundancy. Stinchcombe (1968) advocates using multiple hypotheses to test any theory. The more the tests differ from one another (i.e., the more independent the components are), the more robust the analysis (i.e., the more redundant the system). George and McKeown's (1985) advocacy of process tracing concerns generating and testing subhypotheses to ensure that the proposed causal mechanism truly accounts for the observed outcome. Similarly, King, Keohane, and Verba (1994) advocate using multiple dependent variables to ensure the robustness of analysis.

3. Ireland and Gartner (2001, 549) explicitly state that "we think that it is critical that scholars employ new, additional data sources of democracy and executive constraint to examine international conflict behavior, regime, and institutional effects."

4. An important exception to this statement is the work of Morgan and Campbell (1991), who conceptualize constraint as an independent dimension. However, Morgan and Campbell's empirical test relies on the structural measures in the Polity data sets that are also used to develop the Polity democracy and autocracy indices. Schultz (2001) and Bueno de Mesquita and colleagues (2003) also question this perfect correlation. Bueno de Mesquita and colleagues (2003, 72–73) focus on the "selectorate," and Schultz (2001, 60) focuses on "domestic competition."

5. The model implicitly assumes that the costs are constant across regimes. If autocratic rulers are expected to pay higher costs (e.g., death), the situation becomes

more complex (Schultz 2001, 24). Empirical support for the relationship between failure in war and the loss of political power for wartime leaders is presented in Bueno de Mesquita and Siverson (1995); Bueno de Mesquita, Siverson, and Woller (1992); and Russett and Graham (1989). Bueno de Mesquita and Siverson provide some evidence that democratic leaders are more likely to be punished for costly military adventures.

6. This argument explicitly rejects the extreme form of Allison's (1971) bureaucratic politics model, which assumes that the president is simply first among equals. As Art (1973) and Krasner (1972) emphasize, the utility of the bureaucratic politics model declines as the importance of the decision grows. Decisions to use military force are almost always very important decisions. In terms of these decisions, bureaucratic politics and organizational models are most useful in explaining the flow of information to decision makers and the implementation of the decisions.

7. Allison's model, which describes politics as a tug-of-war between executive decision makers, may, in fact, be most applicable to non-U.S. cases. For an example involving the Soviet decision to invade Czechoslovakia, see Valenta (1975). For a critique of the application of Allison to this case, see Dawisha (1980).

8. If the central party controls the nomination list, party officials can remove renegade members from the list and prevent their reelection. Since 1988, local Conservative associations have been required to choose candidates from a list approved by the national party leaders (Garner and Kelly 1998, 89).

9. Gowa (1999, 33) argues that presidential control of the houses of Congress is a very good measure of institutional constraint within presidential systems such as the United States.

10. Elman also briefly examines British behavior toward Germany before World War II and Israeli behavior toward Lebanon from 1977 to 1981. In a related study, Elman (1997a) examines the Israeli invasion of Lebanon in 1982.

11. A wide variety of data sources were used to code the institutional constraint variables, including both general references and studies of individual countries. The general sources included, among others, country histories from the Library of Congress's *Country Studies—Area Handbook* series, the annual *Europa Yearbook* series, *Keesing's Contemporary Archives*, and the *New York Times*; election data from Mackie and Rose (1974, 1991), Gorvin (1989), and the Council on Foreign Relations' annual *Political Handbook of the World*; party information from the *Greenwood Historical Encyclopedia of the World* political parties series, Degenhardt (1988), and Day (1988); political system data from (Delury 1983), Kurian (1992), and Derbyshire and Derbyshire (1989); and political leader data from Lentz (1994). A fifth hypothesis, which tests the impact of having no legislature, is discussed later. Although this variable is required to test the constraint model, it is not directly derived from the logic of the model.

12. For the sake of clarity, predicted probabilities will be referred to using a percent sign (%), and a change in the predicted probability from X to Y will be referred to as a "Z-percentage-point change." Many would report the fall from 19% to 13% as a "thirty-two-percent" decline in the probability of using force. I believe this overstates the substantive impact of the variables.

13. Other work in this area (e.g., Reiter and Tillman [2002] and Huth and Allee [2002]) do not report nested tests of their models.

14. The India versus Pakistan case study was developed using the following sources: A. Appadorai, *The Domestic Roots of India's Foreign Policy 1947–1972* (Delhi, India: Oxford University Press, 1981); Narottam Gaan, *Indira Gandhi and Foreign Policy Making: The Bangladesh Crisis* (New Delhi, India: Patriot, 1992); Indira Gandhi, *India and Bangla Desh: Selected Speeches and Statements March to December 1971* (New Delhi, India: Orient Longman, 1972); Robert Jackson, *South Asian Crisis: India, Pakistan, and Bangladesh* (New York: Praeger, 1975); Sukhwant Singh, *India's Wars Since Independence, Volume One: The Liberation of Bangladesh* (New Delhi, India: Vikas, 1980).

15. Pakistan was not a democratic state when it initiated the first two military conflicts.

16. The case is one of relative deprivation. Although the economies of both states were growing rapidly by historical standards (6.2 percent per year in the West and 4.2 percent in the East), the rapid and continual relative decline in the eyes of the Easterners triggered increasing unrest.

17. The manifesto was in part triggered by Ayub Khan's military failures during the 1965 war with India. Residents of the East had long questioned the political and economic sacrifices required for the pursuit of the disputed Kashmir territory.

18. Indira Gandhi was the daughter of former Prime Minister Nehru and mother of future Prime Minister Rajiv Gandhi. She was not related to Indian independence leader Mahatma Gandhi.

19. The Congress Party had always been a faction-ridden party (Nicholson 1978). The immediate source of the split was Gandhi's leftist economic policies, which drew the ire of the more conservative members of the party.

20. According to former deputy Prime Minster Desai, regular Indian troops disguised as Mukti Bahini operated in East Pakistan from April to December (Gaan 1992, 130).

21. Pakistan expected a limited offensive by India. Based on this belief, the military chose to dig in around the perimeter of East Pakistan rather than pool its forces behind natural barriers (i.e., rivers) in the center of the state. The Indian army drove around these troops directly toward the capital of Dacca; much of the isolated resistance in the periphery simply melted away. Indian officials stated that by pooling their forces the Pakistani forces could have lasted six to eight weeks—long enough for the anticipated U.N., U.S., or China intervention to materialize.

22. According to the definitions employed in this study, India was the first state to use major force by employing tens of thousands of armed rebels against Pakistan. In contrast, in studies that code only the use of regular army troops, Pakistan would be the initiator of major force with its attack on December 3. Although the use of surrogate forces may, in part, fit a structural model of institutional constraint (i.e., use of surrogates lowers the probability of punishment), it clearly conflicts with normative explanations of the pacific nature of democracies.

23. On the eastern front, Pakistan had 4 divisions, 1 infantry brigade (for a total of 73,000 troops), 100 tanks, and 18 aircraft. India's force on this front consisted of 8 divisions, 3 infantry brigades, 1 airborne brigade, 29 Border Security Force bat-

talions, 3 Mukti Bahini brigades (for a total of 160,000 troops), 180 tanks, and 162 aircraft. In the west, while the forces were more evenly matched, India's defensive strategy greatly enhanced the probability of success.

24. As Visha Menan stated in his interviews with Brecher (1968), the lack of debate in the cabinet was not necessarily evidence of autocratic decision making. Nehru (like Eshkol in the Israeli case) tended to meet with key decision makers outside the formal meetings in order to air views and establish a consensus. Having said this, observers are virtually unanimous in their view that Nehru's opinion always prevailed in the end. Either he was extremely persuasive or he was never challenged in the area in which he considered himself an expert.

25. The El Salvador versus Honduras case study was developed using the following sources: Thomas P. Anderson, *The War of the Dispossessed: Honduras and El Salvador, 1969* (Lincoln: University of Nebraska Press, 1981); Jose Napoleon Duarte with Dianna Page, *Duarte: My Story* (New York: Putnam, 1986); Stephen Webre, *Jose Napoleon Duarte and the Christian Democratic Party in Salvadoran Politics 1960–1972* (Baton Rouge: Louisiana State University Press, 1979).

26. The Small and Singer figures are for battlefield fatalities only. However, Anderson (1981) claims that the military casualties were much lighter and that most of the 4,000 casualties were Honduran civilians. Official government figures (El Salvador claimed 107 killed in action, and Honduras claimed 99) clearly understated the totals (Clodfelter 1992, 1169). Clodfelter estimates that as many as 2,000 Honduran soldiers and civilians may have perished in the conflict. By most measures, the short war was extremely violent. Unfortunately, the inappropriate name for the conflict obscures both the causes and severity of the war.

27. Although these parties were officially outlawed, Rivera allowed them to compete. This leniency triggered much criticism from right-wing groups that supported PCN. PAR participated in the presidential election in 1967, but its election permit was revoked prior to the 1968 legislative elections.

28. Most cabinet members were civilians under Rivera and Sanchez. The exceptions were the internal and external security ministers (Interior and Defense).

29. The subsequent civil war in El Salvador is directly attributable to the failure of the government to address the concerns of opposition groups. These groups resorted to violence to change a system when it became clear to them that the system could not be changed from within.

30. Many U.S. and European elected officials have been former military leaders (e.g., Eisenhower and De Gaulle). However, in the U.S. system the election of a former general never directly followed a military coup. The situation in France following the fall of the Fourth Republic and rise of the Fifth Republic is slightly less clear.

31. Oren's argument that the definition of terms evolve over time is certainly correct. The definition of *republican*, for example, changed significantly in the course of the nineteenth century in the United States as competing economic classes sought to define the term in a manner that suited their interests. However, the terms *democratic* and *constitutional* cannot be used interchangeably in the structural arguments developed in Chapter 2. For example, constitutional states (i.e., states in which rule of law protects specific political rights and private property) that are predominantly

inclusive should behave differently than constitutional states that are relatively exclusive. More important, the identification of "us" (i.e., both are constitutional states or both are democratic states) versus "them" is important only in purely dyadic arguments. The monadic argument postulates that a state's behavior is constant regardless of the regime type of the adversary.

32. The following discussion draws heavily on Anderson (1981).

33. It is unclear why the Salvadoran troops were inside Honduras. Explanations range from attempting to overthrow Lopez Arellano to taking a wrong turn. The behavior of the border guards, who were heavily armed but put up absolutely no resistance to capture, defies explanation. The newspapers dubbed them the "sleeping beauties."

34. The Guatemalan government moved troops to its border and stated that it would not accept border changes in the region.

35. If the territory is consider "sacred" for historical or religious reasons, then dividing the "pie" can be problematic. However, whereas most ideological conflicts are seen in zero-sum terms, this is not true for territorial disputes. For data on the rise of ideological conflicts and the decline of territorial conflicts over the last several centuries, see Holsti (1991).

36. For a discussion of the role of regimes as impartial observers and mediators in ethnic conflicts, see Hopf (1992).

37. The United Kingdom versus the Soviet Union case study was developed using the following sources: Stephen R. Graubard, *British Labour and the Russian Revolution, 1917–1924* (Cambridge, MA: Harvard University Press, 1956); George F. Kennan, *Soviet American Relations, 1917–1920: Volume 2, The Decision to Intervene* (Princeton, NJ: Princeton University Press, 1958); Richard H. Ullman, *Anglo-Soviet Relations, 1917–1921: Volume 1, Intervention and the War* (Princeton, NJ: Princeton University Press, 1961); Richard H. Ullman, *Anglo-Soviet Relations, 1917–1921: Volume 2, Britain and the Russian Civil War* (Princeton, NJ: Princeton University Press, 1968); Stephen White, *Britain and the Bolshevik Revolution: A Study in the Politics of Diplomacy, 1920–24* (London: MacMillan, 1979); Anthony Wood, *Great Britain 1900–1965* (London: Longman, 1978).

38. Although President Wilson rejected calls for an anti-Bolshevik campaign, U.S. troops under the command of British officers clashed with Soviet forces, particularly at Archangel. U.S. troops stationed in Siberia also indirectly supported the White forces.

39. Both the Finnish and Russian civil wars pitted White (conservative) forces against Red (communist) forces.

40. The autonomy versus independence question is discussed below.

41. Some supporters of the eastern strategy, such as Winston Churchill, pushed for the disastrous offensives in the Dardenelles, including the infamous campaign at Gallipoli.

42. The persistent pursuit of the Czecho-Slovak/Japanese front represents a clear case of motivated bias; the cabinet's strong desires made the objective evaluation of incoming information impossible. See Jervis (1976) and Kaufmann (1993) for a discussion of motivated and cognitive biases in the context of foreign policy decision making.

43. Purists, such as Therborn (1977), demand universal suffrage before a country can be labeled a democracy; he contends that the United States cannot be counted as a democracy until the full implementation of the Voter Rights Act of 1964. For a discussion of the impact of war on the voting rights of women and minorities, see Rousseau and Newsome (2004).

44. The decision whether or not to participate in a postwar government split many parties. The ruling coalition included 335 Coalitional Unionists (Conservative), 133 Coalitional Liberals, and 10 Coalitional Labour Party members. The opposition included 23 Conservative, 25 Irish Unionist, 28 Liberals, 63 Labour, 7 Irish Nationalists, 73 Sinn Fein, and 10 others.

45. Democratic polities often choose technologically oriented interventions (such as bombing from a distance) in order to minimize troop losses and exploit their traditional technological superiority. It would be interesting to see if democracies from less developed countries (e.g., India) also avoid battlefield casualties to the same degree. See Reiter and Stam (2002, 134–35) for a related discussion of democracies and technology on the battlefield.

46. For a critique of Peceny, Beer, and Sanchez-Terry (2002), see Reiter and Stam (2003a) and the Peceny and Beer (2003) reply.

47. I would like to thank Finbarr Lane at the State University of New York at Buffalo for helping me prepare this section.

The Saudi Arabian case study was developed using the following sources: Mordechai Abir, *Saudi Arabia: Government, Society and the Gulf Crisis* (New York: Routledge, 1993); Saeed M. Badeeb, *The Saudi-Egyptian Conflict Over North Yemen, 1962–1970* (Boulder, CO: Westview, 1986); William A. Beling (ed.), *King Faisal and the Modernization of Saudi Arabia* (Boulder, CO: Westview, 1980); Ahmed Hassan Dahlan (ed.), *Politics, Administration and Development in Saudi Arabia* (Brentwood, MD: Amana Corporation, 1990); Gerald De Gaury, *Faisal: King of Saudi Arabia* (New York: Praeger, 1966); F. Gregory Gause, *Saudi-Yemeni Relations: Domestic Structures and Foreign Influence* (New York: Columbia University Press, 1990); Stenko Guldescu, "Yemen: The War and the Haradh Conference." *Review of Politics* 28 (1966): 319–31; Helen Chapin Metz (ed.), *Saudi Arabia: A Country Study* (Washington, DC: U.S. Government Printing Office, 1992); James P. Piscatori, "Islamic Values and National Interest: The Foreign Policy of Saudi Arabia." In Adeed Dawisha (ed.), *Islam in Foreign Policy* (Cambridge: Cambridge University Press, 1983): 33–53; Robert R. Sullivan, "Saudi Arabia in International Politics." *Review of Politics* 32 (1970): 436–46; Peter W. Wilson and Douglas F. Graham, *Saudi Arabia: The Coming Storm* (New York: M. E. Sharpe, 1994).

The Jordanian case study was developed using the following sources: Clinton Bailey, *Jordan's Palestinian Challenge, 1948–1983: A Political History* (Boulder, CO: Westview, 1984); Karla Cunningham, *Regime and Society in Jordan: An Analysis of Jordanian Liberalization* (Ph.D. dissertation, SUNY at Buffalo, 1997); Karla Cunningham, "The Causes and Effects of Foreign Policy Decision Making: An Analysis of Jordanian Peace with Israel." *World Affairs* 160:4 (Spring 1998): 192–202; Uriel Dann, *King Hussein and the Challenge of Arab Radicalism: Jordan 1955–1967* (New York: Oxford University Press, 1989); Adam Garfinkle, *Israel and Jordan in the Shadow of War* (New York: St. Martin's, 1992); Fred Khouri, *The Arab-Israeli Dilemma*, third edition (Syracuse: Syracuse University Press, 1985); Yehuda Lukacs, *Israel, Jordan, and the Peace Process* (Syracuse: Syracuse University Press, 1997); Samir A. Mutawi, *Jordan in the 1967 War* (Cambridge: Cambridge University Press, 1987); Robert Satloff, *Troubles on the East Bank: Challenges to Domestic Stability of Jordan* (New York: Praeger, 1986); Bassel F. Salloukh, "State Strength, Permeability, and Foreign Policy: Jordan in Theoretical Perspective." *Arab Studies Quarterly* 18 (Spring 1996): 39–66; Vick Vance and Pierre Lauer, *Hussein of Jordan: My "War" with Israel* (New York: Morrow, 1969); Valerie Yorke, *Domestic Politics and Regional Security: Jordan, Syria and Israel* (Aldershot, UK: Gower, 1988).

48. The closest Saudi Arabia has come to a formal constitution was the proposed but never implemented Organic Law of 1960. This proposed constitution included a 120-member national council (40 appointed and 80 indirectly elected through nomination by provincial councils and approved by a committee of 10 appointed by the king) (Peterson 1988, 113). The commitment to implement this law has been declared whenever the king needs to consolidate power, the last time being after the Gulf War. In 2003, the Council of Ministers announced that elections would be held for local, provincial, and consultative assemblies. However, this has not been implemented to date. For a general discussion of the relationship between war and the expansion of political rights, see Rousseau and Newsome (2004) and Rousseau and Blauvelt (1998).

49. Asir was one of the last pieces of territory incorporated into the Saudi state. It was taken in the 1933–34 Saudi-Yemen war.

50. Both classical realists (Gulick 1955) and neorealists (Waltz 1979) agree that states tend to balance against powerful states rather than bandwagon with them. Walt (1987) emphasizes that states balance against threats rather than power.

51. Peterson (1988, 114) claims that given the regional divisions, "there still is no true Saudi, only Najdis, Hijazis, and 'Aziris tied together by the Al Saud."

52. The Soviet Union vetoed Transjordan's petition to join the United Nations because it claimed Transjordan was not a sovereign state due to institutional ties to the British crown. An additional treaty in 1948 severed the problematic links between Britain and Transjordan. Data sets such as Polity and the Correlates of War project use the 1946 independence date. More important, the Jordanians also use the 1946 date to mark their independence.

CHAPTER 5

Political Norms Versus Institutional Structures

WHY ARE DEMOCRACIES less conflictual? The quantitative analyses in the two preceding chapters demonstrate that democracies are less likely to use force in disputes *regardless* of the regime type of the opposition. Although all the analyses have revealed a strong dyadic effect, a significant monadic effect was found using both the frequently employed Polity democracy-autocracy variables (Chapter 3) and the new institutional constraint variables (Chapter 4). What is the source of this *monadic* constraint in disputes? In this chapter, I investigate this question using a variety of methods, including two statistical models, a laboratory experiment, and four case studies. The results are consistent across each method of inquiry: structures rather than norms are the driving force behind the monadic democratic peace.

The theoretical discussion of the democratic peace model described in Chapter 2 outlines two alternative avenues through which democratic political systems can affect decisions to use military force: a normative explanation and an institutional explanation. The normative approach focuses on the socialization of leaders within the domestic sphere whereas the institutional approach emphasizes the domestic political costs of using force. In the political norms model, individual decision makers are constrained by their internal value systems; the decision maker believes that force is either a legitimate or illegitimate means for resolving political conflicts. In the structural model, political leaders are constrained by their domestic political environment. If opposition groups, regardless of their location in the political system, can punish decision makers for failures or costly successes, decision makers will be reluctant to use force.

Distinguishing the relative importance of structures and norms for foreign policy outcomes has been difficult for several reasons. First, at least to some degree, norms and structures are theoretically interactive. As leaders overseeing a transition to democracy would certainly attest, any attempt to develop stable democratic institutions requires at least some minimal acceptance of norms traditionally associated with democracy (such as resolving disputes within institutions and not resorting to physical force). The interactive relationship also results from the fact that the establishment and maintenance of democratic institutions in a society inevitably shape the socialization of future leaders. Second, developing measures of political norms independent of institutional structures is notoriously difficult. Some researchers have used institutional measures such as those found in the Polity II data set as a proxy for political norms.[1] Finally, most tests attempting to distinguish norms from structures have employed the problematic nondirected dyad (or summed dyad) as the unit of analysis rather than the state unit of analysis used in this project. Isolating the monadic impact of institutions and norms is impossible using the nondirected dyad (for example, United States versus North Korea in 1950) as the unit of analysis. For these three reasons, drawing any firm conclusions about the norms–structure debate from the existing empirical literature is difficult, if not impossible.

Perhaps the best test of the relative power of norms and structures was conducted by Maoz and Russett (1993). These authors lay out the assumptions underlying both models and develop measures designed to isolate the impact of each factor. They test their hypotheses using both the Militarized Interstate Dispute (MID) data set from the Correlates of War project and the International Crisis Behavior (ICB) data set developed by Brecher, Wilkenfeld, and Moser (1988). Maoz and Russett conclude that whereas both the normative and structural explanations are supported by the data, the normative model is superior in terms of robustness and consistency (1993, 636).

However, Maoz and Russett's conclusions cannot be considered definitive for several reasons. First, their analyses focus solely on the relationship between "joint" democracy and constraints on the use of force. That is, they tested only dyadic hypotheses. Having demonstrated in Chapter 3 with the broader dispute data set that more democratic states are less likely to use aggressive force against any type of state in disputes, it behooves us to reexamine the norms–structures debate without restricting our attention to cases of joint democracy.

Second, Maoz and Russett's measurement of norms, though superior to previous operationalizations in many ways, remains problematic. Their first normative variable is the number of years a country has been democratic. They hypothesize that the longer a state is democratic, the more thoroughly the norms of compromise and nonviolence have been absorbed by the public and by foreign policy decision makers. Although this approach is intuitively appealing, the authors acknowledge that because structural measures from Polity II are used to determine whether or not a state is democratic (which is required in order to sum the years in which the state is democratic), the variable still mixes norms and structures. Moreover, this measure mixes the theoretically distinct concepts of stability and democracy. One could logically propose an alternative hypothesis: regime stability reduces the likelihood of aggression. Unstable regimes may be more likely to attack adversaries for diversionary purposes. Conversely, unstable regimes are probably more likely to be attacked by opportunistic neighbors.[2] The non-directed dyad unit of analysis, which makes separating these two avenues to conflict impossible, exacerbates the problem of isolating the effects of democracy from stability.[3]

Maoz and Russett employ a second method for measuring norms: the amount of political violence in a society. They logically propose that the more often that individuals in a society use violence to resolve domestic political disputes, the less likely norms of compromise become deeply entrenched in the culture. Maoz and Russett measure political violence using the average number of political executions and domestic conflicts during the five years preceding the crisis. Unfortunately, this approach is not without its problems. Most U.S. foreign policy leaders were not raised in South Central Los Angeles or in the Cabrini Green public housing project in Chicago; in other words, while the United States as a whole scores very high for domestic violence due to the turmoil of the inner cities, it is not clear that urban violence has fundamentally altered the norms of individuals who go on to hold the most important political offices in the land. Intentional and unintentional segregation of populations can insulate decisions makers from the domestic violence that shapes the norms of specific segments of the population. As I will discuss below, if societal norms are simply an "average" of the population, the link between the norm and the individual president or prime minister becomes extremely tenuous. In addition, data on "political executions" are notoriously difficult to obtain and unreliable, particularly outside the limited set of advanced industrialized democracies. In the course of this study I had difficulty obtaining accurate data on the number of coups in developing countries during the postwar period; presumably, coups are much more significant and reportable events than political executions.

Third, the Maoz and Russett comparison of norms and structures is problematic by virtue of their operationalization of institutional constraint, which combines several sources of constraint (executive, legislative, and even federal-local) into a single trichotomous measure. This aggregation makes it impossible to determine if, for example, legislative or executive constraint can independently influence decision making. Moreover, the original trichotomous variable is transformed into a dummy variable indicating if both participants in the conflict are "highly constrained." This final transformation, which is required for their summed dyad test, neglects the fact that important differences could exist between different types of autocracies or for states at different points along the democracy-autocracy continuum.

Finally, the authors focus only on militarized crises in which military force is threatened or used. Although Maoz and Russett test two independent data sets in order to ensure robustness, both data sets focus on only the most intense conflicts—militarized crises. The dispute data set developed as part of this project allows generalization beyond the rather infrequent set of international crises.

More recently, a number of studies have probed the logical and empirical validity of the normative argument. Gowa (1999, 12) dismisses the argument on the grounds that norms are indistinguishable from interests. From this perspective, norms simply help determine a preference order that actors subsequently use to select policies. For example, if my society believes that using violence is wrong, then I have an interest in not using violence because I may be punished for doing so. Gowa then takes this argument one step further by arguing that all states should prefer to settle disputes short of war because war is costly.[4] Bueno de Mesquita and colleagues (2003, 221) reject the normative argument for two reasons. First, norms appear to be an ad hoc explanation in that proponents use the outcome to infer the presence of norms. Although Bueno de Mesquita and colleagues fail to cite any examples, coding the independent variable based on the dependent variable is an obvious faux pas. Second, they argue that democratic imperialism, the tendency for democracies to pick on the weak, and prevalence of democratic covert action undermine the normative argument.

Reiter and Stam also focus on imperialism and covert action: "The initiation of wars of empire against weaker states to expand democracy's interests and influence at the expense of weaker societies is inexplicable from the liberal norms perspective" (2002, 151). Although it is true that the initiation of violence and the conquering of territory are incompatible with the normative argument, the imperialism argument may not be the best test of the normative argument for three reasons. First, a pro-imperialism norm dominated virtually every middle and large power in the nineteenth and early twentieth centuries. As this competing norm slowly died out with decolonization, the more restrained nature of democracies should have become more apparent. Second, there were even liberal rationales for imperialism. Liberalism is a complex mixture of values that occasionally come into conflict (Rousseau 2004; Doyle 1997). Many liberals believed that civilized states must intervene in the periphery to bring the fruits of civilization to the rest of the world. Third, even if all states are imperialist, democracies could still be less likely to initiate nonimperialist wars relative to nondemocracies. Thus, discussing a handful of imperialist ventures by the United States cannot constitute decisive evidence against a normative argument.

Reiter and Stam (2002, 159) also briefly discuss covert action. They argue that covert action is better explained by institutional arguments than normative arguments. If the use of force is wrong, then whether it is secret or not should not matter. In the final section of this chapter, I probe this argument in a systematic fashion by using a laboratory experiment. My findings provide strong empirical support for Reiter and Stam's theoretical argument.

Cederman (2001a; Cederman and Rao 2001) argues that democracies have learned to cooperate with one another over time. Whereas learning can be interest-based (for example, my neighbors were at peace last year, and they grew rapidly), it can also be rule-based or normative (for instance, democracies should not fight other democracies). Cederman contends that the standard liberal assumption that the impact of institutions is time invariant needs to be questioned because norms can emerge over time through peaceful interaction and learning. Cederman and Rao use a regression model with dynamic coefficients to demonstrate how the peace between democracies has intensified across time. They claim that this can explain why many of the case studies from the nineteenth century and Gowa's statistical analysis of years prior to World War I failed to provide empirical support for the democratic peace argument (Layne 1994; Gowa 1999). In Chapter 7 I will return to this subject of learning and evolution.

Dixon and Senese (2002) argue that democracies are more peaceful with one another due to the presence of peaceful norms of conflict resolution. They argue that all democracies possess norms that restrain competition. Clashes over competing values are settled through mediation, negotiation, and compromise. Moreover, the public resolution of conflict is visible to all actors, domestic and foreign. Thus, Dixon and Senese predict that democratic dyads will be more likely to settle a militarized crisis through negotiation. Using the MID data set and a censored probit model, Dixon and Senese find that the minimum democracy score in the dyad (the "weak link" principle used in much of the nondirected dyad research such as Russett and Oneal [2001]) is positively associated with negotiated settlement even after controlling for alliances, severity of conflict, and duration of the dispute.

Finally, Huth and Allee (2002) explore three models (norms, accountability, and affinity) using a data set of territorial disputes in the twentieth century. They derive several testable propositions, including (1) leaders with nonviolent domestic political norms are more likely to rely on negotiation, more likely to offer concessions, and less likely to escalate a dispute; (2) leaders with nonviolent norms should be less likely to use force even when the balance of forces strongly favors their state; (3) young democracies are more likely to use force; and (4) leaders who violently repress conflicts at home are more likely to use force abroad. Following the empirical analysis of initiation, negotiation, and escalation, Huth and Allee conclude that "we found that the empirical evidence generally supported the expectation of the Accountability model" (2002, 286). The unconditional predictions of the political norms model could not account for the fact that democracies often have trouble conceding to rivals and damping public enthusiasm for aiding co-nationals. Thus, whereas the political accountability model can explain the push and pull within democracies, the norms model cannot.

The theoretical discussion and empirical analyses in the current chapter differ from this existing body of research in a number of ways. First, the statistical models test two causal arguments that have not been extensively studied in the literature. I explore whether the use of violence in other issue areas (such as obtaining office) increases the likelihood of using violence abroad and whether democratic polities are constrained only from using large amounts of violence. Second, the norms versus structures argument is tested with a laboratory experiment for the first time. The experiment probes whether subjects would be willing to use force against a democracy if doing so could be kept secret. Third, the statistical analysis employs the new dispute data set rather than the MID data set employed by Cederman and Dixon and Senese or the more narrow set of territorial disputes examined by Huth and Allee. Finally, the chapter examines a series of case studies to probe the constraining power of norms in both overt and covert settings.

Before turning to the new statistical tests and laboratory experiment, I would like to present a typology of norms that should illuminate the rationale behind the specific tests.

A Typology of Norms

Societal norms constrain behavior in many different ways. Table 5.1 uses a simple typology with two dimensions to illustrate several ways in which social norms can alter human behavior. The first dimension distinguishes the source of enforcement: internal versus external. Individuals adhere to internally enforced norms because they believe obeying the norm is "right"; individuals suffer from guilt or a loss of self-esteem if they violate the norm. In contrast, individuals adhere to externally enforced norms because other members of the group offer either rewards for adherence or threats for deviations. The second dimension distinguishes unconditional (monadic) from

TABLE 5.1

Categorization of norms

	Internally enforced	Externally enforced
Unconditional (monadic)	Quaker pacifism	Prohibitions on interracial marriages
Conditional (dyadic)	Fair trade (i.e., tit-for-tat) policy	Nonuse of chemical weapons by Japan against the U.S. in WWII

conditional (dyadic) norms. Unconditional norms demand adherence regardless of the nature of the situation or the behavior of the second party. In contrast, many conditional norms clearly specify the conditions under which adherence is required by the group.[5]

The two-by-two typology can be used to illustrate a wide variety of normative constraints. Consider, for example, the norm of pacifism in the Quaker religion. "Quaker pacifism" can often be categorized as an unconditional internally enforced norm. Members of this group are socialized to reject the use of violence to resolve political or personal disputes under all circumstances. Many, if not most, Quakers internalize this norm. They reject violence unconditionally; the behavior of the other party is irrelevant to the decision-making process. Quakers in the United States opposed serving in combat units in World War II despite the Japanese attack on U.S. soil and the German declaration of war.[6] Moreover, compliance is based on the belief that the norm is right; threats from other members of the group are not required to ensure that the individual follows the norm.

In contrast, the reciprocity-based fair trade strategy employing a "tit-for-tat" norm provides an example of a conditional internally enforced norm. The adoption of the liberal belief in the benefits of trade by the United States after World War II can be understood as an internally enforced norm (that is, you believe it is the right policy because it makes you and your trading partner better off). However, the fair trade norm is conditional in that if your trading partner does not reciprocate by opening its markets to your goods, you may punish this defection by closing your markets. This explicitly conditional "fair trade" strategy adopted by the United States and institutionalized in the General Agreement on Tariffs and Trade (GATT) in 1947 stands in stark contrast to the unconditional "free trade" strategy adopted by the British in the late nineteenth century. The Manchester Liberals, having internalized the norm of free trade, lowered trade barriers regardless of the behavior of their trading partners.

Norms prohibiting interracial marriages in the United States in the first half of the twentieth century were enforced both internally and externally. Individuals socialized to reject interracial marriage found the idea simply inconceivable; participation in this activity resulted in feelings of guilt and questions of identity. In this situation, the norm is categorically similar to the Quaker norm of nonviolence. However, the norm can also be enforced externally. Some individuals living in the South may have had no internal qualms about marrying someone from a different ethnic group. However, the individuals might have rejected such unions because the action could result in significant personal costs (for example, loss of a job, ostracism by families, and social isolation). These individuals adhered to the norm because of the costs imposed by society for deviating from the norm (Axelrod 1997).

The final example concerns a conditional externally enforced norm. In this situation, individuals adhere to norms because they fear punishment from others. However, the norm is conditional because once your opponent violates the norm, you feel free to follow its lead. An example of a conditional externally enforced norm is Japanese behavior with respect to chemical weapons during World War II. Chemical weapons were used extensively in World War I, and there was great fear they would be used in World War II despite the signing of the 1925 Geneva Protocol outlawing the use (but not development and production) of chemical weapons. Apparently, the Japanese were not internally constrained from using chemical weapons; they used them extensively against ill-equipped Chinese troops and civilians in the late 1930s. However, Japan did not use them against the United States because of the implicit threat that the United States would retaliate in kind (Desch 1998).[7] The external threat rather than internal beliefs dictated Japanese behavior.

Whereas social psychologists have made some progress in categorizing norms, the topic is rarely if ever addressed in the democratic peace literature.[8] Because of the dyadic focus of much of the democratic peace literature, most normative tests have implicitly focused on conditional externally enforced norms. Given that I wish to explore the monadic sources of constraint in order to explain the empirical findings in the previous two chapters, I want to shift the focus to unconditional internally enforced norms.

Test 1: New Political Norms Variables for the Statistical Model

As discussed above, Maoz and Russett employed the best measure of political norms used to date in a quantitative study relating the use of force and regime type—level of domestic violence. Perhaps the biggest drawback of such a measure, however, is its focus on average societal norms rather than norms adhered to by specific individuals. Norms refer to a set of beliefs held by the vast majority of members of a group. Individuals entering into the group, whether by birth, selection, or choice, are socialized through repeated interactions, shared rituals, and peer pressure. This group may be a subset of the total population. For example, Roman Catholics socialized in parochial grammar schools and at weekly masses could hypothetically develop a set of norms distinct from those accepted by society at large. Similarly, Nisbett and Cohen (1996) provide statistical and experimental evidence that southerners socialized to accept the "code of honor" norm are more likely to use violence to resolve personal disputes.

Societal norms, on the other hand, refer to that set of beliefs accepted by the vast majority of members of society at large. The normative explanation of the democratic peace postulates that all leaders within a particular country share common societal norms associated with resolving political conflicts. Maoz and Russett focus on societal norms. *All* political leaders at time X in country Y are expected to possess norms reflecting the average of society (such as the average number of political murders in the previous five years).

However, it is quite clear that individuals and subgroups in a population can operate according to very different norms. This could occur because norms are only weakly adhered to due to the high costs of enforcement by peers (Axelrod 1986). Conversely, as in the Roman Catholic example, adherence to different norms could reflect very different socialization patterns. Regardless of the cause, the variance in norm acceptance across a population implies that using a simple population mean for all individuals can introduce a serious amount of error into the model. For example, Adolf Hitler (National Socialist Party) and Gustav Stresemann (People's Party) were both socialized in the same political systems—a weakly authoritarian imperial system and a democratic Weimar system. Despite this shared experience, they developed very different values regarding the appropriateness of using force to resolve disputes both domestically and abroad. Whereas Stresemann won the Nobel peace prize, Hitler attempted to conquer Western Europe and exterminated millions of innocent people.

An alternative to measuring broad societal norms is to focus on the particular political leaders responsible for deciding whether or not force should be used in a dispute or crisis. In order to estimate norms of nonviolence and compromise for these leaders, I have chosen to focus on perhaps the most important event in their political careers: the attainment of the highest political office in the country. The means they employed in pursuit of one of their most important goals should shed light on how they pursued other political objectives—both domestically and internationally.

Goldgeier (1994) also argues that leaders develop decision-making strategies, or "schemas," for dealing with domestic political opposition. After obtaining the position of chief executive, these leaders naturally tend to rely on these strategies for dealing with international opponents. In his case study analysis of the Soviet Union, Goldgeier finds that Stalin used a "coercive strategy masked by accommodative gestures," Khrushchev employed open confrontation and personal commitments, Brezhnev used a cautious accommodative strategy that kept his options open, and Gorbachev used a confrontational strategy that avoided personal commitments (1994, 113). Goldgeier concludes that learning to use coercive strategies at home undermined the Soviet leaders' ability to conduct crisis management abroad because their aggressive strategies tended to legitimize the U.S. position. This increased public support in the United States and allied support abroad. Thus, how one behaves at home might have a profound impact on the emergence of international conflict.

For each year of a dispute, I identify the political leader in charge of foreign policy. Typically, this is a president, prime minister, or general secretary. However, in some cases, such as Somoza in Nicaragua during the late 1940s, the decision maker with real power holds either no formal position or a behind-the-scenes position with others serving as president or prime minister. For coding purposes, the decision maker with the power to decide whether or not force should be employed is coded, regardless of his or her formal position. If more than one leader held office in a given dispute or crisis year and there was no initiation of force, the leader with the longest tenure is used for coding purposes. However, if an individual authorized the use of force during the year, that person is coded regardless of how long he or she held office. These individual-level data provide the most direct test of the impact of leadership norms on the use of violence abroad.[9]

Leaders can enter office through one of three means: election, designation, and violence. Some chief foreign policy decision makers gained office through formal elections. This category includes free and fair elections as well as those tainted by some fraud and abuse. Although those leaders who stuff the ballot box may not adhere to norms of fair play traditionally associated with democratic systems, they are categorically different from those who reject the principle of elections. Another group of decision makers acquired office by being designated by the outgoing leader, ruling party, or ruling junta. In addition, monarchs are coded as having gained power through formal designation. Finally, leaders who came to power by leading coups or armed rebellions are coded as having used force to obtain office. For example, Ho Chi Minh in Vietnam and Idi Amin in Uganda are coded as having used force.[10]

HYPOTHESIS I

Decision makers who obtain political office through violence are more likely to view violence as an acceptable means for resolving international disputes and, therefore, more likely to use aggressive force.

Obviously, means of entry into office is not a perfect measure of norms. Jimmy Carter and Ronald Reagan both entered office via elections; however, they had very different beliefs about the appropriateness of the use of force to resolve conflicts. An ideal approach would involve developing an extensive case study for each political leader in the dispute data set. This is not feasible for this research design because there are literally several hundred decision makers in the data set. However, I still contend that Carter's and Reagan's belief systems are likely to be more similar to each other than to an individual entering office via a hard-fought civil war or via a coup in which all political opposition is systematically eliminated. Overall, estimating norms by focusing on particular decision makers is in all likelihood a more precise approach to measuring norms than those that rely on aggregate country averages.

It also important to emphasize that the hypothesis tests only norms of conflict resolution among autocratic rulers; by definition, democratic decision makers do not acquire office through force or designation. An analysis of the strength of norms among democratic leaders is deferred until the next section. The correlations between the *Violent Entry into Office* and the *Designated Entry into Office* variables and the *Actor's Net Democracy* are -0.41 and -0.38, respectively. All other variables were defined in chapters 2 and 3.

The results of this first normative test are shown in Table 5.2. The first column presents results using the dispute data set and the dichotomous *Aggressive Use of Force* dependent variable whereas the second column displays results for the crisis data set and the trichotomous *Highest Level of Force* dependent variable.[11] According to the normative argument, the *Violent Entry into Office* variable should be positive; moreover, the marginal effect of this variable should be much stronger than the *Designated Entry into Office* variable (even though both may be positive because autocratic rulers have been shown to be more likely to resort to force in general).

The results using the dispute data set in column one of Table 5.2 do not confirm the hypothesis. Contrary to expectations, the *Violent Entry into Office* coefficient is statistically indistinguishable from zero, and the *Designated Entry into Office* variable in the dispute data set is negative. Thus, the results indicate that autocratic leaders who take office peacefully are less likely to use violence than are other types of autocratic leaders. Although this finding is partially consistent with expectations, the *Designated Entry into Office* variable remains statistically significant in only about half of all sensitivity

TABLE 5.2
Probit analysis incorporating the political norms variables

Independent variables	Dispute data set and aggressive use of force dependent variable Coefficient (SE)	Crisis data set and highest level of force dependent variable Coefficient (SE)
Actor's net democracy (monadic)	−0.022 (0.005)★★★	0.002 (0.009)
Actor's net democracy with democratic opponent (dyadic)	−0.073 (0.015)★★★	−0.062 (0.016)★★
Opponent's net democracy	0.015 (0.004)★★★	0.023 (0.016)★★★
Balance of forces	0.194 (0.073)★★	0.029 (0.271)
Shared alliance ties	−0.114 (0.060)★	−0.139 (0.109)
Satisfaction with the status quo	−0.687 (0.057)★★★	−1.107 (0.118)★★★
Democracy with weak opponent	−0.026 (0.109)	0.540 (0.319)★
Democracy with weak democracy	0.323 (0.487)	−1.114 (0.750)
Opponent initiated force	—	0.742 (0.075)★★★
Violent entry into office	−0.047 (0.076)	0.078 (0.122)
Designated entry into office	−0.146 (0.081)★	0.227 (0.138)
Constant or cut1	−1.592 (0.090)	0.338 (0.216)
Cut2	—	0.693 (0.215)
Number of observations	5,600	667
Log likelihood at convergence	−1830.13	−631.28

NOTE: All significance tests are one-tailed. ★$p < .05$, ★★$p < .01$, ★★★$p < .001$. Robust standard errors.

runs, and its marginal impact is small. As Table 5.3 indicates, a shift from not designated to designated lowers the predicted probability of using force only from 20% to 17%.

The remaining variables in the dispute equation are extremely stable in comparison with the results of the democratic peace model of disputes presented in Chapter 3. The democratic peace variables indicate that democratic polities are significantly less likely to use aggressive force (that is, monadic), particularly when facing other democracies (that is, dyadic). A shift from 0 to 20 on the *Actor's Democracy* variable decreases the predicted probability of using force from 22% to 12%. When facing a democratic opponent, the same shift causes a 29-percentage-point decline in the probability of using force. In terms of marginal effect, the dyadic democracy variable is the strongest factor in the model. Finally, the statistical significance of the three control variables (*Balance of Forces, Shared Alliance Ties*, and *Satisfaction with the Status Quo*) has virtually the same impact as the model in Chapter 3. A favorable military balance increases the probability of using force, and alliance ties decrease uses of aggressive force. However, both these variables have a limited marginal impact (+5 and −3, respectively). In contrast, satisfaction with the status quo strongly decreases a state's likelihood of resorting to violence. A shift from dissatisfied to satisfied lowers the predicted

TABLE 5.3
Marginal effects of the full model with the normative variables

Shift in independent variable	Dispute data set Probability of using aggressive force	Crisis data set Probability of using high levels of force
Actor's democracy		
0	22	n.s.
10	16	n.s.
20	12	n.s.
Total change	**−10**	
Actor's democracy with democratic opponent		
0	30	44
10	7	21
20	1	8
Total change	**−29**	**−36**
Opponent's democracy for fully autocratic state		
0	21	27
10	25	35
20	30	44
Total change	**+9**	**+17**
Balance of forces		
1:9	18	n.s.
1:3	19	n.s.
1:1	20	n.s.
3:1	22	n.s.
9:1	23	n.s.
Total change	**+5**	
Shared alliance ties		
No	20	n.s.
Yes	17	n.s.
Total change	**−3**	
Satisfaction with status quo		
No	20	31
Yes	7	6
Total change	**−13**	**−25**
Opponent initiated force		
0	—	31
10	—	60
20	—	83
Total change		**+52**
Democracy with weak opponent		
Weaker or equal	n.s.	31
Stronger	n.s.	52
Total change		**+21**
Designated entry into office		
No	20	n.s.
Yes	17	n.s.
Total change	**−3**	

NOTE: See Table 2.5 for description of methodology. The probabilities have been collapsed into two categories: the probability of using force at any level and the probability of not using force. The results for the latter, not shown, are simply one minus the former. The abbreviation "n.s." implies the variable is not significant in Table 5.2.

probability of using force by 13 percentage points. Finally, the interactive variables from the selectorate model have no impact.

In the crisis data set, shown in column two of Table 5.2, the *Violent Entry* and the *Designated Entry* variables are statistically insignificant. Once again, it appears that using violence to gain the highest office in the land does not predispose one to using violence to resolve an international conflict. Although the *Designated Entry* is very close to conventional levels of statistical significance, sensitivity analysis with the *Initiation of Force* and the *Aggressive Use of Force* dependent variables introduced in Chapter 2 did not produce significant results. Thus, quantitative findings cast doubt upon the normative hypothesis. The rest of this model is virtually identical to the crisis model presented in Chapter 2.

Test 2: Testing Political Norms with a Logit Model

The second test used to compare the power of political norms with institutional structures relies on an alternative statistical model rather than additional normative variables. Although it is admittedly a more indirect test of the relative strength of the two explanations, the second test, described below, does probe an important difference between the two models. Most analyses of the relationship between domestic political systems and the use of military force abroad have employed categorical dependent variables. Many studies have employed dichotomous dependent variables (in other words, there is either a war or there is not).[12] Other studies have used a multichotomous approach.[13] Some of the preceding analysis employed a three-category version of the *Aggressive Use of Force* dependent variable (no use of force, minor use of force [1–1,000 troops], major use of force [more than 1,000 troops]). The categorical nature of the dependent variable prohibits the use of standard regression procedures, such as ordinary or generalized least squares, because the error term no longer conforms with the underlying assumptions of these models. In response, researchers have relied on probit and logit models that typically employ maximum likelihood methods of estimation. Under typical circumstances, probit and logit models produce very similar results because the two distributions differ only at the extreme ends, or "tails."

There are two types of probit and logit models: ordered and unordered. The appropriate model depends on the dependent variable in question. Some categorical dependent variables have no natural ordering. For example, studies of worker occupation (farming, manufacturing, service, other) typically employ unordered probit and logit models because the categories lack a clear hierarchy. In contrast, an ordered probit or logit model implies a natural ranking of the categories. In the probit analysis used in sensitivity analysis in previous chapters, the trichotomous dependent variable assumed a rising scale from no force to minor force to major force. Whereas the ordered probit model does not require any assumptions about distance between categories (a score of 4 is not necessarily twice the level of a score of 2), it does assume a natural ordering. For this reason, most studies of the use of force that employ multiple categories for the dependent variable have relied on ordered probit and logit models (see Maoz and Russett 1993). As I seek to demonstrate, this quite natural choice may have important repercussions.

The political norms model assumes that decision makers have stable value systems that guide their behavior during disputes. If a decision maker believes that using physical force to coerce a political opponent into complying with a demand is illegitimate, then this decision maker is expected to refrain from initiating violence. Norms of nonviolence and reciprocity imply that force should be reluctantly used and rarely initiated. Such an individual, *constrained from within*, should be less likely to use aggressive force at *any* level (less likely to use both minor force and major force).[14]

Skeptical readers may respond that the degree of adherence to a norm could be directly proportional to the severity of the violation. This is certainly plausible, but it is unlikely because internalized norms tend to be defined with very rigid rules. The rigid rules aid in the transmission and absorption of the norm by young and new members of a society (Berger and Luckmann 1966, 70). Consider, for example, the norm against stealing. There are obviously laws against stealing, but there are also powerful social norms instilled in people during childhood by families, schools, and churches. Does the value of the item matter? Are you more likely to steal a novel from a Borders bookstore than a cuisine art food processor from Williams-Sonoma? Are you more likely to steal the food processor than a car? More likely to steal a car than rob a bank? My guess is that the answer to most of these questions is no. *Stealing anything creates a profound sense of guilt and undermines the individual's self-esteem.* I am suggesting that a norm against using violence to resolve political conflicts has a similar threshold effect.

HYPOTHESIS 2

The normative model predicts that decision makers possessing norms of nonviolence and compromise should be less likely to use aggressive force at any level to resolve an international dispute.

In contrast to the normative explanation, the structural explanation implies that restraint occurs only because of the threat of punishment from the domestic political environment. The structural framework posits that the behavior of leaders varies across political systems precisely because the probability of punishment varies. However, it is also obvious that different uses of military force expose decision makers to very different amounts of political risks. President Reagan's order to bomb Qaddaffi's home in Tripoli in retaliation for allegedly backing the terrorist bombing of a disco in Rome involved very little domestic political risk. The number of Americans at risk was small, as was the probability of conflict escalating or becoming a prolonged engagement. In contrast, President Clinton's decision to commit U.S. forces to Somalia and Bosnia involved much greater political risk; the number of fatalities and the duration of the operations could have grown steadily and resulted in punishment by domestic opposition. As analyses of the Vietnam War have demonstrated, rising casualties lead directly to a decline in public support for the military operation (Mueller 1973, 266; Lorell and Kelley 1985; Gartner and Segura 1998).

Although we still might expect more constrained states to be less likely to initiate force at any level relative to less constrained states, the difference between the two should grow as the expected size and duration of the proposed military operation increases.

HYPOTHESIS 3
The structural model implies that constraint on the use of force in international disputes should be much stronger for major uses of force than for minor uses of force.

Hypotheses 2 and 3 imply that the use of an ordered probit model may in fact obscure information that would allow us to determine the relative strengths of the normative and structural models. An unordered logit model allows us to test the proposition that constrained leaders may be less likely to initiate major violence but quite willing to use small levels of force. In effect, I am arguing that factors which influence decisions to use minor force may be substantially different from the factors affecting decisions to use major force.

The results of the unordered logit test for both the crisis data set (first column) and the dispute data set are shown in Table 5.4.[15] For the crisis equation, I use a trichotomous *Highest Use of Force* dependent variable that distinguishes a major use (more than 1,000 troops), a minor use (1–1,000 troops), and no use of force (0 troops). The dispute equation is estimated with a trichotomous *Aggressive Use of Force* dependent variable using the same thresholds. The baseline category for both models is no use of force. The interactive balance of forces and dyadic democracy variable created to test the selectorate model has been removed because too few observations fall in each category to produce meaningful estimates.

Section A of Table 5.4 examines the probability of using minor force compared to the probability of using no force at all. Section B compares the

TABLE 5.4
Unordered logit analysis of crises and disputes

Independent variables	Crisis data set Dependent variable: Highest use of force	Dispute data set Dependent variable: Aggressive use of force
(A) log [Prob(Minor Force) Prob(No Force)]		
Actor's net democracy (monadic)	0.011	0.016
	(0.016)	(0.012)
Actor's net democracy with	−0.068★	0.096★★
democratic opponent (dyadic)	(0.035)	(0.031)
Opponent's net democracy	0.033	0.023★
	(0.020)	(0.012)
Balance of forces	0.421	−0.287
	(0.602)	(0.217)
Shared alliance ties	−0.396★	−0.389★
	(0.241)	(0.186)
Satisfaction with the status quo	−1.794★★★	1.162★★★
	(0.290)	(0.180)
Opponent's use of force	0.706★★★	—
	(0.182)	—
Democracy with weak opponent	0.137	−0.152
	(0.664)	(0.363)
Constant	0.007	3.648★★★
	(0.401)	(0.224)
(B) log [Prob(Major Force)/Prob(No Force)]		
Actor's net democracy (monadic)	−0.010	−0.053★★★
	(0.017)	(0.010)
Actor's net democracy with	−0.229★★★	−0.288★★★
democratic opponent (dyadic)	(0.045)	(0.086)
Opponent's net democracy	0.063★★	0.036★★★
	(0.020)	(0.011)
Balance of forces	0.044	0.648★★★
	(0.643)	(0.159)
Shared alliance ties	−0.452	−0.236★
	(0.248)	(0.139)
Satisfaction with status quo	−2.610★★★	1.545★★★
	(0.308)	(0.158)
Opponent's use of force	1.732★★★	—
	(0.204)	—
Democracy with weak opponent	0.668	0.216
	(0.694)	(0.253)
Constant	−0.002	−3.668★★★
	(0.430)	(0.194)
Number of observations	674	5600
Log likelihood at convergence	−630.52	−2225.24

NOTE: Robust standard errors appear in parentheses. All significance tests are one-tailed. ★p < 0.05, ★★p < 0.01, ★★★p < 0.001.

probability of using major force to the probability of not using force at all. The political norms model predicts that the coefficients and *t*-statistics found in the top half should parallel those in the lower half; the structural model predicts that the constraint variable should be weak or zero in the top half and strong in the lower half. It is immediately apparent that the data more strongly support the institutional explanation.

In the dispute data on the right, the monadic *Actor's Democracy* variable supports the structural explanation. Whereas a state's level of democracy does not have a statistically significant impact on minor uses of force (B = 0.016; SE = 0.012), it strongly restrains decision makers from using major levels of violence (B = −0.053; SE = 0.010). Democratic leaders appear to be willing to resort to minor uses of force because they are unlikely to be severely punished for the policy. A raid by U.S. aircraft against Libya, which is likely to be popular with the public, has little downside because it is unlikely to result in a prolonged engagement or numerous U.S. casualties. As Stein (1980) has shown, external threats can trigger a rally effect that begins to decay only when mobilization and engagement trigger rising opposition. In sum, minor uses of force can allow leaders to accrue the benefits of the rally effect without the costs of mobilization and body bags.[16]

From a dyadic perspective, the impact of democracy is more consistent when using the dispute data set. When facing a democratic opponent, the more democratic a state, the less likely it is to use either minor or major force. The *Actor's Democracy with a Democratic Opponent* coefficient is negative and statistically significant in both instances. Thus, although democratic leaders appear to be willing to use minor levels of force against autocratic states, they refrain from using force when facing other democracies.

The *Balance of Forces* variable in the dispute model is statistically insignificant in the case of minor uses of force and strongly positive in the case of major uses of force (B = 0.648; SE = 0.159). This combination of results implies that many weak states feel comfortable initiating low levels of violence. An unfavorable military position may not prevent weak states from using minor levels of violence, such as launching small-scale probes or providing limited support of third parties, apparently because these leaders do not expect the situation to spiral into a major conflict. However, weak states are be deterred from using force at major levels. The positive coefficient implies that the stronger a state is, the more likely it is to initiate high levels of violence.

As expected, the *Shared Alliance Ties* variable is negative and statistically significant at the 0.05 level at both levels of violence when using the dispute data set. Alliances decrease the probability that a state will use low or high levels of force. The *Satisfaction with the Status Quo* variable is positive and significant at both levels of violence. As we would expect, states rejecting the status quo are more likely to use both major and minor force in an attempt to resolve a dispute. Unlike the institutional or balance of forces variables, there is no logical reason to expect a shift in the coefficient between low and high levels of aggressive force.

Finally, the interactive balance of forces and democracy variable used to test the selectorate model is once again statistically insignificant. Democracies are not especially likely to pick on weaker states, as the formal model predicts.

The results using the crisis data set, shown in the left-hand column of Table 5.4, parallel both the previous findings involving crises in Chapter 2 and the dispute finding just examined. As shown in Chapter 2, only a dyadic effect of democratic institutions emerges within crises. In both sections A and B, the monadic *Actor's Democracy* variable fails to meet standard thresholds of statistical significance. In contrast, the dyadic *Actor's Democracy with Democratic Opponent* variable is statistically significant in both sections (minor use: B = −0.068; SE = 0.035; major use: B = −0.229; SE = 0.045).

The *Opponent's Democracy* variable is positive and significant only in the case of high levels of force. Whereas autocracies feel free to attack any type of state with low levels of force, they appear more likely to attack democracies when using high levels of force. As in the previous analysis in Chapter 2, the *Balance of Forces* variable is positive but statistically insignificant. Alliance ties only appear to reduce the likelihood of minor uses of force. However, the *t*-statistic falls just short of the 0.05 threshold in the major use of force case, so not much should be made of the difference between sections A and B. As with all of the crisis models examined, *Satisfaction with the Status Quo* reduces the likelihood of conflict, both major and minor. Finally, a use of force by the opponent significantly increases the likelihood that a state will resort to violence.

In summary, the normative hypothesis predicts that democracies will be less likely to use both large- and small-scale force because resorting to violence should be seen as a last resort. In contrast, the structural explanation predicts only that democracies will refrain from initiating large-scale violence. The statistical results strongly support the structural explanation. The monadic constraint of democracy disappears in the case of minor levels of violence.

Test 3: A Laboratory Experiment

In this section, we shift our inquiry from statistical analysis to a laboratory experiment. The use of an experiment will allow us to more easily disentangle the structural causal mechanisms from the normative causal mechanisms. In the experiment, subjects are presented hypothetical international scenarios and are asked whether they support or oppose the use of force to resolve the conflict. By randomly assigning variations of the scenario, we can determine which variables are most important in the decision-making process. For example, half of the subjects read a scenario in which the home state is stronger than the opponent, and half read a scenario in which the home state is weaker. Are subjects more likely to use force from a position of strength? Even against another democracy? As with the statistical analysis, the findings strongly support the structural explanation of the monadic democratic peace.

The use of an experimental method to probe the democratic peace has both advantages and disadvantages. On the positive side of the ledger, the experiment allows the researcher to precisely control the independent variables and dependent variables in order to test subtle differences in causal mechanisms. Moreover, the random assignment of subjects to different scenarios allows the researcher to control for alternative explanations such as the political views of the subjects or their knowledge of international affairs. Although spurious correlations and omitted variable bias always undermine our ability to draw firm conclusions from large-N correlational studies, a well-executed experiment allows us to demonstrate causation. Finally, the standardization of the procedure aids rapid replication, confirmation, and extensions of the analysis.

On the negative side of the ledger, three important critiques of this particular experimental research design stand out. First, critics might argue that the use of student subjects restricts our ability to generalize to other relevant populations, such as foreign policy decision makers. Clearly, students do not make decisions to go to war or to remain at peace. Nor do professors, military officers, or most foreign policy analysts. However, all these groups can have an important impact on foreign policy debates and decisions because political leaders seek to persuade these groups of the merits of their arguments. Understanding how members of the public make sense of foreign policy situations will enhance our understanding of the constraints and opportunities available to foreign policy decision makers. This experiment is clearly a first cut at the issue, but demonstrating the validity of the argument (even with a student sample) can be viewed as a *necessary* first step in the accumulation of knowledge.

Second, critics could claim that the use of hypothetical scenarios undermines our ability to understand real-world crises. Unfortunately, there is always a tension between making a scenario either too "concrete" or too "abstract." If the scenario is too concrete (it strongly resembles a real-world situation), each subject tends to bring unique information into the experiment that is not under the control of the researcher. In contrast, if the scenario is too abstract (such as "alpha state is a neighbor of beta state"), the scenario may fail to engage the respondent in a meaningful way. The current experiment attempts to balance these concerns by providing enough detail to make the story seem plausible without triggering recollections of a particular historical conflict.[17] In the research program overall, the robustness of results should be explored using both concrete cases with real states and abstract cases with highly stylized scenarios.

Third, critics might argue that there are no real consequences for the subjects for choosing to use military force. Unlike real democratic decision makers, the subjects will never have to face an angry public if the policy fails or is a costly success. In such a costless environment, subjects can choose to use force on a whim. However, the lack of costs should make our subjects *more* willing to use force in all conditions (that is, it should work against the proposed hypothesis). The statistically significant results discussed below indicate that even when the costs are low and the opinions are anonymous, individuals are reluctant to initiate a preference for using force against democracies.

In sum, experiments are neither a panacea nor a waste of time. They, like all methods of inquiry, have important strengths and weaknesses. My purpose is to explore the relationship between norms and structures by way of an underused approach in the hopes of complementing the existing large-N and case study literatures.[18]

There are two other experimental investigations of the democratic peace. Mintz and Geva (1993) used an experimental method to assess political incentives for using force against a democracy. Unlike the current study, these authors did not seek to distinguish between normative and structural constraints. Rather, they sought to examine the demand side of the equation: when do leaders benefit from using force? Their results supported a third causal explanation for the democratic peace: democratic political leaders do not use force against democracies because the public views such a policy as a failure: "Leaders of democratic nations are less likely to use force against other democracies to divert attention from domestic problems such as economic crisis, and/or to enhance their popularity" (1993, 501).

Geva and Hanson (1999) used an experimental design to investigate the relationship among cultural similarity, perception of regime type, and willingness to intervene forcibly. Geva and Hanson used a modified version of the abstract Mintz and Geva scenario, in which the island nation of Degania is challenging the island nation of Raggol. In their first study, the authors varied two dimensions: cultural similarity of the challenger to the United

States (similar versus dissimilar) and aggressiveness of the challenger (initiated economic sanctions versus initiated invasion). Rather than telling subjects that the challenger was a democracy, they wished to see how subjects perceived the other state given similar or dissimilar cultural features (such as English speaking versus Arabic speaking).[19] In their second study, the authors substituted the aggressiveness of the United States thus far in the conflict (blockade versus attack) for the aggressiveness of the challenger. The authors concluded that cultural similarity contributes to regime attribution and that the perception of joint democracy decreases willingness to use force.

The current study differs from the work of Mintz and Geva (1993) and Geva and Hanson (1999) in three ways. First, neither of the previous experimental studies focused on distinguishing the normative and the structural explanations of the democratic peace. Whereas Mintz and Geva focused on diversionary war, Geva and Hanson focused on the impact of cultural similarity. Second, the experimental manipulations in the previous studies were quite different from those proposed here. The Mintz and Geva study manipulated a single dimension: the regime type of the adversary (1993, 490). Geva and Hanson manipulated the culture of the other state and the aggressiveness of the other state (or of the United States). In contrast, the current experiment manipulates three dimensions (balance of military forces, domestic political position, and opponent's regime type) in order to examine a competing realist explanation and to disentangle norms and structures. Third, in the previous experiments the opposing state, whether democratic or autocratic, had already triggered a crisis by using military force or an economic blockade.[20] In previous chapters, it was shown that a first use of force by an opponent erodes monadic and dyadic constraints on the use of force by democracies because domestic opposition to the use of violence declines rapidly once blood has been drawn. Therefore, the current experiment begins with an ongoing dispute in which neither side has used force for a number of years. Although none of these differences are intended to be a critique of prior work, they highlight the fact that the current experiment differs significantly in terms of central hypotheses and research design.

HYPOTHESES

The experiment tests four hypotheses:

HYPOTHESIS 1
Balance of Military Forces. If the balance of military forces favors your country, you will be more likely to favor the use of military force.

HYPOTHESIS 2
Opponent's Regime Type. If your opponent is a democratic regime, you will be less likely to use military force.

HYPOTHESIS 3
Domestic Political Position. The stronger your domestic political position, the more likely you are to favor the use of military force.

HYPOTHESIS 4
Secret Use of Force. If you can use force secretly (without discovery by your domestic political opposition or the public at large), you will be more likely to use military force.

The balance of military forces hypothesis probes the realist contention that power, rather than ideas, determines the perception of threat and willingness to use force. Waltz (1979, 102) argues that any asymmetry in power is potentially dangerous because nothing in the anarchic structure of the system prevents another state from using force. Survival depends on a state's ability to amass military power through either domestic military buildups or external alliances. Threats and the use of violence are viewed as effective instruments of state policy in virtually all realist thinking (Machiavelli 1950; Hobbes [1651] 1968; Gulick 1955, chapter 3; Waltz 1979, chapter 8; Mearsheimer 1983).

Built into most realist thinking is the assumption that states will use military force when in a position of strength. Mearsheimer, an offensive realist who assumes that states maximize power, argues that "a great power that has a marked power advantage over its rivals is likely to behave more aggressively, because it has the capability as well as the incentive to do so" (2001, 37). Similarly, in their attempts to develop a "realist" computer model of the world, both Cederman (1997, 85) and Cusack and Stoll (1990, 70) introduce a rule requiring a favorable balance of power position before initiating an attack.

Even defensive realists emphasize the importance of a favorable balance of military power. Although exceptions may occur when states perceive the status quo as unacceptable (Jervis et al. 1985) or believe they can present a *fait accompli* (Paul 1994), most defensive realists would agree that holding all other factors constant, weak states are less likely to initiate direct military conflict than strong states are. Empirical analysis of conflict initiation strongly supports this prediction (Huth 1996). Whereas this reluctance to initiate does not preclude weak states from pursuing alternative means to challenge the threatening state, it does imply that weak states are less likely to initiate a direct military confrontation using regular army forces.[21] Therefore, the Balance of Military Forces hypothesis predicts that individuals will be more willing to use military force if the balance of military power favors their state.[22]

The second hypothesis, opponent's regime type, tests the dyadic version of the democratic peace argument. As discussed, the dyadic version of the democratic peace claims that democracies are more peaceful only with other democracies. How can we isolate this behavior? In all the experimental scenarios, the subject's "home" state was described as democratic.[23] By randomly varying the regime type of the other state in the hypothetical scenarios, we can assess if the regime type of the other state influences the individual's willingness to use violence to resolve a conflict. Given the strong empirical support for the dyadic democratic peace in the quantitative literature, the failure to confirm this hypothesis would call into question the entire experimental design.

The third hypothesis, labeled the domestic political position argument, explores the impact of domestic politics on an individual's willingness to use force. Specifically, the hypothesis tests the monadic structural variant of the democratic peace. If a political leader faces little domestic political opposition, he or she should be more willing to use military force because the probability of punishment remains lower than when the political leader faces intense domestic political opposition. Whereas all leaders can expect to be punished for foreign policy failures (or costly successes), the severity and certainty of punishment are higher in a political system with powerful opposition groups. Conversely, minority governments in democratic polities should be less likely to initiate conflict.[24]

The fourth hypothesis, regarding the secret use of force, explores the normative version of the democratic peace. If internal beliefs about appropriate means of conflict resolution guide an individual's willingness to use force, then whether or not the use of force is publicized should be irrelevant. Individuals should be unwilling to attack democracies because it is wrong rather than because they fear punishment from the political opposition or the public at large. In contrast, the structural version of the democratic peace predicts that if knowledge of the use of force can be kept from the domestic political opposition and the public, then the individual would be more willing to use force.

The issue of covert action has long been tied to the democratic peace debate.[25] Although it is generally accepted that democracies routinely use covert action against nondemocracies, the question of covert action against democracies has been hotly debated. Forsythe claims that the United States has used covert action against "political regimes that were not only elected but which could accurately termed partially or basically democratic" (1992, 392). Many of his cases fall far short of standard thresholds for democracy used by studies employing the Polity data sets (for example, Iran in 1953), but other cases are clearly at least partially democratic (such as Chile in 1973). For example, although the Polity IV Autocracy and Democracy indices for Iran are 4 and 3, respectively, in 1952, the codings for Chile are 0 and 6, respectively, in 1972.[26] Similarly, Sorensen (1992) claims that the United States has used violence short of war, including covert action, due to fears of spreading communism and threats to U.S. economic interests. Finally, James and Mitchell (1995) claim that the use of covert action by democracies against democracies severely undermines the democratic peace argument. Moreover, they explicitly argue that the use of covert action severely undermines the normative (which they refer to as the "cultural") argument:

> In sum, if the shared cultural norms premise of the democratic peace is correct, then why would democratic states fight each other in ways short of open warfare but preclude war itself? The covert attack, the institution of rebellion, the use of political propaganda, the interference in democratic elections, etc. are not tolerant or conciliatory acts. Covert attacks provide a serious challenge to the cultural premise of democratic peace, one that the literature now dismisses because covert attacks do not meet the Small and Singer (1976) definition of war (1995, 91).

Drawing on a modified version of the Bueno de Mesquita and Lalman (1992) *crisis subgame*, James and Mitchell identify the conditions under which democracies are likely to use covert action against other democracies. Specifically, they claim that powerful democracies are likely to use covert action against weak, poorly established democracies (1995, 102).[27] This causal claim, which is also a centerpiece of the selectorate model of Bueno de Mesquita and colleagues, is explored in the empirical analysis.

Finally, Reiter and Stam (2002, 159) argue that covert action provides evidence against the normative version of the democratic peace: "The normative theory in straightforward terms forecasts that democracies would not use any means, overt or covert, to subvert or to overthrow another democratically elected government" (2002, 160). Although Reiter and Stam are speaking about a dyadic peace in this passage, they recognize that the argument should apply to the monadic peace as well. Unfortunately, Reiter and Stam provide only illustrative evidence in support of this argument. In the following section, I provide a more systematic analysis using a laboratory experiment.

RESEARCH DESIGN

The hypotheses are tested using a $2\times2\times2$ between-subject experimental design.[28] Each subject read a hypothetical scenario about a territorial dispute between two contiguous states. An example of one version of the scenario appears in Figure 5.1. The scenarios varied along three dichotomous dimensions: (1) the balance of military forces (strong versus weak), (2) the domestic political position of the leadership (strong versus weak), and (3) the opponent's regime type (democracy versus autocracy).

FIGURE 5.1. One of eight versions of the hypothetical scenario

You are the chief political advisor for the president of your country. Your boss was first elected to office just six months ago. In the presidential election, your boss received 60% of the popular vote while the leading opposition candidate received just 30% of the popular vote. The election also triggered a change in control of the legislature as your political party took control of both houses of Congress (the Senate and House of the People) by large majorities. Your country has a long history of peaceful and fair democratic elections.	Dimension: domestic political opposition Version: strong domestic position
Your country and your southern neighbor dispute the ownership of a 136-square mile stretch of land. This territory includes a very fertile agricultural region and a mountainous region with large mining operations. Although few people lived in the region at one time, it is now home to almost 760,000 people. In 1913, both countries agreed to have King Alfonso XIII of Spain (1886–1931) resolve the dispute. When the king ruled in favor of your country, your southern neighbor rejected the decision and refused to give up its portion of the territory. In response, your country's army occupied the remaining half of the disputed territory. Although negotiations have been attempted on several occasions, no settlement has been reached.	Constant in all scenarios
At the time of the 1913 decision, both countries had armed forces of approximately 30,000 troops, the majority of whom were stationed along the disputed territory. Since that time, the population of your country and the size of your military have grown a lot. Currently, your army has about 300,000 troops, and your air force has about 300 combat aircraft. Your southern neighbor has approximately 150,000 troops and 150 combat aircraft.	Dimension: balance of military power Version: strong military position
Your southern neighbor has been ruled by a democratically elected government since 1972. The military, which ruled the country from 1956 to 1971, is now completely under the control of the civil defense ministers. The next parliamentary elections are scheduled for May 2003, and the next presidential elections are scheduled for May 2005.	Dimension: opponent's regime type Version: democratic opponent

In the strong balance of forces scenario, the army and navy of the opposition state are half the size of those of the "home" state. In the weak balance of forces position, the situation is reversed. In the strong domestic position scenario, the president has been elected with a strong majority (60 percent versus 30 percent), and the president's party controls both houses of the legislature. In the weak domestic political position, the president has been elected by a slim margin (43 percent versus 41 percent), and the opposition party controls both houses of the legislature. In the "democracy" scenario, the opposition state is described as having a "democratically elected government." In the "autocracy" scenario, the opposition state is described as a "single-party dictatorship." Appendix 5.1 contains the exact wording of each version of the three dimensions. Given the 2×2×2 design, there are eight versions of the scenario.

Students (N = 141) enrolled in an introductory political science class at the University of Pennsylvania in the fall of 2002 were required to complete the computer-based exercise as part of a class requirement. The subjects were randomly assigned one of the eight variants of the scenario. After reading the scenario, they proceeded to an online survey. Once they entered the survey, they could not return to the scenario screen. The survey included three manipulation checks: (1) is your southern neighbor an autocracy, democracy, monarchy, or theocracy? (2) does your country or your southern neighbor have a larger army and air force? and (3) does your party or the opposition control both houses of the legislature? After completing the manipulation checks, the subjects responded to a series of questions about the conditions under which they would be willing to use military force to resolve the conflict. The survey instrument appears as Appendix 5.2.

EXPERIMENTAL FINDINGS

All three manipulation checks were statistically significant at better than a 0.001 level. Despite the fact that subjects were not able to return to the scenario screen, the vast majority of subjects were able to correctly identify the balance of military forces, the domestic political position, and the regime type of the other state. Subjects unable to answer these questions were deleted from the analysis on a question-by-question basis (for example, if the subject incorrectly answered the balance of military forces question, he or she was deleted from all analysis involving the balance of military forces).[29]

Hypothesis 1 predicts that a strong balance of power position increases the likelihood of support for military action. To manipulate the balance of forces variable, half the subjects read scenarios in which the balance was

228   *Chapter 5*

TABLE 5.5
Balance of military forces and willingness to use force

Use of force	Weak military position	Strong military position	Totals
Support	19.7%	63.5%	41.9% (52)
Neutral	6.6%	17.5%	12.1% (15)
Oppose	73.8%	19.1%	46.0% (57)
Totals	100% (61)	100% (63)	100% (124)

N O T E : Percentages may not add to 1 due to rounding. Pearson chi square statistic: 37.4; probability < 0.001.

favorable, and half read scenarios in which the balance was unfavorable. The willingness of use force was measured using Question 4 of the post-scenario survey:

> Please respond to the following statement: "If my southern neighbor refuses to resolve the dispute through negotiation, my country should use its army and air force to take back the land."[30]

Table 5.5 strongly supports the balance of military forces proposition. When the country has a 2:1 military advantage over the other state, 63.5 percent of respondents favor using military force to resolve the territorial dispute. In contrast, when the country is at a 2:1 military disadvantage, only 19.7 percent of respondents favor using military force. These results are statistically significant at better than a 0.001 level of significance. As realists predict, the stronger its military position, the more willing a country will be to support the use of military force to resolve international disputes.[31]

Hypothesis 2 predicts that democratic leaders will be less likely to use military force against other democracies (in other words, the dyadic democratic peace). The results in Table 5.6 support this proposition. When the opponent was described as a democracy, about a third of the respondents (32.1 percent) supported using military force to resolve the conflict. In contrast, when the opponent was described as an autocracy, close to half of the respondents (49.2 percent) recommended using force. The difference is statistically significant at the 0.070 level of significance.

Hypothesis 3 predicts that a strong domestic political position increases the likelihood of support for military action. In the scenarios, a strong domestic political position involved both a decisive win in presidential elections and control of both houses of the legislature. Table 5.7 supports this proposition. Although support for a use of military force increases only slightly when shifting from a weak to a strong domestic position (41.9 percent to 46.2 percent), there is a marked decline in opposition to the use of

TABLE 5.6

Opponent's regime type and willingness to use force

Use of force	Autocratic opponent	Democratic opponent	Totals
Support	49.2%	32.1%	41.2% (47)
Neutral	8.2%	20.8%	14.0% (16)
Oppose	42.6%	47.2%	44.7% (51)
Totals	100% (61)	100% (53)	100% (114)

NOTE: Percentages may not add to 1 due to rounding. Pearson chi square statistic: 5.3; probability < 0.070.

TABLE 5.7

Domestic political position and willingness to use force

Use of force	Weak domestic political position	Strong domestic political position	Totals
Support	41.9%	46.2%	43.9% (47)
Neutral	7.3%	19.2%	13.1% (14)
Oppose	50.9%	34.6%	43.0% (46)
Totals	100% (55)	100% (52)	100% (124)

NOTE: Percentages may not add to 1 due to rounding. Pearson chi square statistic: 4.7; probability < 0.096.

military force (50.9 percent to 34.6 percent). However, the conclusion must be treated with caution because the results are statistically significant only at the 0.096 level—implying that there is about a one in ten chance these results are entirely due to chance.

The findings thus far support both realist and liberal arguments: individuals are more likely to initiate when in a position of strength but less likely to initiate when facing either domestic political opposition or a democratic opponent. Given the powerful effect of the balance of military forces variable, one might expect that power considerations will *always* dominate ideational factors such as shared democracy. However, Table 5.8 clearly refutes this line of reasoning. The table isolates the situation in which respondents have a powerful military advantage. The data reveal that even if respondents are likely to possess the necessary military capability to enforce a political decision, they are reluctant to use force against democracies. Whereas 70 percent of respondents were willing to use force against autocracies, only 50 percent were willing to use force against democracies. In fact, the dyadic democracy peace emerges most prominently in situations of strength—when a country is weak, it is unlikely to initiate force regardless

TABLE 5.8

Opponent's regime type and willingness to use force
when facing a favorable military situation

Use of force	Autocratic opponent	Democratic opponent	Totals
Support	70.0%	50.0%	61.5% (32)
Neutral	10.0%	36.4%	21.2% (11)
Oppose	20.0%	13.6%	17.3% (9)
Totals	100% (30)	100% (22)	100% (52)

NOTE: Percentages may not add to 1 due to rounding. Pearson chi square statistic: 5.3; probability < 0.070.

of regime type. This finding strongly refutes the democratic peace predictions of the selectorate model proposed by Bueno de Mesquita and colleagues (2003).

Hypothesis 4 predicts that if the use of force can be kept secret, respondents will be more likely to support a use of military force. If this line of reasoning is correct, we should see a significant weakening or outright evaporation of the results supporting the dyadic democratic peace found in Table 5.7. In other words, statistically significant results support the normative explanation, and insignificant results support the structural explanation. Question 6 of the post-scenario survey specifically asked about the use of covert force:

> Suppose another advisor suggests secretly funneling military aid to opposition groups in the disputed territory. If you could be virtually guaranteed (i.e., 99% chance) that information of the arms program would not be leaked to the either the legislature or the public at large, would you support the FIRST use of SECRET military force?

The results indicate that covert action increases the likelihood of using force. The percentage supporting the use of force jumps from 41.2 percent in the overt action question in Table 5.6 to 54.3 percent in the covert action question in Table 5.9.[32] A test of proportions reveals that the increase is statistically significant at the 0.056 level. How does the covert action question influence the willingness of the individual to use force against other democracies? Table 5.9 indicates that the 17.1-percent gap between the autocracy and democracy in the baseline situation (49.2% − 32.1%) declines to a 9.6-percent gap (58.7% − 49.1%) in the covert situation. The results no longer approach statistical significance. Whereas the open-ended questions reveal that some subjects rejected the use of covert action for balance of power (if you are more powerful, you don't need to use covert action) or moral reasons (covert action is unethical), the appeal of covert action was quite pow-

TABLE 5.9
Opponent's regime type and willingness to use force covertly

Use of force	Autocratic opponent	Democratic opponent	Totals
Support			
covert	58.7%	49.1%	54.3% (63)
Neutral	6.4%	13.2%	4.9% (11)
Oppose			
covert	34.9%	37.7%	36.2% (42)
Totals	100% (63)	100% (53)	100% (116)

N O T E : Percentages may not add to 1 due to rounding. Pearson chi square statistic: 2.0; probability < 0.370.

erful. In sum, the preference for covert action strongly undermines the normative version of the democratic peace argument. If you can use force against democracies without fear of domestic political backlash, you will do so.[33]

Finally, Question 8 of the post-scenario survey explored the implications of a first use of force by the other side. In previous chapters I have argued that democracies are less likely to use force against anyone during the dispute phase of a conflict. However, the case studies and quantitative analyses indicate that if the opposing state uses military force, domestic opposition to the use of force becomes much less constraining. Question 8 of the survey probed this issue:

> Now let's alter the situation. Suppose your southern neighbor was the FIRST to use military force, such as seizing a border outpost with ground troops or bombing border positions with aircraft. Should your country respond with military force?

The percentage supporting a use of force jumps from 41.2 percent in the baseline question to 91 percent in the scenario in which the other side has used force first. The difference is statistically significant at better than a 0.001 level of significance. Table 5.10 displays the willingness to use force against democracies *after* the other democracy has drawn first blood. Although subjects are still less willing to use military force against democracies (88.7 percent) than autocracies (93.4 percent), the results are not statistically significant. In fact, the most striking aspect of the table is that more than 90 percent of the subjects favor using military force after the opposition has launched an attack upsetting the status quo. The results support the empirical findings in previous chapters, but they conflict with the findings of Mintz and Geva (1993), who found subjects less willing to use force even after an iteration of violence by the opposition. The open-ended questions in-

TABLE 5.10

Opponent's regime type and willingness to use force
after a first use of force by the opponent

Use of force	Autocratic opponent	Democratic opponent	Totals
Support			
covert	93.4%	88.7%	91.2% (104)
Neutral	4.9%	1.9%	3.5% (4)
Oppose			
covert	1.6%	9.4%	5.3% (6)
Totals	100% (61)	100% (53)	100% (114)

NOTE: Percentages may not add to 1 due to rounding. Pearson chi square statistic: 4.1; probability < 0.130.

dicated that the other state's reneging on binding arbitration in the scenario was an important factor in the willingness to use force. The unwillingness to employ peaceful norms of conflict resolution coupled with an unprovoked attack to seize territory undermined any constraint on the use of force in retaliation.

Case Studies

Do political norms or domestic structures constrain democratic states from using force? The quantitative tests and the laboratory experiment appear to support the structural explanation, but we need to examine historical cases in order to determine if the process through which institutions influence choice supports the theoretical argument presented in Chapter 2. The case studies, which are drawn from the ICB data set, describe three instances in which democratic states initiate violence against a nondemocratic country: (1) Britain versus Iraq and Iran during World War II, (2) the United States versus Cuba in the 1962 Bay of Pigs Crisis, and (3) the United States versus Grenada in the 1983 invasion of Grenada. The British study presents an extreme case: a state fighting for its very survival. In such a harsh environment, realists appear to be correct in their belief that norms and structures will cease to constrain. The Cuban case highlights how democratic leaders may attempt to circumvent structural constraints through the use of covert action. Such evidence severely undermines the normative argument. The Grenada invasion emphasizes how the nature and duration of the military operation can limit the constraining power of institutions. The Reagan administration succeeded in presenting a *fait accompli* to the political opposition.

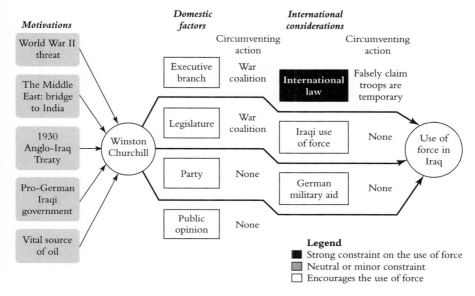

FIGURE 5.2. Middle East campaign (1941): Do norms or structures constrain British behavior?

MIDDLE EAST CAMPAIGN, 1941 (UNITED KINGDOM
VERSUS IRAQ), AND OCCUPATION OF IRAN, 1941
(UNITED KINGDOM VERSUS IRAN)

The United Kingdom faced two related crises during the early stages of World War II: Iraq in the spring of 1941 and Iran later that summer.[34] In both cases, a democratic state resorted to violence to achieve political objectives. Although a plausible case can be made that the British were responding to a first use of force by the Iraqi government, the partition of Iran with Soviet assistance represents a clear example of the initiation of large-scale force by a democratic regime. This raises an interesting question: what role did norms and structures play in British decision making? Figure 5.2 summarizes British motivations, domestic factors, international considerations, and activities designed to circumvent constraints on the use of military force in the case of Iraq.

Motives for British Intervention in Iraq

For Winston Churchill and his cabinet, the decisions to intervene were made after World War II was fully under way. The German-Soviet partition of Poland in September 1939 was followed by a long quiet stretch aptly labeled the "phony war." This period of calm ended in early 1940 with the German invasions of Denmark and Norway, followed shortly by the fall of France and the Low Countries (Belgium, Netherlands, and Luxembourg). From that point forward, the United Kingdom faced a series of aerial attacks, an ongoing naval blockade, and a threat of invasion. Although Hitler's failure to achieve air superiority in the Battle of Britain in 1940 forced him to cancel his invasion plans in the early fall, intermittent air attacks continued in the spring of 1941, and the British Empire continued to be threatened from all sides as Hitler's continental expansion proceeded with vigor. Clearly, the Britain Empire was fighting for its very existence.

Events in 1941 proved equally disheartening for the British. The Balkans became entirely occupied by Axis powers following the fall of Greece and Yugoslavia. Early success against the Italians in Libya had been reversed with the arrival of German forces under General Erwin Rommel. The fall of Egypt and the capture of the Suez Canal, the vital link between the United Kingdom and India, appeared to be a real possibility. It was precisely at this point that the British government was forced to confront the Iraqi crisis.

The British were not extremely popular in the Middle East. Just as with the French in Syria and Lebanon, the legacy of imperialism encouraged anti-British sentiments and Arab nationalism. Although the Iraqi government had broken diplomatic relations with Germany under pressure from the United Kingdom, it had not declared war on Germany. Nor had it even severed relations with Italy despite Italy's attack on the British in Egypt. The Iraqi government sought a neutral course; the government fulfilled the requirements of the 1930 Anglo-Iraqi Treaty, but it did nothing to aid the British war effort. In the meantime, as a neutral country in a sea of unrest, Iraq became the center of Arab nationalism and pro-Axis activity in the Middle East.

The United Kingdom had occupied the territory of Iraq, then part of the declining Ottoman empire, during World War I. Following the war, Britain was assigned a mandate for the territory. The prolonged negotiations over independence culminated in a 1930 treaty that proclaimed Iraq an independent and sovereign state. The British retained the rights to military bases in peacetime and the right to transfer troops through the country in time of war. This legacy of colonialism proved to be the immediate cause of British-Iraqi conflict.

In February 1940, Rashid Ali became prime minister of Iraq. Rashid Ali's pro-Axis position became increasingly dominant within the government over the course of 1940. Five ministers, including the former prime minister, resigned in January 1941 to protest the drift toward a pro-German position. Although Rashid Ali resigned on January 31, 1941, he returned to power via a coup in April with the assistance of the "Golden Square"—four key colonels in the Iraqi military. Rashid Ali quickly solidified his position and opened discussions with Germany; he sought German support for his plan to drive the British completely out of Iraq by force.

For the British, Iraq was important for two reasons: oil and strategic location. The British industrial base and the Royal Navy required imported oil, much of which came from Iraq and Iran, to function.[35] In 1941, 94 percent of world oil production came from eight countries (the United States, Venezuela, Mexico, Romania, Russia, Iran, Iraq, and the Dutch East Indies). Russia and Romania were cut off from the British due to German advances. U.S. neutrality threatened to cut off its markets. Iraq was openly hostile to the British. The Dutch East Indies faced a threat from Japan. From the British perspective, only Iran, Venezuela, and Mexico (recently nationalized) were perceived as secure sources of oil.

From a geographic perspective, German penetration of Iraq threatened Britain's position in Egypt and the vital Suez communication-transport link with the empire east of Suez (India, Hong Kong, etc.). Churchill and his ministers believed that the fall of the Middle East, to either hostile Arab nationalists or Axis forces, would severely undermine the United Kingdom's ability to turn the tide of the war. Finally, U.S. plans to assemble military equipment in Basra for shipment to the Soviet Union added to the British belief in the importance of Iraq's strategic location.

The Crisis

In April 1940, the United Kingdom sent an infantry brigade to Basra. The British claimed that the troops were to be sent to Palestine in support of British operations in Egypt. The Iraqi government, in keeping with the provisions of the 1930 treaty, did not interfere with the shipment. However, the British did not intend for the troops to leave Basra. Although Churchill justified the decision on the grounds that the Iraqi government was established via a coup and had always frustrated the "spirit" of the Anglo-Iraqi accord, it is clear that the move was in violation of the treaty. When the United Kingdom subsequently announced that more troops were entering Basra, the Iraqi government demanded that the first shipment of troops be moved onward prior to further disembarking. Apparently, both sides understood British intentions.[36]

Rashid Ali, fearing a confrontation with the more numerous British in Basra, chose to surround the vital and isolated Habbaniyah air base outside Baghdad with approximately 9,000 troops on April 29, 1941. The air base, which was primarily used as a transport and training facility, contained 2,200 military personnel, 6,000 civilians, and 82 aircraft. Immediately, the British war cabinet dispatched a "rag tag" unit of 6,000 "cooks and drivers" drawn from the already thin forces in Palestine to relieve the airfield (Sachar 1974, 178).

The quick decision to use force was prompted by a fear of German intervention. Hitler had, in fact, approved the shipment of military supplies to Iraq on May 3. Aircraft were ferried from newly conquered Greece, and plans were drawn up for transferring three-quarters of the military supplies of the 55,000-strong Vichy forces in Syria to Iraq. Hitler's Directive No. 30, dated May 23, 1941, stated:

> The Arab Freedom Movement is, in the Middle East, our natural ally against England. In this connection the raising of rebellion in Iraq is of special importance. Such rebellion will extend across the Iraq frontiers to strengthen the forces which are hostile to England in the Middle East, interrupt the British lines of communication, and tie down both English troops and English shipping space at the expense of other theatres of war. For these reasons I have decided to push the development of operations in the Middle East through the medium of going to the support of Iraq. Whether and in what way it may later be possible to wreck finally the English position between the Mediterranean and the Persian Gulf in conjunction with an offensive against the Suez Canal, is still in the lap of the gods. . . . (Churchill 1948, 264)

Unfortunately for the Germans, the quick British victory negated these efforts. British air power from Habbaniyah supported by aircraft from the Shaiba airfield near Basra had dislodged the attackers and destroyed the entire Iraqi air force by the time the relief convoy arrived. On May 30, the relief ground forces pressed on toward Baghdad, causing Rashid Ali and the Golden Square to flee the country. The Iraqi revolt ended with the establishment of a moderate Iraqi government that supported the British war effort. The belated German intervention had proved ineffective. The limited number of aircraft that reached Iraq were never used effectively, and the arms shipments were intercepted in late May, just as the Rashid government was falling.

In June 1941, between the Iraqi and Iranian crises, two events profoundly altered British security interests in the Middle East. First, after unexpectedly intense fighting, British and Free French forces conquered Vichy-controlled Syria. This victory cut off the supply route for opposition forces and thus stabilized the situation in Iraq. Second, the surprise German attack on the Soviet Union on June 22 brought the Soviets into the war on the side of the Allies. The United Kingdom and the Soviet Union signed a mutual-aid pact

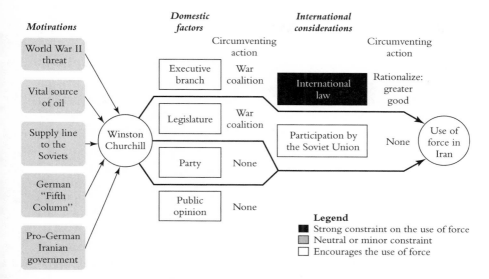

FIGURE 5.3. Occupation of Iran (1941): Do norms or structures constrain British behavior?

in early July. This second event dramatically altered the importance of Iran for both the British and Soviets. Figure 5.3 summarizes British motivations, domestic factors, international considerations, and activities designed to circumvent constraints on the use of military force.

Motives for British Intervention in Iran

Iran, which had long been of strategic interest to the British because of its proximity to India, became increasingly important as a major supplier of oil. However, the German-led surprise attack significantly increased the value of Iran because supporting the Soviet war effort suddenly became a top British priority. The Soviet Union could have been supplied in one of three ways: a northern route through Archangel, a southern route through Iran, or a western route via Vladivostok. However, the northern route was restricted by German submarine activity, and the western route was limited by the long journey across Siberia. Control of Iran became a vital strategic interest.

The pretext for the joint Soviet–U.K. invasion of Iran was the perceived existence of a German "fifth column" in Iran. Germany had become Iran's largest trading partner during the Interwar period. In addition, Germany supplied numerous technicians who supported key sectors of the economy such as energy and railway, and teachers at all levels of the educational system. The British demanded the withdrawal of all Germans because they feared sabotage of the oil facilities, particularly the Abadan processing plant on the shore of the northern Persian Gulf. On August 17, 1941,

> [the United Kingdom issued an] aid-memoire to the Iranian government. It was London's harshest ultimatum yet, and probably the most brutal of its kind (short of Nazi or Soviet terror-diplomacy) ever to be sent by one respectable, constitutional government to another since the Austrian ultimatum to Serbia in the summer of 1914. (Sachar 1974, 219)[37]

The note demanded the withdrawal of 80 percent of all German citizens; informally, the Iranians were given until the end of the month to comply.[38] The Iranian government had long resisted British requests to expel the Germans because the shah believed that Axis powers were going to defeat the British and Soviets quickly. Rather than balance against a potential hegemonic power as many neo-realists would have predicted, the shah attempted to bandwagon with the expected victor.[39] Therefore, prior to the ultimatum, the shah sought to remove Germans at a rate of thirty per month in the hopes of both escaping the wrath of Hitler and placating Churchill and Stalin.

However, the public statements and demands of the British masked the underlying objective of the ultimatum. Had their fear been restricted to the Germans living in Iran, the British would have been open to suggestions by third parties who called for the replacement of German technicians with similarly skilled Americans. However, this outcome would not have been sufficient for the British because the shah also strongly opposed using the Iranian rail system to supply the Soviet Union. The Soviet Union had long been Iran's chief nemesis, and the shah believed its northern neighbor harbored territorial ambitions.[40] Establishing an Iranian government supportive of resupplying the Soviet Union was the primary objective of the British intervention.

The August 25, 1941, invasion of Iran was a quick success. The British, using a force of approximately 19,000, quickly captured the oil fields near the Persian Gulf before marching northward. A second British force entered western Iran from Iraq and moved forward toward Tehran. The Soviets, using a massive force of 120,000 troops, drove southward from both sides of the Caspian Sea.[41] The Iranians offered little resistance and sued for peace after only two days. When the shah continued to refuse to allow the resupply of the Soviet Union, the British and Soviets moved on Tehran. The shah then abdicated in favor of his son, who complied with the British demand for control of the Iranian rail and port systems.

Domestic Constraints on the Use of Force

How can we explain these deviant cases? What factors led to a democratic state initiating large-scale uses of military force against an adversary? Why did norms and institutions fail to constrain the British? The case highlights five reasons that Churchill and his cabinet were not constrained from using force.

First, the existence of a unified war cabinet limited the amount of opposition to the decision. Just as in the Russian Civil War case (see Chapter 4), the existence of a cabinet that included all the major parties significantly decreased the probability that a decision to use military force would be criticized. During World War II, the British war cabinet consisted of members of the Conservative and Labour parties. In the most recent general election (November 14, 1935), these two parties controlled an overwhelming majority, with 586 of the 615 seats in the House of Commons (432 Conservative and 154 Labour). At the time of the crises, the war cabinet consisted of Winston Churchill (leader of Conservatives), Clement Atlee (leader of Labour), Viscount Halifax (Conservative), Anthony Eden (Conservative), Lord Beaverbrook (Conservative—Iraq decision only), O. Lyttelton (Conservative—Iran decision only), and A. Greenwood (Labour). The collective decision to intervene by this multi-party body significantly insulated leaders from potential punishment. A review of the debates in the House of Commons indicates that when the operations were announced, *not a single voice was raised in opposition.*

Second, public opinion played a very minor role due to control of the media by the government during wartime. Although the conflict began on April 29, the first mention of the event in the *Times* did not appear until May 3. Moreover, the information in the report was provided by the military headquarters in Cairo. The first political comment occurred on May 6, when Parliament reconvened. According to the May 8 edition of the *Times*, Churchill's report of the military success in Iraq was greeted with "cheers" from Conservatives and Liberals alike. Government unanimity and control of the press allowed the administration to frame the entire issue: (1) the military action was against the illegitimate leadership of the coup rather than the people of Iraq or the constitutionally elected government that the British were restoring, (2) the Iraqis had initiated violence by surrounding the air base with soldiers, and (3) Rashid Ali was a Nazi collaborator. In the absence of a counterframe to challenge the interpretation of the conflict by Churchill, no opposition to the use of force emerged (Zaller 1992; Schultz 2001; Rousseau 2004).

Third, the British did not expect the operations to be costly from a financial or human perspective. The expectation proved correct; the invasions of Iraq and Iran were over in a matter of weeks and resulted in only a handful of British casualties. Whereas normative constraints should inhibit the use of force at any level, structural constraints should be most powerful with large-scale uses of force.

Fourth, the fact that Britain was in a life-and-death struggle with Germany made the use of force in pursuit of the war effort quite palatable to the legislature and public. In most of the crises in the data set, the democratic or constrained state is not fighting for its very existence. In such extreme situations, one would expect any state to take whatever means necessary to preserve its sovereignty. Wolfers (1962, 13) uses a burning-house analogy. In a burning house, it is quite easy to predict that the occupants will flee; if the house is just warm, however, the occupants have many options, ranging from opening windows to taking off a sweater. The implication is that in extreme situations realists may be quite correct: states act similarly regardless of structure. However, most of the time states are not faced with potential extermination. It is in these less extreme disputes that norms and structures can have a greater impact on decisions to use force.

Just how far a democracy facing extermination is willing to go is captured in a statement by Churchill during the early phases of the war:

> The final tribunal is our own conscience. We are fighting to re-establish the reign of law and to protect the liberties of small countries. Our defeat would mean an age of barbaric violence, and would be fatal, not only to ourselves, but to the independent life of every small country in Europe. Acting in the name of the Covenant, and as virtual mandatories of the League and all it stands for, we have a right, indeed are bound by duty, to abrogate for a space some of the conventions of the very laws we seek to consolidate and reaffirm. Small nations must not tie our hands when we are fighting for their rights and freedom. The letter of the law must not in supreme emergency obstruct those who are charged with its protection and enforcement. It would not be right or rational that the aggressor Power should gain one set of advantages by tearing up all laws, and another set be sheltering behind the innate respect for law of its opponents. Humanity, rather than legality, must be our guide. Of all this history must be the judge. (Churchill 1950, 547; cited in Stewart 1988, 3)

The statement does not conform with either the political norms or institutional structures arguments developed in this project. I have argued that both the normative and structural variants of both arguments emphasize reciprocity. Democracies should be reluctant to initiate violence, but if attacked, they can be expected to respond in kind. However, the Churchill statement indicates a strategy that goes far beyond a tit-for-tat policy. Any state in the system that impedes the defense of the democracy can be dealt with aggressively. In the Iranian case, the threat was not imminent. Many in the Allied camp, such as the United States, did not even believe a threat existed. However, neither international law nor norms of peaceful conflict resolution proved to be barriers to the use of force. Under extreme duress, the United Kingdom acted just as a realist would predict: regardless of institutional structure or international law, a state will use all means necessary to defend itself.[42]

Fifth, the expectation that Germany would intervene very shortly in both crises drove the British to act as quickly as possible. Although Dixon (1993) found empirical support for the proposition that democratic states are more likely to settle conflicts through mediation and arbitration, the British opposed any outside interference because they believed Germany would exploit the delay. Churchill believed that Rashid Ali and the shah had clearly demonstrated their pro-Germany preferences and unwillingness to compromise. Therefore, he shunned negotiation and favored a surprise attack.

In sum, strong motivations and virtually the complete absence of any domestic opposition to the use of force led to the British initiation of violence.

BAY OF PIGS, 1961 (UNITED STATES VERSUS CUBA)

In the spring of 1961 the United States supported a rebel offensive in Cuba designed to topple the revolutionary regime of Fidel Castro.[43] The amphibious landing, which was sponsored by the Central Intelligence Agency (CIA), involved 1,400 Cuban exiles trained in Guatemala and shipped to Cuba under the watchful eye of the U.S. Navy. The U.S. operation represents the initiation of a major initiation of force by a democratic state. Although the United States relied on surrogate forces, it consciously chose to use military force to overthrow a regime that it believed represented an ideological threat to the region. The invasion, initially planned under the Eisenhower administration but ultimately approved by Kennedy during the first months of his administration, was a dramatic failure. Castro's military forces, which responded with unexpected organization and loyalty, crushed the rebel force in a matter of days. The botched invasion resulted in hundreds of deaths (114 rebels, 4 CIA pilots, hundreds of Cuban troops and civilians), more than a thousand captured rebel soldiers, the consolidation of the Castro regime, and, at least temporarily, damage to the prestige of the new administration in the eyes of the world.[44] Figure 5.4 summarizes U.S. motivations, domestic factors, international considerations, and activities designed to circumvent constraints on the use of military force.

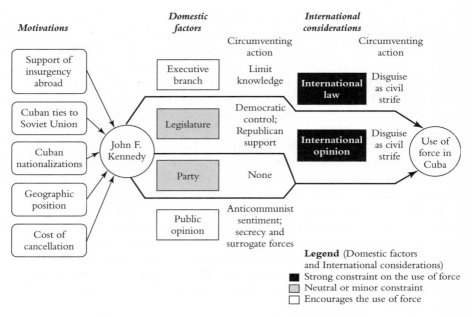

FIGURE 5.4. Bay of Pigs (1961): Do norms or structures constrain U.S. behavior?

Motives for U.S. Intervention

Fidel Castro came to power on January 1, 1959, after a two-year guerrilla war that toppled the dictatorship of Fulgencio Batista—ending almost twenty-six years of oppressive Batista rule. In an attempt to establish a broad political base incorporating several anti-Batista groups, the victorious rebels named Manuel Urrutia as president of the republic. Castro, the behind-the-scenes leader, accepted the position of prime minister on February 16, 1959. In July, differences between Castro and Urrutia resulted in the latter's replacement with Castro supporter Osvaldo Dorticos Torrado. Slowly, the Castro supporters (Fidel Castro himself, his brother Raul Castro, and Che Guevara) eliminated all political opposition in the "coalitional" revolutionary government.

External conflict with the United States sprang from three sources: Cuban support of revolutionary movements abroad, Cuban links with the Soviet Union, and Castro's domestic economic reforms. Upon taking power, the Castro regime quickly began supporting small revolutionary operations abroad. In 1959, Castro-supported rebels attacked several Central American and Caribbean governments including Panama (April), Nicaragua (June), Dominican Republic (June), and Haiti (August). These actions confirmed fears that the revolutionary regime was dedicated to supporting violent political change throughout Central and South America.

Cuban links with the Soviet Union emerged more slowly. In February 1960, Cuba signed agreements with the Soviet Union relating to economic aid and sugar sales. By May 1960, the two states had established full diplomatic relations. In mid-1960, the Castro regime began confiscating sugar lands as part of its domestic economic reforms. The Eisenhower administration responded by canceling Cuba's very favorable sugar quota on July 5, 1960; Castro retaliated by nationalizing many U.S.-owned enterprises. The nationalization of U.S.- and other foreign-owned property without compensation continued throughout the second half of 1960.

The initial decision to overthrow Castro was made in March 1960 by Eisenhower and his advisors (Wyden 1979, 24).[45] In August the Republican administration formally established a thirteen-million-dollar covert operation designed to infiltrate and supply guerrilla forces in Cuba. A training base was set up in Guatemala later that year. On January 3, 1961, shortly before leaving office, Eisenhower formally broke diplomatic relations with Cuba after Castro requested a reduction in personnel at the U.S. embassy. Although Kennedy continued implementation of the plan after he took office on February 2, 1961, he informed the CIA that he reserved the right to cancel the operation up to twenty-four hours before commencement. Kennedy also sought to limit the political risk of the operation (that is, ensure the operation was deniable) and explicitly prohibited the use of regular U.S. forces to meet this end.

The Bay of Pigs invasion began on April 14 with a rebel attack on the Cuban air force from bases in Nicaragua. Although plans called for the destruction of the Cuban air force and complete air superiority by the rebels, the seven-aircraft strike force managed to destroy only five of Castro's thirty planes. The amphibious assault began two days later, when 1,297 Cuban exiles landed at the Bay of Pigs. The Cuban air force quickly established control of the skies, sinking vital ships before they could land and driving the remaining supply ships back to sea. The small invasion force, trapped in a swampy region that precluded escape, was overwhelmed by the 20,000-plus troops mobilized by Castro. The surviving rebel soldiers were quickly captured and eventually exchanged for $53 million worth of medical supplies.

Domestic Constraints on the Use of Force

What drove the democratic government of the United States to be the initiator of force in this case? Why didn't the existence of inclusive political institutions and/or political norms deter Kennedy from using force? The failure of democratic institutions to restrain the president and his advisors

from advocating and authorizing military force can be traced to a single factor—the military operation was expected to have little, if any, political
downside. The estimated low cost was due to four factors: the use of third-
party surrogates, the deniability of responsibility, the low cost of the worst-
case scenario, and the strong public support for an active anticommunist
policy.

Many analyses of the democratic peace focus on the use of regular military forces (for example, Small and Singer 1976; Doyle 1986). Yet political
leaders often have a choice between using regular army troops and employing foreign agents (or mercenaries). Whereas the normative argument implies that a democracy should be less willing to use military force either directly or indirectly, the institutional constraint model implies that that the
use of surrogate forces may be appealing to democratic leaders if it reduces
the costs of war. In the Bay of Pigs situation, the use of Cuban rather than
U.S. personnel reduced domestic costs (inexpensive soldiers and few U.S.
casualties) and international costs (opposition to an imperialist invasion).

The Kennedy administration believed that the covert nature of the operation would allow it to deny involvement should the operation fail to
achieve its objectives. Kennedy was continually concerned about the "noise"
of the operation, which could implicate the United States. Decisions to restrict the scope of the first air strike and to cancel the second air strike alto-
gether stemmed from his desire to make the denial of involvement plausible.[46] The invasion plan was repeatedly scaled back because it looked more
like an invasion than a local uprising (Kornbluh 1998, 262, 294). The United
States also purposefully misled international observers by providing a false
account of the ongoing attack to the United Nations General Assembly. The
U.S. ambassador to the United Nations, Adlai Stevenson, claimed that the
air attacks were being launched by defecting Cuban pilots.[47] However, this
account fell apart within hours because the "defectors" were flying the
U.S., not Cuban, version of the B-26 (Kornbluh 1998, 2–3).[48] The administration's attempt to portray the invasion as an internal "civil war" rather
than an external invasion in violation of international law was beginning to
unravel.

The intense desire to keep the operation secret from domestic and international audiences points to a structural rather than normative explanation.
Norms of peaceful conflict resolution were not constraining decision makers; rather, decisions were made based on the belief that secrecy precluded
domestic punishment for failure. The participants recognized the power of
structural constraints and actively sought to circumvent them. They understood that the logic of the structural model implies that institutional con-

straint breaks down completely if the domestic political opposition has no knowledge of the ruling regime's involvement in aggression.[49]

The rebel landing, which the administration hoped would trigger a popular uprising, was also perceived as a very low-cost policy for overthrowing the first communist regime in the Western Hemisphere.[50] The use of Cuban exiles rather than U.S. troops limited the potential domestic repercussions of the operation; win or lose, body bags containing U.S. soldiers would not be arriving at airports in Lincoln, Nebraska, or Harrisburg, Pennsylvania. Moreover, the rebel operation decreased the probability of a U.S.–Soviet confrontation; Kennedy believed that direct U.S. intervention could have escalated the conflict into a superpower crisis, particularly if the Soviets used the occasion to increase pressure on Berlin (Sorensen 1965, 297). Finally, and perhaps most important, the worst-case scenario was quite palatable to Kennedy: if the invasion attempt failed, the rebels were to "melt" into the Sierra Del Escambray mountains and launch a guerrilla campaign. At the very worst, then, the policy would result in the funding of rebels who would undermine the Castro regime for years to come.

According to Irving Janis (1982), the Kennedy decision to use force represents an example of defective decision making due to the phenomenon known as "groupthink." Decision makers operating in small groups often fail to fully examine the cost, benefits, and viable alternatives for a proposed policy due to the dynamics of group decision making (such as a sense of invulnerability, a propensity for premature consensus, the suppression of personal doubts, the censoring of opposition voices, and an excessive desire for group solidarity). Groupthink may have played some role in the decision-making process, but the fact that all administration decision makers believed the worst-case scenario was an extremely low-cost outcome made the choice quite straightforward.[51] The CIA continually stated that if the beach landing failed, the Cuban (not U.S.) rebels would melt into the mountains and mount a guerrilla campaign. Even after the location of the invasion was switched to the Bay of Pigs, which made escaping into the mountains virtually impossible, the CIA promoted the "melting away" scenario (Schlesinger 1965, 243, 256).[52] The perceived low cost of failure goes a long way toward explaining why Kennedy's advisors failed to probe the assumptions and logistics of the operation more carefully.

Perhaps equally important, Kennedy believed that the cost of canceling the invasion was relatively high. During the presidential campaign, Kennedy had called for support of Cuban freedom fighters and condemned the Eisenhower-Nixon administration for its ineffective Cuban policy. Whereas Schlesinger (1965, 225) argues that Kennedy was merely seeking to build his "tough on communism" image, Nixon believed he had compromised a covert operation for political purposes.[53] The hard-line campaign rhetoric came to haunt Kennedy because canceling the operation created a "disposal" problem; disgruntled Cuban exiles returning to the United States would no doubt reveal the cancellation of the invasion and call into question Kennedy's anticommunist credentials.[54] As CIA Director Allen Dulles later stated, "We had made it very clear to the President that to call off the operation would have resulted in a very unpleasant situation" (Vandenbroucke 1984a, 475). Kennedy was reported to have said,

> "If we have to get rid of these 800 men, it is much better to dump them in Cuba than in the United States, especially if that is where they want to be"—a remark which suggests how much Dulles's insistence on the disposal problem had influenced the decision. . . . (Schlesinger 1965, 258)

Given the potentially high domestic political costs of calling off the attack, Kennedy appeared to prefer failure and "melting into the mountains" to canceling the operation. He told an advisor shortly after the operation that he had valued the failure and guerrilla war as a "net gain" (Sorensen 1965, 297).[55]

Finally, Kennedy was under tremendous pressure to implement the low-cost operation at that time or forgo the opportunity completely (Sorensen 1965, 296). A combination of circumstances created a "use it or lose it" situation. Military aid from the Soviet Union, particularly the arrival of advanced fighter aircraft, would have made an amphibious landing by exiles impossible. Cuban airmen were, in fact, completing training in Eastern Europe around that time. The Guatemalan government was demanding the removal of the Cuban troops; the lack of secrecy had created a public relations nightmare. Finally, the Cuban troops were anxious to complete the long-planned operation; delay or cancellation would have undermined morale and lowered the probability of success.[56]

Kennedy's response to the failed intervention was unapologetic. In a speech before the American Society of Newspaper Editors in Washington on April 20, Kennedy stated:

> I have emphasized before that this was a struggle of Cuban patriots against a Cuban dictator. While we could not be expected to hide our sympathies, we made it repeatedly clear that the armed forces of this country would not intervene in any way.
>
> Any unilateral American intervention, in the absence of an external attack upon ourselves or an ally, would have been contrary to our traditions and to our international obligations. But let the record show that our restraint is not inexhaustible. Should it ever appear that the inter-American doctrine of non-

interference merely conceals or excuses a policy of nonaction—if the nations of this hemisphere should fail to meet their commitments against outside Communist penetration—then I want it clearly understood that this government will not hesitate in meeting its primary obligations which are to the security of our Nation. (*Congressional Quarterly Weekly*, April 28, 1961, 736)

Kennedy went on to state that the forces of communism should not be underestimated and that the country faced a "relentless struggle in every corner of the globe." In a press conference the following day, Kennedy claimed full responsibility for the debacle. Although the statement was intended to defuse intraexecutive efforts to lay the blame on other agencies through a series of costly news leaks, it also reflected Kennedy's belief that he was in large part responsible for the fate of the dead and captured soldiers (Sorensen 1965, 309).

Consequences of Intervention

Did opposition forces punish the president for the failure, as assumed by the institutional explanation? From a structural point of view, the Democratic Party's control of the presidency, the House of Representatives, and the Senate limited potential damage (see Table 5.11). Party members rallied to the president's side during the crisis, and this insulated him from criticism and provided a pro-administration message.

The Republican Party's ability to exploit the issue was also quite limited. Richard Nixon, the president's opponent in the closely contested 1960 election, had been the primary advocate of the covert operation while serving as the vice president in the previous administration. Any attack by Nixon could be easily parried. Moreover, in order to limit attacks from the opposition party, Kennedy met or spoke with each major Republican leader (Nixon, Eisenhower, Rockefeller, and Goldwater) immediately after the crisis. Following the April 20 Kennedy-Nixon discussion, the *New York Times* reported:

> On the Cuban question, [Nixon] joined with the Republican Congressional leaders in a ranks-closing movement to solidify national backing for President Kennedy's decision while the island continued in crisis. This is "obviously a very grave crisis," he said. He has learned from experience, he said, that there is "nothing more irresponsible than for someone from outside the Government," lacking full information on foreign development, "to pop off" at such times. Accordingly, he said, "I will not criticize" Mr. Kennedy. (*New York Times*, April 21, 1961, A4)

Similarly, Eisenhower, who had initiated the operation, stated: "I am all in favor of the United States supporting the man who has to carry the respon-

TABLE 5.11
Distribution of seats in U.S. Congress, 1961

House of Representatives	Seats
Democratic Party (president's party)	259
Republican Party (opposition party)	178
Total	435

Senate	Seats
Democratic Party (president's party)	64
Republican Party (opposition party)	32
Total	100

NOTE: November 1960 elections, January 1961 seating.

sibility for our foreign affairs" (*New York Times*, April 23, 1961, A1). Goldwater, promoting an even more hard-line policy, stated that he would recommend an invasion by U.S. military personnel if all else failed. Governor Rockefeller stated that "the situation in Cuba was a serious threat to the security of the United States," and he urged "all Americans to support President Kennedy in whatever action is needed to meet it" (*New York Times*, April 26, 1961, A1).

Finally, in order to diffuse potential opposition from Republican critics, Kennedy kept Republican appointee Allan Dulles as head of the CIA until he could be quietly forced out after the storm had died down (Schlesinger 1965, 290). Overall, Kennedy's embracing of the Republican Party's traditional hard-line anticommunist policy made political attacks difficult. On the other hand, had the policy failed under a newly elected Republican administration, the Democrats probably would have lost no time in exploiting the failure for domestic political purposes.

Ultimately, Kennedy was not punished for the failure because the public supported a strong stance against communism in Cuban, including supporting use of military force. Schlesinger describes an exchange with Kennedy just after the failure:

> At this point, Evelyn Lincoln brought in an advance on the new Gallup poll, showing an unprecedented 82 per cent behind the administration. Kennedy tossed it aside and said, "It's just like Eisenhower. The worse I do, the more popular I get." (Schlesinger, 1965, 292)

More directly, a full 61 percent of the public specifically approved of "the way President Kennedy [was] handling the situation in Cuba" (Gallup 1972, 1717). The U.S. public, reluctant to commit combat troops throughout the Cold War, supported Kennedy's decision to aid the rebels without interven-

TABLE 5.12
President Kennedy's approval rating, 1961

Month	Percentage approval	Percentage disapproval	Percentage no opinion	
January	69	8	23	(1/12–1/17)
February	72	6	22	(2/10–2/15)
March	72	6	22	(3/10–3/15)
April	83	5	12	(4/28–5/3)★
May	74	11	15	(5/28–6/2)
June	71	14	15	(6/23–6/28)
July	73	13	14	(7/27–8/1)

★ One week after crisis.

SOURCE: Gallup (1972). Interview dates shown in parentheses.

ing directly. As Table 5.12 shows, Kennedy's popularity increased with the crisis—clearly a "rally around the executive" effect.

The Cuban intervention once again demonstrates that when the public and opposition parties support the use of force, decision makers are neither constrained from nor punished for initiating the use of military force in a crisis. The Bay of Pigs also demonstrates that unless the public receives an alternative frame from an opposition elite, it is unlikely to mobilize against a decision (Zaller 1992). Kennedy worked extremely hard to establish a bipartisan line emphasizing "standing up to the red menace" rather than allowing the Republicans to interpret the endeavor as a poorly planned military operation that had virtually no chance of success.

The statements by Nixon, Eisenhower, and Kennedy also provide an interesting perspective on the democratic peace and constraint arguments. Eisenhower and Nixon advocated blind obedience in times of crisis; the common citizen simply lacks the information and skills necessary to evaluate the policy chosen by the chief executive. This mind-set, if possessed by a majority of the populace or elected officials, would undermine any argument concerning democratic constraint, whether monadic or dyadic. Kennedy's statements about traditions and international obligations are equally illuminating. In Kennedy's mind, as long as U.S. troops were not directly involved in the intervention, the United States could not be labeled the aggressor. However, if a man pays a third party to assault his adversary, he is both legally and morally culpable for the act. Indeed, one of the country's "international obligations" was upholding the U.N. Charter, which explicitly prohibits the unprovoked initiation of violence, be it directly or indirectly through third parties. Regardless of how popular the act is, initiating violence through third parties violates norms of peaceful conflict resolution and the spirit of the U.N. Charter.

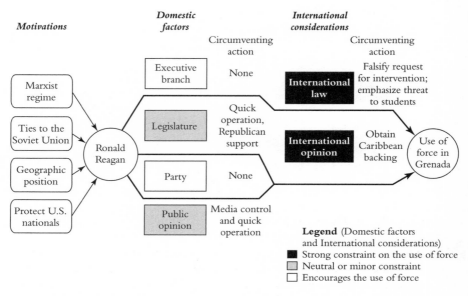

FIGURE 5.5. Invasion of Grenada (1983): Do norms or structures constrain U.S. behavior?

INVASION OF GRENADA, 1983
(UNITED STATES VERSUS GRENADA)

Another crisis in which a democratic state initiated an unprovoked high level of force occurred with the U.S. invasion of Grenada in 1983.[57] Upon taking office in January 1981, Ronald Reagan quickly attempted to fulfill his campaign pledge to take a much more active anticommunist position than that of the outgoing Carter administration. The new administration's massive military build-up and generous support of anticommunist guerrilla movements (such as in Afghanistan and Nicaragua) were manifestations of this new hard-line policy. The Reagan administration dedicated itself not only to containing the spread of communism but also to rolling back communism wherever doing so could be achieved at a reasonable cost. In October 1983, the Reagan administration used domestic turmoil in Grenada as a pretext for overthrowing the militarily insignificant but ideologically troublesome leftist regime in Grenada. Figure 5.5 summarizes U.S. motivations, domestic factors, international considerations, and activities designed to circumvent constraints on the use of military force.

Motives for U.S. Intervention

The small Caribbean island state of Grenada (population 90,000 in 1986) achieved independence from Britain in 1974. The transition was smooth, in large part due to the continued leadership of Sir Eric Gairy, who had been prime minister continuously since 1967.[58] However, the increasingly autocratic and corrupt rule of the Gairy regime provoked widespread domestic opposition. In 1979, in a bloodless coup, Maurice Bishop's New Jewel Movement (NJM) seized power while Gairy was out of the country. Despite its populist rhetoric, the new regime was dedicated to elite-led social and economic reform using a Marxist-Leninist model.

The Carter administration's initial response to changes in Grenada was one of caution. Carter's foreign policy philosophy, which emphasized idealist goals such as respect for human rights in addition to traditional power politics, led to a more conciliatory stance. However, the election of Ronald Reagan shifted U.S. policy to one of intense confrontation. In addition to massive military exercises off the Grenadan coast, the Reagan administration sought congressional approval for a covert CIA operation to destabilize the leftist regime (Schoenhals and Melanson 1985). Although it failed to secure approval for the covert operation, the Reagan administration continued its verbal assault on the Bishop government. In a speech delivered on March 23, 1983, Reagan described Grenada as a serious military threat to the United States due to its links with the Soviet Union and Cuba; Grenada was seen as a platform for projecting Soviet and Cuban power into Latin America during peacetime and for threatening U.S. oil supplies and lines of military communication during war.

Just prior to the invasion, Deputy Assistant Secretary of Defense for Inter-American Affairs Nestor Sanchez argued that the fall of Grenada to the communists raised the distinct possibility of a "a communized Caribbean Basin some years down the road" (Sanchez 1983, 49). Reagan believed Cuba was making a "large-scale attempt to undermine democracy throughout the Americas, financed by its master [the USSR] across the seas" (Payne et al. 1984, 64). Although Soviet-supplied aircraft from bases in Cuba and Nicaragua could not reach key oil supply lines and oil facilities in the Dutch Antilles and Venezuela, aircraft from Grenada would cover these areas (Zakheim 1986, 178). The administration repeatedly emphasized that the new airport on Grenada, which was being built with Cuban assistance, was unnecessarily large for civilian use and was intended for Soviet military use (Payne et al. 1984, 67).[59]

As it turned out, the overthrow of Maurice Bishop was internally rather than externally driven. The NJM was split into two competing factions, one led by the movement's founder, Maurice Bishop, and the other by his deputy, Bernard Coard. The charismatic Bishop emphasized a populist style of politics, a pragmatic approach to policy, and closer ties with Cuba. Conversely, Coard put an emphasis on the importance of party organization, ide-

TABLE 5.13
Timeline of the U.S. invasion of Grenada

Date	Action
October 12	Maurice Bishop placed under house arrest.
October 17	Reagan Administration plans for evacuation of American nationals.
October 19	Bishop executed; General Austin declares military rule and curfew.
October 20	Initial plans for invasion approved; naval task force diverted to Caribbean.
October 21	Organization of Eastern Caribbean States requests U.S. assistance in military intervention.
October 22	Plans for October 25 invasion approved by Reagan.
October 23	Marine bombing in Beirut; final approval of operation.
October 24	Operation begins with Navy Seal infiltration; Reagan informs Thatcher at 6 P.M.; Reagan informs congressional leaders at 8 P.M.
October 25	Full-scale invasion.
December 12	All U.S. combat troops withdrawn.

ological rigidity, and closer links with the Soviet Union. The failure of the young regime to achieve economic and political goals led to charges that Bishop's policies and style of leadership had become barriers to the social and political transformation of the island. In September 1983, the Central Committee of the NJM forced Bishop into a power-sharing relationship with Coard. When Bishop sought to reverse this decision on October 12, he was placed under house arrest. After being briefly freed by a mob of supporters, Bishop was recaptured and executed on orders of the Central Committee. At this point General Austin, head of the People's Revolutionary Army, declared that a revolutionary military council now ruled the island and that a "shoot-on-sight" curfew was in effect.

As outlined in Table 5.13, the Reagan administration formulated, approved, and began executing the invasion of Grenada within the space of several days. The National Security Decision Directive signed by the president stated three objectives for the operation: protection of U.S. citizens, restoration of democracy, and elimination of Cuban influence on the island (Bennett 1984, 75). According to observers, Reagan genuinely feared a hostage situation analogous to the Iranian hostage crisis that had paralyzed the previous administration (Schoenhals and Melanson 1985, 143). Although there was no evidence that U.S. nationals, composed predominantly of medical students, were in imminent danger, the "potential" for harm motivated the administration to act decisively. On October 25, 1983, a military force that ultimately included 7,300 troops began landing on the island of Grenada; the invasion left eighteen U.S. soldiers, twenty-four Cubans, twenty-one Grenadan soldiers, and twenty-four Grenadan civilians dead.

Why would a democracy choose to resort to major levels of military force

TABLE 5.14
Distribution of seats in U.S. Congress, 1983

House of Representatives	Seats
Republican Party (president's party)	166
Democrat Party (opposition party)	269
Total	435

Senate	Seats
Republican Party (president's party)	54
Democrat Party (opposition party)	46
Total	100

NOTE: November 1982 elections, January 1983 seating.

to resolve a political conflict? Reagan, the Republican Party candidate, was elected in November 1980 with a slim 50.7 percent of the popular vote but an overwhelming electoral college vote (489 to 49). The 1980 election also brought the Republican Party to power in the U.S. Senate for the first time since 1952. However, as Table 5.14 shows, the House of Representatives remained firmly in Democratic hands.

Domestic Constraints on the Use of Force

Why didn't the existence of democratic institutions and a powerful opposition party prevent the first large-scale U.S. military intervention in Latin America since the Dominican Republic operation in 1965? Three factors explain the failure of opposition to emerge: (1) the quick victory and low cost of the operation, (2) the effective use of the media by the administration, and (3) the fact that the invasion came on the heels of the tragedy in Beirut.

First, unlike many previous cases, not all parties were united behind the use of military force from the start. The Speaker of the Democratic-controlled House of Representatives strongly denounced the invasion as "gunboat" diplomacy. In an interview with the *New York Times*, Tip O'Neill stated that the Reagan administration had been looking for an excuse to invade Grenada since it came to power. Senator Patrick Moynihan also questioned the administration's motives: "I don't know that you restore democracy at the point of the bayonet" (*New York Times*, October 26, 1983, A22). In the same article, Representative Paul Simon was quoted as commenting: "The military solution seems to be an automatic reflex with this Administration." However, the initial opposition quickly withered due to the rapid military victory, low casualties, and overwhelming public support for the operation. After Reagan's nationally televised speech on October 27, 55 percent of Americans supported the invasion, and only 31 percent opposed it

(*New York Times*, October 29, 1983, A9).[60] The quick victory and broad support immobilized the political opposition:

> On the record, the Democrats denied that they changed their minds when it became clear through public opinion polls that Reagan was winning overwhelming approval for his course. But one House Democratic leader conceded that in the new party position "there is a certain element of jumping on the bandwagon before it rolls over us." (*Congressional Quarterly*, November 12, 1983)

Opposition, which may have effectively mobilized had the invasion taken months to achieve, could not politically attack the quick victory. Unlike the normative explanation, the institutional constraints argument does not predict restraint on decision makers if the military operation is likely to be quick, cheap, and successful (Reiter and Stam 2002).

The debate over the 1973 War Powers Resolution drives this point home. The War Powers Resolution, which was adopted in the wake of the Vietnam War to constrain the executive's ability to wage war without explicit congressional approval, theoretically represents one of the most important institutional constraints across all democratic polities.[61] The resolution requires the removal of troops from the combat zone in sixty days (or ninety days with an extension) unless Congress formally approves of the military operation; the resolution gives Congress the power to terminate a military operation at any time through a concurrent resolution.[62]

Although the House and Senate initially voted to invoke the War Powers Resolution in the Grenada case, the Senate version, which was attached to a debt limit bill, never passed a final vote. As the success and popularity of the operation became apparent, Democratic Party pressure for passage of a bill triggering the War Powers Resolution declined. The fact that the troops were to be removed before the sixty-day limit also undermined efforts to implement the War Powers Resolution. In sum, the quick and popular military operation undermined the mobilization of opposition to the use of force.

Second, the failure of opposition to emerge can be tied to effective use of the media by the Reagan administration. The initial press restrictions limited information available to potential opponents of the regime; unlike previous conflicts, such as the Vietnam War, the press was completely barred from Grenada until after most of the fighting was completed. Initial administration claims, such as massive amounts of weaponry and Cuban-Soviet involvement in Grenada, were accepted by the population. Not only did this disarm opponents; the public's acceptance of the rationale persisted even after the administration admitted the allegations had been hastily made and were ultimately incorrect. Finally, the administration's skillful control of the media reduced the incentive to attack the president for resorting to military force before exhausting all noncoercive approaches and for clearly violating international law. Among the most important of the carefully and consciously controlled messages sent to the U.S. public were the joint announcement of the operation with Prime Minister Eugenia Charles of Dominica, the promotion of the returning of the medical students (and their kissing the ground at the airport), an effective nationally televised address two days after the invasion, and the repeated portrayal of the Grenadan citizens welcoming the troops as liberators. In addition, the restriction of media access to the island until October 30 allowed the administration to monopolize information and to present a single position to the U.S. public.[63]

The United States also attempted to legitimize the invasion in the eyes of domestic and global public opinion by claiming the invasion conformed with international law. The United States presented the invasion as a joint operation with the Organization of East Caribbean States (OECS). U.S. Special Forces secured Governor General of Grenada Sir Paul Scoon and transported him to an U.S. Navy ship, where he produced a note on October 28, but dated October 23, requesting U.S. military assistance through the OECS. Ultimately, the postdating of the memo was revealed in the press. More important, from a legal perspective the governor general has no constitutional right to request outside intervention without first consulting the queen of England. The governor general is a representative of the Commonwealth rather than of the last democratic government of Grenada (Ferguson 1990, 42).

Third, the conflict in Lebanon may have affected public support for the operation. There is no information that Reagan explicitly sought to use the Grenada success to divert attention from the Marine bombing and unpopular peacekeeping operation. Two of three of the formal decisions to intervene were made before the Beirut bombing. Moreover, on the morning of the bombing and the day of the final "go" decision (October 23), Reagan rejected calls to halt the Grenada operation on account of the Beirut tragedy: "If this [Grenada] was right yesterday, it's right today, and we shouldn't let the act of a couple of terrorists dissuade us from going ahead" (Bennett 1984, 75). The U.S. public's frustration with the country's inability to translate potential power into effective policy may have led it to welcome the military success with unusual intensity. When asked to evaluate the statement "I feel good about Grenada because it showed that America can use its power to protect our own interests," a full 74 percent of those surveyed responded with approval.

The decision to use force in Grenada once again supports the structural argument. The overwhelming military position of the United States made

TABLE 5.15
President Reagan's approval rating, 1983

Month	Percentage approval	Percentage disapproval	Percentage no opinion	
June	43	45	12	(6/10–6/13)
July	42	47	11	(7/22–7/25)
August	43	45	12	(8/12–8/15)
September	47	42	11	(9/9–9/13)
October	46	37	17	(9/30–10/16)
Oct.–Nov.	53	31	16	(10/28–11/13)★
November	53	37	10	(11/18–11/21)
December	54	38	8	(12/18–12/21)
January	52	38	10	(1/13–1/16)

★ Just after crisis.

SOURCE: Gallup (1984, 217, 261). Interview dates shown in parentheses.

rapid victory a foregone conclusion; the absence of costs implied that Reagan could use force with relative impunity. Norms of peaceful conflict resolution and the existence of international law failed to restrain the Reagan administration from using force. As Table 5.15 demonstrates, the use of force was not punished by the U.S. public; indeed, the slight rally effect appears to imply that Reagan was rewarded for the decision.[64]

Conclusions

Scholars have posited two causal mechanisms for the relative peace between democratic polities: a normative and a structural mechanism. This chapter assesses the relative importance of the two explanations using three tests. The first test failed to support the normative explanation among autocratic states: autocratic rulers socialized in a world of violence are no more likely to use force compared to other autocratic leaders. The second test produced results consistent with the logic of the structural explanation. Whereas democratic institutions inhibit large-scale uses of force, decision makers in democracies are uninhibited from using minor levels of force, in part because the probability of punishment by domestic opposition is less.[65] Low-level uses of force, particularly if a decision maker can frame the opponent as the aggressor, are not usually politically risky endeavors. Finally, the laboratory experiment supported the structural explanation. If force could be used covertly, the subjects were willing to use violence to resolve the conflict. The case studies of the Bay of Pigs and Grenada support this finding. In the Bay of Pigs, the executive branch embarked on a covert operation via a third party to minimize domestic political costs. In Grenada, the operation was designed to be completed before any potential opposition could arise or any structural constraints could be imposed.

The Middle Eastern cases involving Britain point to another conclusion. When a state's very existence is threatened, norms of peaceful conflict resolution and institutional structures do not constrain decision makers very much. Although realists argue that this level of threat is the norm in a Hobbesian world, history shows that threats of this magnitude are thankfully rare. As the level of threat declines, institutions appear to play an increasingly important role.

The findings have tremendous implications for democratic theory and public policy. If institutions are primarily responsible for the monadic constraint revealed in the preceding chapters, democratic citizens must remain vigilant. The structural explanation implies that democratic leaders should be predisposed to conducting covert operations, employing surrogate forces, relying on high technology to minimize human losses, favoring quick military operations, and selecting weak targets that can be easily overwhelmed. All of these tendencies undermine the democratic process and the democratic system itself.

APPENDIX 5.1

Scenario Wording by Dimension

Balance of Military Forces

STRONG MILITARY POSITION

At the time of the 1913 decision, both countries had armed forces of approximately 30,000 troops, the majority of which where stationed along the disputed territory. Since that time, the population of your country and the size of your military have grown a lot. Currently, your army has about 300,000 troops, and your air force has about 300 combat aircraft. Your southern neighbor has approximately 150,000 troops and 150 combat aircraft.

WEAK MILITARY POSITION

At the time of the 1913 decision, both countries had armed forces of approximately 30,000 troops, the majority of which where stationed along the disputed territory. Since that time, the population of your southern neighbor and the size of its military have grown a lot. Currently, your army has about 150,000 troops, and your air force has about 150 combat aircraft. Your southern neighbor has approximately 300,000 troops and 300 combat aircraft.

Domestic Political Position

STRONG DOMESTIC POLITICAL POSITION

You are the chief political advisor for the President of your country. Your boss was first elected to office just six months ago. In the Presidential election, your boss received 60% of the popular vote while the leading opposition candidate received just 30% of the popular vote. The election also triggered a change in control of the legislature as your political party took control of both houses of Congress (the Senate and House of the People) by large majorities. Your country has a long history of peaceful and fair democratic elections.

WEAK DOMESTIC POLITICAL POSITION

You are the chief political advisor for the President of your country. Your boss was first elected to office just six months ago. In the Presidential election, your boss received 43% of the popular vote while the closest opposition candidate received 41% of the popular vote. A third-party candidate captured the remaining 16% of the vote. The election also triggered a change in control of the legislature as your political opponents took control of both houses of Congress (the Senate and the House of the People) by large majorities. Your country has a long history of peaceful and fair democratic elections.

Regime Type of Opponent

DEMOCRACY

Your southern neighbor has been ruled by a democratically elected government since 1972. The military, which ruled the country from 1956 to 1971, is now completely under the control of the civil defense ministers. The next Parliamentary elections are scheduled for May 2003 and the next Presidential elections are scheduled for May 2005.

AUTOCRACY

Your southern neighbor has been ruled by a single-party dictatorship since 1972. The military, which ruled the country from 1956 to 1971, is now completely under the control of party officials. Although talk of a transition to democracy was discussed during the economic turmoil of the 1980s, the issue has not been seriously discussed for over 15 years.

Experimental Survey Instrument

1. In the scenario you just read, your southern neighbor is a(n) _____.
   ☐ autocracy
   ☐ democracy
   ☐ monarchy
   ☐ theocracy
   ☐ not sure

2. In the scenario, both houses of the legislature are controlled by
   _____.
   ☐ your political party
   ☐ the opposition political party
   ☐ not sure

3. In the scenario, which country has a larger army and air force?
   ☐ your country
   ☐ your southern neighbor
   ☐ not sure

4. Please respond to the following statement: "If my southern neighbor re-
   fuses to resolve the dispute through negotiation, my country should use
   its army and air force to take back the land."
   ☐ Strongly Agree
   ☐ Somewhat Agree
   ☐ Neither Agree Nor Disagree
   ☐ Somewhat Disagree
   ☐ Strongly Disagree
   ☐ Not Sure

5. Why do you support or oppose the First use of military force?

6. Suppose another advisor suggests secretly funneling military aid to op-
   position groups in the disputed territory. If you could be virtually guar-
   anteed (i.e., 99% chance) that information of the arms program would
   not be leaked to either the legislature or the public at large, would you
   support the FIRST use of SECRET military force?
   ☐ Strongly Support First Use of Secret Aid
   ☐ Somewhat Support First Use of Secret Aid
   ☐ Neutral
   ☐ Somewhat Oppose First Use of Secret Aid
   ☐ Strongly Oppose First Use of Secret Aid
   ☐ Not Sure

7. Why do you support or oppose the FIRST use of SECRET military force?

8. Now let's alter the situation. Suppose your southern neighbor was the first to use military force, such as seizing a border outpost with ground troops or bombing border positions with aircraft. Should your country respond with military force?
   - ☐ Definitely Respond with Force
   - ☐ Probably Respond with Force
   - ☐ Neutral
   - ☐ Probably NOT Respond with Force
   - ☐ Definitely NOT Respond with Force
   - ☐ Not Sure

9. Suppose your southern neighbor was the first to use military force *and* the leadership of your political opposition at home called for a military response. Would you be more or less likely to respond with military force after the opposition party's demand?
   - ☐ Much More Likely to Respond with Force
   - ☐ Somewhat More Likely to Respond with Force
   - ☐ About the Same
   - ☐ Somewhat Less Likely to Respond with Force
   - ☐ Much Less Likely to Respond with Force
   - ☐ Not Sure

10. Suppose your southern neighbor was the first to use military force *and* the United Nations Security Council condemned the attack and authorized your country to use "all means appropriate for defending the territory." Would you be more or less likely to respond with military force after United Nations approval?
    - ☐ Much More Likely to Respond with Force
    - ☐ Somewhat More Likely to Respond with Force
    - ☐ About the Same
    - ☐ Somewhat Less Likely to Respond with Force
    - ☐ Much Less Likely to Respond with Force
    - ☐ Not Sure

11. What is your citizenship?

12. If you are a permanent resident of another country, what is it?

Notes

1. This approach may be appropriate as long as no attempt is made to distinguish the relative importance of norms and structures. Dixon's (1993) conclusion that norms are more important than structures is problematic given his reliance on structural variables.

2. Walt (1992, 1996) finds that new revolutionary regimes are often the target of aggression by their neighbors.

3. Bollen and Jackman (1989) demonstrate that using a measure of democracy which captures the effect of political stability can lead one to overestimate the impact of structure or norms. Maoz and Russett recognize this (1993, 630) but choose not to separate the impact of stability as precisely as they had in previous studies (Maoz and Russett 1992).

4. Gartzke (1998) also argues that interests explain cooperation between democracies. Russett and Oneal (2001, 230) counter that joint democracy remains significant even after controlling for shared interests. Moreover, they argue that shared interests are a function of joint democracy and interdependence. Adding Gartzke's measurement of shared interest (i.e., similar United Nations voting patterns) did not change the findings in chapters 3 or 4.

5. For a discussion of these dimensions, see Cialdini and Trost (1998, 160).

6. Some conscientious objectors have been willing to serve in noncombat positions (e.g., medics) in the military. Approximately one-quarter of the 4,000 U.S. conscientious objectors in World War I chose to serve in noncombat roles in the military. Others served in nonmilitary service organizations such as the American Friends Service Committee, founded by the Quakers during World War I (Jones 1971). For a discussion of how conscientious objectors seek to define themselves as "good citizens" despite their unwillingness to serve in the military, see Burk (1995).

7. Price and Tannenwald (1996) propose an alternative normative argument; Duffield and colleagues (1999) debate the two competing arguments. The purpose of the example is simply to illustrate the typology. An examination of the interesting but complex debate is beyond the scope of this project.

8. See, for example, Cialdini and Trost's "Social Influence: Social Norms, Conformity, and Compliance" in the *Handbook of Social Psychology* (1998).

9. These coding rules were developed to conform with the time-series format of the dispute data set. An alternative approach would involve developing a new data set in which the officeholder is the unit of analysis (i.e., one observation for each officeholder). For an example of this approach, see Bueno de Mesquita and Siverson (1995).

10. Leaders who are democratically elected but later overthrow the political system are coded as having used violence in subsequent years. Hitler's consolidation of power in Germany and Duvalier's consolidation of power in Haiti fall within this special category. Similarly, decision makers who help lead a coup and later rotate into office according to a pre-coup plan are coded as having used force to obtain office.

11. Similar results for the dispute data set are produced using either a four-category or three-category version of the *Aggressive Use of Force* variable. The unordered logit model presented later in the chapter requires the use of the trichotomous version. The results in this chapter were produced using STATA 6.0.

12. Examples include Babst (1972), Small and Singer (1976), Chan (1984), Doyle (1986), Bremer (1992), and Spiro (1994).

13. Studies that have relied on multichotomous dependent variables include Maoz and Russett (1993), Bremer (1993), and Senese (1997a, 1997b).

14. For a similar argument, see Maoz and Russett (1993, 634).

15. The statistical program used for portions of this study, STATA 6.0, forces the user to employ a logit model for all unordered dependent variable analysis. In the literature, in fact, the vast majority of analyses with an unordered dependent variable are logit models. Although an unordered probit model would be more consistent with prior chapters, the switch makes no substantive difference because the two distributions differ only slightly in the tails.

16. This result is consistent with Reiter and Stam's (1998, 2002) finding that democratic polities are much more likely to win wars they initiate. Democracies appear less willing to initiate large-scale conflicts that they might lose.

17. In the Mintz and Geva (1993) experiment, over 80 percent of the student subjects believed the scenario was most similar to the 1991 Persian Gulf War. Although the authors argue that the analogy operated against their hypothesis, the readily available historical analogy might have made other information more salient (e.g., the limited loss of life by the U.S.-led coalition).

18. Kinder and Palfrey (1993) argue that experiments should be used more extensively in political science.

19. Oren (1995) argues that the perception of another state as democratic or autocratic is a subjective process that can vary across time. Also see Owen (1997) on this point. In the trilateral conflict, the designation of challenger and target can be confusing (in the Degania-Raggol disputes Degania is the challenger, and in the Degania–United States disputes Degania is the target).

20. In Mintz and Geva (1993) and Study 2 of Geva and Hanson (1999), the challenger has initiated military conflict. In Study 1 of Geva and Hanson, the challenger initiated military force in half the cases and an economic embargo in the other half.

21. Several studies have found a curvilinear relationship between balance of power and initiation of conflict (Sullivan [1976] and Kim and Rousseau [2003]). The inverted U-shaped pattern implies that very weak states are unlikely to initiate because they fear losing and that very strong states are unlikely to initiate because they often get what they want without having to resort to force. In the experimental scenarios employed in this study, we control for this problem by clearly stating that the stronger state is not getting what it wants.

22. Johnston (1995) argues that according to the realist belief system in ancient China, which he labels the Parabellum paradigm, offensive force should be deployed only when in position of strength—accommodation may be necessary when a weak state is marshaling the necessary arms and allies. In contrast to structural realists such as Waltz, Johnston argues that the realist belief system is a product of domestic culture rather than the anarchic structure of the international system. For a comparison of Waltz and Johnston, see Rousseau (2004).

23. This was not a stretch of the imagination for most subjects. Virtually all the subjects were either raised in the United States or another democratic country.

24. Ireland and Gartner (2001) find empirical support for this proposition. Ireland and Gartner (2001, 558) also find that coalitional governments behave no differently from majority governments. This finding is not consistent with the results of the institutional constraint model presented in Chapter 4, which examines coalitions in both democracies and autocracies. The case studies of democratic initiation

in previous chapters demonstrate that democracies often form coalitions prior to using force in order to reduce domestic constraints (e.g., Britain 1917, Israel 1967, and
El Salvador 1969).

25. The covert action debate is part of the broader debate about uses of force
short of war (Cohen 1994). Hermann and Kegley (1996, 2001; Kegley and Hermann
1997) claim that democracies overtly intervene in the affairs of other democracies.
Tures (2001a, 2001b) rejects this claim using the same data. Although some observers
restrict the term *covert action* to low-level influence or violence such as rigging elections or assassinations, the central element of virtually all definitions of covert action
is secrecy designed to hide the identity of the attacker (Goodman and Berkowitz
1992, 30). The scale of covert action can range from small to very large in terms of
total cost (e.g., the CIA covert operation in Afghanistan in the 1980s, with an annual cost over $1 billion) or total personnel (e.g., the 1,400 soldiers in the Bay of Pigs
invasion). Obviously, as the size of the intervention grows, the identity of the attacker is more likely to be exposed. On this point, see Wyden's discussion of the debate within the Kennedy administration about the trade-off between the probability of victory and the probability of maintaining secrecy (1979). Russett and Oneal
(2001, 62) also briefly discuss covert action and its relationship to the democratic
peace. Gibbs (1995) examines the use of secrecy in the United States in the 1960
Congo crisis.

26. The Polity Democracy and Autocracy indices range from 0 to 10. The data
cited are for the year prior to the covert intervention because the intervention years
are coded as periods of transition.

27. Although James and Mitchell add the caveat that the weak democracy is seeking "to escape structural dependency," this variable does not appear in the formal
crisis game model. Therefore, I will focus on the general category of weak democracies that have disputes with powerful democracies.

28. The fourth hypothesis is tested using a within-subject design as well. Subjects
are first asked if they are willing to use overt force and then asked if they would
change their opinion if force could be used covertly.

29. An alterative approach would have involved dropping subjects who incorrectly answered *any* of the three manipulation check questions. Unfortunately, this
approach reduces the sample size by a third. Although about 90 percent of the subjects answered each manipulation check correctly, over the course of three questions
a total of about 30 percent of the subjects (i.e., 10% + 10% + 10%) missed a question. Very few subjects missed more than one question.

30. The response categories "strongly" and "somewhat" were collapsed for all
analyses presented in this chapter.

31. In the Mintz and Geva (1993) and Geva and Hanson (1999) experiments, the
"home" state was always much more powerful than the target state. For example, in
the Mintz and Geva scenario the "home" state had a 12:1 advantage in the invasion
option. In the Geva and Hanson study, the United States was always intervening in
the island nation of Degania.

32. The percentage of those supporting military action varies slightly from table
to table because of the exclusion of subjects who failed the manipulation check on
a question-by-question basis (if subjects got the balance of military forces question

wrong, they were not automatically excluded from the domestic political position analysis).

33. As discussed, James and Mitchell (1995) predict that strong democracies will use covert action against weak democracies. The findings do not support this prediction.

34. The Middle East campaign case studies were developed using the following sources: Winston S. Churchill, *The Second World War: The Gathering Storm* (Boston: Houghton Mifflin, 1948); Winston S. Churchill, *The Second World War: The Grand Alliance* (Boston: Houghton Mifflin, 1950); Christopher Hill, *Cabinet Decisions on Foreign Policy: The British Experience October 1938–June 1941* (Cambridge: Cambridge University Press, 1991); Howard M. Sachar, *Europe Leaves the Middle East, 1936–1954* (London: Allen Lane, 1974); Richard A. Stewart, *Sunrise at Abadan: The British and Soviet Invasion of Iran, 1941* (New York: Praeger, 1988).

35. For a discussion of the limited sources of oil available to Britain at the time, see Yergin (1991).

36. In the coding of this case for the quantitative portion of the study, the landing of British troops in violation of the treaty and against the wishes of the Iraqi government constituted the first use of force in the crisis. However, one could plausibly argue that subsequent rotation of these troops demonstrated compliance with the treaty. From this perspective, Iraqi retaliatory actions constitute the first use of force.

37. Layne (1994) claims that ultimatums should rarely be used by democratic polities because they preclude negotiation and compromise.

38. The combination of the written demand and the informal deadline created an ultimatum. It is clear that the British did not want to put an ultimatum in writing—suggesting that they too believed liberal polities should not resort to such brutal techniques.

39. Although Walt (1987) finds balancing more common than bandwagoning, he identifies several situations in which bandwagoning with the threat is likely. He asserts that "a state may align with the dominant side in wartime in order to share the spoils of victory" (1987, 21). Also see Schweller (1994).

40. Despite Soviet pledges to the contrary in 1941–42, their actions in 1945–46 clearly demonstrated that the shah's fear was well-founded.

41. The scope of the Soviet effort gives some indication of the importance of the Iranian supply route to Soviet leaders. In August 1941 the Soviet forces were in headlong retreat in the face of the German onslaught; even Moscow was threatened by the end of the year. Despite this grave threat, the Soviets chose to deploy 120,000 troops in Iran.

42. Although some may argue that British actions with regard to the developing states of Iraq and Iran were merely a reflection of its imperialist history, this appears not to have been the case. The Churchill statement, in fact, refers more directly to cabinet discussions about whether or not to use force against neutral Norway and Sweden. These democratic states were not small developing nations; Sweden just happened to possess a resource (the Narvik mines) that was essential to the German war effort.

43. The Bay of Pigs case study was developed using the following sources: Irving

Janis, *Groupthink: Psychological Studies of Policy Decisions and Fiascoes*, second edition (Boston: Houghton Mifflin, 1982); James D. Rudolph, *Cuba: A Country Study* (Washington, DC: U.S. Government Printing Office, 1985); Theodore C. Sorensen, *Kennedy* (New York: Harper and Row, 1965); Arthur M. Schlesinger, Jr., *A Thousand Days: John F. Kennedy in the White House* (Boston: Houghton Mifflin, 1965); Peter Wyden, *Bay of Pigs: The Untold Story* (New York: Simon and Schuster, 1979); Peter Kornbluh (ed.), *Bay of Pigs Declassified: The Secret CIA Report on the Invasion of Cuba*, (New York: New Press, 1998).

44. Although Castro provided a figure of 161 total deaths, the rebels claimed 1,650 communist fatalities. The truth is probably somewhere between the two figures (Clodfelter 1992, 1166). Kornbluh argues that the invasion led to closer ties with the Soviet Union and ultimately to the placement of offensive nuclear weapons on the island and the Cuban Missile Crisis (1998, 1).

45. The timing is interesting. Although the decision to overthrow occurs *after* Castro's use of force abroad, it occurs *before* Castro establishes full diplomatic relations with the Soviets and before he begins the land confiscations.

46. The Kennedy administration struggled with the trade-off between maintaining the appearance of U.S. noninvolvement and achieving a military success. A highly noisy landing (e.g., massive air attacks) would increase the probability of success but lower the probability of maintaining secrecy. Kennedy's decision to restrict the number of aircraft sorties in the first strike lowered the appearance of U.S. involvement but raised the prospect of failure. The CIA has long maintained that the administration effort to keep a low profile was the primary cause of the invasion's failure (Vandenbroucke 1984b; Bissell 1984).

47. Stevenson was given the text to read and was repeatedly assured that it was accurate (Wyden 1979, 187).

48. Although the CIA had painted the B-26s with Cuban Air Force markings, the planes had metal noses and a blue stripe on the fuselage: "All of Castro's B-26s had plastic nose cones and no stripes" (Wyden 1979, 176).

49. The secrecy of the operation was obviously compromised when stories of the pending invasion began to appear in major newspapers; the existence of the training camps was common knowledge throughout Latin America (Wyden 1979, 108, 142). However, Kennedy clung to the belief that as long as regular U.S. forces were not directly involved in the fighting, domestic and international observers would accept U.S. denials of responsibility. As events demonstrated, this belief proved erroneous. Although not as extreme an example, Kennedy's unbridled faith in secrecy as a means of circumventing domestic opposition resembles Eden's ill-fated attempt to keep secret his government's collusion with Israel in the 1956 Suez Crisis. As many observers emphasize (Schlesinger 1965; Sorensen 1965; Janis 1982), the obsession with secrecy also kept many potential opponents of the operation, such as the Cuban desk at the State Department, out of the decision-making process.

50. Richard Bissell, the senior CIA planner of the operation, contends that the CIA never claimed that the landing would trigger a spontaneous popular uprising (Bissell 1984). However, the CIA never attempted to correct this misperception held by Kennedy and his advisors.

51. Janis argues that groupthink prevented a complete probe of this rosy "worst-

case" scenario. However, given the information available to the new president and his advisors, the decision process does not appear to deviate radically from a standard rational model.

52. Upon learning in mid-March that the airstrip at the Trinidad site could not accommodate the rebels' B-26 aircraft, the CIA switched the landing site from Trinidad, located next to the Sierra Del Escambray mountains, to the Bay of Pigs. However, the CIA continued to discuss "melting" into the mountains at least until meetings in early April. Kennedy and his advisors believed that retreat into the mountains was the fallback plan until well into the invasion. Bissell admits that the CIA was responsible for the misunderstanding. In fact, the CIA had ceased all guerrilla training as far back as November 1960 (long before the switch in landing sites), and the exiles were instructed to fall back to the beaches rather than flee into the swamps or head for the mountains. Many of the exiles claimed that CIA operatives stated U.S. troops would bail out the operation should a fallback to the beaches be required (Wyden 1979).

53. "For the first and only time in the campaign, I got mad at Kennedy—personally. . . . I had long favored and fought for this line within the Administration, and the covert training of Cuban exiles as well as the new overt quarantine policy were programs due, in substantial part at least, to my efforts. . . . There was only one thing I could do. The covert operation had to be protected at all costs. I must not even suggest by implication that the United States was rendering aid to rebel forces in and out of Cuba. In fact, I must go to the other extreme: I must attack the Kennedy proposal to provide such aid as wrong and irresponsible because it would violate our treaty commitments. . . . I was in the ironic position of appearing to be 'softer' on Castro than Kennedy—which was exactly the opposite of the truth, if only the whole record could be disclosed" (Nixon 1962, 354–55). Nixon felt that he would have won the fourth televised debate had he not been forced into this awkward position.

54. For a discussion of hard-line rhetoric subsequently trapping decision makers in future situations, see Snyder's (1991) discussion of "blowback."

55. On February 14, 1961, Adolph Berle wrote a memo to Secretary Rusk, highlighting a CIA report warning "that dismantling the Cuban operation may mean explosions in three or four countries in Central America" (Kornbluh 1998, 290).

56. In fact, a severe morale problem already existed due to the recruitment of ex-Batista supporters by the CIA. In January 1961, a full-scale mutiny occurred that required the CIA to place several of the most vocal anti-Batista exiles in confinement deep in the Guatemalan jungle. Lyman Kirkpatrick's postmortem, titled "The Inspector General's Survey of the Cuban Operation, October 1961," reported that the Cuban exiles mutinied more than once (Kornbluh 1998, 34). The CIA never informed the administration about the morale problems.

57. The United States versus Grenada case study was developed using the following sources: H. W. Brands, Jr., "Decisions on American Armed Intervention: Lebanon, Dominican Republic, and Grenada." *Political Science Quarterly* 102/4 (1987): 607–24; Michael Rubner, "The Reagan Administration, the 1973 War Powers Resolution, and the Invasion of Grenada." *Political Science Quarterly* 100/4 (1985–86): 627–47; Kai P. Schoenhals and Richard A. Melanson, *Revolution and Intervention*

in Grenada: The New Jewel Movement, the United States, and the Caribbean (Boulder, CO: Westview, 1985); Tony Thorndike, "Grenada." In Peter J. Schraeder (ed.), *Intervention in the 1980's: U.S. Foreign Policy in the Third World* (Boulder, CO: Lynne Rienner, 1989).

58. Gairy was also prime minister briefly in 1962 before being removed by colonial administrators on charges of corruption.

59. One National Security Council staffer stated that the Soviets could place nuclear missiles in Grenada, presumably something they could not do in Cuba given the history of the Cuban Missile Crisis. However, the acquisition of a long-range secure second-strike capability by the Soviets after the 1962 missile crisis eliminated any need for forward-deployed short-range missiles. In addition to being highly improbable, the placement of any additional intermediate-range missiles in Grenada would not have altered the strategic balance between the superpowers, given their highly redundant arsenals in the 1980s.

60. Of those watching the presidential address on October 27, 86 percent favored the intervention after the speech (Rubner 1985–86, 644). Interestingly, public endorsement of the operation was qualified. Whereas 55 percent approved of the use of U.S. troops, 51 percent would have attempted to negotiate with the new leaders or watched the situation closely to see if a crisis did in fact develop; 49 percent felt that the president, in general, resorted to force too quickly; and 51 percent believed Reagan's advisors, rather than the president, ran the administration's foreign policy.

61. The resolution passed over Nixon's veto; every subsequent administration has denied the legality of the resolution on constitutional grounds. The actual effectiveness of the resolution is hotly debated (Zutz 1976; Rubner 1985–86; Glennon 1991).

62. The constitutionality of the concurrent resolution provision in the War Powers Act, which has been described as a legislative veto, has been questioned by constitutional scholars but never formally challenged in the courts.

63. For a discussion of the impact of press restrictions during the Persian Gulf War, see MacArthur (1992) and Gottschalk (1992).

64. The fact that the bombing in Lebanon took place two days before the invasion of Grenada makes separating the rally effect from the Middle Eastern crisis from that attributable to the Caribbean crisis almost impossible. However, it seems reasonable to conclude that at least a portion of the seven-percentage-point rise is due to the success of the Grenada invasion.

65. Also see Senese (1997a) for a discussion of democracy and the use of large-scale violence.

CHAPTER 6

Democratization and International Conflict

IN A PROVOCATIVE and widely cited series of articles, Mansfield and Snyder have claimed that democratization increases the probability of war: "Though mature democratic states have virtually never fought wars against each other, promoting democracy may not promote peace because states are especially war-prone during the transition toward democracy" (1995b, 94). The empirical findings, based on both qualitative and quantitative analysis, stunned the academic and policy communities because the promotion of democracy had become a cornerstone of U.S. foreign policy following the end of the Cold War. Moreover, Mansfield and Snyder's results appear to conflict with the theoretical arguments and empirical findings presented in previous chapters. How could the *process* of becoming more democratic increase the probability of conflict, while simultaneously the *state* of being more democratic decreases the probability of conflict? It is possible for change and state variables to have opposing effects, but the theoretical arguments discussed in prior chapters would not lead one to expect such a divergence. In this chapter, I explore the Mansfield and Snyder argument using quantitative analysis of the unique dispute data set developed as part of this project and case studies from new democracies in Europe during the interwar period (Czechoslovakia versus Hungary and Poland) and Africa after decolonization (Somalia versus Ethiopia). The statistical results do not support the conclusions of Mansfield and Snyder, but the case studies highlight how nationalist mobilization may increase the probability of conflict in specific situations.

Mansfield and Snyder's Theoretical Argument

The empirical support for the dyadic version of the democratic peace has led policy makers to call for the promotion of democracy. President Clinton and his National Security Advisor Anthony Lake have argued, much like Wood-row Wilson did almost a century ago, that the promotion of democracy should be a major U.S. foreign policy objective because it will make the world a safer place in the long run. Logically, if democratic dyads are more peaceful, an expansion of the number of dyads should reduce the amount of conflict in the system. The fact that the same policy (promoting democracy) helped achieve both realist goals (enhancing security) and liberal goals (expanding freedom) explains the rapid emergence of a consensus on the policy.

Mansfield and Snyder question this argument. Whereas mature and stable democracies may be less war prone, transitional regimes with limited democratic control over foreign policy are likely to encourage external conflict (1995a, 5). The logic of their argument draws on Huntington's classic *Political Order in Changing Societies*: "As Samuel Huntington has put it, the typical problem of political development is the gap between high levels of political participation and weak integrative institutions to reconcile the multiplicity of contending claims" (1995a, 22).

The collapse of autocratic institutions leads to the mobilization of interest groups and greater competition for control of government policy. Regulating this competition is difficult due to the weakness of institutions and the absence of democratic norms. In this fluid environment, new interest groups and interests groups associated with the former autocratic government desperately seek to find issues that will allow them to build broad popular coalitions. Those associated with the former ruling government are particularly vulnerable because many traditional uniting issues have lost their legitimacy, and the groups are in danger of losing the economic and political privileges they enjoyed under the previous regime.

What issues tend to be exploited by the old and new elites? Mansfield and Snyder argue that political leaders often create a "belligerent nationalist coalition." The old elite and the military can define themselves as the guardians of the nationalist cause regardless of the political and economic changes made in the transitional environment. Newly emerging interest groups also seize on this issue to both counter the claims made by the old elite and unify the fragmented interest groups just forming in the unstable environment. Although the masses may not be particularly war prone at the start of this process, the appeals to nationalism from across the political spectrum can quickly create a belligerent nationalist mood (1995b, 88). The intensification of this mood can trigger "blowback"—a situation in which leaders feel compelled to behave aggressively as they become trapped by their own rhetoric (Snyder 1991, 41).

Is belligerent nationalism the only policy with which political entrepreneurs can mobilize coalitions? The answer is clearly no. However, it is typically an excellent choice because there is little downside. Most policy choices, such as economic reform, help some groups and hurt others. Thus, using economic reform to mobilize citizens will attract those who will gain from liberalization and repel those who prefer the existing illiberal status quo. Nationalism differs because, unlike most issues, it tends to attract many more than it repels. This is particularly true of new states formed from empires (such as Czechoslovakia), newly independent states after decolonization (such as Somalia), and states facing external threats (such as Wilhelmine Germany).

Using data on wars and regime types from 1811 to 1980, Mansfield and Snyder found "that democratizing states—those that have recently undergone regime change in a democratic direction—are much more war-prone than states that have undergone no regime change, and are somewhat more war-prone than those that have undergone a change in an autocratic direction" (1995a, 8). They conclude that transitioning states have both mobilizing populations and weakly constraining institutions and norms. In this environment, manipulative leaders are able to capture the state and promote aggressive foreign policies that benefit only a narrow constituency.

CRITICS OF MANSFIELD AND SNYDER'S ORIGINAL ANALYSIS

The Mansfield and Snyder theoretical argument and quantitative analysis (1995a, 1995b) was criticized from a number of quarters. Wolf (1996) argued that the theoretical model was most appropriate for the demise of feudal states; consequently, its applicability to the recent demise of communist states in Europe was doubtful. Weede (1996) criticized the analysis on three grounds: (1) the results were statistically weak using conventional levels of significance (particularly weak for inter-state wars); (2) the overly complicated research design made it impossible to distinguish the impact of regime change in general, from democratization (or autocratization) in particular; and (3) and Weede claimed that all democracies, not just democratizing states, suffer from a lack of coherence in foreign policy. Enterline (1996, 1998) argued that conflict initiation rather than conflict involvement is a more direct test of the logic of Mansfield and Snyder's argument. Focusing on regime change along a continuum rather than categorical shifts, Enterline's reanalysis rejected the hypothesis that democratization increases the probability of war and conflict. Rousseau (1997) criticized the lag structure employed in the Mansfield and Snyder model, which allowed a regime change in one year (for example, 1811) to be linked to the outbreak of war almost two decades later (1830). Finally, Thompson and Tucker (1997) demonstrated that Mansfield and Snyder misinterpret their own three-by-two contingency tables. By grouping democratization, autocratization, and no change in a single table, Mansfield and Snyder could not determine if change in either direction was statistically significant. Using Mansfield and Snyder's data, Thompson and Tucker construct a series of two-by-two contingency tables (democratization versus no change, autocratization versus no change). These revised tables demonstrate that in six of eight cases (two measures of war and four measures of democracy), democratization has no statistically significant impact on the use of force even at the more lenient $p < 0.1$ level of significance.

As the debate evolved, a series of new quantitative studies has also called into question the conclusions of Mansfield and Snyder. Using a country-year data set from 1875 to 1996 and a monadic design, Gleditsch and Ward (2000) find that democratization reduces rather than increases the risk of war. The use of a nonlinear model also shows that anocracies are just about as likely to be involved war as autocracies. Thus, it is the state of being an anocracy rather than the process of moving toward it that leads to greater violence.[1] In a dyadic analysis, Russett and Oneal (2001) find no support for the claim that democratization causes war. Using a democratization variable that captures both categorical shifts and the magnitude of the shift, the authors find that "it is the *level* of democratic government achieved by both members of a dyad, not whether this was achieved recently, that affects the likelihood they will experience a dispute" (2001, 120 — emphasis in the original). Finally, using a massive data set of all dyads as well as a smaller data set of politically relevant dyads, Bennett and Stam (2004) find that democratization decreases conflict. In dyads where both states are democratizing, the probability of war declines by 20 to 30 percent (chapter 5, 10).

MANSFIELD AND SNYDER'S RESPONSE

Mansfield and Snyder have responded to these critiques in a number of ways. Snyder (2000) extends the qualitative analysis to former communist states by studying the breakup of the Soviet Union and Yugoslavia and to the developing world by examining nationalism and democracy in Sri Lanka, India, Rwanda, and Burundi. In an analysis of dyads, Mansfield and Snyder (2002b) find that "incomplete democratization," defined as a shift from autocracy to anocracy, increases the probability of involvement in a militarized inter-state dispute (MID). The results remain statistically significant even after controlling for levels of democracy, growth, alliances, contiguity, capability index, and dependency. Only one of the four dependent variables in the paper produced evidence that complete democratization (that is, autocracy to democracy transitions or anocracy to democracy transitions) increased the probability of a dispute. Thus, Mansfield and Snyder's claim has now become more restricted: anocratization increases conflict.[2]

In Mansfield and Snyder (2002a), the authors conduct monadic analysis and reach the same basic conclusions. Using data from both the nineteenth and twentieth centuries and a different set of control variables, they again find that incomplete democratization is the only transition associated with an increase in violence. They argue that this impact is particularly pronounced when the domestic concentration of power is low. Mobilized populations in societies with weak institutions are more likely to become involved in disputes. This finding holds up even when the authors employ a conflict-initiation dependent variable in place of their conflict-involvement variable.

In sum, Mansfield and Snyder have attempted to respond to their critics by placing greater emphasis on the communist and developing worlds, exploring conflict initiation in addition to involvement, shifting to a more traditional lag structure, and disentangling autocratization from democratization. In the process, they have significantly limited the scope of their initial claims. This raises two interesting questions: (1) does anocratization lead to the use of aggressive force in the dispute data set? and (2) what is the relationship between regime transition and the normative-structural debate examined in previous chapters? I tackle the theoretical question first.

Regime Change, Norms, and Structures

The normative explanation of the democratic peace predicts that the regime change variable should reduce the pacifying effect of democratic norms in the short run. Norms are traditionally conceptualized in a dichotomous way: socialization has either etched peaceful norms of conflict resolution into your circuit boards or it has not. The socialization process begins during childhood and continues throughout our lives. Once internalized by individuals, norms tend to be relatively stable; barring catastrophic changes in the environment, norms develop and decay rather slowly. Therefore, the constraining power of democratic norms should develop slowly over time. For example, suppose that a previously stable autocratic regime suddenly becomes a democracy in 1972. The new leaders as well as the entire public were socialized under an autocratic regime. We would not expect them to suddenly shift their normative framework, which is the product of years of conditioning. However, with the rise of a new generation of leaders who have been socialized in a fully democratic polity, we would expect the constraining power of norms to come into full force.

In any particular case, the impact of regime change variable will vary with the new leader in question. In many newly democratic states, the leadership has been long excluded from political power or even exiled from the country. If an exiled leader pressed for democracy from abroad, the emergence of democratic norms might be accelerated. After the ouster of Iraqi dictator Saddam Hussein, some individuals within the U.S. government pushed for the inclusion of Iraqi exiles in the new government because they assumed that the exiles would value democracy and capitalism more than indigenous Iraqis would.[3]

The structural explanation predicts an immediate impact of democratization. As soon as the democratic structures are in place, the domestic opposition should be able to constrain the behavior of foreign policy executives. Returning to the hypothetical example, the new democratic institutions established in 1972 create channels between the legislature and executive, allowing the former to punish leaders for foreign policy mistakes. However, in practice, institutions take time to consolidate. In 1971 the political opposition is united behind a single objective—removal of the autocratic regime. After taking power, this united opposition slowly fragments as differences between groups emerge and initial impetus for the united coalition recedes into history. Distinct opposition parties only slowly emerge. Moreover, essential mechanisms such as a free press typically develop gradually. This scenario implies that the constraining power of political structures may be initially weaker as a stable institutionalized opposition grows over time.

The constraining power of norms and institutions may be further checked by the practice of "pacted democracies" (Karl 1990; Di Palma 1990). Democratic transitions are often negotiated settlements between the conservative autocrats and liberal reformers. In a "pact," the conservatives agree to liberalization but with restrictions that protect elements of the outgoing autocratic regime. Although this speeds the process of transition and can lessen the violence associated with transition, it simultaneously lessens institutional constraint after the transition and makes consolidation of democracy more difficult. An example of a pacted democracy is Chile in the 1980s; although military strongman Pinochet accepted a transition to democracy, he demanded the protection of the military in the new democracy as well as his continued control over the military.

Thus, although it seems reasonable to expect that the full impact of democracy will take some time to develop within a country, in general the normative argument predicts a slower emergence of constraint. Therefore, the normative theory predicts that the democratization coefficient will be strongly positive and statistically significant (that is, increases the *Aggressive Use of Force*). In contrast, the structural explanation predicts a weak substantive effect, a very temporary effect, or no effect of democratization at all.

Conceptualizing Regime Change

In order to identify regime changes, one must first settle on an acceptable measure of regime. As in chapters 2 and 3, I will use the *Democracy Index* minus *Autocracy Index* from the Polity data sets.[4] After adding 10 to the measure in order to ease interpretation, the new variable ranges from 0 to 20. In terms of regime change, the analysis will employ two operationalizations. First, the analysis includes the four measures employed in the most recent Mansfield and Snyder work: (1) *Incomplete Democratization* (a categorical shift from autocracy to anocracy), (2) *Complete Democratization* (a categorical shift from autocracy to democracy *or* a shift from anocracy to democracy), (3) *Incomplete Autocratization* (a categorical shift from democracy to anocracy), and (4) *Complete Autocratization* (a categorical shift from democracy to autocracy *or* a shift from anocracy to autocracy). The thresholds between categories on the 0–20 level of democracy continuum are 4 for autocracy-anocracy and 16 for anocracy-democracy.[5]

Mansfield and Snyder remain adamant that a correct test of their theory requires a focus on categorical shifts (Mansfield and Snyder 1996, 201; 2002a, 309; 2002b, 534). That is, the predicted rise in violence occurs only when a state in transition crosses one of the two thresholds (located at 4 and 16 in my data set). Yet many, if not most, remain unconvinced of this claim (Rousseau 1997; Enterline 1998; Gleditsch and Ward 2000; Russett and Oneal 2001; Bennett and Stam 2004). Why wouldn't a shift from 5 to 15 on the democracy scale trigger rising political mobilization and limited institutionalization of democracy? Although Mansfield and Snyder test the robustness of their analysis by varying the thresholds (2002a, 313), a robust analysis of the impact of regime change would include tests of both categorical and continuous shifts. For this reason, I provide a second test that includes any change in the democratic direction and the autocratic direction on the 0–20 scale. As we shall see, neither the continuous nor the categorical versions support the conclusions of Mansfield and Snyder.

THE DATA SET, HYPOTHESES, AND VARIABLES

The baseline model is identical to that presented in Chapter 3. It includes the three levels of democracy variables (*Actor's Democracy, Opponent's Democracy,* and the *Actor's Democracy with Democratic Opponent*) and five control variables (*Balance of Forces, Alliance Ties, Satisfaction with the Status Quo, Democracy with Weak Opponent,* and *Democracy with Weak Democracy*). The dependent variable is *Aggressive Use of Force,* and the data set is the population of international disputes from 1960 to 1988. In their original analysis, Mansfield and Snyder use conflict involvement rather than conflict initiation as their dependent variable. Unfortunately, involvement is not a precise enough measure because it fails to distinguish aggressors from victims. For example, Iran experienced a regime change with the fall of the Shah in 1979, and it was attacked by its neighbor Iraq the following year. In the Mansfield and Snyder framework, these events constitute evidence in support of their theory. However, it is quite clear that the regime undergoing the regime change did not initiate this war. Mansfield and Snyder (1996, 207) criticize Enterline for attempting to focus on initiation rather than conflict involvement because "mass nationalism (among other factors) that tends to characterize democratizing states may provoke other states to launch wars." In their most recent work, they reiterate this point (2002a, 330). However, although provocation may indeed occur, it seems virtually inevitable that the errors associated with systematically including all victims of aggression will outweigh the errors associated with omitting a handful of cases of provocation.[6]

In response to their critics, Mansfield and Snyder include an initiation of war dependent variable as part of a sensitivity analysis in their monadic analysis (2002a, 332). Although the authors claim that the initiation results support their general conclusions, two important differences emerge. First, *Complete Democratization* has a positive and statistically significant impact in lag years 1 and 2 (but not with lags 3 through 10). Second, *Incomplete Democratization* increases war only with lags of seven years or greater. This implies, for example, that we should expect an Iranian revolution in 1979 to trigger the initiation of war in 1986. As Rousseau (1997) demonstrates, the longer the lag period used in the analysis, the more likely the *process* of anocratization will become mixed with the *state* of being an anocracy.

The dependent variable used in this chapter is *Aggressive Use of Force,* which measures whether regular troops or surrogate forces cross international borders. As discussed in Chapter 3, this variable is more closely tied to initiation than involvement because victims of aggression are not coded as having used force. From the perspective of Mansfield and Snyder, this dependent variable should be better than initiation because it captures many (but not all) conflicts triggered by provocation.

The baseline model from Chapter 3 is augmented with two regime change hypotheses. Based on the finding of Mansfield and Snyder, I hypothesize the following:

HYPOTHESIS 1

Democratizing states are more likely to use aggressive force to resolve an international dispute.

HYPOTHESIS 2

Autocratizing states are more likely to use aggressive force to resolve an international dispute.

Following Russett and Oneal (2001) and Mansfield and Snyder's recent work (2002a), I employ a five-year lag model in the baseline model. In the sensitivity analysis, I examine models using one-, three-, and ten-year lags. For all the variables, in order to minimize the number of missing observations triggered by the introduction of lags, shorter lags were used for the first five years of the time series.[7] This method, which is commonly used in time-series analysis (Oneal and Russett 1997), restricts the loss of information to the first year in each dispute. Given that the average dispute lasts about ten years, the standard five-year lag operationalization would require the discarding of almost half of the data set.

The estimated coefficients and robust standard errors for the two multivariate models are shown in Table 6.1. Model 1 in the table tests the logic of the Mansfield and Snyder argument using the international dispute data set ($N = 5,137$), a dichotomous *Aggressive Use of Force* dependent variable ($1 = 12\%$; $0 = 88\%$), and a five-year lag period for the regime change variables. Contrary to the predictions of Mansfield and Snyder, the *Incomplete Democratization* is negative and statistically significant. Movement from autocracy to anocracy appears to lower, rather than raise, the probability of violence. Table 6.2, which displays the marginal impacts of both models, indicates that a categorical shift from autocracy to anocracy lowers the probability of using force by 7 percentage points. In terms of the *Complete Democratization* and *Incomplete Autocratization* variables, the findings in Model 1 are identical to the findings of Mansfield and Snyder: neither variable has an impact on the use of force.[8] Finally, the *Complete Autocratization* variable is negative and statistically significant. The marginal impact is identical to the anocratization variable: a shift decreases the probability of using aggressive force by 7 percentage points.

The estimated coefficients and marginal impacts of the remaining variables in Model 1 are virtually identical to those shown in Chapter 3. The monadic *Actor's Net Democracy* variable and the dyadic *Actor's Net Democracy with Democratic Opponent* are both negative and statistically significant. A shift from 0 to 20 with a democratic opponent reduces the probability of using aggressive force by 27 percentage points, and a shift from 0 to 20 with any type of opponent reduces the probability of using aggressive force by 9 per-

TABLE 6.1

Probit analysis using the aggressive use of force dependent variable (0,1), the international dispute data set (1960 – 88), and a five-year lag on the regime change variables

Independent variable	Mansfield and Snyder model (1)	Continuous model (2)
Incomplete democratization	−0.292★	—
	(0.167)	
Complete democratization	0.189	—
	(0.185)	
Incomplete autocratization	0.080	—
	(0.328)	
Complete autocratization	−0.256★★	—
	(0.096)	
Continuous democratization	—	−0.001
		(0.018)
Continuous autocratization	—	−0.031★★
		(0.010)
Actor's net democracy (monadic)	−0.020★★★	−0.019★★★
	(0.004)	(0.004)
Actor's net democracy with democratic opponent (dyadic)	−0.075★★★	−0.076★★★
	(0.016)	(0.016)
Opponent's level of democracy	0.013★★	0.014★★★
	(0.004)	(0.004)
Balance of forces	0.183★★	0.178★★
	(0.075)	(0.074)
Shared alliance ties	−0.135★	−0.120★
	(0.064)	(0.064)
Satisfaction with the status quo	−0.695★★★	−0.7693★★★
	(0.060)	(0.060)
Democracy with weak opponent	−0.090	−0.073
	(0.115)	(0.116)
Democracy with weak democracy	0.451	0.509
	(0.502)	(0.518)
Constant	−1.622★★★	−1.163★★★
	(0.079)	(0.079)
Number of observations	5,137	5,137
Log likelihood	−1656.48	−1658.42

N O T E : Robust standard errors appear in parentheses below the coefficient estimates. All significance tests are one-tailed. ★p < .05, ★★p < .01, ★★★p < .001. Results generated with STATA 6.0.

centage points. As with earlier models, the dyadic democracy variable is by far the most powerful in the model.

The *Balance of Forces* variable is positive and statistically significant; the more the military balance favors a state, the more likely it is to send troops across the border. However, the impact of the variable is quite limited. A shift from a position of overwhelming inferiority to one of overwhelming superiority increases the probability of using force by only 4 percentage points. The *Shared Alliance Ties* coefficient is negative and statistically significant. However, an alliance decreases the probability of using force by only

TABLE 6.2

Marginal impacts using the estimated coefficients from multivariate analysis in Table 6.1

Shift in independent variable	Mansfield and Synder model	Continuous model
Incomplete democratization		
No	20	—
Yes	13	—
Total change	**−7**	
Complete autocratization		
No	20	—
Yes	13	—
Total change	**−7**	
Continuous autocratization		
0 to 5 point change	—	19
5 to 10 point change	—	15
10 to 15 point change	—	12
Total change		**−7**
Actor's net democracy		
0	21	21
10	16	16
20	12	11
Total change	**−9**	**−10**
Actor's democracy with democratic opponent		
0	28	28
10	6	6
20	1	1
Total change	**−27**	**−27**
Opponent's democracy for fully autocratic state		
0	20	20
10	24	24
20	28	28
Total change	**+8**	**+8**
Balance of forces		
1:9	18	17
1:3	18	18
1:1	20	19
3:1	21	20
9:1	22	21
Total change	**+4**	**+4**
Alliance		
No	20	19
Yes	16	16
Total change	**−4**	**−3**
Satisfaction with status quo		
No	20	19
Yes	6	6
Total change	**−14**	**−13**

NOTE: See Table 2.3 for methodology. Only statistically significant coefficients in Table 6.2 are presented in the table. Clarify software was used to calculate the marginal impacts (Tomz et al. 2003).

4 percentage points. The *Satisfaction with the Status Quo* variable is negative and statistically significant. A shift from dissatisfied to satisfied decreases the predicted probability of using force by 14 percentage points. Finally, neither of the interactive terms used to test the selectorate model is statistically significant.

In Model 2 in Table 6.1, the continuous regime change variables are substituted for the four categorical autocratization and democratization variables. Overall, the results are very similar to those from Model 1; the coefficients, standard errors, and marginal impacts of the nonregime change variables are virtually identical to Model 1 and need no further elaboration. The *Continuous Democratization* variable is negative, but it fails to achieve statistical significance. Apparently, combining all three types of categorical shifts into a single measure reduces the impact of the variable. In contrast, the *Continuous Autocratization* is negative and statistically significant at better than the 0.01 level. The marginal analysis shows that a shift from a full democracy to a full autocracy reduces the probability of violence by 7 percentage points.

Thus, both models call into question the most recent findings of Mansfield and Snyder. Neither anocratization nor democratization appears to increase the probability of conflict. This implies that attempting to promote democratization has no downside. If it works, the mature democracy will be less likely to use force. If it doesn't, there is either no impact or a reduction in the use of violence. How stable are these results? The results of the sensitivity analysis, which vary either the lag structure (models 1–4) or the control variables (models 5–11), are shown in Table 6.3. In order to simplify the table and focus on general trends, statistically significant negative coefficients are depicted with a minus sign (−) and statistically significant positive coefficients are depicted with a plus sign (+). The strength of the statistical relationship is indicated by the number of minus and plus signs (one symbol implies $p < .05$, two symbols imply $p < .01$, and three symbols imply $p < .001$). Coefficients that fail to achieve statistical significance are labeled "n.s." ("not significant").

The *Incomplete Democratization* remains negative and significant in all but four cases: 1-year lag, 10-year lag, with a cubic spline, and with all the new variables in the same model. Interestingly, the only case in which the variable is statistically significant in the positive direction is when the cubic spline peace years function is included. (See Chapter 3 for a discussion of this model.) The same pattern emerges for the other two statistically significant variables. Unlike the democracy variables, which remain substantively and statistically significant when all the sensitivity analysis variables are thrown into a single equation, the regime transition variables disappear entirely.[9]

TABLE 6.3

Robustness of the estimated coefficients in the regime change model

Regime change variable	Model 1 1-year lag	Model 2 3-year lag	Model 3 5-year lag	Model 4 10-year lag	Model 5 Great power	Model 6 Nuclear weapons	Model 7 Inter-dependence	Model 8 Trade	Model 9 Contiguity	Model 10 Cubic spline	Model 11 All new variables
Incomplete democratization	n.s.	–	–	n.s.	–	–	–	–	–	+	n.s.
Complete democratization	n.s.	n.s.	n.s.	n.s.	n.s.	n.s.	n.s.	n.s.	n.s.	n.s.	n.s.
Incomplete auocratization	n.s.	n.s.	n.s.	n.s.	n.s.	n.s.	n.s.	n.s.	n.s.	n.s.	n.s.
Complete autocratization	n.s.	–	–	–	–	–	–	–	–	n.s.	n.s.
Continuous democratization	n.s.	n.s.	n.s.	n.s.	n.s.	n.s.	n.s.	n.s.	n.s.	n.s.	n.s.
Continuous autocratization	–	–	– –	– – –	– – –	– – –	– – –	– – –	– –	n.s.	n.s.

NOTE: A five-year lag is used for tests with all the new independent variables. The direction of the coefficient (+ or –) and the statistical significance of the coefficients (one symbol implies p < .05, two symbols imply p < .01, and three symbols imply p < .001) are shown with various lags and control variables. Coefficients that fail to achieve statistical significance are labeled "n.s." (not significant).

In conclusion, the statistical analysis supports neither Mansfield and Snyder's original fears about the dangers of democratization (1995a, 1995b) nor their current fears about autocratization (2002a, 2002b). Rather, *Incomplete Democratization* and *Complete Autocratization* appear to lower the probability of violence. These findings are generally consistent with those of Gleditsch and Ward (2000) and Bennett and Stam (2004), despite the use of a new data set and an alternative dependent variable. Given the limited robustness of the regime transition coefficients, the findings should be treated with caution. However, even if the weakly negative coefficients were in fact zero, the results would support the institutional model. There doesn't appear to be a long lag between regime change and the emergence of the constraining power of democracy. Although the normative model predicts strongly positive coefficients for the democratization variables, this outcome emerges only once in the twenty-two separate models.

Case Studies

Two case studies allow further exploration of the impact of regime change on decisions to use military force: (1) Somalia versus Ethiopia and (2) Czechoslovakia versus Poland and Hungary. As with the previous case studies, these cases represent instances in which democratic states initiated large-scale military force against their neighbors. In the final chapter, we will examine all the cases simultaneously in order to identify patterns of democratic initiation.

Somalia and Ethiopia have been engaged in a territorial dispute since Somalia became an independent state.[10] The case is particularly illuminating because over time Somalia transitioned from a colonial dependency into a democratic regime into an autocratic regime. The results of the quantitative model just presented predict that in the short run the probability of conflict decreases and that in the long run it increases. Autocratizing regimes are less likely to use force, but stable autocracies are more likely to use force. The case study supports this contention.

A second case explores the behavior of the new Czechoslovak republic following the end of World War I.[11] In this case democratization is correlated with a use of force, as Mansfield and Snyder predict. As with other states emerging from heterogeneous empires, overwhelmingly popular support for securing "historic" lands prevented the emergence of domestic opposition to the use of force.

SOMALIA VERSUS ETHIOPIA

Somalia and Ethiopia have long disputed the ownership of the Ogaden territory. The area, which is inhabited by ethnic Somalis, was conquered by

Ethiopia between 1886 and 1892. Since that time, Somali leaders have consistently called for the return of the territory. Following independence in 1960, every Somali government, whether democratic or autocratic, has pursued a policy of irredentism. However, as will be discussed, the means used by various governments to achieve this end differed greatly.

The territorial dispute, which continues to this day, results from a unique geographic situation and the legacy of imperialism. Most Somalis, even today, are nomadic herders; during the dry seasons (July–September and December–March), many inhabit natural springs located near the coast around the Horn of Africa. During the rainy seasons (April–June and October–November), these herders drive their animals to the lush Haud pastures located in the Ogaden region in present-day Ethiopia (Laitin and Samatar 1987, 3). This ancient migration pattern was interrupted in the late 1800s, when Italian, British, and French forces colonized the coastal regions. Simultaneously, Menelik II of Ethiopia conquered the Ogaden region using guns and ammunition supplied by Italy and Russia as part of their unsuccessful attempt to manipulate independent Ethiopia into becoming a protectorate. By 1900, the imperial expansion of the four powers had severed the Haud pastures from the coastal wells. Ethnic Somalis had become the subjects of four different states.

Therefore, the Ethiopian-Somali conflict was just one piece of a broader conflict. Somalia also claimed territory occupied by its ethnic kindred in the western portion of Djibouti (formerly French Somaliland) and northern Kenya (formerly a British colony). In terms of the number of individuals and square miles of territory, however, the Ogaden claim is by far the largest. Although the exact number of Somali in the Ogaden is unclear due to the continual migration, estimates range from one million at independence to three million today (Touval 1963, 132; Day 1982, 114).

The only time the vast majority of ethnic Somalis have been under a single political administration occurred during World War II. After the British removed the Italians from Ethiopia and the Horn of Africa in 1941, they restored Ethiopian Emperor Haile Selassie to his throne. However, the British continued to administer the Ogaden region. In addition, the British administered British Somaliland, Italian Somaliland, and the Northern Frontier District (NFD) of Kenya. In 1948 British Foreign Secretary Ernest Bevin called for the creation of a greater Somalia, but the combination of little international support and vehement Ethiopian opposition doomed the enlightened proposal. Suspicion that the plan promoted British imperialism coupled with Haile Selassie's image as a victim of fascism appears to have contributed to opposition to the plan.[12] On November 29, 1954, the British announced that the Ogaden would be handed back to Ethiopia.

In an effort to resolve the geographic and migration problems, the new 1954 treaty reaffirmed the "access" provision originally stipulated in Annex 3 of the 1897 Anglo-Ethiopian Treaty, which had established the boundary between British Somaliland and Ethiopia. The annex stated that both sides agreed "the tribes occupying either side of the line shall have the right to use the grazing grounds on the other side, but during their migrations it is understood that they shall be subject to the jurisdiction of the territorial authority" (Day 1982, 115). However, when Somalia became independent in 1960, the Ethiopian government assumed a convenient but inconsistent position: the treaty-established boundary was deemed valid, but the grazing rights provision was revoked. The position only inflamed the Somali-Ethiopian dispute.

On July 1, 1960, the democratic Republic of Somalia was born. On this date the 33-member British Somaliland assembly merged with the 90-member Italian Somaliland assembly. The composition of the National Assembly at independence is shown in Part C of Table 6.4. The new 123-member National Assembly, which was dominated by the Somali Youth League (SYL), elected Osman Dar (SYL, Hawiye clan, southerner) as president of the republic and Abdirashid Ali Shermarke (SYL, Majeerteen clan, southerner) as prime minister. Despite the official rejection of tribalism, the new government established an ethnically balanced cabinet.[13]

Was the Republic of Somalia a democracy? Despite the somewhat uncomfortable merging of traditional politics with modern democratic institutions, the answer is an unqualified yes.[14] The constitution, ratified a short time later, provided all the structural components necessary for a democratic polity, such as the protection of political rights and universal adult suffrage. From a normative perspective, the question is slightly more difficult to answer. The British and Italians, like other colonial powers, did not socialize the local populations in strongly democratic environments. The only election in British Somaliland occurred in February 1960; the British literally provided "crash courses" (public seminars) on democracy just prior to independence. More important from a socialization perspective, the British had banned political parties until 1959. In Italian Somaliland the experience was slightly better, with municipal elections beginning in 1956. However, even under Italian supervision irregularities persisted, as evidenced by the boycott of the 1958 general elections by Hisbia Destour Mustaquil Somali (HDMS) and the Greater Somali League (GSL) in response to harassment by SYL members.

Despite these caveats, the Somali political system was democratic from 1960 through 1969. It allowed for widespread participation and encouraged open political debate. In part, the early success of democracy in Somalia

TABLE 6.4
Legislative elections in Somalia

	Italian Somalia 1956 (regional)	Italian Somalia 1959 (regional)	British Somalia 1960 (regional)	Independent Somalia 1960 merged	Somalia 1964 elected	Somalia 1969 elected	Somalia 1969 after defections
Somali Youth League (SYL)	43	83	—	83	69	73	110
Somali National Congress (SNC)	—	—	20	20	22	11	11
United Somali Party (USP)	—	—	12	12	9	—	—
Hisbia Destour Mustaquil Somali (HDMS)	13	5*	—	5	—	3	—
Liberal Somali Youth Party (LSYP)	—	2	—	2	—	3	—
National United Front (NUF)	—	—	1	1	—	—	—
Somali Democratic Union (SDU)	—	—	—	—	15	2	2
Somali African Union (SAU)	3	—	—	—	—	6	—
Somali Democratic Party (SDP)	1	—	—	—	—	—	—
Marehan Union (MU)	—	*	—	—	—	—	—
Greater Somali League (GSL)	10	—	—	—	—	—	—
Reserved	—	—	—	—	—	—	—
Other	—	—	—	—	8	25	—
Total	70	90	33	123	123	123	123

NOTE: An asterisk indicates that the entire party or a portion of the party boycotted the election. Reserved seats included seats for minority groups such as Italians (4), Arabs (4), Indians (1), and Pakistanis (1). The Greater Somali League transformed into the Somali Democratic Union.

reflected the egalitarian clan culture that existed long before the country was conquered and colonized. The Somali nomadic culture emphasized individualism and rejected hierarchical control (Laitin and Samatar 1987, 41). Moreover, the apparent domination of the SYL in the National Assembly was quite limited due to clan-based factionalism within the party. In both 1961 and 1962, the government narrowly escaped a vote of no confidence despite the fact that the SYL had 67 percent of the seats in the legislature and the ruling coalition (SYL, Somali National Congress [SNC], and United Somali Party [USP]) possessed 93 percent of the seats in the legislature.

Opposition clearly existed on many issues, such as economic development and the formation of a national language. However, our interest is in opposition with respect to the use of force to resolve the territorial dispute with Ethiopia. On this issue there was virtual unanimity. The overriding policy goal of the new state was unification of Somali-inhabited territory (Potholm 1970, 222; Laitin and Samatar 1987, 69). The constitution explicitly called for the unification of ethnic Somalis into a "greater" Somalia by legal and peaceful means. The new flag consisted of a five-point star on a blue background; the five points represented the five pieces of Somalia held in captivity prior to independence. The unification of the British and Italian spheres implied that three pieces remained to be incorporated: western French Somaliland, the Ogaden in Ethiopia, and the NFD in Kenya. Unification was universally demanded by both elites and masses. Moreover, the rhetoric of democracy and self-determination implied that this national goal was both morally correct and historically inevitable.

Did the political structure of the new state alter its foreign policy behavior? Given that no opposition to the overriding goal existed, did the political structure influence the means used to achieve this goal? Somalia's conflicts with its neighbors represent a uniquely informative case because we have a common policy pursued by both a democratic and, following the military coup by Siad Barre in 1969, an autocratic regime.

Somalia pursued its goal of national unification through both coercive and noncoercive means. On the diplomatic front, it pressed the issue through both bilateral and multilateral channels. Above all else, Somalia demanded a plebiscite for each occupied region: let the residents of the territory decide for themselves. The Somali government demanded this in the United Nations, in the Organization of African Unity (OAU), and in negotiations with the British. The sincerity of this position was demonstrated in the mid-1970s, when ethnic Somalis in present-day Djibouti indicated a preference for independence over incorporation into Somalia. Somalia, as it had long promised, was one of the first states to recognize Djibouti's independence.

Self-determination rather than imperialism was the force behind Somali demands.

In all these forums, the Republic of Somalia was unsuccessful in its efforts. The OAU provides an interesting case. The Somali government pressed its claims in the OAU shortly after the organization was founded in 1963. The petition put the OAU in an awkward position. Given the arbitrariness of colonial boundaries and the existence of overlapping ethnic groups throughout Africa, the organization feared that any indication that borders were not permanently fixed would result in widespread secessionist and irredentist movements. In July 1964 the OAU assembly adopted a resolution declaring "that all member states pledge themselves to respect the borders existing on their achievement of national independence" (Day 1982, 117). Ironically, at the very same meeting the OAU established its permanent headquarters in Addis Ababa, Ethiopia. Over time the persistent Somali demands for border revisions and plebiscites in the disputed territories alienated it from the OAU and isolated it from other African states.

On the Kenyan question, the demand for self-determination appeared to make some headway. A British colonial commission determined that ethnic Somalis, who constituted 60 percent of the Northern Frontier District, almost unanimously favored merging with Somalia. However, on March 8, 1963, just before granting independence to Kenya, the British government declared that Kenya would retain the Northern Frontier District. The British faced a value trade-off: promoting self-determination versus maintaining good post-independence relations with Kenya. They chose interests over principles.

The British action triggered harsh words from the Somali government. Somalia broke diplomatic relations with the United Kingdom. This step was costly because Britain supplied a significant portion of its foreign aid; the Somali government was willing to pay a hefty price for unification. Although the Somali inhabitants of Kenya initiated a guerrilla resistance upon news of the British decision, the government appeared to support the uprising more with rhetoric than material:

> The Somali Republic did not aggressively supply the fighters with weapons, and the rebellion was quickly put down. Leaders of the Somali resistance in Kenya felt embittered and abandoned by the Somali Republic's weak material support. (Laitin and Samatar 1987, 135)

Although some observers, such as Gorman (1981), have emphasized that Somalia lacked the resources to support the rebels, it appears that there was a clear decision not to use force. Guerrilla warfare is a poor man's game; certainly, resources could have been sacrificed given the importance of the issue at stake. The breaking of diplomatic relations demonstrated a willingness to pay for the achievement of this goal. However, very small amounts of aid appear to have been supplied to rebels during 1963 to 1967, and the Somali government primarily restricted itself to rhetoric through radio broadcasts and in international forums.

On the Ethiopian front, the means selected were very similar. The Somali government supported ethnic Somalis through a steady stream of rhetoric and some minor material support. However, the increasing efforts by the Ethiopian government to both extract resources from its Somali residents and to forcibly assimilate them into Ethiopian society provoked a much stiffer resistance in the Ogaden. The natural migration patterns provided rebel Somalis with a sanctuary inside Somalia. This situation led to border clashes as Ethiopian troops often crossed into Somalia in "hot pursuit" raids. Who exactly initiated these conflicts is often unclear. The spirals of hostility followed a typical pattern: Somali rebel–Ethiopian army clashes leading to Somali army–Ethiopian army clashes. When clashes occurred during a coup attempt in Ethiopia in January 1961, the Ethiopian monarch accused the Somali government of initiating the conflict to probe Ethiopian resolve (Gorman 1981, 37).

Conflict peaked once more during 1964, when the regular armed forces of both sides clashed repeatedly. Again, the initiator of the conflict was unclear; each side blamed the other, and no impartial third party observed the origin of the conflict. Regardless of who was at fault, the two countries fought a minor war until mediators were able to produce a cease-fire.

The year 1964 also marked a turning point in Somali domestic politics. Following the 1964 elections, in which the SYL party retained its sizable majority, President Osman named Hussen as prime minister rather than Shermarke. The roots of the dispute had to do with prioritizing goals. The Osman-Hussen faction desired to place economic development ahead of irredentism; the Shermarke coalition wanted to pursue unification even at the expense of development. This conflict created the interesting situation in which the opposition advocated greater use of force than the chief executive; ironically, an autocracy headed by Osman would not have felt the pressure to use greater force.[15]

Osman's presidential term ended in 1967, and the National Assembly elected Shermarke president and Egal prime minister. Despite the fact that Shermarke's main criticism of Osman was the lack of pressure for unification, the new regime followed a more conciliatory path. Farer (1979, 107) gives four reasons for this pragmatic policy shift. First, the confrontational approach had not produced any results and had isolated the regime from the OAU and its African neighbors. Second, the United States was pushing a regional economic plan for Somalia, Ethiopia, Kenya, Tanzania, and Uganda that promised accelerated economic growth. Third, the 1967 Arab-Israeli war had eliminated any hope of substantial Arab assistance against the Christian Ethiopian Empire. Fourth, the closing of the Suez Canal had hurt Somali exports of agricultural goods by removing its European markets. Makinda (1992, 26) adds a fifth factor: all previous prime ministers had been from the Darod clan, which had close ties with the Ogadan. In contrast, Egal was from the Isaaq clan, which did not have as large a contingent in the Ogadan.[16]

Although Prime Minster Egal's trip to Kenya was bitterly denounced on the streets and in the halls of the legislature, the change in policy was approved by the National Assembly. In response, Kenya offered amnesty to the rebels and opened the borders for the first time since declaring a state of emergency in 1964. Shortly after Egal's visits to Addis Ababa and Paris, tensions with remaining neighbors eased substantially. The sporadic fighting that continued in the Ogaden clearly indicated that Mogadishu had never been dictating terms to the independent Somalis in the Ogaden; armed nomadic herders in the periphery could trigger conflict regardless of the stated policy of the center. However, in this region tension gradually declined as well. Although the Republic of Somalia never wavered from its position on plebiscites, it did pledge to refrain from using force to encourage self-determination.

Unfortunately, both the conciliatory policy and Somalia's young democracy did not endure much longer. In October 1969, following the assassination of Shermarke, the military seized power. The military and the population in general had become disillusioned with the parliamentary government that consistently failed to address their perceptions of the most pressing societal problems. The military created the twenty-five-member Supreme Revolutionary Council (SRC), which took over all legislative and executive powers. Decisions were to be based on majority vote. Siad Barre was named president of the SRC and commander and chief of the armed forces. Although Siad Barre wielded considerable influence, he was not an absolute dictator at that point in time. During the first years of the regime, while Barre sought to consolidate his power, the SRC promoted both economic development and a military buildup. Unification of all ethnic Somalis remained a central state goal. Ominously, while the preamble of the revolutionary socialist state's constitution reiterated its demand for unification, talk of pursuing the goal through "legal and peaceful means" had been removed from the text.

However, despite the change in phrasing, there was not a drastic change in policy. The more autocratic regime did not quickly resort to force to resolve its outstanding territorial disputes. There were three reasons for this delay. First, the military regime set out to rebuild the country's small and antiquated conventional military forces. Most of this aid came from external sources; over time the external source increasingly became the Soviet Union.

Second, Barre continued to consolidate power within the SRC. Although factionalism within the SRC remained hidden from view for the most part, it did occasionally explode to the surface. The vice president of the SRC, Jaama Ali Qoorsheel, was charged with treason and arrested in April 1970. Qoorsheel led a more conservative faction within the SRC and resisted the more revolutionary policies of the Barre faction. A second conflict surfaced in May 1971, when SRC members Major General Ainanche and Lieutenant Colonel Salah Gaveire Kedie were arrested along with several army officers on charges of plotting to assassinate Barre. The two leaders were quickly executed. However, the power struggles within the SRC appeared to diminish as Barre consolidated his position. By 1974, Barre was secure enough to release Qoorsheel and the democratic leaders who had been in prison since the coup in 1969.

Third, the delay also appears to have been linked to the regime in power in Ethiopia. Although the specifics are not exactly clear, Somali leaders apparently believed that the fall of the emperor in Ethiopia would reopen the issue of unification. Perhaps they believed that the monarchy, which had conquered the territory almost a hundred years ago, would never willingly part with the prize. Or they may have believed that a new regime, dedicated to the ideal of self-determination, would be more open to compromise.

A regime change did in fact occur; Haile Selassie was overthrown by the military in 1974. The new military regime was compelled to cope with both violent internal factionalism and secessionist movements throughout the heterogeneous state. The Barre regime exploited the situation by increasing its support for the Somali Ogaden resistance movement around 1975. By 1977, the Somali government was releasing regular army troops to "volunteer" for guerrilla operations. By June 1977, the rebels controlled approximately 60 percent of the disputed Ogaden territory.

At this point Barre and the SRC chose to use massive force to free the Ogaden. The timing appeared appropriate. The Ethiopian political system seemed to be on the verge of disintegration as it desperately fought off internal opposition. The Ethiopian government, which previously had been supplied military aid by the United States, was beginning to receive increasing amounts of military aid from the Soviet Union. Having completed its military buildup with Soviet assistance, Somalia expected to see the balance of military forces deteriorate as Ethiopia absorbed the planned deliveries of Soviet equipment.[17]

The initial Somali attack included 10,000 regular army troops; by the end of October 1977, Somalia had committed most of its army to the operation. In the short run, the operation was extremely successful: Somalia captured the entire Ogaden. However, the victory was short-lived. Massive Soviet aid, coupled with 15,000 Cuban troops, stabilized the lines. The Ethiopian counterattack, using Cuban troops, began in February 1978. By March, the Somali army had been crushed; Barre announced the withdrawal of the remnants of his army and his acceptance of a cease-fire.

If the logic of the balance of forces argument is correct, why didn't Somalia attack in 1975 or 1976, at the peak of its relative power? Although guerrilla operations did increase during this period, Farer (1979) argues that the severe drought of 1975 caused hundreds of thousands of refugees to flee the Ogaden. The Somali army was a major supplier of aid to the refugee camps during this period, which decreased the likelihood of intervention. Moreover, the fact that Barre committed the regular army only after the guerrillas had been successful indicates that he may have been simply exploiting a somewhat unexpected opportunity. Barre recognized that a long war was impossible due to the military's lack of spare parts and the likely suspension of Soviet aid. He believed that a successful *fait accompli* could have pressured the Ethiopian government to sue for peace on the Ogaden front in order to concentrate on the much more valued Eritrean conflict.

Did institutional constraints or political norms play any role in the evolution of the Somali-Ethiopian conflict? Did the breakdown of democracy increase (as Mansfield and Snyder predict) or decrease (as my models predict) the probability that Somalia would turn to violence? Although the evidence appears to support the proposition that inclusive institutional structures inhibit the use of force, the case study does raise some interesting points that a purely quantitative analysis would miss. I will begin the dyadic-monadic discussion and then turn to the question of regime change.

At first glance, the case appears to support both the dyadic and monadic arguments of the democratic peace. The fact that a democratic Somalia did not use force against the democratic states of France and Kenya, but resorted to violence twice against the autocratic Ethiopian monarchy, appears to support the dyadic argument. Moreover, the fact that a democratic Somalia used only minor levels of force in the Ogaden, whereas the autocratic revolutionary regime of Barre used major levels of military force, appears to support the monadic argument.

However, on closer inspection it appears that other factors played an important role in the pattern of outcomes, particularly with respect to the dyadic case. Although the democratic Republic of Somalia did rely on a co-ercive strategy against a democratic Kenya, several other factors can explain the lack of conflict.[18] First, in stark contrast to the Ogaden situation, the Somali clans in Kenya did not have close links with the most powerful clans in Somalia (Laitin and Samatar 1987, 135). The major Ogaden clans (Ogaadeen, Isaaq, and Dir) were also the most powerful clans in Somalia. The closer ties increased the desire to aid the Somalis in the Ogaden. Moreover, Ogaadeen, Isaaq, and Dir clan leaders in Somalia recognized that unification would have expanded their political power in domestic politics.[19] Second, the British and Kenyan military forces in Kenya could physically prevent the small Somali military from forcibly seizing the territory. Third, the mistreatment of Somalis in Ethiopia was much more severe than anything that had occurred in the Northern Frontier District (Laitin and Samatar 1987, 136).

Nor does the Somali decision not to use force against French Somaliland seem to be due to "shared" democratic norms and the expectation of peace between democracies.[20] The lack of Somali aggressiveness can be traced to three factors. First, the Issa inhabitants of French Somaliland were the largest ethnic group in the territory; unification would have reduced their status to just one powerful clan among many. Second, France maintained at least 5,000 well-trained troops in French Somaliland and indicated on more than one occasion that reinforcements would be forthcoming if force were used by the Republic of Somalia. Third, unlike the Ogaden, with its economically valuable pastures, Djibouti had very little economic value. High-paying jobs existed, but these were the result of French subsidies and control of the railway to the Ethiopian capital of Addis Ababa. Somalis in Djibouti and Mogadishu realized that these revenues would cease to exist following the use of force. France would certainly halt subsidies, and Ethiopia was unlikely to continue to rely on a single railway, the head of which was controlled by its primary adversary.

Overall, the case study lends greater support to the monadic argument. Although the 1960 and 1964 clashes represent deviations from the model because a democracy initiated force, the level of violence was significantly below the 50,000 regular army troops used later by an autocratic regime. Moreover, Osman Dar and others in the democratic regime clearly opposed the use of force to resolve the dispute (despite sharing the goal of unification). One can only surmise that the proportion of decision makers devoted to peaceful unification declined as the regime transitioned to a military government. Overall, therefore, although the cases deviate from expectations, structural constraints appear to have played an important role in the evolution of the dispute.

However, two pieces of evidence at least partially undermine the monadic argument. First, the opposition strongly favored an aggressive stance to resolve the territorial dispute. In 1961 it appears that democratic decision makers in Somalia attempted to probe the resolve of the Ethiopian army during the internal crisis in Ethiopia. Second, the balance of forces may have had a pivotal role in decisions to use force. If Somalia had possessed a decisive military advantage in the early 1960s, would it have initiated major rather than minor uses of force? In sum, although there is evidence supporting the monadic argument, the case is not ironclad.

With respect to the democratization-autocratization debate, the results are much clearer. First, as predicted by Mansfield and Snyder, political leaders from across the spectrum in the newly independent state chose to embrace nationalism and irredentism. However, the means employed to achieve this end varied significantly. Leaders such as Osman Dar sought to use democratic means to promote voluntary unification. Second, in the short run autocratization appears to dampen the probability of conflict. Autocratic leaders such as Siad Barre need to consolidate power before embarking on any major policy initiative—whether it be domestic or foreign. Third, in the long run autocratic institutions raise the probability of violence. As Table 6.1 demonstrated, stable autocratic regimes are much more likely to use violence than either regimes experiencing autocratization or stable democracies. Only after consolidating his regime and removing democratic leaders opposed to using force to resolve the territorial conflict did Barre commit tens of thousands of troops to the field.

THE TESCHEN CRISIS, 1919 (CZECHOSLOVAKIA VERSUS POLAND), AND THE HUNGARIAN WAR, 1919 (CZECHOSLOVAKIA VERSUS HUNGARY)

As with the Russian Civil War crisis, the causes of both the Teschen Crisis and the Hungarian War can be traced to the destructiveness of World War I. This first "total war" triggered the collapse of three massive heterogeneous empires: the Austro-Hungarian empire, the Russian empire, and the Ottoman empire. The splintering of the Austro-Hungarian empire led to the creation of four entirely new states (Austria, Hungary, Czechoslovakia, and what became Yugoslavia) and significantly altered the boundaries of three others (Romania, Poland, and Italy). With competing historical claims to territory and intermingled ethnic populations, these states quickly became involved in conflict with one another. In the Teschen Crisis, a territorial dispute led to armed conflict between Czechoslovakia and Poland. The conflict soured relations throughout the interwar period and contributed to the outbreak of World War II. In the Hungarian War of 1919, the belated addition of ideology to an already volatile mixture led to a violent struggle among three of these new states (Hungary versus Romania and Czechoslovakia). From the perspective of the constraint model, why did a democratic and theoretically constrained Czechoslovakian state initiate high levels of military force against both Poland and Hungary?[21]

Few observers, even ardent Czech and Slovak nationalists, expected that World War I would trigger the breakup of the Hapsburg Dual Monarchy. Before the war, the most prominent Czech leaders, such as Tomas Masaryk and Karel Kramer, simply envisioned a more autonomous Czech state within a larger monarchal empire. Masaryk hoped for greater autonomy within the dual monarchy whereas Kramer looked toward a pan-Slavic empire led by the Russian tsar. The Allies, hoping to turn the Austro-Hungarian empire against Germany, did not actively support dismemberment of the empire until the last year of the war, 1918.[22] Despite these expectations and desires, the Austro-Hungarian empire unraveled with astonishing rapidity in 1918 in the face of mounting battlefield losses, increasing Allied support of minorities, and ill-fated attempts by the new emperor to placate minorities.[23]

As the empire's defeat became likely, the Paris-based provisional government of Masaryk and Benes merged forces with the Prague-based council led by Kramer. The three leaders agreed that Masaryk would hold the post of president and Kramer that of prime minister. Rejecting last-minute appeals for unity in exchange for autonomy, Masaryk declared independence on October 28, 1918. The dual monarchy left the war on November 3; eight days later the abdication of Emperor Charles signaled the formal end of the empire.[24] An independent Czech state existed for the first time since the incorporation of the kingdom of Bohemia into the Hapsburg empire in 1526.

Poland also began the war as a nation within a heterogeneous empire— in this case a subject of the Russian empire.[25] Poland, which remained a puppet state under German control following the Brest Litovsk Treaty in the spring of 1918, became completely independent following the Allied armistice with Germany on November 11, 1918. General Joseph Pilsudski, recently released from prison in Germany, arrived in Warsaw three days later and took control of the provisional Polish government. Pilsudski was immediately forced to confront several territorial disputes, including conflicts with Germany (Posnia, Pomerania, and German Silesia), Lithuania (Vilnus), the Ukraine (East Galicia), the Soviet Union (eastern border), and Czechoslovakia (Teschen).

Both the newly independent states of Poland and Czechoslovakia claimed a small enclave historically known as Austrian Silesia, which included the Duchy of Teschen. Although the Polish-speaking inhabitants formed a majority of the inhabitants, the territory was of great economic importance to Czechoslovakia because it contained key rail links with Slovakia and the coal upon which all Czech industry depended.[26]

After the collapse of Austro-Hungarian authority, two local organizations (the Polish National Council and the Czech National Local Committee for Silesia) temporarily divided the duchy into two regions based on ethnic groupings until a formal agreement could be reached. Of the four districts in the duchy, the Polish Zone contained Bielitz, Teschen, and portions of Frystat whereas the Czech Zone contained Frydek and portions of Frystat. A majority of the coal pits fell within the Czech Zone (twenty-six versus ten). A central body composed of seven Czechs, seven Poles, and five Germans organized food supplies for the entire duchy (Temperley 1921, 356).

The crisis erupted in December 1918, when the Polish government announced that elections for the Polish Sejm would be held on January 26, 1919, and that seats in the body had been created for the occupied territories. The election, coupled with the presence of Polish troops in their occupation zone, led the Czechs to believe that the Poles were attempting to unilaterally transform the temporary division into a permanent settlement. The Czech government suspected that Poland would claim that participation in the vote constituted evidence of the public's acceptance and the legitimacy of Polish rule.

The Czechs attempted to open negotiations by sending a special courier to Warsaw with a request for the withdrawal of Polish troops from the area. However, the courier was arrested in Cracow and did not reach Warsaw until January 26, 1919, after the commencement of hostilities. Having received no reply by January 23, Czech troops led by four Allied officers (one each from France, the United Kingdom, Italy, and the United States) marched approximately ten miles into the Teschen Duchy and demanded a Polish withdrawal.[27] Czech troops also advanced into Oderberg, triggering a small skirmish. On February 5 the adversaries signed an armistice and established a new temporary frontier. The Czechs then controlled almost half the duchy (up from one-fifth) and all the coal fields. An inter-allied commission, which was sent by the Paris Peace Conference at the outbreak of conflict, separated the hostile forces and began negotiations. After direct negotiations broke down during July over the Czech refusal to participate in a plebiscite, the Poles demanded that the issue be resolved by the Allied Supreme Council.

On July 28, 1920, the Conference of Ambassadors, under whose jurisdiction the issue fell after the close of the peace conference, ordered the territory divided between the two states. Under heavy pressure from the French, the ruling granted Czechoslovakia even more territory than it had seized in January 1919. Poland, in the midst of a desperate struggle with the Soviet Union and extremely dependent on French military aid, accepted the decision grudgingly. Czechoslovakia, which retained control of all the coal pits and rail links, was required to ensure flow of coal to Poland equal to the quantity that had been transferred in 1913.

Shortly after the outbreak of violence in the Teschen case, Czechoslovakia became involved in a bitter conflict with its new southern neighbor, Hungary. On October 17, 1918, the Hungarian parliament declared its independence from the collapsing Austro-Hungarian empire. The declaration led to the Hungarian Revolution, in which Count Michael Karolyi, a democrat and pacifist, was made prime minister. Hungary was declared a republic on November 16; Karolyi was appointed president in January 1919. Despite the appearance of institutional change, the French refused to recognize the new government or permit it to participate in the Paris Peace Conference.[28] On March 21, 1920, Karolyi resigned in response to the Allied ultimatum demanding further withdrawal from Transylvanian territory. Although the territory was populated by ethnic Hungarians, the Allies had pledged the territory to Romania in 1916 in exchange for Romania reentering the war on the side of the Entente. Karolyi clearly stated to Allied representatives that domestic opposition to further dismemberment made any concessions impossible for the liberal regime (Perman 1962, 214).[29]

Karolyi's departure led to the formation of a coalition government that included the Socialist and Communist parties. The Communists, under the leadership of Bela Kun, quickly established a dictatorship. The Hungarian Republic of Councils proclaimed its ideological and spiritual ties to the Soviet Union and requested a military alliance with the Bolshevik regime. The communist government was actively supported by the demobilizing Hungarian army because of Kun's dedication to the retrieval of all lost territory.[30] The irredentist goal was supported by an overwhelming majority of the population, and it instantly triggered alarm in the capitals of the beneficiaries of Hungary's dismemberment (Czechoslovakia, Romania, Yugoslavia, and Austria).

The new state of Czechoslovakia was carved from portions of both the Austrian and Hungarian sides of the dual monarchy. Determining the Austrian piece was relatively straightforward because Bohemia, Moravia, and Austrian Silesia were administrative districts within the Austrian half of the dual empire. Determining the appropriate size of the portion from the Hungarian side of the empire proved to be much more difficult. Ethnic Hungarians were a bare majority in the old Hungarian empire. In an attempt to preserve their political position, Hungarian officials had long pursued a ruthless Magyarization program. One plank in this program was the creation of a centralized, rather than federalized, state. The Hungarian government feared that federalism encouraged the development of a national identity among minority groups that would lead to demands for greater autonomy or outright independence. Therefore, there was no easily defined "Slovak province" that could be merged with the Czech lands. The Czechoslovak leader in exile, Tomas Masaryk, had persuaded the French to establish a line based on military and economic rationales rather than ethnic considerations.[31] On November 18, 1918, Marshal Foch, commander of Allied forces, drew a preliminary boundary based on input from Masaryk. The decision resulted in the transfer of 700,000 ethnic Hungarians to a foreign state.

Although some armed clashes occurred in November 1918 as Czech volunteers entered Slovakia and encountered "reluctantly" retreating forces, Hungary quickly complied with the armistice under pressure from France. Trouble erupted the following spring, when the Czechs requested permission to occupy additional territory. Foch's hastily drawn line did not exactly match either Masaryk's request or the March 1919 boundary set by the Commission on Czechoslovak Affairs established at the Paris Peace Conference. Czechoslovak Foreign Minister Benes requested a change in the armistice line that would have allowed the incorporation of a strategic rail line. On April 27, without notifying either the Big Four (the United Kingdom, France, Italy, and the United States), which were meeting in Paris, or the Hungarian government, Foch authorized the boundary change: "Czech troops took possession of the railroads as authorized by Marshal Foch, and without any authorization whatever also occupied the coal basins near Salgotarjan, in the Matra foothills" (Perman 1962, 221).

According to Juhász (1979, 22), the simultaneous entry of Czech and Romanian forces into Hungary was a plot to overthrow the new Bolshevik regime. French generals Foch and Esperey presented plans for a military occupation of Hungary involving French, Romanian, and Czechoslovak troops; the French military desired to crush the Hungarian communist regime before turning on the Bolsheviks in the Soviet Union. However, Wilson, Lloyd George, and Clemenceau rejected the use of force as long as Hungary did not initiate armed aggression.[32] By May, the Romanian forces had penetrated all the way to the Tisza River, and Czech forces had captured Miskolc and the coal basin of Salgotarjan (Perman 1962, 221; Juhász 1979, 23; Vondracek 1937, 35). Romanian forces finally halted after a demand by the Big Four to suspend the offensive and a mobilization by the Soviet Union on the Bessarabian border.[33]

The Hungarians chose to counterattack against the weaker of the two intruders—Czechoslovakia. By early June, Hungarian forces had occupied a third of Slovakia, and the Czechoslovak forces were in full retreat (Volgyes 1971, 148). Only Clemenceau's June 7 and June 13 ultimatums threatening occupation of Budapest halted the attack. Although the United States and the United Kingdom continued to blame Czechoslovakia and Romania for the conflict, the French position was adopted by the Allied Powers due to the presence of French forces in the region and Clemenceau's demand for the preservation of an eastern threat to balance against Germany. Hungary accepted the ultimatum and withdrew from Slovakia.

Although Clemenceau's ultimatum called for Romania to withdraw from Hungarian territory upon the latter's compliance, Romania refused to withdraw unless the new Hungarian Red Army was demobilized to the six infantry and two cavalry units specified in the November armistice agreement.[34] The French and Romanians convinced representatives of the Peace Conference of the need for demobilization. In July, after receiving no response to demands that Romania comply with the Clemenceau ultimatum, the Hungarians attacked the Romanian forces. The Romanian army quickly counterattacked and began to march toward Budapest. The Allied Powers then demanded the installation of a democratic government in Hungary as a condition for peace. On August 1, 1919, Bela Kun fled to Vienna as the Romanians approached Budapest. Although the conflict officially ended with the signing of the Treaty of Trianon on June 4, 1920, irredentism continued to shape alliance patterns and international conflict throughout the interwar period.[35]

Was Czechoslovakia a democracy? Did institutional constraints influence the behavior of its leaders in these territorial disputes? Whereas the following discussion will demonstrate that Czechoslovakia was slowly consolidating a democratic regime, the institutional structures did not constrain decision makers because the public overwhelmingly supported irredentist policies.

After the establishment of the dual monarchy in the Austro-Hungarian empire in 1867, the Czechs and other minorities were represented in the Austrian Reichsrat through proportional representation. Universal male suffrage, which was adopted for the 1906 elections, greatly expanded political participation in the regime. In 1911, the last election before the outbreak of war, Czech parties held forty seats in the Austrian Reichsrat. These political parties were highly developed and possessed a strong mass following. Czech lands constituted the industrial heart of the Austro-Hungarian empire, and they contained a large and highly educated middle class. Although the monarchy continued to wield considerable power in the empire, the constitutional system and economic situation proved conducive to the development of strong political parties and regularized party competition in Czech lands.

Under much more repressive Hungarian rule, the Slovaks had experienced little political development. Despite constituting 10 percent of the Hungarian population, Slovaks won only three seats in the last pre–World War I parliamentary elections, held in 1910. Unlike the Austrian side of the empire, suffrage was extremely limited in Hungary. Few of the predominantly peasant Slovak population possessed the right to vote. Moreover, the Hungarian government used majority voting rules to minimize minority representation and power. Only a single Slovak political party developed in the prewar era—the Slovak National Party. Even this party lacked a mass basis of support.

During the disintegration of the empire in early November 1918, the Prague-based National Committee headed by Kramer and the Paris-based National Council headed by Masaryk united under a single banner. The leadership agreed on a distribution of power: Kramer as prime minister, Masaryk as president, and Benes as foreign minister. The leadership formed a provisional national assembly to run the government until elections could be held. Using the percentage breakdown of party seats from the Reichsrat election in 1911, the 268-member provisional legislature included the Agrarian Club (55), Social Democratic Party (53), State Rights Democrats (46), Czech Socialists (29), Czech Populist Party (24), Czech Progressive Party (6), and the Slovak Club (53).

Although the use of the 1911 election results was arguably the best approach in the short run, the provisional legislature was not perfectly representative of the population for two reasons. First, neither the Austrian elections nor the Hungarian parliament could be used to choose Slovakian representatives. For this reason, Slovakian leader Vavro Srobar was designated to select all 54 representatives. Second, tremendous social and economic changes since 1911 inevitably made the body more conservative than the population in 1918, as demonstrated by the leftward shift of the electorate in the local elections in June 1919. In response, Prime Minister Kramer (State Rights Party) was replaced by Vlastimil Tusar (Social Democratic Party) in July 1919.

In sum, at the points in time when Czechoslovakia chose to use force against Poland (January 1919) and Hungary (April 1919), it was transitioning toward a democratic state. A broadly representative legislative body existed, and the chief executives (president and prime minister) were elected by, and perceived themselves as accountable to, the legislature. However, Czechoslovakia did not ratify a constitution or hold general elections until 1920. These factors, coupled with the exclusive selection process for Slovakian delegates, led Czechoslovakia to be coded as only partially democratic in the quantitative portion of the study.

The evidence suggests that the existence of the developing institutional channels did not constrain the chief executive from using force. This lack of constraint had five sources. First, the opposition in the legislature pushed for more aggressive policies than the chief executive. In the Teschen case, President Masaryk and Foreign Minister Benes strongly opposed the use of force

(Mamatey and Luza 1973, 34; Perman 1962, 106). However, Prime Minister Kramer and his nationalist supporters from the States Rights and Agrarian parties controlled the cabinet and were strongly supported by public opinion. Kramer argued that previous uses of force, such as the *fait accomplis* in Sudetenland and Slovakia, had not triggered a hostile international reaction. Masaryk and Benes, having spent years in exile, rejected the narrow "Czech first" perspective of the prime minister. These leaders believed that the first use of force would undermine Allied support for the independent Czechoslovak state at that critical juncture. However, faced with intense domestic opposition, Masaryk reluctantly agreed to the demands of the legislature, and force was used to resolve the disputes.

Would the outcome have been different if the crisis occurred after the adoption of a constitution and a full general election? The most likely answer is no for several reasons. First, while the Agrarian parties were the most nationalistic, the spirit of uncompromising nationalism infected all parties, including the Social Democrats. Although the April 1920 elections increased leftist representation in the Red-Green coalition (Social Democrat-Agrarian), the parties that supported the use of force in 1919 were reelected in 1920. The citizens in the newly independent state demanded the incorporation of historic territories; the leadership (with the exception of Masaryk and Benes) enthusiastically complied.[36]

Second, a regime just transitioning to democracy has very little time to instill political norms associated with democracy in either the leadership or the masses. The normative explanation emphasizes the socialization of political leaders within the domestic political environment. This socialization process can take generations to complete; however, the age of the transitional Czechoslovak regime was measured in months rather than generations. The Czech leaders, through participation in the Austrian Reichsrat, had some experience in the "give and take" associated with the peaceful resolution of political conflict within democracies. The Slovak leadership, in contrast, had no such experience. In sum, a generic societal norms argument would imply that constraints would be the weakest in a new polity transitioning to democracy.

The weakness of "societal" norms measures is highlighted by this case. According to a generic societal norms argument, the longer a state is democratic, the more ingrained democratic norms of conflict resolution become. However, in the case of Czechoslovakia the two leaders had been socialized in the same political system (the Austrian constitutional monarchy) but adhered to very different norms of conflict resolution. Masaryk was a humanist and pacifist; he believed that force, should it ever be necessary, was justifiable only in self-defense. Kramer, on the other hand, was determined to use force to acquire all historically Czech lands. A complete test of the normative hypotheses requires extensive information about the belief systems of individual leaders rather than aggregate societal measures.[37] Whereas the research design used in the previous chapter represents a first step in this direction, more work needs to be done before we can make any definitive conclusions about the importance of political norms.

Third, the expectation of imminent hostility from the Hungarians justified the preemptive strike in the minds of the leadership. Bela Kun and his military supporters had openly rejected the tentative borders with Romania and Czechoslovakia. Moreover, Kun and the army were rapidly building a large army in direct defiance of the November 13, 1918, armistice that Hungary had signed with the local French military commander (Perman 1962, 218). Facing an enemy with hostile intentions and growing capability, Romania and Czechoslovakia struck the first blow.[38]

Finally, the low expected cost of the operations encouraged the Czechoslovak leaders to take aggressive action. The structural argument posits that leaders of democratic or constrained states should be willing to engage in "cheap" uses of force. In the Teschen case, the Czechoslovaks struck while three-fourths of the Polish army was engaged in full-blown war in eastern Galicia with Ukrainian separatists. The probability of a Polish counterattack at that moment was virtually nil. In the Hungarian case, the balance of forces was much more equal because the Czech armies from Italy, France, and Siberia had yet to fully return. However, in this case Czechoslovakia was supported by the Romanian army, which unlike the defeated, demoralized, and demobilized Hungarian army, was an integrated fighting force. Moreover, in both cases, the Czechs expected no international opposition to the use of force because previous *fait accomplis* had triggered no response.

Conclusions

Mansfield and Snyder concluded their landmark 1995 essay with an alarming proclamation: promoting democratization may be a dangerous policy choice. Although their recent analysis limits this fear to anocratization (that is, moving from autocracy to anocracy), they still worry about democratization because it can stumble to a halt halfway through the process. The statistical findings from the dispute data set presented here strongly contravene their central conclusions and policy recommendations. First, democratization does not increase the likelihood of resorting to violence. Only the categorical incomplete democracy variable was statistically significant, and it was negative rather than positive. Second, the quantitative analysis demonstrates that autocratization lowers rather than raises the probability of using force. This is important because it means states need not fear the failure of democratization in their neighbors. A reversion to full autocracy in Russia, for example, is likely to decrease rather than increase the probability that Russia uses force abroad in the short run.

However, the qualitative analysis of the Czechoslovak cases supports key elements of Mansfield and Snyder's theoretical framework. The mobilization of interests groups coupled with weak institutions increased the probability of violence. Thus, the causal process outlined by the authors may be particularly important for newly independent states emerging from heterogeneous empires. Future research should be devoted to examining the conditions under which the thesis might hold.

Finally, the Somali case supports the contention that autocratization decreases the probability of violence as new leaders consolidate power. The case also supports the monadic argument that once this autocratic regime consolidates, it is more likely to resort to major uses of force because of the systematic elimination of opposition groups.

Notes

1. See Rousseau (1997) for a similar point.

2. Mansfield and Snyder persist in warning about the dangers of "democratization" (2002a, 334). Whereas this may seem appropriate given that anocratization is a subset of democratization, it is potentially misleading because the careless reader (or policy analyst) may erroneously believe that the current research supports their earlier findings about democratization in general. More important, the term *democratization* refers to all types of transitions (that is, autocracy to democracy, anocracy to democracy, and autocracy to anocracy). Only the third of the three transitions is problematic according to the current study.

3. See Susan Baer, "Iraqi Exiles, Pentagon Unite to Plan Rebuilding; Expatriates: Former Citizens Jump at the Chance to Help Country Move from Oppression to Democracy." *Baltimore Sun*, April 26, 2003, 1a.

4. In their original analysis, Mansfield and Snyder also use a Polity II–based index developed by Maoz and Russett (1993): Power Concentration Index $\star$ (Democracy Index minus Autocracy Index). This operationalization was criticized for a lack of a theoretical basis (Oneal and Russett 1997, 274), nonmonotonicity in the dyadic measure (Ray 1995; Rummel 1995), and inconsistencies in the monadic measure (Thompson and Tucker 1997, 447). In their new work, Mansfield and Snyder (2002a) separate power concentration from categorical regime change.

5. Mansfield and Snyder (2002a, 311) use identical thresholds, but without the addition of the 10 to the index. The addition of a constant will not change the results.

6. In the Iran example, the shift on the 0–20 scale is from 0 to 4; therefore, it falls entirely within the autocratic category and would not be considered a regime change by Mansfield and Snyder (but would by Enterline and me). However, the

logic of the argument demonstrates the shortcoming of a conflict-involvement variable. The assumption that provocation is relatively rare is supported in the data set by the fact that defenders rarely initiate aggressive force.

7. The following example specifies the operationalization of the lagged variables:

Observations	Variable X	5-Year Lag (Standard)	5-Year Lag (Minimize Loss)	Actual Lag Used with Minimized Loss
1	5	missing	missing	—
2	6	missing	5	1-year
3	7	missing	5	2-year
4	8	missing	5	3-year
5	9	missing	5	4-year
6	9	5	5	5-year
7	9	6	6	5-year
8	9	7	7	5-year

8. In the Mansfield and Snyder analysis, the *Complete Democratization* variable was statistically significant only when using the "Constraints on the Chief Executive" dependent variable (2002a, 324). In stark contrast to their earlier work, this variable is positive.

9. Following Gleditsch and Ward (2000) and Bennett and Stam (2004), I also ran sensitivity analysis using three variables measuring the direction, magnitude, and variance of regime change. Regardless of the lag employed, none of the variables were statistically significant.

10. The Somalia versus Ethiopia case study was developed using the following sources: A. A. Castagno, "Somali Republic." In James S. Coleman and Carl G. Rosberg (eds.), *Political Parties and National Integration in Tropical Africa* (Berkeley: University of California Press, 1970); Tom J. Farer, *War Clouds on the Horn of Africa: The Widening Storm*, 2nd rev. ed. (New York: Carnegie Endowment for International Peace, 1979); Robert F. Gorman, *Political Conflict on the Horn of Africa* (New York: Praeger, 1981); David D. Laitin and Said S. Samatar, *Somalia: Nation in Search of a State* (Boulder, CO: Westview, 1987); I. M. Lewis, *A Modern History of Somalia: Nation and State in the Horn of Africa*, rev. ed. (Boulder, CO: Westview, 1988); Christian P. Potholm, *Four African Political Systems* (Englewood Cliffs, NJ: Prentice-Hall, 1970); Saadia Touval, *Somali Nationalism: International Politics and the Drive for Unity in the Horn of Africa* (Cambridge, MA: Harvard University Press, 1963).

11. The case studies for the Teschen Crisis and the Hungarian War were developed using the following sources: Gyula Juhász, *Hungarian Foreign Policy* (Budapest: Akademiai Kiado, 1979); Victor S. Mamatey and Radomir Luza (eds.), *A History of the Czechoslovak Republic, 1918–1948* (Princeton, NJ: Princeton University Press, 1973); Dagmar Perman, *The Shaping of the Czechoslovak State* (Leiden, Netherlands: E. J. Brill, 1962); Ivan Volgyes (ed.), *Hungary in Revolution, 1918–1919* (Lincoln: University of Nebraska Press, 1971); Harold W. Temperley, *A History of the Paris Peace Conference, Volume IV* (London: Institute of International Affairs, 1921); Felix John Vondracek, *The Foreign Policy of Czechoslovakia, 1918–1935* (New York: Columbia University Press, 1937).

12. Selassie passionately pleaded with the League of Nations to collectively halt Italian aggression against his country. The Great Powers refused to enforce the collective provision of the treaty militarily.

13. The cabinet consisted of four Daaroods (two Dulbahantes, one Majeerteen, and one Mareehaan), two Isaaqs (one Habar Awal and one Habar Yoonis), three Hawiyes (one Habar Gidir and two Abgaals), and three Digil and Rahanwayn.

14. Ethnic parties have long existed in many democracies. For example, three Social Democratic parties existed in Czechoslovakia during the interwar period: a German, a Czechoslovak, and a Hungarian party. However, no one would claim that Czechoslovakia was not a democracy at the time.

15. The factional split over policy supports the contention that Somalia was not a monolithic single-party state.

16. Future leader Siad Barre was also a member of the Darod clan.

17. Some have argued that statements by the United States about forthcoming aid encouraged the initiation of force by Barre. However, Farer (1979) logically argues that the regular army troops had been committed to the campaign well before the State Department and President Carter made vague statements about the level of U.S. assistance.

18. Some may question the democratic credentials of Kenya. Although Kenya was dominated by the Kenya African National Union (KANU) after independence, opposition existed in the form of the Kenya's Peoples Union until Kenyetta established a one-party state following an assassination attempt on the president in 1969.

19. Although I found no evidence to support the proposition, one might expect Somali clans, which would likely lose power following unification, to be less enthusiastic about the policy.

20. Colonial cases are difficult cases to code; whereas France was a democracy in the period of dispute, the local administration in French Somaliland was not. In colonial situations in the quantitative analysis, I code the institutional variables using the motherland because decisions to use force, either initiating or retaliating, were typically made in the European capitals rather than in the colonies. Once again, conflicts falling solely within one colonial empire were considered civil wars and were excluded from the analysis.

21. Although Romania played a much larger role than Czechoslovakia in the Hungarian War, the autocratic nature of the Romanian regime makes its behavior less central to this chapter.

22. Despite Woodrow Wilson's calls for self-determination, he remained opposed to the creation of many small states in central Europe until 1918.

23. Ironically, the offering of concessions by the emperor in 1918 demonstrated the severity of the crisis and actually accelerated the dissolution of the empire.

24. Charles had become the emperor of Austria and Hungary following the death of Franz Joseph in 1916.

25. The largest portion of what was to become Poland fell within the Russian empire; the Austro-Hungarian and German empires also contained portions of historical Poland following the three separate partitions of Poland in 1772, 1793, and 1795.

26. Although all sources indicate a Polish majority, the exact percentages of Poles,

Czechs, and others groups is unclear. Mamatey and Luza (1973) report 65 percent Polish, 18 percent Czech, and 12 percent German. Temperley (1921, 353) reports that only 55 percent of the population was Polish. The situation is even more confusing because many of the inhabitants described themselves as Silesian rather than one of the three historical occupants.

27. The Czechs consciously used the officers from the Great Powers to lessen the probability of an armed Polish response. The Allies condemned the action. It is not clear why the officers consented to accompany the Czech troops.

28. The situation is similar to the Rhineland dispute between France and Germany in the interwar period (Rousseau 1996). In that case, the French absolutely rejected the proposition that regime type influenced the foreign policy objectives of states. The change in political structure in Hungary (and Germany) made no difference to the French (Juhász 1979, 19; McDougall 1978). In essence, they did not accept the democratic peace proposition.

29. Although the withdrawal was supposedly tied to French plans to militarily halt the spread of communism in Russia, the Hungarians correctly perceived that the action implied the historically Hungarian territory of Transylvania would eventually be completely transferred to Romania by the Allies (Juhász 1979, 21; Perman 1962, 214).

30. Nagy (1971) rejects the contention that Bela Kun was a revisionist in foreign policy. However, if he was not dedicated to irredentism, it is difficult to explain the army's support of the radical leftist regime.

31. The French desired a strong ally to balance Germany after World War I. For the same reason, French Prime Minster Clemenceau rejected transferring the Sudetenland Germans to Germany. Although the German government did not press its claim to this land in 1920, Adolf Hitler revisited the issue in 1938.

32. Although no direct evidence exists, some speculate the French encouraged the Romanians and Czechoslovaks in the hope of provoking a Hungarian response that would justify an Allied occupation of Budapest (Low 1971, 146). The Allies had also instituted an economic blockade of Hungary; although not a use of force as defined by this study, the coercive tactic may have implicitly encouraged a use of force by third parties.

33. Langer (1968, 1019) incorrectly indicates that Hungary initiated violence.

34. Although Austria-Hungary signed an armistice on November 3, the newly independent Hungarian state did not sign a cease-fire until November 13. The demobilization conditions were specified in the second armistice.

35. Although France viewed the Little Entente as a mechanism designed to balance against Germany, its three members (Czechoslovakia, Romania, and Yugoslavia) were more immediately concerned with reemerging Hungarian irredentism.

36. A critic of this line of argument could argue that the foreign policy successes caused the reelection of the ruling coalition. However, the Hungarian intervention resulted in 2,000 Czechoslovak deaths (Clodfelter 1992, 620), triggered Allied condemnation, and required outside intervention to prevent complete defeat. It is difficult to see why the public would view the operation as a success. It should be noted that the near defeat was in part caused by the slow return of the Czech army, which had fought with distinction in France, Italy, and Siberia during World War I.

37. See, for example, the work of Margaret Hermann (1978, 1984, 1987).

38. The behavior of the Romanians seems to conform with this explanation because their drive toward Budapest was designed to topple the Kun regime. The small seizure of land by the Czechoslovaks, unless it was done to secure a more defendable position or provoke the Hungarians, remains more puzzling.

CHAPTER 7

The Evolution of Conflicts, Institutions, and Norms: An Agent-Based Simulation

THE EMPIRICAL ANALYSES in the preceding chapters reveal a complex causal process linking domestic politics to international behavior. Specifically, the qualitative and quantitative analyses indicate that democratic states are constrained at the initiation phase by the presence of domestic political opposition that can punish a chief executive for using military force. However, the use of force by the international opponent reduces domestic opposition to the escalation of conflict once democracies are engaged in militarized crises. The chief exception to this process is the dyadic democratic peace: even when they enter a rare crisis, democracies are less likely to escalate against other democracies.

Did this complex pattern of behavior emerge in anarchy by chance? Is it an idiosyncratic outcome that would not recur if history were allowed to repeat itself? Or is it the likely outcome of an evolutionary process that has encouraged the proliferation of liberal states in the international system? In this chapter I use a computer simulation to explore these questions. In the agent-based model, actors residing in an anarchic environment must decide whether or not to use military force to maximize national wealth. Each agent is composed of a government that decides whether or not to fight and a political opposition that can punish the government for military defeats and costly victories. Agents learn over time from their mistakes and from the successes (and failures) of other agents in their neighborhood. Using just a handful of assumptions drawn from the preceding analysis, the model reveals several interesting patterns. First, the simulation indicates that democracies are less likely to initiate military conflict than are autocracies. Second, democratic dyads are less likely to engage in war than are either autocratic dyads or mixed dyads. Third, even when the repressive capability of autocratic states is minimal, major differences in the level of domestic opposition arise across time, and this opposition has a significant impact on the war prone-ness of states. Overall, the model contributes to the democratic peace liter-ature by demonstrating the evolutionary nature of conflict and constraint. As discussed below, it represents an important advancement over existing simulations by incorporating a model of domestic politics and identifying mechanisms that can trigger the emergence of the democratic peace.

Strengths and Weaknesses of Agent-Based Computer Simulations

Computer simulations, like formal models, fall within the category of math-ematical models of social behavior. Within the category of computer simu-lations, a large number of approaches exist, ranging from macro-level sys-temic modeling (such as Globus, developed by Bremer and his colleagues [1987]) to micro-level agent-based models (for example, Cusack and Stoll [1990]). Whereas macro-level models dominated the social sciences during the three decades after World War II, the rapid expansion in computing power in the last two decades has encouraged the proliferation of agent-based models. Agent-based simulations are "bottom–up" models that probe the micro-foundations of macro-patterns. Agent-based models assume that actors are autonomous, interdependent, simple rule followers, and adaptive or backward looking (Macy and Willer 2002, 146). The agent-based mod-els are micro-level in that the user simply defines the attributes of the agents (states in our case) and the rules for interaction. Upon executing the simu-lation, the attributes and rules can evolve as agents seek to improve their po-sition relative to others. These bottom–up simulations often reveal interest-ing and unexpected patterns due to complex interactions and nonlinear relationships. Macy and Willer claim that agent-based models are "most ap-propriate for studying processes that lack central coordination, including the emergence of organizations that, once established, impose order from the top down" (2002, 148).

Although both agent-based and formal models fall within the category of mathematical modeling, they differ in important respects. In most formal models, the developer makes assumptions about preference orders and the sequence of interactions. The model is then solved in order to identify an equilibrium or "expected" outcome. By increasing or decreasing the value of a particular variable, the modeler can identify changes in the equilibrium. In contrast, agent-based models can allow preferences and interactions to vary and evolve across time. Whereas the simulation may reveal a stable equilibrium, this need not occur because many situations are characterized by cycles rather than stability. The important point to remember is that the two methods of inquiry are complements rather than substitutes. Formal models are ideal for deductively determining expected behavior given a fixed set of conditions, but simulations are ideal for exploring the evolutionary processes across long time spans. Within the democratic peace literature, formal models have been much more common than computer simulations. In this chapter I hope to contribute to correcting this imbalance.

As with all methods of investigation, computer simulations have strengths and weaknesses.[1] On the positive side of the ledger, five strengths stand out. First, as with formal mathematical models, simulations compel the researcher to be very explicit about assumptions and decision rules. Second, simulations allow us to explore extremely complex systems that often have no analytical solution. Third, simulations resemble controlled experiments in that the researcher can precisely vary a single independent variable (or isolate a particular interaction between two or more variables). Fourth, although other methods of inquiry primarily focus on outcomes (for example, do democratic dyads engage in war?), simulations allow us to explore the processes underlying the broader causal claim (for example, how does joint democracy decrease the likelihood of war?). Fifth, simulations provide a nice balance between induction and deduction. Although the developer must construct a logically consistent model based on theory and history, the output of the model is explored inductively by assessing the impact of varying assumptions and decision rules.

On the negative side of the ledger, two important weaknesses stand out. First, simulations have been criticized because they often employ arbitrary assumptions and decision rules (Johnson 1999, 1512). In part, this situation stems from the need to explicitly operationalize each assumption and decision rule. However, it is also due to the reluctance of many simulation modelers to empirically test assumptions using alternative methods of inquiry. In the model developed below, I attempt to minimize this problem by using assumptions and interaction rules based on the case studies, statistical analysis, and laboratory experiments presented in earlier chapters. Second, critics often question the external validity of computer simulations. Although one of the strengths of the method is its internal consistency, it is often unclear if the simulation captures enough of the external world to allow us to generalize from the artificial system we have created to the real world we inhabit. However, this shortcoming is not limited to agent-based modeling; all models (formal and statistical) are simplifications designed to isolate the essential elements of complex systems or processes. Moreover, the purpose of the simulation developed here is to demonstrate how simple institutional structures can produce the patterns that emerged in the previous empirical work. Therefore, this chapter focuses on the processes that led to the emergence of the behavioral patterns already documented.

Cederman's Agent-Based Model

Although most of the democratic peace literature has avoided the issue of historical evolution, the work of Cederman and his colleagues (Cederman 1997, 2001a, 2001b, 2003; Cederman and Rao 2001; Cederman and Gleditsch 2002) has tackled the thorny problem head-on through the use of so-phisticated statistical models and computer simulations. Cederman and Rao (2001) employ a regression model with dynamic coefficients to demonstrate that the dyadic democratic peace has grown more powerful during the last two centuries as democracies have learned to cooperate with one another. They claim that the gradual strengthening of the democratic peace can explain why realist critiques such as Gowa (1999) failed to find evidence of the democratic peace in the pre–World War I era. In other work, Cederman employs an agent-based simulation to explore the implications of strategic tagging, regime-influenced alliance formation, and collective security for the emergence of a peaceful liberal world. He concludes that the three causal mechanisms, first proposed by Kant over two centuries ago, can collectively increase the probability of the emergence of a liberal world. Finally, Ceder-man and Gleditsch (2002) employ an agent-based model to explore the diffusion of democracy across time.

Cederman's agent-based simulation model has evolved across time in terms of decision rules, scope, and programming platform. His earliest work focused on the emergence of polarity in an anarchic environment (Ceder-man 1997). Using Pascal-based specification, his agent-based model consisted of a 10-by-10 lattice landscape in which states grew over time by conquering the territory of neighbor states. Contrary to conventional wisdom, he demonstrated that alliances encouraged power concentration and that revisionism discouraged a reduction in the number of states in the system. Later he migrated the model to Repast, a Java-based simulation package developed at the University of Chicago, to explore the democratic peace (Cederman 2001b). Most recently, the simulation model has evolved into GeoSim, which has been used to explore the power laws and the sizes of wars (Cederman 2003).

Although Cederman's innovative research has increased our understand-ing of the evolution of conflict and the emergence of the modern liberal order, much work remains to be done. For example, whereas Cederman's model of the democratic peace illustrates the conditions under which a stable democratic peace emergences, he assumes that the dyadic democratic peace exists (2001b, 480). In his simulation, democratic states cannot attack other democratic states by definition. In contrast, the model described in this chapter analyzes the conditions under which the dyadic and monadic democratic peaces are likely to emerge. Democracies can (and do) fight one another in the new simulation; the question explored is whether over time democracies learn to stop fighting one another. Thus, whereas Cederman explored the consequences of the democratic peace, I examine the causes of its emergence.

My simulation builds upon Cederman's GeoSim model by adding a domestic politics component to his geopolitical simulation model. This approach has advantages and disadvantages. On the positive side, Cederman's model has been widely published in leading journals. This implies that many readers will be familiar with the model's basic decision rules and baseline results. In addition, the development of the model for other purposes ensures that I cannot strategically select decision rules designed to produce a desired outcome. On the negative side, the model (like all simulations) contains a number of decision rules I might not have chosen were I to develop a model from scratch. My solution to the dilemma involves three steps: (1) replicate the Cederman model as closely as possible, (2) transform all key assumptions hardwired into the model into parameters that can be manipulated by the user, and (3) extend the model to incorporate domestic politics.[2] Thus, whereas Cederman's GeoSim model contains twenty user-definable parameters, my simulation contains seventy-seven parameters. By extending the number of parameters, we can explore the robustness of both models. Given the debt I owe Cederman for making his Repast code available to me, I will refer to the new model as "DomGeoSim."[3]

The agent-based model consists of a population of "agents" that interact on a lattice "landscape." Each agent possesses certain attributes (such as power, institutions, and norms) that are modified through interaction with other agents in the landscape. Figure 7.1 provides two examples of the landscape at initialization. Panel A displays a 50-by-50 landscape with 2,500 evenly sized "primitive" actors; Panel B displays a 50-by-50 landscape with 200 variously sized "composite" actors. Aggregation takes place by identifying a "capital" and linking all primitive agents within the borders to the capital; these primitive agents are analogous to provinces that can become free if the capital falls during warfare. Thus, the model is in reality a network in which provinces are connected to a capital and capitals interact with one another. The user can define any initial polarity, but all the simulations reported in this chapter were run using randomly created landscapes with

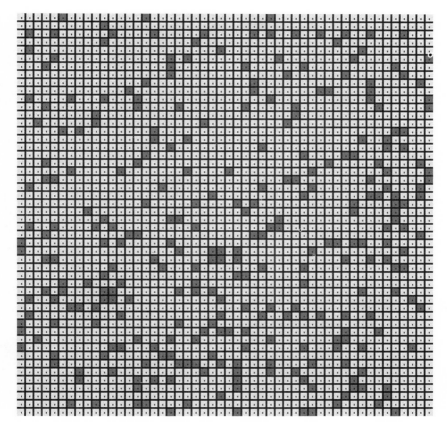

Panel A

FIGURE 7.1. Landscapes at initialization

200 actors similar to that shown on Panel B. Autocratic agents are displayed in off-white, and democratic agents are displayed in gray. In both landscapes, the initial frequency of democratic states is set at 10 percent of the population.

Each agent in the landscape can go to war with any contiguous agent. Thus, the autocratic agent in the upper-left-hand corner of Panel B can go to war with any of the four autocratic states it is touching. Each agent can ally with either a contiguous agent or an agent contiguous to a contiguous agent. This rule permits two-front conflicts, which are common in the history of international relations (such as the Polish–French alliance versus Ger-

Panel B

FIGURE 7.1. (*continued*)

many prior to World War II). Thus, the autocratic agent in the upper-left-hand corner of Panel B has nine potential alliance partners.[4] Whether or not an alliance is consummated depends on the alliance formation algorithm discussed below.

Each simulation is run for a series of rounds or iterations; the simulations reported here were run for 5,000 iterations. If we think of each iteration as a period of time such as a calendar month, then each run of the simulation models the rise and spread of democracy across 400 years of human history. In each iteration of the simulation, agents must complete four tasks: (1) tax their provinces (at a rate of 25 percent of resources available in the default simulation), (2) allocate a portion of the tax revenue to battlefronts along the

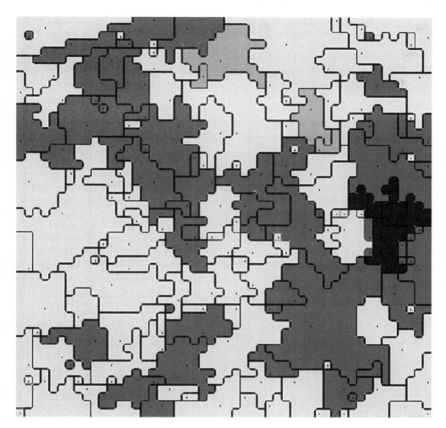

FIGURE 7.2. Landscape at iteration 2,311

borders (with movable resources limited to 50 percent of tax revenue in the default simulation), (3) update the alliance portfolio by adding or subtracting alliance partners, and (4) decide whether or not to attack neighbors. If an attack takes place, the costs of war are subtracted from the battlefront. If the balance of power shifts decisively on the front, the "primitive" province falls to the attacker and becomes a new province within the borders of the attacker. Victory is probabilistic once the attacker achieves a 3 : 1 advantage on the front.

Figure 7.2 displays a typical landscape after 2,311 iterations. The number of states has fallen from 200 to 168, and the percentage of democracies has grown from 10 to 39 percent. Agents at war appear in darker colors (dark gray for democracies and light gray for autocracies); the landscape reveals that there are four wars involving eight states. These wars involve pairs of autocracies (at about 12 o'clock and 1 o'clock) and pairs of democracies (both at about 3 o'clock).

In GeoSim, alliances are made by identifying the most important threat facing an agent based on the balance of power and status of relations (at war or peace). If one state is identified as the *most* important threat by two alliance-available states, they form an alliance. During warfare, there is only a 50-percent chance that the ally will fulfill its obligation (buckpassing can occur).[5] The decision to wage war in GeoSim is based on three rules: (1) when at peace, there is a 10-percent chance of initiating an unprovoked attack on a neighbor; (2) when on "alert status," which is triggered by the outbreak of war in the neighborhood, agents attempt an unprovoked attack in every period; and (3) when at war, states employ a "grim trigger" strategy in which agents attack until victory, defeat, or a draw (Cederman 2003, 139).

ADDING DOMESTIC POLITICS TO THE SIMULATION

Cederman's models address certain "domestic" issues. For example, as states grow, they add "provinces" composed of conquered territory. The provinces are taxed, and border provinces receive additional resources to help defend the state. However, Cederman black-boxes domestic politics because his theoretical interests lay elsewhere.[6] In DomGeoSim, domestic politics are incorporated into the model in three ways: (1) the conflict is divided into phases to allow (but not require) domestic politics to affect each phase differently, (2) state characteristics are a function of traits that can evolve over time, and (3) domestic political opposition can influence decisions to use force.

EXPANDING PHASES OF CONFLICT

In GeoSim, states can be in one of three phases: peace, alert status, and war. In DomGeoSim, the interactions between the challenger and target are separated more clearly, using a simple bargaining decision tree found extensively in the formal modeling literature.[7] As displayed in Figure 7.3, the bargaining game has four phases: (1) peace or status quo, (2) dispute, (3) crisis, and (4) war. Peace is the baseline condition, in which agents face no threats or violence. A dispute phase begins when the challenging state initiates with a demand on the target state. The dispute ends when the target state rejects the demand or concedes to it, or the dispute diffuses peacefully. A target state can also do nothing, in which case the dispute remains ongoing. A crisis phase begins when either the target rejects the demand of the challenger or a challenger becomes impatient with the target's delaying tactics. The crisis ends when the challenger escalates the conflict to war or concedes, or the crisis diffuses peacefully. In addition, a challenging state can do nothing, in which case the crisis remains ongoing. War can proceed for many rounds

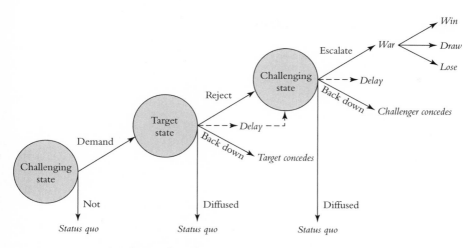

FIGURE 7.3. The phases of conflict

and ends in victory, defeat, or a draw. After the war ends, the dyad enters a peace phase.

INCORPORATING A TRAIT STRUCTURE

In GeoSim, agent characteristics are generally fixed or change randomly. For example, the decision process is fixed for taxation, resource allocation, and alliance formation. As discussed, the decision process for conflict initiation changes based on the status of the dyad rather than the character of the unit. Thus, behavior is homogeneous in that all states at "war" or all states on "alert" behave in the same way. Other characteristics change randomly. For example, regime type varies randomly based on a complex logistic function that permits a small amount of autocratization via coups and democratization (Cederman and Gleditsch 2002).[8] Similarly, the tax and technology shocks, which increase an agent's ability to extract and allocate resources over great distances, are random variables in GeoSim. Therefore, although the agents in GeoSim react to a changing environment, they do not evolve or learn. In contrast, DomGeoSim permits a wide variety of decision strategies and social learning. Each agent has a set of traits that evolve through random mutation and copying from more successful neighbors (that is, learning).[9]

Traits

DomGeoSim uses a genetic algorithm to model the evolution of agents and the system.[10] The behavior of agents is determined by the eleven traits summarized in Table 7.1. The first three traits determine the role of power

TABLE 7.1
Trait structure of the model

Trait name	Number	Attribute	Description
Peace: Power	0	0	Ignore power dimension in peacetime
		1	Initiate demand against weak agents in peacetime
Dispute: Power	1	0	Ignore power in disputes
		1	Reject against weak agents in disputes
Crisis: Power	2	0	Ignore power dimension in crises
		1	Escalate against weak agents in crises
Peace: Alliance	3	0	Ignore alliances in peacetime
		1	Initiate demand against allies in peacetime
Dispute: Alliance	4	0	Ignore alliances in disputes
		1	Reject against allies in disputes
Crisis: Alliance	5	0	Ignore alliances in crises
		1	Escalate against allies in crises
Peace: Regime type	6	0	Ignore regime type in peacetime
		1	Initiate demand against autocracies in peacetime
		2	Initiate demand against democracies in peacetime
Dispute: Regime type	7	0	Ignore regime type in disputes
		1	Reject against autocracies in disputes
		2	Reject against democracies in disputes
Crisis: Regime type	8	0	Ignore regime type in crises
		1	Escalate against autocracies in crises
		2	Escalate against democracies in crises
Regime type	9	0	Autocracy
		1	Democracy
Satisfaction	10	0	Revisionist
		1	Status quo

in the decision-making process. Trait 0 determines whether an agent uses the dyadic balance of power to initiate a challenge. If the attribute on Trait 0 is 0, then that agent initiates demands against all states regardless of the balance of power. If the attribute on Trait 0 is 1, then the agent initiates demands only against weaker agents. Realist theory predicts that over time, successful agents would acquire attribute 1 and other agents would emulate these more successful agents (Waltz 1979, 118). Bueno de Mesquita and colleagues (2003) predict that democracies will be particularly sensitive to the balance of power. Traits 1 and 2 determine whether the balance of power influences decisions to "reject" and "escalate," respectively. Creating distinct traits for each phase of the conflict allows variation in the power of variables across decision stages. Reed (2000, 88), for example, finds that estimated coefficients can vary significantly between the onset and escalation stages of conflict.

Traits 3, 4, and 5 govern the role of alliances in decisions to use force. An attribute value of 0 implies that the agent will not initiate (or reject or escalate) against current allies. Alliances are typically formed in the face of a common threat and can therefore indicate a degree of shared interest (Bueno de Mesquita 1981). Numerous scholars predict that states will be less likely to initiate against allies than against nonallies (for example, Gowa [1999] and Bennett and Stam [2004]). The quantitative analysis in the preceding chapters provided some support for the alliance variable at the dispute stage. In the literature overall, the alliance hypothesis has received mixed support because neighbors are both more likely to ally and more likely to fight.

Traits 6, 7, and 8 allow the regime type of the opponent to influence decisions to use force. For example, if the attribute on Trait 6 is 0, then the agent ignores regime type in decisions to initiate conflict. If the attribute is 1, the agent will initiate only against autocratic opponents. Finally, if the attribute is 2, the agent will initiate demands only against democratic opponents. Traits 7 and 8 operate in an analogous fashion for decisions to "reject" and "escalate," respectively.

Trait 9 governs the regime type of the agent. If the attribute is a 0, the agent is an autocratic polity. Conversely, if the attribute is a 1, the agent is a democratic polity. As discussed below, democratic and autocratic polities differ with respect to their ability to repress domestic political opposition.

Finally, Trait 10 governs the satisfaction of the agent. If the attribute is 1, the agent is satisfied with the status quo. If the attribute is 0, the agent is a revisionist state. Status quo and revisionist states differ in two ways. First, revisionist states ignore domestic opposition when calculating whether or not to initiate conflict. Therefore, holding everything else constant, revisionist states are more likely to initiate conflict than status quo states. Second, revisionist states opportunistically attack neighbors that are already under attack. This opportunistic rule implies that revisionist states are likely to gang up on states under threat. The initial percentage of revisionist states and the frequency of opportunistic behavior are parameters that are set at 0.20 and 0.25, respectively, in the default simulations. Revisionist states suffering a regime change transform into a status quo state. For example, the war-induced regime changes in Germany after the world wars transformed the state into a status quo power, temporarily after World War I and permanently after World War II.

The eleven-trait string consists of eight dichotomous and three trichotomous traits. This implies that there are 6,912 possible strategies for maximizing growth and security in the anarchic environment ($2 \times 2 \times 2 \times 2 \times 2 \times 2 \times 3 \times 3 \times 3 \times 2 \times 2$). Agents search among these possible strings through mutation and learning. It is important to remember that the fitness of strings is often a function of the current environment. This implies that there may be no movement toward a global optimum over the course of the simulation. For example, a strategy that aids an agent in rapid growth in the short run may be undermined by the adoption of the same strategy by other agents in the neighborhood.

Mutation

In the real world, states constantly shift strategies as new politicians and bureaucrats take office. Good ideas are both forgotten and stumbled upon in the process. In the simulation, this process is captured by random mutation. If the *Mutation* parameter is set at 0.01, there is a 1-percent chance that the attribute for each trait is switched during an iteration. Given that there are eleven traits in the string, there is an 11-percent chance of a single attribute changing during each iteration because the probability of mutation for each trait is an independent event. Although mutation allows agents to stumble upon good strategies that might not be available in the immediate neighborhood, it can also be lethal by making the agent unsuited for survival in a competitive environment. In the default simulation, the *Mutation* rate is set at 0.01.

Learning

In the real world, states that are performing poorly often study the strategies of their neighbors in the hope of identifying and adopting a more successful strategy. In the simulation, agents update their strategies using one of three decision rules. The "look to the most successful" rule implies that agents copy from the most successful agent in the neighborhood, defined as the agent with the most power. This rule leads to the rapid diffusion of traits. The "if below mean, look above the mean" rule implies that agents first determine if their power is below the average in the neighborhood. If so, the agents copy from any agent with power above the average of the neighborhood. This rule, which is employed in the default simulation, slows the evolutionary process because only half the agents learn in each iteration and agents do not always learn from the most successful agent in the neighborhood. Finally, the "if the worst, look to anyone else" rule implies that agents look to see if they are the most unsuccessful in the neighborhood in terms of total power. If so, the agent copies from any other agent in the neighborhood. This rule results in very slow learning because few agents learn in each iteration and agents often copy from other pretty unsuccessful agents.

Agents do not immediately change strategies if they are doing poorly. This reflects the fact that in the real world it often takes some time for a consensus to emerge that a problem exists. For this reason, the *UpdateProb* parameter sets the probability an agent updates in a given round (for all three decision rules). In the default simulation the *UpdateProb* parameter is set at 0.10, implying that states have a 10-percent chance of updating each trait if they meet the criterion of the *UpdateRule*. The fact that each trait is treated independently implies that copying every trait of a neighbor is possible, but it should be extremely rare (the probability equals 0.10^{11}). If the *UpdateProb* and *Mutation* rates are set to zero, agents never change their traits. This allows us to compare a world in which learning takes place to one in which it does not.

In sum, traits determine an agent's characteristics and the interaction rules it adopts. The string of traits determines the strategy an agent uses to cope with anarchy. Traits evolve across time due to the diffusion of successful strategies from neighbor to neighbor and random mutation within a particular agent. As we shall see, traits play a central role in filtering the impact of domestic political opposition on the behavior of agents.

INCORPORATING DOMESTIC POLITICAL OPPOSITION

The domestic politics component of the model is based on three core assumptions. These assumptions, which have extensive theoretical and empirical support, are similar to those discussed in the structural model of the democratic peace discussed in Chapter 2 and the institutional constraint model discussed in Chapter 4. The power of the model stems from the fact that even a very simple institutional structure can have a profound impact on foreign policy behavior.

ASSUMPTION 1
All states, whether autocratic or democratic, have domestic political opposition (Bueno de Mesquita et al. 2003). Whereas the extent of opposition can vary from state to state, it exists to some degree in all states.

ASSUMPTION 2
Although there is great variance in the repressive power of autocratic states, autocratic states, on average, can repress domestic political opposition more than democratic states.

ASSUMPTION 3
Domestic political opposition reduces the probability of initiation and escalation for status quo states. In contrast, revisionist states ignore domestic political opposition.

At the initialization of the simulation, each agent is randomly assigned a level of domestic opposition drawn from a uniform distribution bounded by a minimum and a maximum (0.20 and 0.60, respectively, in the default simulation). Democracies and autocracies *do not* differ with respect to the initial levels of opposition. Domestic opposition then rises and falls over the course of the simulation between the bounds of 0 and 1.0 based on four factors: (1) the rate of economic growth, (2) the level of repression, (3) the severity of military conflict, and (4) the "rally around the flag" effect.[11]

First, domestic political opposition changes in proportion to changes in economic growth. For example, if the economy grows by 2.5 percent in a year, domestic political opposition declines by 5 percent. Economic growth is a function of the growth rate minus the rate of consumption and the costs of war. During each round of the simulation, a growth rate is randomly selected from a normal distribution with a mean and a standard deviation (set at .0025 and .005, respectively, in the default simulation).[12] The economic growth factor captures the fact that random factors outside of military conflict can influence domestic politics.

Second, political repression reduces domestic opposition. The extension of economic and political civil liberties in democratic polities coupled with respect for rule of law implies that domestic political opposition is less likely to be silenced by censorship and coercion. The ability to repress in autocracies is a function of their "repressive power endowment" and regime stability. Repressive power endowment is randomly assigned for each agent at the initialization of the simulation by drawing from a normal distribution with a mean (.02) and a standard deviation (.05). Regime stability is a function of how long the democracy has been a democracy (or the autocracy has been an autocracy). In the simulation, this is operationalized by creating a *Stability* variable that is equal to 1 divided by the number of years since the last regime change. On average, the longer the regime has existed, the more it is able to repress the political opposition. Therefore, the ability to repress is equal to repressive power endowment minus stability. For example, in an autocratic state, a repressive power endowment of .02 will reduce domestic opposition by 1 percent in the first year of existence and 1.99 percent during the hundredth year of existence.

Third, domestic political opposition grows during military conflicts and in response to military defeats (Stein 1980). During military conflicts, domestic political opposition rises in proportion to the cost of war. For example, if the cost of war in a particular iteration is 1.25 percent of GNP, then domestic opposition rises by this amount. In the military defeat, the domestic opposition rises in proportion to the amount of GNP lost by the defeated state. Finally, if the state concedes, domestic opposition rises in proportion to the loss in power resulting from the loss of the province.

Fourth, domestic political opposition declines due to a "rally around the flag" effect. Numerous studies of public opinion have shown that the popularity of chief executives rises during times of military conflict, whether the state is the aggressor or the target (Mueller 1973, 1994; Cotton 1987; Page and Shapiro 1992). In the simulation, domestic political opposition declines at the start of a dispute, crisis, or war by a random number drawn from a uniform distribution bounded by a minimum and maximum defined by the user. In the default simulation, the rally minimum and the rally maximum are set at 0 percent and 5 percent, respectively.

Regime change occurs when the attribute on Trait 9 shifts from 0 to 1 (democratization) or 1 to 0 (autocratization). Regime change is a function of four factors: (1) rising domestic political opposition, (2) regime stability, (3) random shocks (such as a coup) in the form of mutation of the regime type trait, and (4) learning from successful agents in the neighborhood. Having addressed mutation and learning, all that needs to be specified is the impact of rising domestic political opposition and regime stability.

Opposition and stability are combined into a single function because of their countervailing properties. In general, the higher the level of domestic political opposition, the greater the probability of regime change. However, the longer an agent has been a democracy (or autocracy), the less likely it is to experience a regime change holding all else constant (such as domestic opposition). Therefore, a long-lived democracy such as the United States is more likely to weather a period of high political opposition than a young democracy such as Panama or South Korea. In the simulation, the probability of regime change is equal to $(((\text{DomesticOpposition}/2) + \text{Stability})/2)^2$. The division of domestic opposition by two implies that the maximum is .50; this ensures that stability and domestic opposition are equally weighted in the function. It also guarantees that the sum of the two factors never exceeds one. The averaging of the two factors implies that stability can offset domestic opposition and vice versa. Finally, the squaring of the term reduces the probability of change and implies that there is a nonlinear relationship. For example, if a regime is in its second year and the domestic opposition is .75, there is a 19-percent chance of a regime change. However, if the regime has been in place for 100 years, the probability falls to 4 percent despite the same level of opposition. Although there are obviously an infinite number of ways to formulate the impact of opposition and stability on regime change, the proposed function addresses the tension between stability and opposition in a simple manner. Moreover, the fact that the same rule is applied to all types of regimes reduces the probability that the developer surreptitiously builds a model that automatically produces desired results. In fact, the only difference between democracies and autocracies is the presence of repressive capabilities within autocracies. This single difference produces important differences in behavior.

SIMULATION RESULTS

Each run of the simulation lasted 5,000 iterations. Due to the large variation across the runs, I focus on differences in mean values over 50 runs of the simulation using *t*-tests. A typical example of the landscape after 5,000

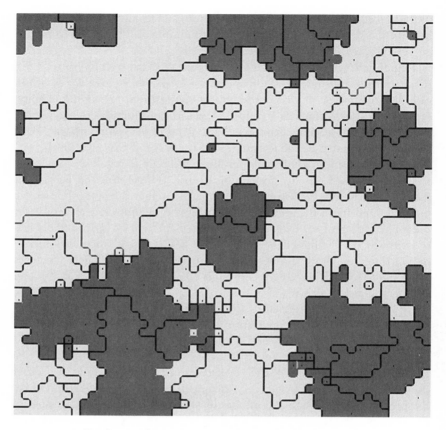

FIGURE 7.4. Landscape after 5,000 iterations with default parameters

LEGEND: Democratic states appear in dark gray, and autocratic states appear in off white. Darker colors imply that agents are at war. In this landscape, no agents are at war. Light-colored borders imply that actors share an alliance. Medium-colored borders imply that agents are on opposite sides of an alliance. In the simulation, colors are used to highlight differences.

iterations using the default parameters appears in Figure 7.4. (See Appendix 7.1 for a description of the default parameters.) The landscape exhibits significant territorial consolidation and the clustering of a number of democratic states. Although the simulation model can be used to test literally dozens of hypotheses, I will focus on seven causal claims that directly relate to the empirical analysis in the prior chapters.

HYPOTHESIS I
Democratic states are less likely to initiate conflict regardless of the regime type of the opponent.

This monadic hypothesis is strongly supported by the data. Although the number of initiations per opportunity in the simulation is very low for both types of states, this simply reflects the rarity of war and the large number of contiguous states. The mean number of initiations for democracies across the 50 runs of 5,000 iterations is .01198. The mean score for autocracies is .01270. If we assume 8 interactions per iteration and 5,000 iterations, a democracy would be expected to initiate 479 conflicts, and an autocracy would be expected to initiate 509 conflicts.[13] This difference is statistically significant at better than the .001 level of significance. Thus, the simulation reveals that democracies are less likely to initiate regardless of the regime type of the opposition.

HYPOTHESIS 2
Democratic dyads are less likely to engage in war than either mixed dyads or autocratic dyads.

This dyadic hypothesis is also strongly supported by the data. The mean number of democracy-democracy wars over the 50 runs of the simulation was 0.00380. The mean values for mixed dyads and autocracy-autocracy dyads were .00400 and .00451, respectively. Assuming 8 interactions per iteration and 5,000 iterations, we would expect to have 152 democracy-democracy wars, 160 mixed-dyad wars, and 182 autocracy-autocracy wars. Therefore, no autocratic peace emerges in the simulation. The difference between democratic and autocratic dyads is significant at the 0.000 level of significance. The difference between democracy and mixed dyads is significant at 0.065 level, or just above a standard level of significance.

Does the existence of so many democracy-democracy wars undermine our faith in the model? Critics might argue that it does because the democratic peace is a "law" proposition (Levy 1988). There has never been a case of large-scale violence between two democratic states. In part, the number of wars is a function of the simplicity of the model—both regime type and war are dichotomous variables. If we were to create a range of regime types and if we restricted the term *war* to cases of major losses on the battlefront, the number of wars would drop drastically. However, the simplicity of the model is one of its strengths. It is not intended to make point predictions about particular historical eras or the future. The purpose is to determine whether a handful of simple assumptions can shape the evolution of agents over long periods. Therefore, the important point to take from the model is the fact that democratic dyads are involved in significantly fewer wars than other types of dyads.

HYPOTHESIS 3
States with a favorable balance of power are more likely to initiate conflict than states facing an unfavorable situation.

This realist hypothesis is strongly supported by the data at every level of conflict. The mean value for the attribute is virtually always above 50 percent, indicating that a majority of states in the system learn to focus on weak rather than strong states. The differences are statistically significant at the 0.001 level of significance for all levels of conflict. However, the results do not indicate that democracies are especially likely to adopt the "only pick on weak states" attribute, as predicted by Bueno de Mesquita and colleagues (2003). At the rejection and escalation points, there are no differences between the two types of regimes. At the initiation level, contrary to expectations, the results indicate that autocracies are slightly more likely to adopt the weak-power-only rule. Therefore, the simulation results are consistent with the quantitative tests in chapters 2 and 3, which demonstrated that although the balance of forces matters in general, it holds no special significance for democratic polities.

HYPOTHESIS 4
States are less likely to initiate conflict against allies than against nonallies.

This hypothesis is not supported by the data. Agents are just as likely to initiate against allies as nonallies. The statistical analysis in previous chapters found mixed support for the alliance variable. In the crisis analysis, alliances tended not to have much impact on suppressing conflict. In the dispute chapter, there was a greater impact of alliances, but the marginal effect was still rather limited. In the simulation, the lack of an impact of alliances appears to be tied to the correlation between allies and contiguous states. In the real world, most alliance partners are neighbors or near neighbors because alliances are typically created to deal with a common enemy. In the simulation, alliances were limited by definition to contiguous states or states contiguous to contiguous states in order to allow for checkerboard alliances, such as the Polish-Franco alliance against Germany before World War I. Given that agents in the simulation are restricted to fighting wars with contiguous states, it is not surprising that many allies today become adversaries tomorrow.[14]

HYPOTHESIS 5
Democratic states will cluster spatially.

This monadic hypothesis is strongly supported by the data. A visual inspection of virtually any run of the simulation shows that the vast majority of democracies tend to cluster near democracies. An example of spatial clustering appears in Figure 7.4. Although a handful of democracies exist in isolation, these are the exception rather than the rule. The spatial cluster appears to be due to two forces. First, the diffusion of traits to contiguous states tends to lead to clustering. If there are several democracies in the neighborhood and they are doing very well, the agent is more likely to adopt their regime type (attribute 1 on Trait 9). If learning is local, small and relatively homogeneous clusters are likely to emerge before spreading across the entire landscape. For example, if Spain in the 1970s was more likely to learn from its European neighbors than from either African or Asian states, then it was more likely to become a democracy due to its geographic location.[15] Second, the spatial clustering appears to be a function of the lack of democracy–democracy war. If an agent clusters with states that are less likely to attack it, it can both avoid the costs of war and allocate forces to fronts that are more likely to become engaged. Thus, democracies, which are less likely to initiate in general and less likely to become involved in democracy–democracy wars, are likely to cluster together in the anarchic environment. This result is consistent with Deutsch's explanation of the emergence of security communities (1957).

HYPOTHESIS 6
Democratic states are less likely to be revisionist.

At the start of the simulation, the revisionist trait is randomly distributed to both democracies and autocracies. Over time, states become revisionist due to diffusion and mutation. Although revisionist states appear to have some advantages, such as the ability to ignore domestic opposition when deciding whether to use force and the ability to launch predatory attacks on neighbors weakened by war, revisionist states do not thrive in the anarchic environment, as some might expect. Whereas these states do well when they are able to gobble up weak states in the neighborhood, their war proneness inevitably leads them to collide with more powerful states at some point. Serious military defeats leading to a rise in political opposition can lead to the fall of the revisionist regime, either on the battlefield or at the hands of the domestic opposition. The rise and fall of Hitler nicely illustrates this phenomenon. Although Hitler pursued a relatively conservative strategy by focusing on relatively weak and diplomatically isolated states at the start of his imperial expansion, his early successes brought him into conflict with a collection of more powerful states, including the United States and the Soviet Union, in the longer term. Democracies are less likely to be revisionist because the inability to repress domestic opposition that arises during warfare is likely to trigger a regime change (and the end of revisionism in the state). The difference in revisionism between democratic and autocratic states is statistically significant at the 0.001 level.

HYPOTHESIS 7
Democratic norms will emerge in response to the constraints of democratic institutional structures.

The simulation contains elements that resemble both norms and structures. I hypothesize that the norms and structures are complementary and mutually reinforcing. That is, the existence of structures creates incentives for the adoption of norms, which then reinforce the cooperative behavior among democracies. The model incorporates institutional constraints via the absence of repressive capabilities in democracies and the linking of initiation to domestic opposition in all status quo states. These decision rules are common to all democracies. The norms are represented by traits 6 and 8, which govern behavior with other types of regimes. As with norms in the real world, norms in the simulation are socially constructed by the spread of ideas through interaction and diffusion. I hypothesize that the gradual acquisition of attribute 2 on these traits by democratic polities will inhibit initiation and escalation against democracies.

The data do not support the hypothesis. Democratic states are no less likely to acquire the "initiate against democracies" attribute or the "escalate against democracies" attribute. In fact, more agents in the overall population acquire this attribute than either the "ignore regime type" attribute or "initiate/escalate against autocracies" attribute. Agents appear to prefer challenging and attacking democracies. Although this finding supports the statistical results in chapters 2 and 3 with respect to autocratic states, it does not conform with the dyadic democratic peace. However, it is important to remember that despite the apparent targeting of democracies by all states, democratic-democratic dyads are still less likely to enter disputes and to escalate to war than either mixed dyads or autocratic dyads. Thus, the unexpected finding is statistically significant, but it does not have a large substantive impact on aggregate behavior due to countervailing forces.

In sum, in the absence of the emergence of dyadic norms, we must conclude that the monadic peace and the dyadic peace are the products of institutional constraint.

Conclusions

The quantitative, qualitative, and experimental analyses in chapters 2 through 6 indicated a monadic effect of democracies at the dispute phase and a dyadic effect of democracy at the dispute and crisis phases. I argued that this unique result was due to the evolution of institutions, norms, and conflicts. In this chapter I have probed the plausibility of the argument using an agent-based model. The results strongly support the evolutionary argument. Using just a handful of assumptions, most important the assumption that autocracies have greater power to repress domestic political opposition than democracies do, the model produces both a monadic and dyadic impact of democratic institutions. Sensitivity analysis involving randomly varying parameters such as economic growth within a maximum and minimum did not alter the findings.

The beauty of the model is its simplicity. I did not have to make powerful assumptions such as those often postulated in the democratic peace literature. I did *not* assume that democracies suddenly drop their peaceful norms of conflict resolution when facing an autocratic opponent (Maoz and Russett 1993). I did *not* assume that political opposition exists only in democratic polities. I did *not* assume that democratic polities behave differently because they expect their democratic opponents to behave differently (Bueno de Mesquita and Lalman 1992). I did *not* assume that autocratic leaders are more likely to focus on private benefits than their democratic counterparts (Bueno de Mesquita et al. 2003). I did *not* assume that democracies will not fight other democracies (Cederman 2001b). I did *not* assume that democracies were more likely to settle disputes through mediation and arbitration (Dixon 1993, 1994; Raymond 1994). I did *not* assume that democracies form perfectly efficient collective security organizations (Cederman 2001b). I did *not* assume that democracies ally only with other democracies. *Although many of these dyadic causal mechanisms may in fact reinforce the monadic and dyadic peace, the simulation demonstrates that they are not necessary for its emergence.* Only three relatively uncontroversial assumptions are necessary: domestic political opposition exists in all states, autocratic states have greater powers of repression, and domestic political opposition inhibits the use of force.

It is not obvious that these three assumptions would produce the monadic and dyadic democratic peace. It was quite possible that realists such as Waltz would have been correct: if domestic politics limit a state's ability to balance threats, then the state will be eliminated from the gene pool in the long run. However, the simulation revealed the exact opposite: agents with greater domestic interference thrived within the anarchic system. The proportion of democratic states rose, on average, from 10 percent to 48 percent of the system. Why? The successful performance of democratic states led to their emulation by other states.

Although the results are encouraging, it should be emphasized that the simulation developed here is a first cut at the problem. It is designed to be a preliminary rather than definitive test of the evolutionary argument. Additional empirical research, both qualitative and quantitative, will be required to probe the robustness of the assumptions, decision rules, and predictions. Simulations are useful tools, but they must be used in conjunction with alternative methods of inquiry to ensure a comprehensive analysis.

DomGeoSim Parameter Dictionary and Comparison of Parameters with GeoSim

TABLE 7.2

WarAndPeace parameter dictionary

Name	Description	Type	Default	Cederman
1. Simulation set-up				
WorldXSize	Horizontal dimension of the world grid.	Integer (1 . . . 100)	50	50
WorldYSize	Vertical dimension of the world grid.	Integer (1 . . . 100)	50	50
WrapHorizontal	Whether the world wraps around left to right.	true/false	false	false (n.a.)
WrapVertical	Whether the world wraps around top to bottom.	true/false	false	false (n.a.)
MaxRounds	Number of rounds (steps, ticks) to run the system.	Integer (1 . . .)	5000	10500
StartStationary	Round in which to start monitoring system for output, and also possibly to restructure the system by turning some states into democracies.	Integer, less than MaxRounds	20	500
Cederman	Whether to run an approximation of Lars-Erik Cederman's Geosim2 model.	true/false	false	n.a. (but true)
CountWars	Whether to keep track of wars and their size (*warCounting* in Geosim2).	true/false	true	true
DemocracyMatters	Whether to keep track of governance type (democracies vs. autocracies) (*democracy* in Geosim2).	true/false	true	false
2. Initialization specs				
InitSystem	Whether to reduce the number of states in the system at the start (if not, every grid location is a state at the start).	true/false	true	true
InitPolarity	Number of states desired at the start.	Integer (1 . . . WorldXSize* WorldYSize)	200	200

Parameter	Description	Range		
P_hegemon	Probability that a state will receive 10 times the standard quantity of resources at initialization time. (Note that this may not matter much if InitSystem is true, since the amalgamation of states will make resource disparities at the individual-territory level rather less noticeable.)	Fraction (0 . . . 1)	0.2	0.2
P_revisionist	The probability of becoming a revisionist state at startup.	Fraction (0 . . . 1)	0.2	n.a.
S_neighbourhoodType	The connectivity structure of the world: • 0—von Neumann neighborhood (only the 4 straight-line neighbors) • 1—hexagonal neighborhood (6 of the 8 possible neighbors, in an alternating pattern from row to row, to mimic a hexagonal structure) • 2—Moore neighborhood (all 8 neighbors, including the 4 diagonal ones)	0, 1, or 2	0	0
F_democracies	Fraction of states to turn into democracies at the start (*propDem* in Geosim2).	Fraction (0 . . . 1)	0.1	0.1
InitDemsAtStart	Whether to turn states into democracies at the start, or (if set to false) at the start of the stationary period.	true/false	true	false
InitDemocracyBias	Whether to make democracies stronger at the start. If set to true, pick half of the democracies at random from among the 5% most powerful (richest in resources) states, and the other half at random from among the other 95% of states. Will go wrong if F_democracies exceeds 10%.	true/false	false	false
3. Agent specs				
S_updateRule	How to learn from neighboring states: 0—unless richer than all neighbors, learn from richest neighbor 1—unless richer than average neighbor, learn from a neighbor whose wealth is above average 2—if poorer than all neighbors, learn from a randomly selected neighbor	0, 1, or 2	1	n.a.
P_updateType	Probability of an attempt to learn from neighboring states.	Fraction (0 . . . 1)	0.1	n.a.
P_changeType	Probability of a random change in strategy (e.g., exploration/mutation).	Fraction (0 . . . 1)	0.001	n.a.

(continued)

TABLE 7.2
(Continued)

Name	Description	Type	Default	Cederman
4. Resource settings				
CumulativeResources	Whether resource gathering is cumulative from round to round. Variable used only for Cederman's model (WarAndPeace model is always cumulative; Geosim uses the complementary parameter *terRes*, true if resources noncumulative).	true/false	true	false
TaxRate	Fraction of a territory's resources a capital can extract.	Fraction (0 . . . 1)	0.025	1.0
M_growth	Mean growth rate of a territory's resources, per round.	Fraction (0 . . . 1)	0.0025	n.a.
SD_growth	Standard deviation of the growth rate.	Fraction (0 . . . 1)	0.005	n.a.
M_harvest	Mean harvest size for setups with cumulative resources (Geosim uses *mRes* and *mHarvest* here).	Positive real (0 . . .)	10.0	100.0 at start, 1.0 thereafter
SD_harvest	Standard deviation of the harvest size (Geosim uses *sRes* and *sHarvest* here).	Positive real (0 . . .)	5.0	50.0 at start, 5.0 thereafter
F_fixedResources	Fraction of resources fixed from one round to the next. Used only for Cederman's model when resources noncumulative (Geosim uses a complementary parameter, called *resChange*, representing the fraction that changes from one round to the next).	Fraction (0 . . . 1)	0.0	0.99
ProDemocracyBias	Resource extraction bias modifier for democracies. A state's total extraction of resources is multiplied by this value (e.g., a value below 1 means democracies extract fewer resources; above 1 means they extract more than autocracies). Used only if Cederman is true (*demBias* in Geosim2).	Positive real (0 . . .)	1.0	1.0
5. Distance settings				
S_distanceCosts	The way in which a state's ability to extract resources from distant provinces as well as its ability to mobilize forces in those provinces to face opponents there are affected by distance (comparable parameter in Geosim2 is *distRes*). • 0—no costs associated with distance • 1—costs follow a geometric pattern (distance^gradient). With the default settings, the fraction of resources extractable/mobilizable at successive integer distances is 1 — 1, 2 — 0.5, 3 — 0.33, 4 — 0.25, 5 — 0.2, 6 — 0.17.	0, 1, or 2	1	2

• 2—costs (apart from offset) follow a logistic pattern: $1/(1+e^{(slope*\ln(distance/threshold))})$. With the default settings, the fraction of resources extractable/mobilizable at successive integer distances is 1 — 0.90, 2 — 0.55, 3 — 0.31, 4 — 0.2, 5 — 0.15, 6 — 0.13, 7 — 0.12.

Parameter	Description	Range		
DistanceGradient	Used when S_distanceCosts = 1. Extractive and mobilizing ability are calculated as (distance from province to capital)^DistanceGradient. So for the default value of −1, this is 1/(distance from province to capital).	Positive real (0 . . .)	−1.0	0.0
T_distance	Threshold of distance at which the inflection point of the logistic curve occurs (distDrop in Geosim2).	Positive real (0 . . .)	2.0	2.0
SD_distance	Standard deviation of the initial distance threshold, relevant for distance-loss functions that are state-specific, i.e., as a result of shocks (distDropSD in Geosim2).	Positive real (0 . . .)	0.0	0.0
DistanceSlope	Slope of logistic distance-loss curve.	Positive real (0 . . .)	3.0	3.0
DistanceOffset	The fraction of resources unaffected by the logistic distance loss function.	Fraction (0 . . . 1)	0.1	0.1
6. Conflict initiation				
P_unprovokedAttack	The probability of initiating an unprovoked conflict.	Fraction (0 . . . 1)	0.05	0.01
P_selectWeakest	The probability, when initiating a conflict, of selecting the weakest possible target, as opposed to a randomly selected possible target.	Fraction (0 . . . 1)	0	0
P_revOpportunism	The probability that a revisionist state will behave opportunistically and attack a neighboring state already embroiled in a conflict.	Fraction (0 . . . 1)	0.25	n.a.
Campaigns	Whether to allow campaigns. If true, states will keep fighting against opponents even after a territory changes hands. The "unit" of a war is a single-territory conflict. If true, states will go on attacking the target of their campaign as long as they share a border (governed, of course, by the value of P_dropCampaign).	true/false	true	true
P_dropCampaign	The probability of dropping a campaign against a state.	Fraction (0 . . . 1)	0.2	0.2
P_twoFrontWar	The probability a state will initiate another conflict (i.e., without provocation) if already involved in a conflict.	Fraction (0 . . . 1)	0	0

(continued)

TABLE 7.2
(*Continued*)

Name	Description	Type	Default	Cederman
MonitorNeighbours	Whether to go on the alert when a neighboring state is currently embroiled in a conflict (*activeNeighs* in Geosim2).	true/false	true	true
P_dropAlert	Once on the alert (for example, because a neighbor is in a conflict, the probability that alert status will be dropped (*dropActive* in Geosim2).	Fraction (0 . . . 1)	0.1	0.1
7. Conflict implementation				
F_mobile	The fraction of resources in a state's war chest that is mobile and can be allocated according to the strength of opposing forces. The remaining fraction is evenly divided across all fronts (*mobil* in Geosim2).	Fraction (0 . . . 1)	0.5	0.5
F_warCost	Cost of a war to one's opponent, expressed as a fraction of the resources one has mobilized at the front.	Fraction (0 . . . 1)	0.33	0.1
NoisyWar	Whether the outcome of a battle (win/loss) is deterministic or stochastic (in Geosim2, not a separate parameter, but true unless VictorySlope = 0).	true/false	true	true
BalanceFront	Whether to consider only the resources a state has mobilized at our mutual front, or instead against the sum total of the resources it has in its war chest (not a variable in Geosim2—always balance against front only; in WarAndPeace balancing against a front is not meaningful since a front only exists if a war is being fought).	true/false	false	true
SuperiorityRatio	The superiority ratio used to decide whether to attack an opponent (*sup* in Geosim2). Depending on the presence of alliances and the value of parameter *BalanceFront*, if the relevant resources of a state are X times greater than those that can be mustered by the target, a state will consider the target attackable.	Positive real (0 . . .)	3.0	3.0
SuperioritySlope	The slope of the logistic function used to decide whether to attack an opponent (if 0, then simply use the SuperiorityRatio value) (*supC* in Geosim2). The logistic function is analogous to that for distance loss, apart from the offset: $1/(1+e^{\wedge}(\text{slope}* \ln(\text{SuperiorityRatio}/\text{actualPowerRatio})))$. With the default values, this means that the probability a state will find a target attackable, for various power ratios is: $1 - 3E\text{-}10$, $2 - 0.0003$, $3 - 0.5$, $4 - 0.997$, $5 - 0.99997$.	Positive real (0 . . .)	20.0	20.0

SD_superiority	Standard deviation of the superiority ratio, relevant for ratios (and thus attack decisions) that are state-specific, i.e., as a result of shocks (*supSD* in Geosim2).	Positive real (0 . . .)	0	0
VictoryRatio	Functions analogously to SuperiorityRatio above, but now for deciding whether a state will win (*vict* in Geosim2). When shocks apply, and thus state-specific ratios, a state's victory ratio is always kept equal to its superiority ratio.	Positive real (0 . . .)	3.0	3.0
VictorySlope	Functions analogously to SuperioritySlope above, but now for deciding whether a state will win (*victC* in Geosim2).	Positive real (0 . . .)	20.0	20.0
8. Conflict resolution				
P_peace	The probability that a given dispute, crisis, or war will end suddenly in any given round.	Fraction (0 . . . 1)	0.5	0
Patience	The number of rounds a state will allow its opponent in a dispute or crisis simply to delay taking further action.	Integer	100	n.a.
MaxWarMemory	The number of rounds after a war is over that a state will remember it was in a war (called *maxShadow* in Geosim2).	Integer	2	20
DisintegrateCutoffs	When a capital is conquered, or when a section of a state is cut off from the rest, whether to keep cut-off or head-less provinces together as one or more new states, or instead to atomize them all into states with a single province.	true/false	false	true
KeepConnected	Whether to keep all territories in a state contiguous.	true/false	true	true
9. Alliance settings				
AllowAlliances	Whether to allow alliances	true/false	true	false
T_invokeAlliance	The resource ratio beyond which one is willing to join an alliance against an opposing state. For example, if 5, then we join an alliance against an opponent if that opponent has 5 times as many resources as we do in our war chest or at our mutual front (depending on the value of *BalanceFront*) (in Geosim2, this parameter is called *minThreat* and is negative, but otherwise with the same implications).	Integer	5	2.8

(*continued*)

TABLE 7.2
(Continued)

Name	Description	Type	Default	Cederman
P_aidAllies	The probability that one will come to the aid of one's allies (i.e., defect against an alliance target) (*prOblig* in Geosim2)	Fraction (0 . . . 1)	0.5	0.5
AllyContribution	The proportion of the forces of states allied with a target that a state takes into account when deciding whether or not to attack that target (*contrib* in Geosim2).	Fraction (0 . . . 1)	0.5	0.5
10. Democracy settings				
Democratize	Whether states are subject to coups and democratizations (*democratization* in Geosim2).	true/false	true	false
P_democratize	The probability that an autocracy will turn into a democracy in any given round. In Geosim2, this probability is modified by a complicated ad hoc function involving a logistic calculation based on the degree to which a state is surrounded by democracies. The parameter value is multiplied by the resulting value, which, for different fractions of surrounding democracy, is: 0.1 — 0.56, 0.2 — 0.62, 0.5 — 0.77, 0.9 — 0.89, 1.0 — 0.91. In WarAndPeace, regime change may also take place based on learning, domestic opposition, instability, or random exploration (see P_changeType above).	Fraction (0 . . . 1)	0.002	0.002
P_coup	The probability that a democracy will turn into an autocracy in any given round. In Geosim2, modified in the same way as P_democratize, except now we count the fraction of surrounding states that are already autocracies. Comments for WarAndPeace are the same as under P_democratize.	Fraction (0 . . . 1)	0.001	0.001
P_losePariahStatus	The probability that a state marked as a pariah will lose its pariah status. If 0, states will never be marked as pariahs (*collSec* in Geosim2).	Fraction (0 . . . 1)	0	0
11. Domestic opposition				
F_domOpp_DemMin	Min. level of domestic opposition for a new democratic state.	Fraction (0 . . . 1)	0.20	n.a.
F_domOpp_DemMax	Max. level of domestic opposition for a new democratic state.	Fraction (0 . . . 1)	0.60	n.a.

Name	Description	Type		
F_domOpp_AutMin	Min. level of domestic opposition for a new autocratic state.	Fraction (0 . . . 1)	0.20	n.a.
F_domOpp_AutMax	Max. level of domestic opposition for a new autocratic state.	Fraction (0 . . . 1)	0.60	n.a.
SD_opposition	Standard deviation of the normal function from which the next round's initial opposition level is drawn (with mean equal to the current round's opposition level).	Fraction (0 . . . 1)	0.05	n.a.
RepressOpposition	Reduction in the opposition level that autocracies can achieve in a given round (will be modified by their length of tenure as an autocracy), expressed as a fraction of the maximum possible reduction.	Fraction (0 . . . 1)	0.02	n.a.
RallyMin	Minimum level by which domestic opposition will fall if a state is attacked (expressed as a fraction of the maximum possible drop).	Fraction (0 . . . 1)	0	n.a.
RallyMax	Maximum level by which domestic opposition will fall if a state is attacked.	Fraction (0 . . . 1)	0.05	n.a.

12. Shock settings

Name	Description	Type		
P_shock	Probability that a state will be subjected to a shock in any given round, starting from StartStationary (see above).	Fraction (0 . . . 1)	0.0001	0.0001
TaxShock	Size of the extractive shock. The shock affects the distance threshold (i.e., the inflection point of the logistic distance loss function). A shocked state's distance threshold is set to the default model threshold plus the fraction of the shock size that corresponds to the fraction of the period between StartStationary and MaxRounds that has elapsed. In other words, the threshold will gradually increase over time, meaning extraction ability improves over time.	Real	20.0	20.0
TechnoShock	If true, a shocked state's victory and superiority ratios will be reset to the result of a random draw from a normal distribution with mean SuperiorityRatio and standard deviation Superiority Ratio*SD_superiority.	true/false	false	false
ProDemBias_Shocks	Degree to which democracies are more or less likely to be shocked. Multiplied by the shock probability, so that a value below 1 means democracies are less likely to be shocked, and a value above 1 means they are more likely to be.	Positive real (0 . . .)	1.0	1.0

(continued)

TABLE 7.2
(*Continued*)

Name	Description	Type	Default	Cederman
13. Output choices				
S_WarSizeMeasure	The measure used to gauge the size of wars: 0—the cost of the war 1—the duration of the war, in rounds 2—the total number of states involved in the war 3—the duration * the total number of states 4—the number of state-rounds (less than 3, since not every state will be involved in every round the war is ongoing). All of these values are written to the output, but only the selected one is displayed, if the war-size chart is displayed during the run.	0, 1, 2, 3, or 4	4	0
ReportInterval	The interval at which data gets written to a file. Data about wars is written out for each war, but tracking data about the number of states, ongoing conflicts, and so on are written out only every ReportInterval rounds.	Integer	20	n.a.

Notes

1. For a more extensive discussion of strengths and weakness of agent-based modeling, see Rousseau (2004), Johnson (1999), and Axtell (2000).

2. Axtell and colleagues (1995) refer to this process as "alignment" and "docking." They discuss extending Axtell and Epstein's Sugarscape model to subsume Axelrod's cultural diffusion model. My approach is similar in that I reproduced Cederman's model before extending it in new directions.

3. For a complete description of GeoSim, see Cederman (2001b, 2003). DomGeoSim was programmed by Maurits van der Veen. Appendix 7.1 contains a parameter dictionary that highlights the links between the two models. Whereas DomGeoSim can produce results very similar to those of GeoSim with the appropriate parameter settings, the results will not be identical due to van der Veen's correction of a few minor problems that do not alter Cederman's substantive findings. I would like to thank Lars-Erik Cederman for generously providing the original code to me. DomGeoSim is available for downloading at www.international-affairs.org/rousseau/research.htm.

4. In "nonwrapping" landscapes, agents on the edge of the landscape interact with fewer agents than actors in the middle of the landscape. In "wrapping" landscapes, agents on the left (and/or top) of the shape interact with actors on the right (and/or bottom) of the shape, implying that all agents interact with the same number of other agents. DomGeoSim permits wrapping, but the landscapes reported in this chapter are nonwrapping. Although several neighborhood types are available in the model—for example, von Neumann (only the four neighbors located north, south, east, and west), hexagonal (six of the eight possible neighbors in an alternating pattern from row to row), and Moore (all eight neighbors including diagonals)—all the results reported are based on the von Neumann neighborhood used in the GeoSim model.

5. Waltz (1979) argues that buckpassing and chainganging help make the multipolar world more conflictual than a bipolar world. Christensen and Snyder (1990) use the offense-defense balance to explain when each phenomenon is likely to occur. Specifically, they argue that chainganging is more likely in an offense-dominant world and that buckpassing is more likely in a defense-dominant world. The hypotheses can be explored in the simulation by varying the probability that allies aid the state ($P\_aidAllies$), the margin of power needed for victory (*VictoryRatio*), and the costs of war ($F\_warCost$).

6. In earlier work, Cederman studied nationalism and secession (1997). These parameters are not available in GeoSim.

7. Kinsella and Russett (2002, 1046) argue that empirical models are beginning to test the stages of conflicts employed in formal models. Thus, introducing stages into the simulation will aid comparative analysis of formal models, large-N quantitative studies, and computer simulations.

8. In the default version of GeoSim, the "coup" parameter is set at .001 and the "democratize" parameter is set at .002. These settings trigger the slow democratization of the system across time.

9. The trait structure and evolutionary process were modeled on Macy and Skvoretz (1998) and Rousseau and Cantor (2003).

10. Many authors prefer to restrict the use of the term *gene* to situations involving death and reproduction. For these individuals, the learning model proposed here would be more appropriately labeled a "meme" structure (Dawkins 1976). I have chosen to use the terms *traits* and *attributes* in order to both sidestep the debate and reduce confusion.

11. Although not addressed in this chapter, each of these factors is parameterized in the model, allowing the user to conduct sensitivity analysis by selectively zeroing out individual factors.

12. If each iteration is analogous to a month, then the growth rate is about 3 percent per year. In future versions of the model we plan to incorporate temporal correlation in order to model the impact of economic cycles. The large standard deviation relative to the mean implies that recessions take place in the model.

13. Although the number of conflicts may seem high, the Militarized Interstate Dispute (MID) data set (version 3.01) reveals that in just under 200 years the United States has been involved in 344 disputes and the United Kingdom has been involved in 263 disputes.

14. Realists such as Waltz (1979) and Grieco (1988) have strongly argued that cooperation among allies will be limited because concerns about relative gains persist due to the fact that alliances are temporary measures.

15. On the spatial diffusion of democracy, see Gleditsch and Ward (2000), Cederman and Gleditsch (2002), and Gleditsch (2002).

THIS BOOK BEGAN with a general question: *do domestic institutions and political norms influence decisions to use military force to resolve international conflicts?* In every chapter we have found strong support for the constraining power of domestic political institutions. Although normative constraint may still be important in particular situations and for particular individuals, it appears that, in general, institutions are the driving force behind the democratic peace. We arrived at this conclusion by examining six specific questions that have been debated without resolution in the international relations literature.

First, are more democratic states less likely to initiate violence regardless of the regime type of their opponent, or are democracies more pacific only when dealing with other democracies? Whereas researchers have generally accepted the notion of a dyadic democratic peace, the idea of a monadic peace has been much more controversial. The quantitative analyses in this study have demonstrated a powerful monadic effect. When using the data set of international *disputes*, employing the institutional constraint variables, in the laboratory experiment, and with the computer simulation, democracies were less likely to use force regardless of the regime type of the international opponent. The presence of domestic political opposition coupled with the existence of institutional channels through which chief executives can be punished for defeats and costly victories reduces enthusiasm for the use of military power.

Second, has the literature, which has focused almost exclusively on wars and militarized crises, underestimated the importance of institutions by neglecting the fact that democratic institutions may inhibit the escalation of a nonmilitarized dispute into a war or militarized crisis? Yes. The analyses indicate that the dyadic democratic peace exists at both the dispute and crisis stages of international conflict. However, the monadic constraint emerges only at the dispute stage. This

.ttern occurs because the monadic constraint evaporates as the opponents of democracies use or threaten the use of violence to resolve the conflict. Therefore, the selection process implies that an analysis restricted to wars or crises will neglect the fact that democracies are less likely to end up in the situation to begin with.

Third, has the almost exclusive focus on regime type led to a neglect of how domestic institutions can either constrain or encourage armed conflict? Yes. Although it is easy to recall instances in which a belligerent democratic public (and political opposition) bullied a reluctant chief executive into war, few theories specify the causal mechanisms required to both push and pull democratic leaders. The chief exception is the work of Schultz (2001), who argues that the domestic opposition can restrain democratic leaders from bluffing and confirm signals of resolve. The quantitative and qualitative analyses presented in the preceding chapters are consistent with this argument. However, I have also shown how the behavior of the international opponent can influence the rise and fall of domestic opposition. Moreover, whereas both Schultz and I assume identical preferences across types of states in the short run, the evolutionary argument explains how different institutional mechanisms can lead to divergences in preferences over strategies in the long run.

Fourth, are institutional structures or political norms more important in constraining democracies from using force? The evidence strongly supported the institutional structure argument. Autocratic leaders who obtained power through violence were no more likely to resolve conflicts violently than those who achieved office through peaceful selection. Democratic leaders appeared constrained only from using large-scale violence, implying that their behavior was driven by fear of body bags rather than abhorrence of violence. Both President Kennedy and experimental subjects were willing to use force if it could be kept secret from the public and political opposition. Finally, young democracies were not more likely to use force than old democracies. In sum, no strong empirical support emerged for the normative argument across a wide variety of very different tests.

Fifth, does regime transformation, the process of becoming more or less democratic, influence decisions to resolve an ongoing dispute with force? No. Although Mansfield and Snyder have been arguing for nearly a decade first that democratization (1995a, 1995b, 1996) and second that anocratization (2002a, 2002b) increases the probability of military violence, the analysis of disputes provides no support for the claims. However, the case studies of Czechoslovakia do indicate the combination of political mobilization without institutionalization can increase the probability of military conflict in particular cases. Thus, future research must focus on identifying the conditions under which the causal process described by Mansfield and Snyder is likely to operate (such as after the fall of empires rather than African military coups).

Defining scope conditions for the theory will allow us to predict if, and when, democratization will be problematic.

Sixth, how does the evolution of conflicts, institutions, and norms influence decisions to use force and the amount of violence in the system overall? The evolutionary aspect of the democratic peace, long neglected by the field, needs to be pushed to the forefront of the research. The importance of addressing the evolution of conflicts emerged in the comparison of disputes and crises. The evolution of conflict has an important impact on the strength of domestic opposition and, therefore, the constraining power of institutions. The importance of addressing the evolution of institutions surfaced in the analysis of regime transitions and the computer simulation. The quantitative analysis indicated that movement from the democratic end of the spectrum toward the autocratic end of the spectrum temporarily reduced the likelihood that a state will use force. The agent-based model linked the war-related rise of political opposition to regime change. Although the existence of institutional constraints reduces violence in the short run, it also can affect the evolution of acceptable strategies in the long run. For example, the simulation demonstrated that democratic regimes eschewed revisionist strategies because such policies were likely to trigger regime change in the long run.

The individual findings are revealing in and of themselves, but it is the collection of quantitative and qualitative findings as a whole that allows us to push the democratic peace literature in new directions. The synthesis of findings points to a dynamic and evolutionary model of the relationship between regime type and external conflict. We will now examine how the collection of cases as a whole sheds light on this evolutionary model. This lays the groundwork for future research.

Synthesizing Across Cases: The Breakdown of Structural and Normative Constraints

In the International Crisis Behavior (ICB) data set used in Chapter 2, twenty-four democratic states initiated high levels of violence against their adversaries. These cases represent deviations from the monadic model, which predicts that democracies should be less likely to turn to force. Over the course of the previous seven chapters, seventeen of these twenty-four cases have been explored in greater depth.[1] As a whole, the case studies highlight several reasons why and when institutional and normative constraints failed to restrain decision makers. By probing for across-case patterns, we can both identify weaknesses in the quantitative models and generate hypotheses for future research.

The deviant cases are displayed in Table 8.1. The table highlights several interesting observations about democratic initiation of violence. First, the

TABLE 8.1
Summary of democratic aggressors: Patterns of initiation

Country	Dispute	Year	Issue	Balance of forces	Expected cost	Legislative opposition	Public
United Kingdom	Russian Civil War	1918	antiregime	favorable	low	supports	not informed
Czechoslovakia	Teschen	1919	territorial	favorable	low	strongly supports	strongly supports
Czechoslovakia	Hungarian War	1919	territorial and antiregime	even (favorable with allies)	low	strongly supports	strongly supports
Poland	Russo-Polish War	1920	territorial	unfavorable	moderate	supports	supports
Poland	Vilna	1920	territorial	extremely favorable	low	strongly supports	strongly supports
France	Rhenish Rebellion	1920	treaty violation	extremely favorable	low	strongly supports	strongly supports
France	German reparations	1921	treaty violation	extremely favorable	low	strongly supports	strongly supports
France	Ruhr I	1923	treaty violation	extremely favorable	low	strongly supports	strongly supports
United Kingdom	Middle East campaign	1941	antiregime	extremely favorable	low	strongly supports	strongly supports
United Kingdom	Occupation of Iran	1941	antiregime	extremely favorable	low	strongly supports	strongly supports
United Kingdom	Suez Crisis	1956	antiregime	very favorable	low	strongly opposes	divided
France	Suez Crisis	1956	antiregime	very favorable	low	strongly supports	strongly supports
Israel	Suez Crisis	1956	antiregime and pre-ventative	favorable (with allies)	low	strongly supports	strongly supports
Somalia	Ethiopia-Somalia	1960	territorial	unfavorable	low	strongly supports	strongly supports
Somalia	Ogaden I	1964	territorial	unfavorable	low	strongly supports	strongly supports
United States	Bay of Pigs	1961	antiregime	extremely favorable	low	no knowledge	no knowledge
Israel	Six Days' War	1967	preemption	favorable (with surprise)	moderate	strongly supports	strongly supports
El Salvador	Football War	1969	treatment of nationals	favorable	low	strongly supports	strongly supports
India	Bangladesh	1971	antiregime and territorial	favorable	moderate	strongly supports	strongly supports
Turkey	Cyprus III	1974	territorial and antiregime	extremely favorable	low	strongly supports	strongly supports
United States	Grenada	1983	antiregime	extremely favorable	low	no prior knowledge	no prior knowledge
United States	Panama	1989	antiregime	extremely favorable	low	strongly supports	supports
Ecuador	Peruvian Border	1995	territorial	unfavorable	low	strongly supports	strongly supports
United States	Kosovo	1999	antiregime and human rights	extremely favorable	low	majority supports	supports

TABLE 8.1
(*continued*)

Secret from		Unified government	Military outcome	Political outcome	Punished	Years democratic	Prior disputes	Related disputes
(a) opposition	(b) public							
no	yes	yes	failure	irrelevant	no	52 (1867)	no	yes
no	no	no	success	success	no	>1 (1919)	no	yes
no	no	no	failure	unknown	no	>1 (1919)	no	yes
no	no	no	failure	success	no	1 (1919)	yes	yes
no	no	no	success	success	no	1 (1919)	no	yes
no	no	no	success	success	no	46 (1875)	yes	yes
no	no	no	success	success	no	47 (1875)	yes	yes
no	no	no	success	failure	yes	49 (1875)	yes	yes
no	yes	yes	success	success	no	75 (1867)	no	yes
no	yes	yes	success	success	no	75 (1867)	no	yes
yes	yes	no	failure	failure	yes	90 (1867)	yes	yes
?	yes	no	failure	success	no	82 (1875)	yes	yes
no	yes	yes	success	success	no	9 (1948)	yes	yes
?	yes	yes	failure	success	no	>1 (1960)	no	no
no	no	no	failure	success	no	5 (1960)	yes	yes
yes	yes	no	failure	failure	yes	134 (1828)	no	no
no	no	yes	success	success	no	20 (1948)	yes	yes
no	no	yes	failure	success	no	6 (1964)	yes	no
no	no	no	success	success	no	24 (1948)	yes	yes
no	no	no	success	success	no	2 (1972)	yes	yes
yes	yes	no	success	success	no	156 (1828)	no	no
no	no	no	success	success	no	162 (1828)	no	no
no	no	no	limited success	success	no	17 (1979)	yes	no
no	no	no	success	success	no	171 (1828)	no	no

table indicates that in most cases opposition leaders and their followers supported the use of force. For example, the political opposition strongly supported the British interventions in the Middle East in 1941, the Somali intervention in Ethiopia in 1960, and the Israeli preemptive strike in 1967. The frequency of this occurrence is one of the most significant findings of this study. It demonstrates that institutional constraints are not sufficient for restraining decision makers; if opposition to the use of force does not emerge within the institutional channels, leaders will not fear punishment and thus will not act with restraint. Moreover, in several other cases, such as France in the 1920s and El Salvador in the Football War, the opposition compelled the chief executives to take a more aggressive position than they wished to pursue.

Second, Table 8.1 demonstrates that in most cases the democratic initiators were militarily much stronger then their targets. In Iran in 1941 and Grenada in 1983, the democratic challengers possessed infinitely more resources than their opponents. This finding points to a structural explanation of institutional constraint. Decision makers did not abhor violence; they feared being punished for failure. Therefore, democratic leaders can be expected to choose their battles carefully—if they are going to use force, they want to ensure that the probability of success is very high (Reiter and Stam 2002). This is the lesson that many civilian and military leaders in the United States drew from the Vietnam experience. In subsequent military operations, from Panama to the First Persian Gulf War, military leaders strove to apply massive force in order to ensure a quick victory.

It is important to emphasize that the balance of forces argument does not negate the importance of institutional structures. Constrained states are, on average, still less likely to use force. However, as the balance of forces increasingly favors a constrained state, the more likely it is to use force aggressively. The only important exception to the argument that democracies tend to initiate from a favorable balance of forces position is the Polish attack on the Soviet Union in 1920. However, Pilsudski believed that the balance of forces would only get worse and that a Soviet attack was inevitable. In his mind, he initiated while the balance of forces was most favorable.

If this argument is correct, why didn't the selectorate model proposed by Bueno de Mesquita and colleagues (2003) perform better in the quantitative analysis? There was no evidence that stronger democracies were willing to use violence against weak democracies. Nor did we find democracies willing to use force against weak states in general. The reason is that a favorable military balance is a necessary but not sufficient condition for using force. A democratic polity is likely to initiate violence when the belligerent behavior of the international opponent reduces domestic political opposition *and* when the balance of forces is favorable.[2]

Third, the case studies point to a more complex relationship between coalition government and propensity to use force than examined in the quantitative model. I had hypothesized that due to the presence of potential opposition within the executive, coalitions should be less likely to use force aggressively. I had envisioned an underlying linear relation: the more cabinet seats held by other parties, the less likely a state would be to attack. However, the cases demonstrate that democratic polities often form unity cabinets in time of war or in expectation of war. These "war" cabinets may, in fact, be more likely to use force because all parties participate in decision making; this joint decision making renders it very unlikely that a foreign policy failure will be exploited by the opposition and thereby minimizes one of the perceived risks of initiating violence. The "unity" or "war" government appears in numerous cases, including Britain in 1917, Israel in 1967, and El Salvador in 1969. Future research should carefully distinguish "unity" coalitional governments from more typical coalitional governments.

Fourth, the cases also highlight the degree to which the crises are interrelated. In the statistical model, I assume that each dispute (and crisis) is an independent event.[3] This is a standard assumption in the field. However, in almost every case the evolution of the crisis was significantly related to the dynamics and outcome of other crises. For example, French decisions in the Suez Crisis were made based on the impact that the outcomes were expected to have on the Algerian war of independence. Similarly, the British decision to use force against Iraq and Iran was inextricably tied to the ongoing war with Germany. Although I had expected to find relations between crises within a dispute (for example, the dynamics of the first Arab-Israel war influenced decisions during the second war), I did not anticipate the degree of dependency found across disputes.

Fifth, several of the cases highlight (as does the laboratory experiment) the degree to which secrecy plays an important role in the decision to use force. Again, this points to a structural rather than normative explanation of the constraint model. If your domestic opponents do not know the government has used force, they cannot punish you should the operation fail. President Kennedy in the Bay of Pigs invasion explicitly sought "plausible denial"—the rebels were to disappear into the hills should the operation go astray. Similarly, Anthony Eden believed that by keeping the collusive aspect of the operation secret, he could rally public opinion to his side.

In U.S. history, the executive has consistently sought to execute covert operations outside the purview of the legislature. Secrecy was driven by domestic considerations rather than military rationales. In the Bay of Pigs, the training of Cuban exiles was common knowledge in both Guatemala and Cuba; the cloak of secrecy was required for Congress and the U.S. public. When President Reagan found the CIA too open to legislative scrutiny due to changes resulting from the Church Committee, he brought the operation into the White House under the National Security Council. The structural model implies that citizens and legislators in democracies must always be on their guard against covert operations designed to minimize the costs of a foreign policy.

Sixth, in several cases the democratic leader sought to present both its foreign adversary and domestic opposition with a *fait accompli*. A quick and successful use of force is unlikely to provoke criticism. Eden in Suez and Reagan in Grenada believed that the public would strongly support a victory and that the opposition would be reluctant to criticize the chief executive for a military success. Once again, this points to a structural explanation.

Seventh, one pattern that does not emerge from the examination of democratic initiators is preemption. The only clear case of democratic preemption is the Israeli attack on Egypt in the Six Days' War of 1967. Democracies do not typically attack because they fear their opponents are about to attack; they attack because there is no domestic opposition to the use of force. It will be interesting to see if the events of September 11, 2001, alter this historical pattern. The United States has explicitly adopted a preventative war strategy that is far more aggressive than a preemptive strategy.[4] (Preemption involves attacking an opponent that is likely to attack you; preventative war involves attacking a state that might someday acquire the capability to harm you.) This strategy, if adopted by other democratic powers, would in all likelihood erode the monadic relationship discovered in this project. The long-term success of the preventative strategy will depend on how much domestic opposition it triggers. If all the wars are against extremely weak states and the battlefield victory is followed by the rapid creation of a stable government, the public is likely to endorse the radical change in strategy. However, as with the revisionist strategy in the simulation, if the policy drags the United States into a number of conflicts with long-term commitments, the public is likely to punish leaders for adopting the strategy.

Eighth, the cases point out that of all government decisions, foreign policy questions are determined by a very restricted number of people. In Lloyd George's war cabinet, five individuals determined policy toward the Soviet Union. In the Suez Crisis, decision making in both France and the United Kingdom was restricted to a handful of decision makers. The limited number of perspectives brought to the table and the potential for the small group to be dominated by a single individual indicate that decision making within these bodies may not be optimal. Moreover, the small decision-making group highlights the fact that democratic institutions constrain retrospectively, if at all. On domestic issues, many different viewpoints are typically provided as policy is formulated over a long period of time. On foreign policy questions, the legislature and public are restricted to an after-the-fact judgment role. A bad policy simply becomes one that has failed.

Ninth, the cases highlight the importance of individuals. Most models testing propositions associated with the democratic peace totally neglect the decision makers who actually chose to use force.[5] Estimates of norms based on societal averages, for example, fail to capture the fact that Masaryk and Kramer, both socialized in the same political system, held radically different philosophies on the use of force. Although the normative tests presented in Chapter 5 serve as a first step in this direction, the case studies indicate that much more work must be done to "bring the decision makers" back into the picture.

Tenth, the cases point to a surprising number of democratic initiations against revolutionary regimes. Previous studies that have looked at the conflict involvement of revolutionary regimes have concluded that they are more conflictual. However, as Walt (1992, 1996) points out, if the revolutionary states are targets of aggression, the high involvement may not be a product of their own aggressiveness. In the crisis data set, Britain initiated violence against the revolutionary Bolshevik regime led by Lenin; Czechoslovakia attacked Bela Kun's revolutionary communist republic; Britain, France, and Israel colluded against Nasser's revolutionary Arab socialist state; and the United States invaded revolutionary Grenada. In each case a democratic capitalist state feared the revolutionary propaganda and agitation of an autocratic socialist country. If democracies socialize their publics to fear socialism and socialist states, then they (consciously or unconsciously) manufacture a situation in which the use of force against leftist states is unlikely to be punished.

Future Research

The findings of this project point to a number of important directions for future research. One issue insufficiently explored in the analysis is the role of individuals in the decision-making process. As Hermann and Kegley (1995) observe, most of the democratic peace literature neglects the democrats—all leaders socialized or operating in a "democratic" environment are assumed to behave similarly. However, the case studies demonstrate that the beliefs and orientations of particular decision makers can have a dramatic influence on decisions to resort to force. A pragmatic-idealist such as Jimmy

Carter was much less likely to resort to force against Grenada than a revisionist-realist such as Ronald Reagan, despite the fact that both were socialized in the same political system. Similarly, although Czechoslovak President Tomas Masaryk was reluctant to use force to resolve disputes, his political adversary Prime Minister Karel Kramer believed that military force was both effective and appropriate for resolving territorial conflicts with Czechoslovakia's neighbors.

A preliminary step toward exploring this individual-level influence was taken in this study. I hypothesized that leaders who used violence to acquire the chief executive position are more likely to resort to violence in external conflicts than those who did not. The test required the identification of the leader in power for each year of the dispute, his or her method of attaining power, and the state's behavior within international conflicts. Although the results did not support the prediction, the groundwork has been laid for more thorough analysis of individual-level hypotheses. Further specifications might explore whether a military career or attendance at a military academy increases the likelihood that a decision maker resorts to force. Related questions include (1) are pragmatic leaders less likely to initiate violence? and (2) are decision makers who have been socialized in unstable political periods or systems more likely to resort to diversionary war? This individual-level analysis can be used to test independent hypotheses as well as explore the underlying causal mechanisms associated with the domestic institution analysis.[6]

A second issue requiring greater exploration is constraint within autocratic polities. The findings of this study show that some autocratic structures appear to constrain decision makers from using force. Military juntas and factional ruling parties encourage the existence of opposition groups, which raises the likelihood of punishment for failed foreign policy ventures. In order to probe this finding in greater depth, case studies of these constrained autocracies must be completed to ensure that the opposition is in fact a central reason for the reluctance to use force.

A third issue requiring greater study is the connection between institutions and the extraction and mobilization of resources. Numerous studies have examined the relationship among war, resource extraction, and political development (Tilly 1975; Levy 1988; Organski and Kugler 1980; East et al. 1978; Rasler and Thompson 1989). Although resource extraction as an avenue through which institutions can constrain decision makers was not a major focus of the study, several findings suggest that it should be incorporated into the analysis. For example, the finding that an absence of a legislature inhibits the use of force is much more closely related to an extraction-mobilization argument than a constraint argument. In fact, the constraint model would predict that the lack of a legislative channel should *increase* the propensity for violence. The inclusion of an extraction–mobilization perspective would aid a more complete analysis of the relationship between institutions and external violence.

Finally, in the terms of neo-realist Kenneth Waltz (1959, 1979), the analysis has focused on the "second image," or domestic level of analysis: how do domestic institutions influence the external behavior of states? As with all analyses in the democratic peace literature, the research design implies that domestic institutions (the independent variables) *cause* states to initiate violence (the dependent variable). However, this causal arrow could easily be reversed—an extremely violent or peaceful international environment can shape the political development of states (Thompson 1996; Rousseau and Blauvelt 1998; Rousseau and Newsome 2004: Lasswell 1941; Klinkner and Smith 1999). Writing at the turn of the century, Otto Hintze ([1906] 1975) claimed that Imperial Germany's autocratic structure was attributable to its geographic position in the center of war-plagued Europe. Until the debacle of World War I, Hintze believed that the autocratic state of Germany was optimized for survival in a harsh environment; continual external threats forced states to adopt autocratic structures that enhanced their military efficiency and probability of survival in an anarchic world. Similarly, other scholars have argued that the insulated position of states such as the United Kingdom and the United States has allowed them to develop in a relatively peaceful environment; this peaceful environment has allowed democratic institutions to flourish. Given that statistical models of the democratic peace are misspecified should an interactive relationship exist, further investigation of the issue is absolutely essential.

In sum, there is much to be done.

Notes

1. Summaries of five additional cases can be found in Rousseau (1996). Two recent cases, the United States versus Yugoslavia in 1999 and the United States versus Panama in 1989, are not examined in detail.

2. It is also possible that the material balance of forces, which is used in this study, is not the sole factor upon which decision makers calculate the probability of victory. Case studies could be used to identify variables that decision makers employ, and then a broader data set of material and ideation variables could be collected to further test the theory.

3. In more technical language, I assumed that there was no spatial autocorrelation, which can affect the estimates of the standard errors but not the coefficients.

4. "The National Security Strategy of the United States," September 2002, produced by the Bush White House.

5. For a similar point, see Hermann and Kegley (1995) and Elman (1997b). Gelpi and Grieco (2001) collect data on the length of tenure for democratic leaders. They find that leaders with short tenures are more likely to be militarily challenged.

6. Although earlier work has followed this line of thinking (e.g., the CREON project), the new effort would require the development of indicators explicitly created for testing causal arguments within the democratic peace literature.

Bibliography

Abir, Mordechai. 1993. *Saudi Arabia: Government, Society and the Gulf Crisis.* New York: Routledge.

———. 2002. "Toward a New Political Methodology: Microfoundations and ART." *Annual Review of Political Science* 5:423–50.

Ahmad, Feroz. 1977. *The Turkish Experiment in Democracy, 1950–1975.* London: Royal Institute of International Affairs.

Alker, Hayward R., and Frank L. Sherman. 1986. *International Conflict Episodes.* Ann Arbor, MI: Inter-university Consortium for Political and Social Research.

Allison, Graham T. 1971. *The Essence of Decision: Explaining the Cuban Missile Crisis.* Boston: Little, Brown.

Allison, Paul D. 1995. *Survival Analysis Using the SAS System: A Practical Guide.* Cary, NC: SAS Institute.

Anderson, Thomas P. 1981. *The War of the Dispossessed: Honduras and El Salvador, 1969.* Lincoln: University of Nebraska Press.

Andreski, Stanislav. 1980. "On the Peaceful Disposition of Military Dictatorships." *Journal of Strategic Studies* 3 (3): 3–10.

Appadorai, A. 1981. *The Domestic Roots of India's Foreign Policy 1947–1972.* Delhi, India: Oxford University Press.

Art, Robert J. 1973. "Bureaucratic Politics and American Foreign Policy: A Critique." *Policy Studies* 4:467–90.

Auerswald, David P. 2000. *Disarmed Democracies: Domestic Institutions and the Use of Force.* Ann Arbor: University of Michigan Press.

Avery, William P. 1984. "Origins and Consequences of the Border Dispute Between Ecuador and Peru." *Inter-American Economic Affairs* 38 (Summer): 65–77.

Axelrod, Robert. 1986. "An Evolutionary Approach to Norms." *American Political Science Review* 80 (4):1095–1111.

———. 1997. *The Complexity of Cooperation: Agent-Based Models of Competition and Collaboration.* Princeton, NJ: Princeton University Press.

Axtell, Robert. 2000. "Why Agents? On the Varied Motivations for Agent Computing in the Social Sciences." *Working Paper No. 17.* Washington, DC: Brookings Institution, Center on Social and Economic Dynamics.

Axtell, Robert, Robert Axelrod, Joshua M. Epstein, and Michael D. Cohen. 1995. "Aligning Simulation Models: A Case Study and Results." Unpublished manuscript dated July 21, 1995.

Babst, Dean V. 1972. "A Force for Peace." *Industrial Research* (April): 55–58.

Badeeb, Saeed M. 1986. *The Saudi-Egyptian Conflict over North Yemen, 1962–1970.* Boulder, CO: Westview.

Bahcheli, Tozun. 1990. *Greek-Turkish Relations Since 1955.* Boulder, CO: Westview.

Bailey, Clinton. 1984. *Jordan's Palestinian Challenge, 1948–1983: A Political History.* Boulder, CO: Westview.

Bar-On, Mordechai. 1994 [Hebrew: 1992]. *The Gates of Gaza: Israel's Road to Suez and Back, 1955–1957.* New York: St. Martin's.

Beasley, William G. 1990. *The Rise of Modern Japan.* New York: St. Martin's.

Beck, Nathaniel, David Epstein, Simon Jackman, and Sharyn O'Halloran. 2001. "Alternative Models of Dynamics in Binary Times-Series-Cross-Section Models: The Example of State Failure." Paper presented at the annual meeting of the Society for Political Methodology, Emory University, October 2001.

Beck, Nathaniel, Jonathan N. Katz, and Richard Tucker. 1997. "Beyond Ordinary Logit: Taking Time Seriously in Binary Time-Series-Cross-Section Models." Paper presented at the annual meeting of the American Political Science Association, Washington, DC.

———. 1998. "Taking Time Seriously in Binary Time-Series-Cross-Section Models." *American Journal of Political Science* 42 : 1260–88.

Beling, William A. (ed.). 1980. *King Faisal and the Modernization of Saudi Arabia.* Boulder, CO: Westview.

Bennett, D. Scott, and Allan C. Stam. 2000. "Research Design and Estimator Choices in the Analysis of Interstate Disputes." *Journal of Conflict Resolution* 44 (5): 653–85.

———. 2004. *The Behavioral Origins of War.* Ann Arbor: University of Michigan Press.

Bennett, Ralph K. 1984. "Grenada: Anatomy of a 'Go' Decision." *Reader's Digest* 124 (February): 72–77.

Benoit, Kenneth. 1996. "Democracies Really Are More Pacific (in General): Reexamining Regime Type and War Involvement." *Journal of Conflict Resolution* 40 (4): 636–57.

Berger, Gordon M. 1988. "Politics and Mobilization in Japan, 1931–1945." In Peter Duus (ed.), *The Cambridge History of Japan.* Cambridge: Cambridge University Press.

Berger, Peter L., and Thomas Luckmann. 1966. *The Social Construction of Reality: A Treatise in the Sociology of Knowledge.* New York: Anchor.

Bissell, Richard M. 1984. "Response to Lucien S. Vandenbroucke, 'The Confessions of Allen Dulles: New Evidence on the Bay of Pigs.'" *Diplomatic History* 8 (4): 377–80.

Bligh, Alexander. 1984. *From Prince to King: Royal Succession in the House of Saud in the Twentieth Century.* New York: New York University Press.

Bloomfield, Lincoln P., and Amelia C. Leiss. 1969. *Controlling Small Wars: A Strategy for the 1970's.* New York: Knopf.

Bollen, Kenneth A., and Robert W. Jackman. 1989. "Democracy, Stability, and Dichotomies." *American Sociological Review* 54 : 612–21.

Box-Steffensmeier, Janet M., and Christopher Zorn. 2002. "Duration Models for Repeated Events." *Journal of Politics* 64 (4): 1069–94.

Brands, H. W., Jr. 1987. "Decisions on American Armed Intervention: Lebanon, Dominican Republic, and Grenada." *Political Science Quarterly* 102 (4): 607–24.

Brecher, Michael. 1968. *India and World Politics: Krishna Menon's View of the World.* Oxford: Oxford University Press.

———. 1980. *Decisions in Crises: Israel, 1967 and 1973.* Berkeley: University of California Press.

———. 1999. "International Studies in the Twentieth Century and Beyond: Flawed Dichotomies, Synthesis, and Cumulation." *International Studies Quarterly* 43 (2): 213–64.

Brecher, Michael, Jonathan Wilkenfeld, and Sheila Moser. 1988. *Crises in the Twentieth Century.* Vol. 1, *Handbook of International Crises.* New York: Pergamon.

Bremer, Stuart A. (ed.). 1987. *The GLOBUS Model: A Computer Model of Long Term Global Political and Economic Processes.* Boulder, CO: Westview.

———. 1992. "Dangerous Dyads: Conditions Affecting the Likelihood of Interstate War, 1816–1965." *Journal of Conflict Resolution* 36 (2): 309–41.

———. 1993. "Democracy and Militarized Interstate Conflict, 1816–1965." *International Interactions* 18 (3): 231–49.

Budge, Ian, Ivor Crewe, David McKay, and Ken Newton. 1998. *The New British Politics.* Essex, UK: Longman.

Bueno de Mesquita, Bruce. 1981. *The War Trap.* New Haven, CT: Yale University Press.

———. 2002. "Domestic Politics and International Relations." *International Studies Quarterly* 46 (1): 1–9.

Bueno de Mesquita, Bruce, and David Lalman. 1992. *War and Reason.* New Haven, CT: Yale University Press.

Bueno de Mesquita, Bruce, James D. Morrow, Randolph M. Siverson, and Alastair Smith. 1999. "An Institutional Explanation of the Democratic Peace." *American Political Science Review* 93 (4): 791–807.

Bueno de Mesquita, Bruce, and Randolph Siverson. 1995. "War and the Survival of Political Leaders: A Comparative Analysis of Regime Type and Accountability." *American Political Science Review* 89 (4): 841–55.

Bueno de Mesquita, Bruce, Randolph Siverson, and Gary Woller. 1992. "War and the Fate of Regimes." *American Political Science Review* 86 (3): 638–46.

Bueno de Mesquita, Bruce, Alastair Smith, Randolph M. Siverson, and James D. Morrow. 2003. *The Logic of Political Survival.* Cambridge, MA: MIT Press.

Burk, James. 1995. "Citizenship Status and Military Service: The Quest for Inclusion by Minorities and Conscientious Objectors." *Armed Forces and Society: An Interdisciplinary Journal* 21 (4): 503–30.

Bustamante, Fernando. 1992/93. "Ecuador: Putting an End to the Ghosts of the Past." *Journal of Interamerican Studies and World Affairs* 34 (4): 195–225.

Butterworth, Robert L., with Margaret E. Scranton. 1976. *Managing Interstate Conflict, 1945–74.* Pittsburgh, PA: University Center for International Studies.

Campbell, John C. 1989. "The Soviet Union, the United States, and the Twin

Crises." In William R. Louis and Roger Owen (eds.), *Suez 1956: The Crisis and Its Consequences*. Oxford: Clarendon.

Carlton, David. 1988. *Britain and the Suez Crisis*. Oxford: Blackwell.

Carment, David, and Patrick James. 1998. "The United Nations at 50: Managing Ethnic Crises—Past and Present." *Journal of Peace Research* 35 (1): 61–82.

Castagno, A. A. 1970. "Somali Republic." In James S. Coleman and Carl G. Rosberg (eds.), *Political Parties and National Integration in Tropical Africa*. Berkeley: University of California Press.

Cederman, Lars-Erik. 1997. *Emergent Actors in World Politics: How States and Nations Develop and Dissolve*. Princeton, NJ: Princeton University Press.

———. 2001a. "Back to Kant: Reinterpreting the Democratic Peace as a Macrohistorical Learning Process." *American Political Science Review* 95 (1): 15–31.

———. 2001b. "Modeling the Democratic Peace as a Kantian Selection Process." *Journal of Conflict Resolution* 45 (4): 470–502.

———. 2003. "Modeling the Size of Wars: From Billiard Balls to Sandpiles." *American Political Science Review* 97 (1): 135–50.

Cederman, Lars-Erik, and Kristan Gleditsch. 2002. "Conquest and Regime Change: An Evolutionary Model of the Democratic Peace." Paper presented at the annual meeting of the American Political Science Association, Boston, August 31, 2002.

Cederman, Lars-Erik, and Mohan Penubarti Rao. 2001. "Exploring the Dynamics of the Democratic Peace." *Journal of Conflict Resolution* 45 (6): 818–33.

Chan, Steve. 1984. "Mirror, Mirror on the Wall . . . Are the Freer Countries More Pacific?" *Journal of Conflict Resolution* 28 (4): 617–48.

Chicago Council on Foreign Relations. 1977. *American Public Opinion and U.S. Foreign Policy 1975*. Ann Arbor, MI: Inter-university Consortium for Political and Social Research.

Child, Jack. 1985. *Geopolitics and Conflict in South America: Quarrels Among Neighbors*. New York: Praeger.

Christensen, Thomas, and Jack Snyder. 1990. "Chain Gangs and Passed Bucks: Predicting Alliance Patterns in Multipolarity." *International Organization* 44 (2): 137–68.

Churchill, Winston. 1948. *The Second World War: The Gathering Storm*. Boston: Houghton Mifflin.

———. 1950. *The Second World War: The Grand Alliance*. Boston: Houghton Mifflin.

Cialdini, Robert B., and Melanie R. Trost. 1998. "Social Influence: Social Norms, Conformity, and Compliance." In Daniel T. Gilbert, Susan T. Fiske, and Gardner Lindzey (eds.), *The Handbook of Social Psychology*. Boston: McGraw-Hill.

Clark, David H. 2000. "Agreeing to Disagree: Domestic Institutional Congruence and U.S. Dispute Behavior." *Political Research Quarterly* 53 (2): 375–400.

Clodfelter, Micheal. 1992. *Warfare and Armed Conflicts: A Statistical Reference to Casualty and Other Figures, 1618–1991*. Vol. 2. Jefferson, NC: McFarland.

Cohen, Raymond. 1994. "Pacific Unions: A Reappraisal of the Theory That Democracies Do Not Go to War with Each Other." *Review of International Studies* 20 (July): 207–23.

Conaghan, Catherine M. 1985. "Politicians Against Parties: Discord and Disconnection in Ecuador's Party System." In Scott Mainwarin and Timothy R. Scully (eds.), *Building Democratic Institutions: Party Systems in Latin America.* Stanford, CA: Stanford University Press.

————. 1994. "Loose Parties, 'Floating' Politicians, and Institutional Stress: Presidentialism in Ecuador, 1979–1988." In Juan J. Linz and Arturo Valenzuela (eds.), *The Failure of Presidential Democracy: The Case of Latin America.* Baltimore: Johns Hopkins University Press.

Conybeare, John C. 1994. "Arms Versus Alliances: The Capital Structure of Military Enterprise." *Journal of Conflict Resolution* 38 (2): 215–35.

Cotton, Timothy Y. 1987. "War and American Democracy." *Journal of Conflict Resolution* 30 (4): 616–35.

Couloumbis, Theodore A. 1983. *The United States, Greece, and Turkey: The Troubled Triangle.* New York: Praeger.

Cunningham, Karla. 1997. *Regime and Society in Jordan: An Analysis of Jordanian Liberalization.* Ph.D. dissertation, SUNY at Buffalo.

————. 1998. "The Causes and Effects of Foreign Policy Decision Making: An Analysis of Jordanian Peace with Israel." *World Affairs* 160 (4): 192–202.

Cusack, Thomas R., and Richard Stoll. 1990. *Exploring Realpolitik: Probing International Relations Theory with Computer Simulations.* Boulder, CO: Lynne Rienner.

Dahl, Robert A. 1971. *Polyarchy: Participation and Opposition.* New Haven, CT: Yale University Press.

Dahlan, Ahmed Hassan (ed.). (1990). *Politics, Administration and Development in Saudi Arabia.* Brentwood, MD: Amana Corporation.

Dann, Uriel. 1989. *King Hussein and the Challenge of Arab Radicalism: Jordan 1955–1967.* New York: Oxford University Press.

Dassel, Kurt. 1998. "Civilians, Soldiers, and Strife: Domestic Sources of International Aggression." *International Security* 23 (1): 107–41.

Dassel, Kurt, and Eric Reinhardt. 1999. "Domestic Strife and the Initiation of Violence at Home and Abroad." *American Journal of Political Science* 43 (1): 56–85.

Dawisha, Karen. 1980. "The Limits of the Bureaucratic Politics Model: Observations on the Soviet Case." *Studies in Comparative Communism* 13 (Winter): 300–346.

Dawkins, Richard. 1976. *The Selfish Gene.* New York: Oxford University Press.

Day, Alan J. (ed.). 1982. *Border and Territorial Disputes.* Essex, UK: Longman.

————. 1988. *Political Parties of the World.* Chicago: St. James.

De Gaury, Gerald. 1966. *Faisal: King of Saudi Arabia.* New York: Praeger.

Degenhardt, Henry W. 1988. *Political Parties of the World.* Detroit: Gale.

Delury, George E. 1983. *World Encyclopedia of Political Systems.* New York: Facts on File.

Derbyshire, J. Denis, and Ian Derbyshire. 1989. *Encyclopedia of World Political Systems.* Armonk, NY: Sharpe Reference.

Desch, Michael C. 1998. "Culture Clash: Assessing the Importance of Ideas in Security Studies." *International Security* 23 (1): 141–71.

————. 2002. "Democracy and Victory: Why Regime Type Hardly Matters." *International Security* 27 (2): 5–47.

Deutsch, Karl. 1957. *Political Community and the North Atlantic Area.* Princeton, NJ: Princeton University Press.

Dion, Douglas. 1998. "Evidence and Inference in the Comparative Case Study." *Comparative Politics* 30 (2): 127–45.

Di Palma, Giuseppe. 1990. *To Craft Democracies: An Essay on Democratic Transitions.* Berkeley: University of California Press.

Dixon, William J. 1993. "Democracy and the Management of International Conflict." *Journal of Conflict Resolution* 37 (1): 42–68.

———. 1994. "Democracy and the Peaceful Settlement of International Conflict." *American Political Science Review* 88 (1): 14–32.

Dixon, William J., and Paul D. Senese. 2002. "Democracy, Disputes, and Negotiated Settlements." *Journal of Conflict Resolution* 46 (4): 547–71.

D'Lugo, David, and Ronald Rogowski. 1993. "The Anglo-German Naval Race and Comparative Constitutional 'Fitness.'" In Richard Rosecrance and Arthur A. Stein (eds.), *Domestic Bases of Grand Strategy.* Ithaca, NY: Cornell University Press.

Downing, Brian M. 1992. *The Military Revolution and Political Change.* Princeton, NJ: Princeton University Press.

Doyle, Michael W. 1983. "Kant, Liberal Legacies, and Foreign Affairs," parts 1 and 2. *Philosophy & Public Affairs* 12 (3–4): 205–35, 323–53.

———. 1986. "Liberalism and World Politics." *American Political Science Review* 80 (4): 1151–69.

———. 1997. *Ways of War and Peace: Realism, Liberalism, and Socialism.* New York: Norton.

Duarte, Jose Napoleon, with Dianna Page. 1986. *Duarte: My Story.* New York: Putnam.

Duffield, John S., Theo Farrell, Richard Price, and Michael C. Desh. 1999. "Isms and Schisms: Culturalism Versus Realism in Security Studies." *International Security* 24 (1): 156–80.

East, Maurice A., Stephen A. Salmore, and Charles F. Hermann, eds. 1978. *Why Nations Act: Theoretical Perspectives for Comparative Foreign Policy Studies.* Beverly Hills, CA: Sage.

Eckstein, Harry. 1975. "Case Study and Theory in Political Science." In Fred I. Greenstein and Nelson W. Polsby (eds.), *Strategies of Inquiry.* Vol. 7, *Handbook of Political Science.* Reading, MA: Addison-Wesley.

Elman, Colin. 1996. "Horses for Courses: Why *Not* Neorealist Theories of Foreign Policy?" *Security Studies* 6 (1): 7–53.

Elman, Colin, and Miriam Fendius Elman. 1997. "Lakatos and Neorealism: A Reply to Vasquez." *American Political Science Review* 91 (4): 923–26.

Elman, Miriam Fendius. 1997a. "Israel's Invasion of Lebanon, 1982: Regime Change and War Decisions." In Miriam Fendius Elman (ed.), *Paths to Peace: Is Democracy the Answer?* Cambridge, MA: MIT Press.

———. 2000. "Unpacking Democracy: Presidentialism, Parliamentarianism, and Theories of the Democratic Peace." *Security Studies* 9 (4): 91–126.

——— (ed.). 1997b. *Paths to Peace: Is Democracy the Answer?* Cambridge, MA: MIT Press.

Enterline, Andrew J. 1996. "Correspondence: Democratization and the Danger of War." *International Security* 20 (4): 183–96.

————. 1998. "Regime Changes and Interstate Conflict, 1816–1992." *Political Research Quarterly* 51 (2): 385–409.

Epstein, Leon D. 1964. *British Politics in the Suez Crisis*. Urbana: University of Illinois Press.

Ertekun, N. M. 1981. *The Cyprus Dispute and the Birth of the Turkish Republic of Northern Cyprus*. Nicosia, Northern Cyprus: K. Rustem and Brothers.

Eyerman, Joe, and Robert A. Hart. 1996. "Empirical Evidence of the Audience Cost Proposition: Democracy Speaks Louder Than Words." *Journal of Conflict Resolution* 40 (4): 597–616.

Farber, Henry S., and Joanne Gowa. 1995a. "Common Interests or Common Polities? Reinterpreting the Democratic Peace." *National Bureau of Economic Research Working Paper No. 5005*, Cambridge, MA.

————. 1995b. "Politics and Peace." *International Security* 20 (2): 123–46.

Farer, Tom J. 1979. *War Clouds on the Horn of Africa: The Widening Storm*, 2nd rev. ed. New York: Carnegie Endowment for International Peace.

Fearon, James D. 1994. "Domestic Political Audiences and the Escalation of International Disputes." *American Political Science Review* 88 (3): 577–92.

Ferguson, James. 1990. *Grenada: Revolution in Reverse*. London: Latin America Bureau.

Fisher, Louis. 1995. *Presidential War Power*. Lawrence: University of Kansas Press.

Foot, Rosemary. 1985. *The Wrong War: American Policy and the Dimensions of the Korean Conflict, 1950–53*. Ithaca, NY: Cornell University Press.

Forde, Steven. 1995. "International Realism and the Science of Politics: Thucydides, Machiavelli, and Neorealism." *International Studies Quarterly* 39 (2): 141–60.

Foreign Broadcast Information Service. 1974. "Middle East & North Africa: Special Cyprus Issue." 5,140a (July 21).

Forsythe, David P. 1992. "Democracy, War, and Covert Action." *Journal of Peace Research* 29 (4): 385–95.

Gaan, Narottam. 1992. *Indira Gandhi and Foreign Policy Making: The Bangladesh Crisis*. New Delhi, India: Patriot.

Gallup, George H. 1972. *The Gallup Poll: Public Opinion 1935–1971*. Vol. 3, *1959–1971*. New York: Random House.

————. 1976a. *The Gallup International Public Opinion Polls: France 1939, 1944–1975*. New York: Random House.

————. 1976b. *The Gallup International Public Opinion Polls: Great Britain 1937–1975*. New York: Random House.

————. 1984. *The Gallup Poll: Public Opinion 1983*. Wilmington, DE: Scholarly Resources.

Gandhi, Indira. 1972. *India and Bangla Desh: Selected Speeches and Statements March to December 1971*. New Delhi, India: Orient Longman.

Garfinkle, Adam. 1992. *Israel and Jordan in the Shadow of War*. New York: St. Martin's.

Garner, Robert, and Richard Kelly. 1998. *British Political Parties Today*, 2nd ed. Manchester, UK: Manchester University Press.

Gartner, Scott Sigmund, and Gary M. Segura. 1998. "War, Casualties, and Public Opinion." *Journal of Conflict Resolution* 42 (3): 278–300.

Gartner, Scott Sigmund, Gary M. Segura, and Michael Wilkening. 1997. "All Politics Are Local: Local Losses and Individual Attitudes Toward the Vietnam War." *Journal of Conflict Resolution* 41 (5): 669–94.

Gartzke, Erik. 1998. "Kant We All Just Get Along? Opportunity, Willingness, and the Origins of the Democratic Peace." *American Journal of Political Science* 42 (1): 1–27.

Gates, Scott, and Sara McLaughlin. 1996. "Rare Events and the Democratic Peace." Unpublished manuscript.

Gaubatz, Kurt Taylor. 1999. *Elections and War: The Electoral Incentive in the Democratic Politics of War and Peace.* Stanford, CA: Stanford University Press.

Gause, F. Gregory. 1990. *Saudi-Yemeni Relations: Domestic Structures and Foreign Influence.* New York: Columbia University Press.

Gelb, Leslie H., with Richard K. Betts. 1979. *The Irony of Vietnam: The System Worked.* Washington, DC: Brookings Institution.

Gelpi, Christopher. 1997. "Democratic Diversions: Governmental Structure and the Externalization of Domestic Conflict." *Journal of Conflict Resolution* 41 (2): 255–82.

Gelpi, Christopher, and Joseph M. Grieco. 2001. "Attracting Trouble: Democracy, Leadership Tenure, and the Targeting of Militarized Challenges, 1918–1992." *Journal of Conflict Resolution* 45 (6): 794–817.

George, Alexander, and Timothy J. McKeown. 1985. "Case Studies and Theories of Organizational Decision Making." *Advances in Information Processing in Organizations* 2:21–58.

Geva, Nehemia, and D. Christopher Hanson. 1999. "Cultural Similarity, Foreign Policy Actions, and Regime Perception: An Experimental Study of International Cues and Democratic Peace." *Political Psychology* 20 (4): 803–27.

Gibbs, David N. 1995. "Secrecy and International Relations." *Journal of Peace Research* 32 (2): 213–28.

Gleditsch, Kristian S. 2002. *All International Politics Is Local: The Diffusion of Conflict, Integration, and Democratization.* Ann Arbor: University of Michigan Press.

Gleditsch, Kristian S., and Michael D. Ward. 2000. "War and Peace in Space and Time: The Role of Democratization." *International Studies Quarterly* 44 (1): 1–29.

Glennon, Michael J. 1991. "The Gulf War and the Constitution." *Foreign Affairs* 70 (2): 84–101.

Gochman, Charles S., and Zeev Maoz. 1984. "Militarized Interstate Disputes, 1816–1976." *Journal of Conflict Resolution* 28 (4): 585–617.

Golani, Motti. 1998. *Israel in Search of a War: The Sinai Campaign, 1955–56.* Brighton, UK: Sussex Academic Press.

Goldgeier, James. 1994. *Leadership and Soviet Foreign Policy.* Baltimore: Johns Hopkins University Press.

Goodman, Allan E., and Bruce D. Berkowitz. 1992. "Background Paper." In the Twentieth Century Fund's *The Need to Know: The Report of the Twentieth Century Fund Task Force on Covert Action and American Democracy.* New York: Twentieth Century Fund.

Gorman, Robert F. 1981. *Political Conflict on the Horn of Africa.* New York: Praeger.

Gorst, Anthony, and Lewis Johnman. 1997. *The Suez Crisis.* New York: Routledge.

Gorvin, Ian (ed.). 1989. *Elections Since 1945: A Worldwide Reference Compendium*. Essex, UK: Longman.

Gottschalk, Marie. 1992. "Operation Desert Cloud: The Media and the Gulf War." *World Policy Journal* 9 (3): 449–87.

Gowa, Joanne. 1995. "Democratic States and International Disputes." *International Organization* 49 (3): 511–22.

———. 1999. *Ballots and Bullets: The Elusive Democratic Peace*. Princeton, NJ: Princeton University Press.

Graubard, Stephen R. 1956. *British Labour and the Russian Revolution, 1917–1924*. Cambridge, MA: Harvard University Press.

Greene, William H. 1990. *Econometric Analysis*. New York: Macmillan.

Grieco, Joseph M. 1988. "Anarchy and the Limits of Cooperation: A Realist Critique of the Newest Liberal Institutions." *International Organization* 42:485–507. Reprinted in David A. Baldwin (ed.), *Neorealism and Neoliberalism: The Contemporary Debate*. New York: Columbia University Press, 1993.

Guldescu, Stenko. 1966. "Yemen: The War and the Haradh Conference." *Review of Politics* 28:319–31.

Gulick, Edward V. 1955. *Europe's Classical Balance of Power*. New York: Norton.

Gurr, Ted Robert, Keith Jaggers, and Will H. Moore. 1989. "Polity II Codebook." Center for Comparative Politics, Department of Political Science, University of Colorado.

Haas, Ernst B., Robert L. Butterworth, and Joseph S. Nye. 1972. *Conflict Management by International Organizations*. Morristown, NJ: General Learning Press.

Hagan, Joe D. 1987. "Regimes, Political Oppositions, and the Comparative Analysis of Foreign Policy." In Charles F. Hermann, Charles W. Kegley, and James N. Rosenau (eds.), *New Directions in the Study of Foreign Policy*. Boston: Allen and Unwin.

———. 1993. *Political Opposition and Foreign Policy*. Boulder, CO: Westview.

Halperin, Morton H. 1974. *Bureaucratic Politics and Foreign Policy*. Washington, DC: Brookings Institution.

Hanratty, Dennis (ed.). 1991. *Ecuador: A Country Study*. Washington, DC: Federal Research Division, Library of Congress.

Hanushek, Eric A., and John E. Jackson. 1977. *Statistical Methods for Social Scientists*. San Diego, CA: Academic Press.

Head, Richard G., Frisco W. Short, and Robert C. McFarlane. 1978. *Crisis Resolution: Presidential Decision Making in the Mayaguez and Korean Confrontations*. Boulder, CO: Westview.

Henderson, Errol A. 2002. *Democracy and War: The End of an Illusion?* Boulder, CO: Lynne Rienner.

Hensel, Paul R. 2001. "Contentious Issues and World Politics: The Management of Territorial Claims in the Americas, 1816–1992." *International Studies Quarterly* 45:81–109.

Hensel, Paul R., Gary Goertz, and Paul F. Diehl. 2000. "The Democratic Peace and Rivalries." *Journal of Politics* 62 (4): 1173–88.

Hermann, Margaret G. 1978. "The Effects of Personal Characteristics of Political

Leaders on Foreign Policy." In Maurice East et al. (eds.), *Why Nations Act.* Beverly Hills, CA: Sage.

———. 1984. "Personality and Foreign Policy Decision Making: A Study of Fifty-Three Heads of Government." In Donald Sylvan and Steve Chan (eds.), *Foreign Policy Decision Making: Perception, Cognition, and Artificial Intelligence.* New York: Praeger.

———. 1987. "Leaders' Foreign Policy Orientations and the Quality of Foreign Policy Behavior." In Stephen G. Walker (ed.), *Role Theory and Foreign Policy Analysis.* Durham, NC: Duke University Press.

Hermann, Margaret G., and Charles W. Kegley. 1995. "Rethinking Democracy and International Peace: Perspectives from Political Psychology." *International Studies Quarterly* 39 (4): 511–34.

———. 1996. "Ballots, a Barrier Against the Use of Bullets and Bombs: Democratization and Military Intervention." *Journal of Conflict Resolution* 40 (3): 436–60.

———. 2001. "Democracies and Intervention: Is There a Danger Zone in the Democratic Peace?" *Journal of Peace Research* 38 (2): 237–45.

Herrmann, Richard K., Philip E. Tetlock, and Penny S. Visser. 1999. "Mass Public Decisions to Go to War: A Cognitive-Interactionist Framework." *American Political Science Review* 93 (3): 553–73.

Herzog, Chaim. 1982. *The Arab-Israeli Wars: War and Peace in the Middle East from the War of Independence to Lebanon.* London: Arms and Armour.

Hewitt, J. Joseph, and Jonathan Wilkenfeld. 1995. "Democracies in International Crisis." Paper presented at the annual meeting of the International Studies Association, Chicago.

Hey, Jeanne A. K. 1995. "Ecuadorean Foreign Policy Since 1979: Ideological Cycles or a Trend Towards Neoliberalism." *Journal of Interamerican Studies and World Affairs* 37 (4): 57–88.

Hill, Christopher. 1991. *Cabinet Decisions on Foreign Policy: The British Experience October 1938–June 1941.* Cambridge: Cambridge University Press.

Hintze, Otto. [1906] 1975. *Historical Essays of Otto Hintze.* New York: Oxford University Press.

Hobbes, Thomas. [1651] 1968. *Leviathan.* Harmondsworth, UK: Penguin.

Holsti, Kalevi J. 1991. *Peace and War: Armed Conflicts and International Order, 1648–1989.* Cambridge: Cambridge University Press.

Holsti, Ole R., and James N. Rosenau. 1990. "The Structure of Foreign Policy Attitudes Among American Leaders." *Journal of Politics* 52 (1): 94–125.

Hopf, Ted. 1992. "Managing Soviet Disintegration: A Demand for Behavioral Regimes." *International Security* 17 (1): 44–75.

———. 1998. "The Promise of Constructivism in International Relations Theory." *International Security* 23:171–200.

Hudson, Rex A. 1991. "Government and Politics." In Dennis Hanratty (ed.), *Ecuador: A Country Study.* Washington, DC: Federal Research Division, Library of Congress.

Huth, Paul K. 1996. *Standing Your Ground.* Ann Arbor: University of Michigan Press.

Huth, Paul K., and Todd L. Allee. 2002. *The Democratic Peace and Territorial Conflict in the Twentieth Century.* Cambridge: Cambridge University Press.

International Institute for Strategic Studies. 1981. *The Military Balance, 1981–82.* London: International Institute for Strategic Studies.

Ireland, Michael J., and Scott Sigmund Gartner. 2001. "Time to Fight: Government Type and Conflict Initiation in Parliamentary Systems." *Journal of Conflict Resolution* 45 (5): 547–68.

Isaacs, Anita. 1993. *Military Rule and Transition in Ecuador, 1972–92.* Pittsburgh, PA: University of Pittsburgh Press.

Jackman, Simon. 2000. "In and Out of War and Peace: Transitional Models of International Conflict." Unpublished manuscript dated January 27, 2000.

Jackson, Robert. 1975. *South Asian Crisis: India, Pakistan, and Bangladesh.* New York: Praeger.

James, Patrick, and Glenn E. Mitchell. 1995. "Targets of Covert Pressure: The Hidden Victims of the Democratic Peace." *International Interactions* 21(1): 85–107.

Janis, Irving L. 1982. *Groupthink: Psychological Studies of Policy Decisions and Fiascoes,* 2nd ed. Boston: Houghton Mifflin.

Jervis, Robert. 1976. *Perception and Misperception in International Politics.* Princeton, NJ: Princeton University Press.

———. 1978. "Cooperation Under the Security Dilemma." *World Politics* 30 (2): 167–214.

Jervis, Robert, Richard Ned Lebow, and Janice Stein. 1985. *Psychology and Deterrence.* Baltimore: Johns Hopkins University Press.

Johnson, Loch K. 1989. "Covert Action and Accountability: Decision-Making for America's Secret Foreign Policy." *International Studies Quarterly* 33:81–109.

Johnson, Paul E. 1999. "Simulation Modeling in Political Science." *American Behavioral Scientists* 42 (10): 1509–30.

Johnston, Alastair Iain. 1995. *Cultural Realism: Strategic Culture and Grand Strategy in Chinese History.* Princeton, NJ: Princeton University Press.

Jones, Mary Hoxie. 1971. *Swords into Ploughshares: An Account of the American Friends Service Committee, 1917–1937.* Westport, CT: Greenwood.

Juhász, Gyula. 1979. *Hungarian Foreign Policy.* Budapest: Akademiai Kiado.

Kacowicz, Arie M. 1995. "Explaining Zones of Peace: Democracies as Satisfied Powers?" *Journal of Peace Research* 32 (3): 265–76.

Kahl, Colin H. 1998/99. "Constructing a Separate Peace: Constructivism, Collective Liberal Identity, and Democratic Peace." *Security Studies* 8 (2): 94–119.

Kant, Immanuel. [1795] 1971. "Perpetual Peace: A Philosophical Essay." In Hans Reiss (ed.), *Kant: Political Writings,* 2nd ed. London, UK: Cambridge University Press.

Karl, Terry L. 1990. "Dilemmas of Democratization in Latin America." *Comparative Politics* 23 (1): 1-21.

Kaufmann, Chaim D. 1993. *Deterrence and Rationality in International Crises.* Ph.D. dissertation, Columbia University.

Keesing's Contemporary Archives. Various Years. (Continued as Keesing's *Record of World Events After 1987*). London: Keesing's Limited.

Kegley, Charles W., and Margaret G. Hermann. 1997. "A Peace Dividend? Democracies' Military Interventions and Their External Political Consequences." *Cooperation and Conflict: Nordic Journal of International Relations* 32 (4): 339–68.

Kegley, Charles W., and Richard A. Skinner. 1976. "The Case-for-Analysis Problem." In James N. Rosenau (ed.), *In Search of Global Patterns*. New York: Free Press.

Kennan, George F. 1956. *Soviet American Relations, 1917–1920*. Vol. 1, *Russia Leaves the War*. Princeton, NJ: Princeton University Press.

———. 1958. *Soviet American Relations, 1917–1920*. Vol. 2, *The Decision to Intervene*. Princeton, NJ: Princeton University Press.

Khouri, Fred. 1985. *The Arab-Israeli Dilemma*, 3rd ed. Syracuse, NY: Syracuse University Press.

Kim, Hyung Min, and David L. Rousseau. 2003. "The Classical Liberals Were Half Right (or Half Wrong): New Tests of the 'Liberal Peace,' 1960–88." Unpublished manuscript.

Kinder, Donald R., and Thomas R. Palfrey. 1993. "On Behalf of an Experimental Political Science." In Donald R. Kinder and Thomas R. Palfrey (eds.), *Experimental Foundations of Political Science*. Ann Arbor: University of Michigan Press.

King, Gary, Robert O. Keohane, and Sidney Verba. 1994. *Designing Social Inquiry*. Princeton, NJ: Princeton University Press.

King, Gary, and Langche Zeng. 2001. "Explaining Rare Events in International Relations." *International Organization* 55 (3): 693–715.

Kingdon, John W. 1984. *Agendas, Alternatives, and Public Policy*. Boston: Little, Brown.

Kinsella, David, and Bruce Russett. 2002. "Conflict Emergence and Escalation in Interactive International Dyads." *Journal of Politics* 64 (4): 1045–68.

Kirshner, Jonathan. 1995. *Currency and Coercion: The Political Economy of International Monetary Power*. Princeton, NJ: Princeton University Press.

Kissinger, Henry. 1999. *Years of Renewal*. New York: Simon & Schuster.

Klinkner, Philip A., and Rogers M. Smith. 1999. *The Unsteady March: The Rise and Decline of Racial Equality in America*. Chicago: University of Chicago Press.

Koch, H. W. 1984. *A Constitutional History of Germany*. London: Longman.

Kornbluh, Peter (ed.). 1998. *Bay of Pigs Declassified: The Secret CIA Report on the Invasion of Cuba*. New York: New Press.

Krasner, Stephen D. 1972. "Are Bureaucracies Important? (Or Allison Wonderland)." *Foreign Policy* 7 (Summer): 159–79.

Krehbiel, Keith. 1992. *Information and Legislative Organization*. Ann Arbor: University of Michigan Press.

Krieg, William L. 1986. *Ecuadorean-Peruvian Rivalry in the Upper Amazon* (2nd ed., enlarged to include the Paquisha incident, 1981). Washington, DC: U.S. Department of State.

Kurian, George T. 1992. *Encyclopedia of the Third World*. New York: Facts on File.

Kyle, Keith. 1991. *Suez*. New York: St. Martin's.

Laipson, Ellen B. 1986. "Cyprus: A Quarter Century of US Diplomacy." In John T. Koumoulides (ed.), *Cyprus in Transition, 1960–1985*. London: Trigraph.

Laitin, David D., and Said S. Samatar. 1987. *Somalia: Nation in Search of a State*. Boulder, CO: Westview.

Lake, David A. 1992. "Powerful Pacifists: Democratic States and War." *American Political Science Review* 86 (1): 24–37.

Langer, William L. 1968. *An Encyclopedia of World History*. Boston: Houghton Mifflin.

Laquer, Walter. 1968. *The Road to War 1967: The Origins of the Arab Israel Conflict.* London: Weidenfeld and Nicolson.

Lasswell, Harold D. 1941. "The Garrison State." *American Journal of Sociology* 46 (4): 455−68.

Layne, Christopher. 1994. "Kant or Cant: The Myth of the Democratic Peace." *International Security* 19 (2): 5−94.

———. 1997. "Lord Palmerston and the Triumph of Realism: Anglo-French Relations, 1830−48." In Miriam Fendius Elman (ed.), *Paths to Peace: Is Democracy the Answer?* Cambridge, MA: MIT Press.

Lebow, Richard Ned. 1981. *Between Peace and War: The Natures of International Crisis.* Baltimore: Johns Hopkins University Press.

Leeds, Brett A., and David R. Davis. 1999. "Beneath the Surface: Regime Type and International Interactions, 1953−1978." *Journal of Peace Research* 36 (1): 5−21.

Leng, Russell. 1993. "Reciprocating Influence Strategies in Interstate Crisis Bargaining." *Journal of Conflict Resolution* 37 (1): 3−41.

Lentz, Harris. 1994. *Heads of States and Governments.* Jefferson, NC: McFarland.

Levy, Jack S. 1988. "Domestic Politics and War." In Robert I. Rotberg and Theodore K. Rabb (eds.), *The Origin and Prevention of Major Wars.* Cambridge: Cambridge University Press.

———. 1989. "The Diversionary Theory of War: A Critique." In Manus I. Midlarsky (ed.), *Handbook of War Studies.* Boston: Unwin Hyman.

Levy, Jack S., and Joseph R. Gochal. 2002. "Democracy and Preventive War; Israel and the 1956 Campaign." *Security Studies* 11 (2): 1−49.

Lewis, I. M. 1988. *A Modern History of Somalia: Nation and State in the Horn of Africa,* rev. ed. Boulder, CO: Westview.

Lijphart, Arend. 1977. *Democracy in Plural Societies: A Comparative Exploration.* New Haven, CT: Yale University Press.

———. 1984. *Democracies: Patterns of Majoritarian and Consensus Government in Twenty-One Countries.* New Haven, CT: Yale University Press.

Lillard, L., J. P. Smith, and F. Welch. 1986. "What Do We Really Know About Wages? The Importance of Nonreporting and Census of Imputation." *Journal of Political Economy* 94:489−506.

Lippmann, Walter. 1922. *Public Opinion.* New York: Harcourt, Brace.

———. 1925. *The Phantom Public.* New York: Harcourt, Brace.

Lorell, Mark, and Charles Kelley. 1985. "Casualties, Public Opinion, and Presidential Policy During the Vietnam War." Rand Report (R-3060-AF).

Louis, William R., and Roger Owen (eds.). 1989. *Suez 1956: The Crisis and Its Consequences.* Oxford: Clarendon.

Low, Alfred D. 1971. "Soviet Hungary and the Paris Peace Conference." In Ivan Volgyes (ed.), *Hungary in Revolution, 1918−1919.* Lincoln: University of Nebraska Press.

Lucas, W. Scott. 1991. *Divided We Stand: Britain, the US, and the Suez Crisis.* London: Hodder & Stoughton.

Lukacs, Yehuda. 1997. *Israel, Jordan, and the Peace Process.* Syracuse, NY: Syracuse University Press.

MacArthur, John R. 1992. *Second Front: Censorship and Propaganda in the Gulf War.* Berkeley: University of California Press.

Machiavelli, Niccolo. 1950. *The Prince and the Discourses.* New York: Random House.

Mackie, Thomas T., and Richard Rose. 1974. *The International Almanac of Electoral History.* London: Macmillan.

————. 1991. *The International Almanac of Electoral History*, 3rd ed. Washington, DC: Congressional Quarterly.

Macy, Michael, and John Skvoretz. 1998. "The Evolution of Trust and Cooperation Between Strangers: A Computational Model." *American Sociological Review* 63 (5): 638–61.

Macy, Michael W., and Robert Willer. 2002. "From Factors to Actors: Computational Sociology and Agent-Based Modeling." *American Review of Sociology* 28, 143–66.

Makinda, Samuel M. 1992. *Security in the Horn of Africa.* Adelphi Paper no. 269. London: Brassey's/International Institute of Strategic Studies.

Mamatey, Victor S., and Radomir Luza (eds.). 1973. *A History of the Czechoslovak Republic, 1918–1948.* Princeton, NJ: Princeton University Press.

Mansfield, Edward, and Jack Snyder. 1995a. "Democratization and the Danger of War." *International Security* 20 (1): 5–38.

————. 1995b. "Democratization and War." *Foreign Affairs* 74 (3): 79–97.

————. 1996. "Correspondence: Democratization and the Danger of War." *International Security* 20 (4): 196–207.

————. 2002a. "Democratic Transitions, Institutional Strength, and War." *International Organization* 56 (2): 297–337.

————. 2002b. "Incomplete Democratization and the Outbreak of Military Disputes." *International Studies Quarterly* 46: 529–49.

Maoz, Zeev, and Nasrin Abdolali. 1989. "Regime Type and International Conflict." *Journal of Conflict Resolution* 33 (1): 3–35.

Maoz, Zeev, and Bruce M. Russett. 1992. "Alliance, Contiguity, Wealth, and Political Stability: Is the Lack of Conflict Among Democracies a Statistical Artifact?" *International Interactions* 17 (3): 245–67.

————. 1993. "Normative and Structural Causes of Democratic Peace, 1946–1986." *American Political Science Review* 87 (3): 624–38.

Marcella, Gabriel. 1995. *War and Peace in the Amazon: Strategic Implications for the United States and Latin America of the 1995 Ecuador-Peru War.* Carlisle, PA: Strategic Studies Institute.

Marcella, Gabriel, and Richard Downes. 1999. *Security Cooperation in the Western Hemisphere: Resolving the Ecuador-Peru Conflict.* Coral Gables, FL: North-South Center, University of Miami.

Mares, David R. 1996–97. "Deterrence Bargaining in the Ecuador-Peru Enduring Rivalry: Designing Strategies Around Military Weakness." *Security Studies* 6 (2): 91–123.

Markides, Kyriacos C. 1977. *The Rise and Fall of the Cyprus Republic.* New Haven, CT: Yale University Press.

Martz, John D. 1996. "Ecuador: The Fragility of Dependent Democracy." In

Howard J. Wiarda and Harvey F. Kline (eds.), *Latin American Politics and Government*. Boulder, CO: Westview.

Masani, Zareer. 1975. *Indira Gandhi: A Biography*. London: Hamish Hamilton.

Mayer, Arno J. 1971. *Dynamics of Counter Revolution in Europe, 1870–1956*. New York: Harper and Row.

McClintock, Cynthia. 1994. "Presidents, Messiahs, and Constitutional Breakdowns in Peru." In Juan J. Linz and Arturo Valenzuela (eds.), *The Failure of Presidential Democracy: The Case of Latin America*. Baltimore: Johns Hopkins University Press.

McDougall, Walter A. 1978. *France's Rhineland Diplomacy, 1914–1924*. Princeton, NJ: Princeton University Press.

Mearsheimer, John J. 1983. *Conventional Deterrence*. Ithaca, NY: Cornell University Press.

———. 2001. *The Tragedy of Great Power Politics*. New York: Norton.

Mendelson, Sarah E. 1993. *Explaining Change in Foreign Policy: The Soviet Withdrawal from Afghanistan*. Ph.D. dissertation, Columbia University.

Metz, Helen Chapin (ed.). 1992. *Saudi Arabia: A Country Study*. Washington, DC: U.S. Government Printing Office.

Mintz, Alex, and Nehemia Geva. 1993. "Why Don't Democracies Fight Each Other? An Experimental Study." *Journal of Conflict Resolution* 37 (3): 484–503.

Morgan, T. Clifton, and Sally H. Campbell. 1991. "Domestic Structure, Decisional Constraints, and War." *Journal of Conflict Resolution* 35 (2): 187–211.

Morgan, T. Clifton, and Valerie L. Schwebach. 1992. "Take Two Democracies and Call Me in the Morning: A Prescription for Peace?" *International Interactions* 17 (4): 305–20.

Morgenthau, Hans J. 1973. *Politics Among Nations*, 5th ed. New York: Praeger.

Mowat, Charles L. 1955. *Britain Between the Wars, 1918–1940*. London: Methuen.

Mueller, John E. 1973. *War, Presidents, and Public Opinion*. Lanham, MD: University Press of America.

———. 1994. *Policy and Opinion in the Gulf War*. Chicago: University of Chicago Press.

Mutawi, Samir A. 1987. *Jordan in the 1967 War*. Cambridge: Cambridge University Press.

Nagy, Zsuzsa. 1971. "Problems of Foreign Policy Before the Revolutionary Governing Council." In Ivan Volgyes (ed.), *Hungary in Revolution, 1918–1919*. Lincoln: University of Nebraska Press.

Nicholson, Norman K. 1978. "Factionalism and Public Policy in India: The Vertical Dimension." In Frank P. Belloni and Dennis C. Beller (eds.), *Political Parties and Factionalism in Comparative Perspective*. Santa Barbara, CA: ABC-Clio.

Nisbett, Richard E., and Dov Cohen. 1996. *Culture of Honor: The Psychology of Violence in the South*. Boulder, CO: Westview.

Nixon, Richard M. 1962. *Six Crises*. Garden City, NY: Doubleday.

Notter, Harley. 1965. *The Origins of the Foreign Policy of Woodrow Wilson*. New York: Russell & Russell.

Nye, Joseph S. 1971. *Peace in Parts: Integration and Conflict in Regional Organization*. Boston: Little, Brown.

Nyrop, Richard F. 1979. *Turkey: A Country Study*. Washington, DC: U.S. Government Printing Office.

Oneal, John R., and Bruce M. Russett. 1997. "The Classical Liberals Were Right: Democracy, Interdependence, and Conflict, 1950–1985." *International Studies Quarterly* 41 (2): 267–94.

Oren, Ido. 1995. "The Subjectivity of the 'Democratic' Peace: Changing U.S. Perceptions of Imperial Germany." *International Security* 20 (2): 147–84.

Oren, Michael B. 2002. *Six Days of War: June 1967 and the Making of the Modern Middle East*. New York: Oxford University Press.

Organski, A. F. K., and Jacek Kugler. 1980. *The War Ledger*. Chicago: University of Chicago Press.

Owen, John M. 1993. *Testing the Democratic Peace: American Diplomatic Crises, 1794–1917*. Ph.D. dissertation, Harvard University.

———. 1994. "How Liberalism Produces Democratic Peace." *International Security* 19 (2): 87–125.

———. 1997. *Liberal Peace, Liberal War*. Ithaca, NY: Cornell University Press.

———. 2000. "Review of *Ballots and Bullets: The Elusive Democratic Peace*." *American Political Science Review* 94 (2): 509.

Page, Benjamin I., and Robert Y. Shapiro. 1992. *The Rational Public*. Chicago: University of Chicago Press.

Paige, Glenn D. 1968. *The Korean Decision, June 24–30, 1950*. New York: Free Press.

Palmer, David Scott. 1997. "Peru-Ecuador Border Conflict: Missed Opportunities, Misplaced Nationalism, and Multilateral Peacekeeping." *Journal of Interamerican Studies and World Affairs* 39 (3), 109–48.

Parker, Richard B. 1996. *The Six-Day War: A Retrospective*. Gainesville: University Press of Florida.

Paul, T. V. 1994. *Asymmetric Conflicts: War Initiation by Weaker Powers*. Cambridge: Cambridge University Press.

Payne, Anthony, Paul Sutton, and Tony Thorndike. 1984. *Grenada: Revolution and Invasion*. London: Croom Helm.

Peceny, Mark, and Caroline C. Beer. 2003. "Peaceful Parties and Puzzling Personalists." *American Political Science Review* 97 (2): 339–42.

Peceny, Mark, Caroline C. Beer, and Shannon Sanchez-Terry. 2002. "Dictatorial Peace?" *American Political Science Review* 96 (1): 15–26.

Perman, Dagmar. 1962. *The Shaping of the Czechoslovak State*. Leiden, Netherlands: E. J. Brill.

Peterson, J. E. 1988. *The Arab Gulf States: Steps Toward Political Participation*. New York: Praeger.

Peterson, Susan. 1996. *Crisis Bargaining and the State: The Domestic Politics of International Conflict*. Ann Arbor: University of Michigan Press.

Pickering, Jeffrey. 2002. "Give Me Shelter: Reexamining Military Intervention and the Monadic Democratic Peace." *International Interaction* 28:293–324.

Piscatori, James P. 1983. "Islamic Values and National Interest: The Foreign Policy of Saudi Arabia." In Adeed Dawisha (ed.), *Islam in Foreign Policy*. Cambridge: Cambridge University Press.

Political Handbook of the World. Various Years. (Published as *Political Handbook and Atlas of the World* prior to 1975). New York: McGraw-Hill.

Potholm, Christian P. 1970. *Four African Political Systems.* Englewood Cliffs, NJ: Prentice-Hall.

Price, Richard, and Nina Tannenwald. 1996. "Norms and Deterrence: The Nuclear and Chemical Weapons Taboos." In Peter J. Katzenstein (ed.), *The Culture of National Security: Norms and Identity in World Politics.* New York: Columbia University Press.

Prins, Brandon C., and Christopher Sprecher. 1999. "Institutional Constraints, Political Opposition, and Interstate Dispute Escalation: Evidence from Parliamentary Systems, 1946–89." *Journal of Peace Research* 36 (3): 271–87.

Putnam, Robert D. 1988. "Diplomacy and Domestic Politics: The Logic of Two-Level Games." *International Organization* 42 (3): 427–61.

Rasler, Karen, and William R. Thompson. 1989. *War and State Making: The Shaping of the Global Powers.* Boston: Unwin Hyman.

———. 2001. "Rivalries and the Democratic Peace in the Major Power System." *Journal of Peace Research* 38 (6): 659–83.

Ray, James L. 1995. *Democracy and International Politics.* Columbia: University of South Carolina Press.

Raymond, Gregory A. 1994. "Democracies, Disputes, and Third-Party Intermediaries." *Journal of Conflict Resolution* 38 (1): 24–42.

Reed, William. 2000. "A Unified Statistical Model of Conflict Onset and Escalation." *American Journal of Political Science* 44 (1): 84–93.

Reiter, Dan. 1995. "Exploding the Powderkeg Myth: Preemptive Wars Almost Never Happen." *International Security* 20 (2): 5–34.

Reiter, Dan, and Allan C. Stam. 1998. "Democracy, War Initiation, and Victory." *American Political Science Review* 92 (2): 377–89.

———. 2002. *Democracies at War.* Princeton, NJ: Princeton University Press.

———. 2003a. "Identifying the Culprit: Democracy, Dictatorship, and Dispute Initiation." *American Political Science Review* 97 (2): 333–37.

———. 2003b. "Understanding Victory: Why Political Institutions Matter." *International Security* 28 (1): 168–79.

Reiter, Dan, and Erik R. Tillman. 2002. "Public, Legislative, and Executive Constraints on the Democratic Initiation of Conflict." *Journal of Politics* 64 (3): 810–26.

Richardson, Louise. 1996. *When Allies Differ: Anglo-American Relations During the Suez and Falklands Crises.* New York: St. Martin's.

Rioux, Jean-Sebastien. 1998. "A Crisis-Based Evaluation of the Democratic Peace Proposition." *Canadian Journal of Political Science* 31 (2): 263–84.

Risse-Kappen, Thomas. 1995. *Cooperation Among Democracies: The European Influence on U.S. Foreign Policy.* Princeton, NJ: Princeton University Press.

Ritcher, James. 1994. *Khrushchev's Double Bind.* Baltimore: Johns Hopkins University Press.

Robinson, Thomas W. 1981. "The Sino-Soviet Border Conflict." In Stephen S. Kaplan (ed.), *Diplomacy and Power: Soviet Armed Forces as a Political Instrument.* Washington, DC: Brookings Institution.

Rock, Stephen R. 1997. "Anglo-U.S. Relations, 1845–1930: Did Shared Liberal Values and Democratic Institutions Keep the Peace?" In Miriam Fendius Elman (ed.), *Paths to Peace: Is Democracy the Answer?* Cambridge, MA: MIT Press.

Roeder, Philip. 1984. "Soviet Politics and Kremlin Politics." *International Studies Quarterly* 28 (June): 171–93.

Rousseau, David L. 1996. *Domestic Political Institutions and the Evolution of International Conflict.* Ph.D. dissertation, University of Michigan.

———. 1997. "Regime Change and International Conflict: Is Democratization Really So Dangerous?" Paper presented at the annual meeting of the American Political Science Association, Washington, DC.

———. 2004. "Identifying Threats and Threatening Identities: The Social Construction of Realism and Liberalism." Unpublished book manuscript dated August 1, 2004.

Rousseau, David L., and Timothy Blauvelt. 1998. "War, Mobilization, and Democratization: The Experience of Minority Groups." Paper presented at the annual meeting of the International Studies Association, Minneapolis.

Rousseau, David L., and Max Cantor. 2003. "The Evolution of Trading and Military Strategies: An Agent-Based Simulation." Paper presented at the annual meeting of the American Political Science Association, Philadelphia.

Rousseau, David L., Christopher Gelpi, Dan Reiter, and Paul Huth. 1996. "Assessing the Dyadic Nature of the Democratic Peace, 1918–1988." *American Political Science Review* 90 (3): 512–33.

Rousseau, David L., and Bruce Newsome. 2004. "Women, Minorities and War: The Impact of Wartime Mobilization on Political Rights in Europe, 1900–1955." Unpublished manuscript.

Rubner, Michael. 1985–86. "The Reagan Administration, the 1973 War Powers Resolution, and the Invasion of Grenada." *Political Science Quarterly* 100 (4): 627–47.

Rudolph, James D. 1985. *Cuba: A Country Study.* Washington, DC: U.S. Government Printing Office.

Rummel, R. J. 1983. "Libertarianism and International Violence." *Journal of Conflict Resolution* 27 (1): 27–72.

———. 1985. "Libertarian Propositions on Violence Within and Between Nations." *Journal of Conflict Resolution* 29 (September): 419–55.

———. 1995. "Democracies Are Less Warlike Than Other Regimes." *European Journal of International Relations* 1:457–79.

Russett, Bruce M. 1970. "International Behavior Research: Case Studies and Cumulation." In M. Haas and H. Kariel (eds.), *Approaches to the Study of Political Science.* San Francisco: Chandler.

———. 1993. *Grasping the Democratic Peace: Principles for a Post-Cold War World.* Princeton, NJ: Princeton University Press.

Russett, Bruce M., and Thomas Graham. 1989. "Public Opinion and National Security Policy." In Manus Midlarsky (ed.), *Handbook of War Studies.* Boston: Unwin Hyman.

Russett, Bruce, and John Oneal. 2001. *Triangulating Peace: Democracy, Interdependence, and International Organizations*. New York: Norton.

Russett, Bruce M., and James L. Ray. 1995. "Raymond Cohen on Pacific Unions: A Response and Reply." *Review of International Studies* 21:319–25.

Sachar, Howard M. 1974. *Europe Leaves the Middle East, 1936–1954*. London: Allen Lane.

———. 1979. *A History of Israel: From the Rise of Zionism to Our Time*. New York: Knopf.

Salamore, Barbara G., and Stephen A. Salamore. 1978. "Political Regimes and Foreign Policy." In Maurice A. East, Stephen A. Salamore, and Charles F. Hermann (eds.), *Why Nations Act: Theoretical Perspectives for Comparative Foreign Policy Studies*. Beverly Hills, CA: Sage.

Salloukh, Bassel F. 1996. "State Strength, Permeability, and Foreign Policy: Jordan in Theoretical Perspective." *Arab Studies Quarterly* 18 (2): 39–66.

Sanchez, Nestor. 1983. "The Communist Threat." *Foreign Policy* 52 (Fall): 43–50.

Satloff, Robert. 1986. *Troubles on the East Bank: Challenges to Domestic Stability of Jordan*. New York: Praeger.

Schlesinger, Arthur M., Jr. 1965. *A Thousand Days: John F. Kennedy in the White House*. Boston: Houghton Mifflin.

Schoenhals, Kai P., and Richard A. Melanson. 1985. *Revolution and Intervention in Grenada: The New Jewel Movement, the United States, and the Caribbean*. Boulder, CO: Westview.

Schultz, Kenneth A. 1998. "Domestic Opposition and Signaling in International Crises." *American Political Science Review* 92 (4): 829–44.

———. 1999. "Do Democratic Institutions Constrain or Inform? Contrasting Two Institutional Perspectives on Democracy and War." *International Organization* 53 (2): 233–66.

———. 2001. *Democracy and Coercive Diplomacy*. Oxford: Oxford University Press.

Schweller, Randall L. 1992. "Domestic Structure and Preventive War: Are Democracies More Pacific?" *World Politics* 44 (2): 235–69.

———. 1994. "Bandwagoning for Profit: Bringing the Revisionist State Back In." *International Security* 19 (1): 72–108.

Sellers, J. A. 1990. "Military Lessons: The British Perspective." In Selwyn Ilan Troen and Moshe Shemesh (eds.), *The Suez-Sinai Crisis 1956: Retrospective and Reappraisal*. New York: Columbia University Press.

Senese, Paul D. 1997a. "Between Dispute and War: The Effect of Joint Democracy on Interstate Conflict Escalation." *Journal of Politics* 59 (1): 1–28.

———. 1997b. "Costs and Demands: International Sources of Dispute Challenges and Reciprocation." *Journal of Conflict Resolution* 41 (3): 407–28.

Seymour-Ure, Colin. 1984. "British 'War Cabinets' in Limited Wars: Korea, Suez and the Falklands." *Public Administration* 62 (Summer): 181–200.

Shepsle, Kenneth A., and Barry A. Weingast. 1981. "Structure Induced Equilibrium and Legislative Choice." *Public Choice* 37:503–19.

Sherman, Frank. 1987. *Partway to Peace: The United Nations and the Road to Nowhere*. Ph.D. dissertation, Pennsylvania State University.

————. 1994. "SHERFACS: A Cross-Paradigm, Hierarchical and Contextually Sensitive Conflict Management Data Set." *International Interactions* 20 (1–2): 79–100.

Signorino, Curtis S., and Jeffrey M. Ritter. 1999. "Tau-b or Not Tau-b: Measuring the Similarity of Foreign Policy Positions." *International Studies Quarterly* 43 (1): 115–44.

Singh, Sukhwant. 1980. *India's Wars Since Independence*. Vol. 1, *The Liberation of Bangladesh*. New Delhi, India: Vikas.

Small, Melvin, and J. David Singer. 1976. "The War Proneness of Democratic Regimes." *Jerusalem Journal of International Relations* 1 (1): 50–69.

————. 1982. *Resort to Arms: International and Civil Wars, 1816–1980*. Beverly Hills, CA: Sage.

Snyder, Jack. 1991. *Myths of Empire*. Ithaca, NY: Cornell University Press.

————. 2000. *From Voting to Violence: Democratization and Nationalist Conflict*. New York: Norton.

Solsten, Eric (ed.). 1993. *Cyprus: A Country Study*. Washington, DC: U.S. Government Printing Office.

Sorensen, Georg. 1992. "Kant and Processes of Democratization: Consequences for Neorealist Thought." *Journal of Peace Research* 29 (4): 397–414.

Sorensen, Theodore C. 1965. *Kennedy*. New York: Harper and Row.

Spiro, David E. 1994. "The Insignificance of the Democratic Peace." *International Security* 19 (2): 50–86.

St. John, Ronald Bruce. 1994. "The Ecuador-Peru Dispute: A Reconsideration." In Pascal O. Girot (ed.), *World Boundaries*. Vol. 4, *The Americas*. London: Routledge.

Stein, Arthur A. 1980. *The Nation at War*. Baltimore: Johns Hopkins University Press.

Stewart, Richard A. 1988. *Sunrise at Abadan: The British and Soviet Invasion of Iran, 1941*. New York: Praeger.

Stinchcombe, Arthur. 1968. *Constructing Social Theories*. New York: Harcourt, Brace.

Stolzenberg, Ross M., and Daniel A. Relles. 1990. "Theory Testing in a World of Constrained Research Design: The Significance of Heckman's Censored Sampling Bias Correction for Nonexperimental Research." *Sociological Methods and Research* 18 (4): 395–415.

Sullivan, Michael P. 1976. *International Relations: Theories and Evidence*. Englewood Cliffs, NJ: Prentice-Hall.

Sullivan, Robert R. 1970. "Saudi Arabia in International Politics." *Review of Politics* 32:436–60.

Temperley, Harold W. 1921. *A History of the Paris Peace Conference*. Vol. 4. London: Institute of International Affairs.

Therborn, Goran. 1977. "The Rule of Capital and the Rise of Capitalism." *New Left Review* 103:3–41.

Thompson, William. 1996. Democracy and Peace: Putting the Cart Before the Horse." *International Organization* 50 (1): 141–74.

Thompson, William R., and Richard Tucker. 1997. "A Tale of Two Democratic Peace Critiques." *Journal of Conflict Resolution* 41 (3): 428–54.

Thorndike, Tony. 1989. "Grenada." In Peter J. Schraeder (ed.), *Intervention in the 1980's: U.S. Foreign Policy in the Third World*. Boulder, CO: Lynne Rienner.

Tilly, Charles (ed.). 1975. *The Formation of States in Western Europe*. Princeton, NJ: Princeton University Press.

Tomz, Michael, Jason Wittenberg, and Gary King. 2003. "Clarify: Software for Interpreting and Presenting Statistical Results." Unpublished paper dated January 5, 2003.

Touval, Saadia. 1963. *Somali Nationalism: International Politics and the Drive for Unity in the Horn of Africa*. Cambridge, MA: Harvard University Press.

Trowen, Selwyn Ilan, and Moshe Shemesh (eds.). 1990. *The Suez-Sinai Crisis 1956: Retrospective and Reappraisal*. New York: Columbia University Press.

Tures, John A. 2001a. "Addressing Concerns About Applying the Democratic Peace Arguments to Interventions." *Journal of Peace Research* 38 (2): 247–49.

———. 2001b. "Democracies as Intervening States: A Critique of Kegley & Herman." *Journal of Peace Research* 38 (2): 227–35.

Ullman, Richard H. 1961. *Anglo-Soviet Relations, 1917–1921*. Vol. 1, *Intervention and the War*. Princeton, NJ: Princeton University Press.

———. 1968. *Anglo-Soviet Relations, 1917–1921*. Vol. 2, *Britain and the Russian Civil War*. Princeton, NJ: Princeton University Press.

Unterberger, Betty Miller. 1989. *The United States, Revolutionary Russia, and the Rise of Czechoslovakia*. Chapel Hill: University of North Carolina Press.

Vaisse, Maurice. 1989. "France and the Suez." In William R. Louis and Roger Owen (eds.), *Suez 1956: The Crisis and Its Consequences*. Oxford: Clarendon.

Valenta, Jiri. 1975. "Soviet Decisionmaking on Czechoslovakia, 1968." *Studies in Comparative Communism* 8 (Spring/Summer): 147–73.

———. 1984a. "Soviet Decisionmaking on Czechoslovakia, 1968." In Jiri Valenta and William C. Potter (eds.), *Soviet Decisionmaking for National Security*. London: George Allen & Unwin.

———. 1984b. "Soviet Decision Making and the Hungarian Revolution." In Bela K. Kiraly, Barbara Lotze, and Nandor F. Dreisinger (eds.), *The First War Between Socialist States: The Hungarian Revolution of 1956 and Its Impact*. New York: Brooklyn College Press/Columbia University Press.

Vance, Vick, and Pierre Lauer. 1969. *Hussein of Jordan: My "War" with Israel*. New York: Morrow.

Vandenbroucke, Lucien S. 1984a. "Anatomy of a Failure: The Decision to Land at the Bay of Pigs." *Political Science Quarterly* 99 (3): 471–91.

———. 1984b. "The Confessions of Allen Dulles: New Evidence on the Bay of Pigs." *Diplomatic History* 8 (4): 365–75.

Van Evera, Stephen. 1997. *Guide to Methods for Students of Political Science*. Ithaca, NY: Cornell University Press.

Vasquez, John A. 1997. "The Realist Paradigm and Degenerative Versus Progressive Research Programs: An Appraisal of Neotraditional Research on Waltz's Balancing Position." *American Political Science Review* 91 (4): 899–934.

Volgyes, Ivan (ed.). 1971. *Hungary in Revolution, 1918–1919*. Lincoln: University of Nebraska Press.

Vondracek, Felix John. 1937. *The Foreign Policy of Czechoslovakia, 1918–1935.* New York: Columbia University Press.

Walt, Stephen. 1987. *The Origins of Alliances.* Ithaca, NY: Cornell University Press.

———. 1992. "Revolution and War." *World Politics* 44 (April): 321–68.

———. 1996. *Revolution and War.* Ithaca, NY: Cornell University Press.

———. 1997. "The Progressive Power of Realism." *American Political Science Review* 91 (4): 931–34.

Waltz, Kenneth N. 1959. *Man, the State, and War: A Theoretical Analysis.* New York: Columbia University Press.

———. 1979. *Theory of International Politics.* Reading, MA: Addison-Wesley.

———. 1996. "International Politics Is Not Foreign Policy?" *Security Studies* 6 (1): 54–61.

———. 1997. "Evaluating Theories." *American Political Science Review* 91 (4): 913–17.

Webre, Stephen. 1979. *Jose Napoleon Duarte and the Christian Democratic Party in Salvadoran Politics 1960–1972.* Baton Rouge: Louisiana State University Press.

Weede, Erich. 1984. "Democracy and War Involvement." *Journal of Conflict Resolution* 28 (4): 649–64.

———. 1996. "Correspondence: Democratization and the Danger of War." *International Security* 20 (4): 180–83.

Werner, Suzanne. 2000. "The Effects of Political Similarity on the Onset of Militarized Disputes, 1816–1985." *Political Research Quarterly* 53 (2): 343–74.

White, Stephen. 1979. *Britain and the Bolshevik Revolution: A Study in the Politics of Diplomacy, 1920–24.* London: Macmillan.

Wiener, Sharon A. 1980. *Turkish Foreign Policy Decision-Making on the Cyprus Issue: A Comparative Analysis of Three Crises.* Ph.D. dissertation, Duke University.

Wilson, Peter W., and Douglas F. Graham. 1994. *Saudi Arabia: The Coming Storm.* New York: M. E. Sharpe.

Wittkopf, Eugene R. 1986. "On the Foreign Policy Beliefs of the American People: A Critique and Some Evidence." *International Studies Quarterly* 30 (4): 425–45.

———. 1987. "Elites and Masses: Another Look at Attitudes Toward America's World Role." *International Studies Quarterly* 31 (3): 131–59.

———. 1994. "Faces of Internationalism in a Transitional Environment." *Journal of Conflict Resolution* 38 (3): 376–401.

Wolf, Reinhard. 1996. "Correspondence: Democratization and the Danger of War." *International Security* 20 (4): 176–80.

Wolfers, Arnold. 1962. *Discord and Collaborations: Essays on International Politics.* Baltimore: Johns Hopkins University Press.

Wood, Anthony. 1978. *Great Britain 1900–1965.* London: Longman.

Wood, Bryce. 1978. *Aggression and History: The Case of Ecuador and Peru.* Ann Arbor: UMI.

Wright, Quincy. [1942] 1965. *A Study of War.* Chicago: University of Chicago Press.

Wyden, Peter. 1979. *Bay of Pigs: The Untold Story.* New York: Simon and Schuster.

Yergin, Daniel. 1991. *The Prize: The Epic Quest for Oil, Money, and Power.* New York: Simon and Schuster.

Yorke, Valerie. 1988. *Domestic Politics and Regional Security: Jordan, Syria and Israel.* Aldershot, UK: Gower.

Young, Peter. 1967. *The Israeli Campaign 1967*. London: William Kimber.

Zakheim, Dov. 1986. "The Grenada Operation and Superpower Relations: A Perspective from the Pentagon." In Jiri Valenta and Herbert J. Ellison (eds.), *Grenada and Soviet/Cuban Policy: Internal Crisis and US/OECS Intervention*. Boulder, CO: Westview.

Zaller, John R. 1992. *The Nature and Origins of Mass Opinion*. Cambridge: Cambridge University Press.

Zutz, Robert. 1976. "The Recapture of the S.S. Mayaguez: Failure of the Consultation Clause of the War Powers Resolution." *New York University Journal of International Law and Politics* 8 (3): 457–78.

Index

Italic page numbers indicate material in tables or figures.